Coast to Coast
PATH

109 large-scale maps & guides to 33 towns and villages
PLANNING – PLACES TO STAY – PLACES TO EAT

ST BEES TO ROBIN HOOD'S BAY

HENRY STEDMAN

TRAILBLAZER PUBLICATIONS

INTRODUCTION

About the Coast to Coast path

PART 1: PLANNING YOUR WALK

Practical information for the walker

Budgeting 32

Itineraries

What to take

Getting to and from the Coast to Coast path

PART 2: THE ENVIRONMENT & NATURE

Conserving the Coast to Coast path

Flora and fauna

PART 3: MINIMUM IMPACT WALKING & OUTDOOR SAFETY

Minimum impact walking

Outdoor safety

Contents

PART 4: ROUTE GUIDE & MAPS

Contents

ABOUT THIS BOOK

This guidebook contains all the information you need. The hard work has been done for you so you can plan your trip from home without the usual pile of books, maps and guides.

When you're all packed and ready to go, there's comprehensive public transport information to get you to and from the trail and 109 detailed maps and town plans to help you find your way along it. The guide includes:

● All standards of accommodation with reviews of campsites, bunk-houses, hostels, B&Bs, guesthouses and hotels
● Walking companies if you want an organised tour and baggage-carrying services if you just want your luggage carried
● Itineraries for all levels of walkers
● Answers to all your questions: when to go, degree of difficulty, what to pack, and how much the whole walking holiday will cost
● Walking times and GPS waypoints
● Cafés, pubs, tearooms, takeaways, restaurants and shops for buying supplies
● Rail, bus and taxi information for all villages and towns along the path
● Street plans of the main towns: St Bees, Grasmere, Shap, Orton, Kirkby Stephen, Reeth, Richmond, Grosmont and Robin Hood's Bay
● Historical, cultural and geographical background information

❏ MINIMUM IMPACT FOR MAXIMUM INSIGHT

Man has suffered in his separation from the soil and from other living creatures ... and as yet he must still, for security, look long at some portion of the earth as it was before he tampered with it.
Gavin Maxwell, *Ring of Bright Water*, 1960

Why is walking in wild and solitary places so satisfying? Partly it is the sheer physical pleasure: sometimes pitting one's strength against the elements and the lie of the land. The beauty and wonder of the natural world and the fresh air restore our sense of proportion and the stresses and strains of everyday life slip away. Whatever the character of the countryside, walking in it benefits us mentally and physically, inducing a sense of well-being, an enrichment of life and an enhanced awareness of what lies around us.

All this the countryside gives us and the least we can do is to safeguard it by supporting rural economies, local businesses, and low-impact methods of farming and land-management, and by using environmentally sensitive forms of transport – walking being pre-eminent.

In this book there is a detailed and illustrated chapter on the wildlife and conservation of the region and a chapter on minimum-impact walking, with ideas on how to tread lightly in this fragile environment; by following its principles we can help to preserve our natural heritage for future generations.

INTRODUCTION

In devising a walk that would span the north of England from the Cumbrian coast to the North Sea, the legendary fell walker, guidebook writer and illustrator, Alfred Wainwright, created an enduring concept that 40 years later continues to inspire hikers in ever-growing numbers.

Despite not being an official National Trail with all the support that entails, the Coast to Coast path has almost certainly become the most popular long-distance footpath in England. At about 190 miles (see box p18) it's not the longest in the country and certainly doesn't, as some mistakenly think, cross the country at its widest point. It makes no claim to being especially tough (though we can safely predict that those who attempt it in one go will find it sufficiently challenging). Nor does it, unlike the long-distance paths that run alongside Hadrian's Wall or Offa's Dyke, follow any ancient construction or border.

> It's almost certainly become the most popular long-distance path in England

In truth, the Coast to Coast is but one of an infinite number of routes that could be devised by joining the various footpaths and byways to form a trail across northern England and in doing so providing those who follow it with a snapshot of the country.

But what a magnificent snapshot that is! Around two-thirds of the walk is spent in the national parks of the Lake District, the Yorkshire Dales and the North York Moors. These parks encompass the most dramatic upland scenery in England, from its highest fells to its largest lakes, some of its most beautiful woods and parts of its bleakest, barest moors. The walk also passes through areas alive with some of Britain's rarest wildlife, including red squirrels and otters, and even skirts around the eyrie of England's last surviving golden eagle.

> Around two-thirds of the walk is spent in national parks

Furthermore, where man has settled on the trail he has, on the whole, worked in harmony with nature to produce some of England's finest villages, from idyllically situated Grasmere to unspoilt Egton Bridge. The trail itself is a further example of this harmony; these paths and bridleways have existed for centuries and though man-made, do not feel or look like an imposition on the landscape but are very much part of it. While these paths and villages continue to thrive

At St Bees, 'Mile Zero' (**above**) is clearly marked. It's become a tradition to collect a pebble, carry it with you as a keepsake and then drop it into the North Sea at Robin Hood's Bay to mark your journey's end.

under the steady stream of Coast to Coasters, in other places nature has reclaimed the poignant ruins of mills and mines, ancient Iron Age sites and mysterious stone circles which between them bear witness to thousands of years of human endeavour. They punctuate the path and provide absorbing highlights along the way.

But the walker on the Coast to Coast path experiences additional, unquantifiable rewards. There is the pleasure of acquiring a developing level of fitness, the satisfaction of unravelling a route-finding conundrum and the relief when a hard-won day finally ends at the doorstep of a cosy B&B or in a centuries-old hostelry. Most memorably, it's the cheery camaraderie shared by your fellow pilgrims bound for Robin Hood's Bay and the window into the lives of the people who live and work in this fabulous landscape that stay with you as you transit the country from coast to coast.

Wainwright's 'AW' monogram on a fingerpost on the North Yorks Moors.

❑ Mr Coast to Coast – Alfred Wainwright

The popular perception of the man who devised the Coast to Coast path is that of a gruff, anti-social curmudgeon with little time for his fellow men, though one who admittedly knew what he was doing when it came to producing guidebooks. It's an unflattering portrait, but one that the man himself did little to destroy. Indeed, many say that he deliberately cultivated such a reputation in order to make himself unapproachable, thus allowing him to continue enjoying his beloved solitary walks without interruptions from the cagoule-clad masses who trudged the fells in his wake. Yet this unflattering and rather dull two-dimensional description disguises a very complex man: artist, father, divorcé, pipe smoker, accountant, part-time curator at Kendal Museum, TV personality, romantic and cat-lover.

Alfred Wainwright was born in Blackburn on 17 January 1907, to a hardworking, impoverished mother and an alcoholic father. Bright and conscientious, his early years gave little clue to the talents that would later make him famous, though his neat handwriting – a feature of his guidebooks – was frequently praised by his teachers. Leaving school to work in accounts at the Borough Engineer's Office in Blackburn Town Hall, he regularly drew cartoons to entertain his colleagues. When, in December 1931, he married Ruth Holden, it seemed that Wainwright's life was set upon a course of happy – if humdrum – conformity. Wainwright, however, never saw it like that. In particular, he quickly realised that his marriage had been a mistake.

Wainwright's Coast to Coast path

The Coast to Coast path owes its existence to one man: Alfred Wainwright. It was in 1972 that Wainwright, already renowned for his exquisitely illustrated guides to walking in the Lake District, finally completed a trek across the width of England along a path of his own devising. It was an idea that he had been kicking around for a time: to cross his native land on a route that, as far as he was aware, would 'commit no offence against privacy nor trample on the sensitive corns of landowners and tenants'. The result of his walk, a guidebook, was originally printed by his long-time publishers, *The Westmoreland Gazette*, the following year. It proved hugely successful. Indeed, a full twenty years after the book was first published, a television series of the trail was also made in which Wainwright himself starred, allowing a wider public to witness first-hand his wry, abrupt, earthy charm.

Wainwright reminds people in his book that his is just **one of many such trails** across England that could be devised, and since

It was in 1972 that Wainwright finally completed a trek across the width of England along a path of his own devising

Wainwright felt stifled and bored with his home life; feelings that not even the arrival of a son, Peter, could erase. His wife, though loyal, good and obedient, left Wainwright unfulfilled and any trace of romantic love that had been in the marriage at the beginning quickly drained away.

To escape the misery at home, Wainwright threw himself into his new-found hobby, fellwalking. He first visited the Lakes in 1930 and soon after was making detailed notes and drawings on the walks he made. Initially, these visits were few and far between, but a move to Kendal ten years later to take up a position as an accounting assistant allowed Wainwright to visit the Lakes virtually every weekend. Yet it wasn't until the early 1950s that Wainwright struck upon the idea of shaping his copious notes and drawings into a series of walking guides. The idea wasn't a new one: guides to the Lakes had existed since at least the late 18th century and previous authors had included such literary luminaries as William Wordsworth. Where Wainwright's guides differed, however, was in their detail and the unique charm of their production.

For Wainwright was a publisher's dream: his writing was concise and laced with a wry humour, his ink sketches were delightful, and every page was designed by the author himself, with the text justified on both sides (and without hyphens!) around the drawings. As a result, all the publisher really needed to do was crank up the printing press, load in the paper, and hey presto! They had another bestseller on their hands.

His first seven books, a series of guides to the Lakeland fells, took fourteen years to produce and by the end he had built up quite a following amongst both walkers and those who simply loved the books' beauty. *(cont'd overleaf)*

❏ **Mr Coast to Coast – Alfred Wainwright** *(cont'd from p9)* Further titles followed, including one on the Pennine Way (a walk that he seemed to have enjoyed rather less than the others, possibly because at one point he had needed to be rescued by a warden after falling into a bog). As an incentive to walkers, however, he offered to buy a pint for every reader who completed the entire walk, telling them to put it on his bill at the Border Hotel at the end of the Pennine Way. The Coast to Coast was the follow-up to the Pennine Way, with the research starting in 1971 and the book published in 1973. It was a project that Wainwright seemed to have derived much greater enjoyment from (though, unfortunately, there was no offer of a free drink this time!).

While all this was going on, however, Wainwright's private life was in turmoil. Though his home life with Ruth remained as cold as ever, Wainwright had found the love of his life in Betty McNally, who had visited him in his office on official matters sometime in 1957. For Wainwright, it was love at first sight, and he began courting Betty soon after. They married eventually in 1970, and by all accounts this union provided Wainwright with the contentment and happiness he had so signally failed to find in his first marriage. She also accompanied Wainwright on his forays into television, where his gruff, no-nonsense charm proved a big hit.

At the time of their marriage Wainwright, already 63, promised Betty ten happy years. In the event, he was able to provide her with 21, passing away on Sunday, January 20, 1991. His last wish, fulfilled two months later by Betty and his long-time friend Percy Duff, was to have his ashes scattered on Hay Stacks. At the end of his autobiography, *Ex-Fellwanderer*, he sums his life up thus:

I have had a long and wonderful innings and enjoyed a remarkable immunity from unpleasant and unwelcome incidents. ... I never had to go to be a soldier, which I would have hated. I never had to wear a uniform, which I also would have hated. ... I was never called upon to make speeches in public nor forced into the limelight; my role was that of a backroom boy, which suited me fine. I never went bald, which would have driven me into hiding. ... So, all told, I have enjoyed a charmed life, I have been well favoured. The gods smiled on me since the cradle. I have had more blessings than I could ever count.

Wainwright's book other Coast to Coast walks have indeed been established. Yet it is still *his* trail that is by far and away the most popular, and in order to distinguish it from the others, it is now commonly known as Wainwright's Coast to Coast path.

The route has been amended slightly since 1973 mostly because, though careful to try to use only public rights of way, in a few places Wainwright's original trail actually intruded upon private land. Indeed, even today the trail does in places cross private territory and it's only due to the largesse of the landowners that the path has remained near-enough unchanged throughout its course.

Though the trail passes through three national parks, crosses the Pennine Way and at times joins with both the Lyke Wake Walk and the Cleveland Way, it's not itself one of the 15 national trails in the UK, nor is it likely to become one anytime soon. What is certain is that despite this lack of official support, the Coast to Coast has become one of the most popular of Britain's long-distance paths, with estimates of up to 10,000 people attempting it annually.

(**Opposite**) Looking down Greenup, on the trail between Borrowdale and Grasmere; Skiddaw in the distance.

How difficult is the Coast to Coast path?

INTRODUCTION

Undertaken **in one go**, the Coast to Coast path is a long, tough walk. Despite the presence of some fairly steep gradients, every mile is 'walkable' and no mountaineering

> From seashore to seashore you'll have ascended and of course descended the equivalent height of Mount Everest

or climbing skills are necessary. All you need is some suitable clothing, a bit of money, a backpack full of determination and a half-decent pair of calf muscles. In the 190-odd miles from seashore to seashore you'll have ascended and of course descended the equivalent height of Mount Everest.

That said, the most common complaint we've received about this book, particularly from North American readers, is that it doesn't emphasise how tough it can be. So let us be clear: **the Coast to Coast is a tough trek**, **particularly if undertaken in one go**. Ramblers describe it as 'challenging' and they're not wrong. When walkers begin to appreciate just how tough the walk can be, what

they're really discovering is the reality of covering a daily average of just over 14 miles or 23km, *day after day*, for two weeks, in fair weather or foul and while nursing a varying array of aches and pains. After all, how often do any of us walk 14 miles in a day, let alone continuously for *two weeks*?

The Lake District, in particular, contains many steep sections that will test you to the limit; however, there are also plenty of genteel tearooms and places to stay in this section should you prefer to break your days into easier sections.

The topography of the eastern section is less extreme, though the number of places with accommodation drops too, and for a couple of days you may find yourself walking 15 miles or more in order to reach a town or village on the trail that has somewhere to stay.

Regarding safety, there are few places on the regular trail where it would be possible to fall from a great height, save perhaps for the cliff walks that book-end the walk. On some of the high-level Lakeland alternatives (see p123 and p133), however, there is a chance of being blown off a ridge. In 2009 a walker suffered this fate and broke his ankle, as did the rescuer who came in a helicopter, though sustaining such a serious injury by being blown over is highly unusual. The greatest danger to trekkers is, perhaps, the likelihood of **losing the way**, particularly in the Lake District with its greater chance of poor visibility, bad weather and a distinct **lack of signposting**. A compass and knowing how to

use it is vital, as is appropriate clothing for inclement weather and most importantly of all, a pair of boots which you ease on each morning with a smile not a grimace.

Not pushing yourself too hard is important, too, as this leads to fatigue with all its inherent dangers, not least poor decision making. In case all this deters you from the walk bear in mind that in 2009 a 71-year-old finished the walk for the fifth time, and a 7-year-old girl once completed the walk with her father – and they all managed it in 13 days! At the same time young men with all the right kit and a previous crossing under their belt were finished after storming across to Shap in three days.

How long do you need?

We've heard about an athlete who completed the entire Coast to Coast path in just 37 hours and a walker who managed it in eight days. We also know somebody who did it in ten and another guy who did four four-day stages over four years. Continuously or over several visits, for most people, the Coast to Coast trail takes a minimum of 14 walking days, in other words an average distance of just over 14 miles (23km) a day. Indeed, even with a fortnight in

For most people, the Coast to Coast trail takes a minimum of 14 walking days

which to complete the trail, many people still find it tough going, and it doesn't really allow you time to look around places such as Grasmere or Richmond which can deserve a day in themselves. So, if you can afford to build a couple of rest days into your itinerary or even break it up into shorter stages over several weeks, you'll be very glad you did.

Of course, if you're fit there's no reason why you can't go a little faster if that's what you want to do, though you'll end up having a different sort of trek to most of the other people on the route. For where theirs is a fairly relaxing holiday, yours will be more of a sport as you try to reach the finishing line on schedule. There's nothing wrong with this approach, though you obviously won't see as much as those who take their time; *chacun à son goût*, as the French probably say. However, what you mustn't do is try to push yourself beyond your body's ability; such punishing challenges often end prematurely in exhaustion, injury or, at the absolute least, an unpleasant time.

When deciding how long to allow for their trek, those intending to camp and carry their own luggage shouldn't underestimate just how much a heavy pack can wear you down. On pp34-5 there are some suggested itineraries

See pp34-5 for some suggested itineraries covering different walking speeds

covering different walking speeds. If you've only got a few days, don't try to walk it all; concentrate, instead, on one area such as the Lakes or North York Moors. You can always come back and attempt the rest of the walk another time.

(**Opposite**): From The Cape (see p136) there are superb views across to Ullswater.

When to go

SEASONS

Britain is a notoriously wet country and the north-west of England is an infamously damp part of it. Rare indeed is the trekker who manages to walk the Coast to Coast path without suffering at least one day of rain; three or four days per trek is more likely, even in summer. That said, it's equally unlikely that

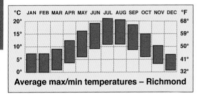

Average max/min temperatures – Richmond

you'll spend a fortnight in the area and not see any sun at all, and even the most cynical of walkers will have to admit that, during the walking season at least, there are more sunny days than showery ones. That **walking season**, by the way, starts at Easter and builds to a

crescendo in August, before quickly tailing off in September. By the end of that month there are few trekkers on the trail, and in late October many places close down for the winter.

Spring

Find a couple of dry weeks in springtime and you're in for a treat. The wild flowers are beginning to come into bloom, lambs are skipping in the meadows and the grass is green and lush. Of course, finding a dry fortnight in spring (around the end of March to mid-June) is not easy but occasionally there's a mini-heatwave at this time. Another advantage will be fewer trekkers on the trail so finding accommodation without booking is relatively easy. Easter is the exception, the first major holiday in the year when people flock to the Lake District and other national parks.

Summer

Summer, on the other hand, can be a bit *too* busy and, in somewhere like the Lakes over a weekend in August, at times depressingly congested. Still, the chances of a prolonged period of sunshine are of course higher at this time of year than any other, the days are much longer and the heather is in bloom, too, turning the hills a fragrant purple. If you like the company of other trekkers summer will provide you with the opportunity of meeting scores of them, though do remember that you'll need to book your accommodation well in advance or be prepared to camp occasionally. Despite the higher-than-average chance of sunshine, take clothes for any eventuality – it's bound to rain at some point.

Autumn

September can be a wonderful time to walk; many of the families have returned home and the path is clear although accommodation gets filled up in early

September by a wave of older visitors who've been waiting for the new school term. The weather is usually sunny, too, at least at the beginning of September. By the end of the month the weather will begin to get a little wilder and the nights will start to draw in. For most mortals the walking season is almost at an end.

Winter

A few people trek the Coast to Coast in winter, putting up with the cold, damp conditions and short days for the chance to experience the trail without other tourists and maybe even under snow. Much of the accommodation will be closed too but whilst it may also be a little more dangerous to walk at this time, particularly on the high-level routes through the Lakes, if you find yourself walking on one of those clear, crisp, wintry days it will all seem absolutely worth it.

RAINFALL

At some point on your walk, it will rain; if it doesn't, it's fair to say that you haven't really lived the full Coast to Coast experience properly. At nearly 4.7 metres (185 inches), the hills over Borrowdale on Stage 2 record the **highest rainfall in England**; a

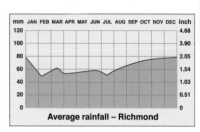

Average rainfall – Richmond

staggering eight times more than the south-east of England, for example! In December 2015 there was serious flooding in the Lake District. The question, therefore, is not whether you will be rained on, but how often and how hard. But as long as you dress accordingly and take note of the safety advice given on pp81-5, this shouldn't be a problem.

Do, however, think twice about tackling some of the high-level alternatives if the weather is bad and visibility poor, and don't do so on your own.

DAYLIGHT HOURS

If walking in autumn, winter or early spring, you must take account of how far you can walk in the available light. It won't be possible to cover as many miles as you would in summer. Remember though, that you'll get a further 30-45 minutes of usable light before sunrise and after sunset depending on the weather. In June, because the path is in the far north of

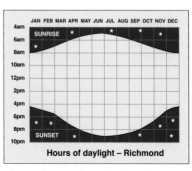

Hours of daylight – Richmond

England, those coming from the south may be surprised that there's enough light for walking until at least 10pm. Conversely, in early spring, late autumn and winter you'll be equally amazed how quickly the nights draw in.

❑ FESTIVALS AND ANNUAL EVENTS

Thanks largely to its undying appeal with tourists, **Grasmere** has become something of a mecca for those interested in those peculiarly Lakeland sports such as fell running, and Cumberland and Westmoreland wrestling.

In addition to the events outlined below, all kinds of **agricultural shows** take place annually in towns and villages on the Coast to Coast trail. These shows are an integral and traditional part of life all over rural England and particularly in the Lake District. Too numerous to list here, details of all the shows can be found by looking at the websites of the places concerned. For further information about events in the southern Lake District see 🖥 applications.southlakeland.gov.uk/eventsearch.

Being aware of the bigger festivals is also useful when planning your walk as there's a good chance that available accommodation will be all the more in demand should you turn up on a busy weekend. For example early June's Appleby Horse Fair (🖥 www.applebyfair.org) can drain accommodation opportunities in Kirkby Stephen and Orton.

January to March
Grasmere hosts an annual Art and Book Festival (🖥 www.wordsworth.org.uk; click on What's on) at one of Wordsworth's old houses, Dove Cottage (or at a hotel very near by). The festival usually takes place in January, is residential and consists of lectures, surgeries and workshops.

April to June
The villages of Swaledale, which include Keld, Muker, Thwaite, Gunnerside and Reeth, hold an annual music festival (Swaledale Festival); this usually takes place at the end of May to early June. The festival has an annual theme (eg stringed instruments), and in addition to the music there are all kinds of other activities from art exhibitions and guided walking trails to craft workshops; information can be found and tickets bought on the dedicated website 🖥 www.swaledale-festival.org.uk. Another event in June is the Swaledale Marathon (🖥 www.swaledaleoutdoorclub.org.uk; click on Swaledale Marathon) so accommodation in the area can dry up.

Robin Hood's Bay hosts a folk music weekend (🖥 www.robin-hoods-bay.co.uk – click on What's on), usually on the first or second weekend of June.

July to September
Richmond Live (🖥 www.richmondlive.org) is a pop music festival usually held over one weekend in late July or early August. Some readers have advised that if you want a quiet night's sleep, Richmond can be well worth avoiding at this time.

The Grasmere Lakeland Sports and Show (🖥 www.grasmeresports.com) has taken place every year since 1868, except during World Wars I and II. Held on August Bank Holiday Sunday, sports featured include wrestling, tug-of-war, hound-trailing and the more recent addition of mountain biking.

After the walk many people will head for Whitby to catch a train or bus. If you're there at the end of August consider staying on for Whitby Folk Week (🖥 www.whit byfolk.co.uk) when the pubs and other venues are abuzz with fiddles and bodhrans.

October to December
If you happen to be in Robin Hood's Bay in winter don't miss the Victorian weekend (🖥 www.robin-hoods-bay.co.uk – click on What's on) at the beginning of December, where the town turns out in 19th-century costume. It's all good fun, with quizzes, recitals, concerts and demonstrations, and it's all in aid of charity, too.

PLANNING YOUR WALK

1

Practical information for the walker

ROUTE FINDING

The presence of signposts and waymarking varies along the path. Once over the Pennines and into Yorkshire the trail becomes fairly well signposted and finding the way shouldn't be a problem. In the Lakes, on the other hand, there are few Coast to Coast signposts and you'll have to rely on the descriptions in this book to find the way. For much of the time the path is well trodden and obvious, though of course there are situations where there are a number of paths to choose from, and other occasions where the ground is so boggy no clear path is visible at all. Misty conditions are another problem, particularly in the Lake District. In these instances a compass or GPS will help you move in the right direction or follow the correct path. (See the box on pp91-3 for more details.)

In the Lakes in particular there are a number of high-level alternatives to the main route, and on a clear day fit trekkers should consider taking them. Though obviously more tiring, the rewards in terms of the views and sense of achievement are all worthwhile.

GPS

I never carried a compass, preferring to rely on a good sense of direction... I never bothered to understand how a compass works or what it is supposed to do ... To me a compass is a gadget, and I don't get on well with gadgets of any sort.
Alfred Wainwright

While Wainwright's acolytes may scoff, other walkers will accept GPS technology as an inexpensive, well-established if non-essential navigational aid. To cut a long story short, within a minute of being turned on and with a clear view of the sky, **GPS receivers** will establish your position as well as elevation in a variety of formats, including the British OS grid system, anywhere on earth to an accuracy of within a few metres. These days, most **smartphones** have a GPS receiver built in and mapping software available to run on it (see p46).

One thing must be understood however: **treating GPS as a replacement for maps, a compass and common sense is a big mistake**. Every electronic device is susceptible to battery failure or some electronic malfunction that might leave you in the dark. GPS is primarily a navigational aid or backup to conventional route finding and, in almost all cases, is best used in conjunction with a paper map.

At its most basic level a GPS stops you exacerbating navigational errors and saves you time in correcting them. Newer units may come with some inbuilt mapping, but while it's possible to buy **digital mapping** (see box p46) to import into a regular GPS unit with sufficient storage capacity, it might be considered as practical as having internet on a mobile phone – you still end up scrolling and zooming across a tiny screen.

Using GPS with this book – tracklog and waypoints

The easiest way to avoid getting lost is to install a **tracklog** of the route on either a GPS unit or a smartphone running GPS. A tracklog is a continuous line like a path that appears on your GPS screen; all you have to do is keep on that line. If you lose it on the screen you can zoom out until it reappears and walk towards it. To download the GPS tracklog on which this sixth edition's maps are based, see the Trailblazer website – ⌨ www.trailblazer-guides.com.

Where a tracklog is a continuous line, **waypoints** are single points like cairns. This book identifies key waypoints on the route maps. It's anticipated you won't tramp along day after day, ticking off the book's waypoints, transfixed by the screen on your GPS or smartphone; the route description and maps are more than adequate most of the time. Only when you're unsure of your position or which way to go might you feel the need to even turn on the unit for a quick affirmation. You'll find more waypoints in the book across bleak mountain and moorland sections where the walk can degenerate into a prolonged stumble through thick mist.

The book's waypoints correlate to the list on pp258-63 which gives the OS grid reference and a description. You can either simply read off the nearest presumed waypoint from the list as and when the need arises and work out where you are in relation to it or, less confusingly, key it in as a new point and press 'go to'. As there will probably be only a handful of times you need to do this, for most that will suffice but, with less margin for keystroke error, you can

---

❑ Just how long is Wainwright's Coast to Coast path?

The figure of **191¹/₂ miles** has been bandied around for years as this is close to the 190 miles which Wainwright's original edition quoted back in 1972. Disregarding the fact that these days his exact route is no longer followed, for this guidebook each stage was logged using a suitably calibrated GPS odometer and after editing the final tally showed the actual distance walked to be around **189¹/₂ miles** (305km) via the most used routes. This, of course, doesn't account for walking to the pub or B&Bs off the track, going the wrong way and even, as some Pythagorians like to consider, the fact that walking up and down hills technically covers more ground than if the terrain was flat.

The precise total length of Wainwright's Coast to Coast (and doubtless many other long-distance paths) is not of great import in the big picture as you'll walk the walk, but a day's true distance is something worth knowing when psyching yourself up for a long stage. Other guides, maps and local signposts will show differing distances, often constrained to fit the immutable figure estimated by Alfred Wainwright. This is the first Coast to Coast path guidebook to use satellite technology to closely estimate the actual distance walked.

download the complete list as a GPS-read-able .gpx file of grid references (but with no descriptions) from 🖥 www.trailblazer-guides.com

Using GPS with this book, be it a track-log, all the waypoints or just the key way-points, is *an option*. Without them you could find yourself staggering around a mist-clad moor, or ambling confidently down the wrong path. With GPS, when the need arises, you can reliably establish your position in relation to the path, or quickly find out how far and in what direction it is to a known point on the trail.

It's worth repeating that 98% of people who've ever walked the Coast to Coast did so without GPS so there's no need to rush out and buy one – or a new GPS-enabled smartphone, for that matter. Your spending priorities ought to be on good waterproofs and above all, footwear. However, correctly using this book's GPS data could get you back on track and dozing in front of the pub fireplace or tucked up in bed all the sooner.

For more on how not to lose your way, see pp91-3.

In the Lakes there's little in the way of Coast to Coast signposting but once over the Pennines and into Yorkshire the trail is well signposted.

© Chris Scott

Since 2012 the Wainwright Society has been marking fingerposts at public road crossings with a special C2C logo featuring Wainwright's 'AW' monogram.

ACCOMMODATION

From one coast to the other, businesses and families alike today owe a lot to Wainwright's inspired concept. Smaller towns and villages as well as isolated farms far from the reliable Lakeland honeypots have come to rely on accom-modating and feeding the seasonal flow of coastbound walkers.

The route guide (Part 4) lists a fairly comprehensive selection of places to stay along the trail. The three main options are: camping, staying in hostels/bunkhouses, or using B&Bs/pubs/hotels. Few people stick to just one of these the whole way, preferring, for example, to camp most of the time but spend every third night in a hostel, or perhaps take a hostel where possible but splash out on a B&B or hotel every once in a while.

The table on pp36-7 provides a snapshot of what type of accommodation and services are available in each of the towns and villages, while the tables on pp34-5 provide some suggested itineraries. The following is a brief introduction as to what to expect from each type of accommodation.

Camping

It's possible to camp all along the Coast to Coast path, though few people do so every night. You're almost bound to get at least one night where the rain falls relentlessly, sapping morale; it's then that most campers opt to spend the next night drying out in a hostel or B&B somewhere. There are, however, many advantages with camping. It's more economical, for a start, with most campsites charging somewhere between £5 and £10. Best of all there's **rarely any need to book**, except possibly in the very high season, and even then you'd be highly unlucky not to find somewhere, even if it means camping discreetly in the woods. The campsites vary and you get what you pay for: some are just pub gardens or a farmer's spare field with basic toilet/shower facilities; others are full-blown caravan sites with security access codes and sparkling ablutions blocks and a few spaces put aside for tents. Showers are usually available, occasionally for a fee, though more often than not for free. Note that most YHA hostels on the Coast to Coast path now accept campers again following a hiatus of a few years. Note, too, that the biggest town en route, Richmond, does not have a recognised campsite, with the nearest being at least three miles away.

Wild camping (ie camping not in a regular campsite; see p79) is also possible along the route but please don't do so in a field without first gaining permission from the landowner. Some good wild camping locations include the level areas surrounding mountain lakes such as Innominate Tarn (on the high route to Borrowdale), Grisedale Tarn (out of Grasmere) and Angle Tarn (two miles from Patterdale). Further east old mine ruins, such as those on the high route to Reeth, provide good shelter and 'cover' as well as patches of level grass and nearby running water. Beyond there, wild camping might be misconstrued as 'vagrancy' so woodland or plantations will be your best bet.

Remember that camping, wild or 'tame', is not an easy option, especially for a solo walker. Walked continuously, the route is wearying enough without carrying the means to sleep and cook with you. Should you decide to camp at campsites, consider employing one of the baggage-carrying companies mentioned on pp28-9, though this does mean the loss of spontaneity which is the whole point of camping – and of course they can't deliver to Angle Tarn!

Bunkhouses and camping barns

A bunkhouse and a camping barn are different things. In most cases a **camping barn** is pretty much what it sounds like: an old barn in the corner of a farmer's field with a couple of wooden benches to sleep on; sleeping bags and usually sleeping mats are thus necessary, though bedding is provided in many of the YHA-franchised camping barns. A camping barn is probably the nearest non-campers will get to sleeping outside, while at the same time providing shelter from the elements. Note also that camping barns are sometimes booked for sole occupancy and thus it is essential to call in advance to check availability.

Bunkhouses can be much more agreeable places, with fluffed-up bedding, bathrooms you'd be happy to show to your parents and even kitchen and lounge areas. The description 'bunkhouse' is often used in place of 'small hostel' or 'independent hostel' to distinguish a private enterprise from lodgings under the YHA banner (see below) which can sometimes be huge properties with scores of beds, hyperactive school groups and, depending on your age, unhappy memories of a long-gone institutional past.

Hostels

Youth hostels are plentiful along the Coast to Coast path and if you haven't visited one recently – and thus the words 'youth' and 'hostel' still conjure up images of limited opening hours, crowded dorms, lousy food and staff who really wish you'd move on – we advise you to take a second look. Hostels, whether owned by the Youth Hostel Association (YHA) or independent, offer some of the best-located and most interesting accommodation along the path. In fact there are now as many independent hostels as YHA ones along the Coast to Coast path, several having passed from YHA into private ownership in recent years as the YHA reviews its portfolio of properties.

Despite the name, anyone of any age can join the YHA. This can be done at any hostel, or by contacting the **Youth Hostels Association of England and Wales** (☎ 01629-592700 or 0800-0191 700, 🖥 www.yha.org.uk). The cost of a year's membership is £20 for an adult (£15 if you pay by Direct Debit), £10/5

□ Should you book your accommodation in advance?

With the trend in recession-beating 'staycations' and the general rise in the popularity of walking holidays, the Coast to Coast path could be entering something of a boom time and some have predicted that accommodation may struggle to cope. In the high season of **June to August**, unless camping, it's essential you have your night's accommodation secured. Nothing is more deflating than arriving at the end of a long day only to find that you've then got to walk another few miles or even take a detour off the route, because everywhere is booked up.

How soon you start booking is up to you but doing so the night before is no longer dependable. If you start booking **up to six months** in advance you'll have a good chance of getting precisely the accommodation you want. Booking so early does leave you vulnerable to changing circumstances of course, but with enough notice it's likely your deposit will be returned as they can easily fill your bed; ask on booking.

Outside the high season and away from weekends, as long as you're **flexible** and willing to take what's offered, you might get away with booking just a couple of weeks or even just days in advance. Having said that, some establishments we've spoken to told us that May and September were in fact their busiest months, early September being dubbed 'Saga week' when older hikers return to the hills once the schools have re-absorbed all the kids. However, **weekends** are busy everywhere, especially in **the Lakes** and in places like Keld or Blakey Moor where conveniently close accommodation is limited.

If you've left it too late and can only get accommodation for parts of the walk but are set on a certain period, **consider camping** to fill in the gaps. It's not to everyone's taste and it helps if you already own the gear, but it can save you money which you can lavish on yourself later without guilt and, if using a baggage service, they can cart the gear from door to door at no extra effort to yourself.

If you're planning on staying in hostels the same applies, though do be careful when travelling out of high season as many **hostels** close during the week and shut altogether from around November to February. Once again, it's well worth booking in advance.

Campers, whatever the time of year, should always be able to find somewhere to pitch their tent, though ringing in advance can't hurt and will at least confirm that the campsite is still open.

for anyone under 26. Having secured your membership, youth hostels are easy to book, either online or by phone through the contact details above. Since non-members have to pay around £3 more per night it is worth joining if you expect to stay in a YHA hostel for more than six nights in a year. You'll also get free wi-fi. However, one reader has written in to say that at least one hostel (the one in Osmotherley), though approved by the YHA, no longer offers discounts to YHA card holders as they are now a private hostel.

Hostels come equipped with a whole range of facilities, from drying rooms to washing machines, televisions to pool tables and fully equipped kitchens. Some have a shop selling a selection of groceries, snacks and souvenirs and may even have internet access. Many offer breakfast and/or dinner (of varying quality), some offer a packed lunch, and several have a licence to sell alcohol. They are also great places to meet fellow walkers, swap stories and compare blisters.

P L A N N I N G   Y O U R   W A L K

❑ Information for foreign visitors

● **Currency** The British pound (£) comes in notes of £100, £50, £20, £10 and £5, and coins of £2 and £1. The pound is divided into 100 pence (usually referred to as 'p', pronounced 'pee') which come in silver coins of 50p, 20p 10p and 5p and copper coins of 2p and 1p.

● **Rates of exchange** Up-to-date exchange rates can be found at 🖥 www.xe.com/ucc.

● **Business hours** Most **shops** and main **post offices** are open at least from Monday to Friday 9am-5pm and Saturday 9am-12.30pm. Many choose longer hours and some open on Sundays as well. However, some also close early one day a week, often Wednesday or Thursday. **Banks** are usually open 10am-4pm Monday to Friday. **Note that some cash machines do not accept foreign cards (eg at St Bees).**

Pub opening hours have become more flexible – up to 24 hours a day seven days a week – so each pub may have different times. However, most pubs on the Coast to Coast route continue to follow the traditional 11am to 11pm and some still close in the afternoon.

● **National (Bank) holidays** Most businesses are shut on 1 January, Good Friday (March/April), Easter Monday (March/April), the first and last Monday in May, the last Monday in August, 25 December and 26 December.

● **School holidays** School holiday periods in England are generally as follows: a one-week break late October, two weeks around Christmas, a week mid-February, two weeks around Easter, a week in late May and from late July to early September.

● **Documents** If you are a member of a National Trust organisation in your country bring your membership card as you should be entitled to free entry to National Trust properties and sites in the UK. English Heritage, who look after Richmond Castle, also have a membership card allowing free access to their sites.

● **Travel/medical insurance** The European Health Insurance Card (EHIC) entitles EU nationals (on production of the EHIC card) to necessary medical treatment under the UK's National Health Service while on a temporary visit here. However, this is not a substitute for proper medical cover on your travel insurance for unforeseen bills and for getting you home should that be necessary. Also consider cover for loss or theft of personal belongings, especially if you're camping or staying in hostels, as there will be times when you'll have to leave your luggage unattended.

● **Weights and measures** The European Commission is no longer attempting to ban the pint or the mile: so, in Britain, milk can be sold in pints (1 pint = 568ml), as can

Weighed against these advantages is the fact that even though many hostels now have rooms with two to four beds you may have to share your night with a heavy snorer. A couple of the hostels also suffer from uncomfortably small dorms when they're full. Some rooms now have en suite facilities but in others you have to share a shower room and in a couple of cases facilities may be limited. Nor is it possible to stay in hostels every night on the trail, for there are some areas where hostels don't exist and when they do they're occasionally at least a mile or two off the path.

If you're travelling out of the main season (particularly between November and February) you may find some hostels are shut to walkers during the week, or completely. Even in high season some are not staffed during the day and walkers may have to wait until 5pm before checking in, though you may be able to access the kitchen and leave luggage in a secure room before 5pm. And finally,

---

beer in pubs, though most other liquid including petrol (gasoline) and diesel is sold in litres. Distances on road and path signs will also continue to be given in miles (1 mile = 1.6km) rather than kilometres, and yards (1yd = 0.9m) rather than metres.

The population remains split between those who still use inches (1 inch = 2.5cm), feet (1ft = 0.3m) and yards and those who are happy with millimetres, centimetres and metres; you'll often be told that 'it's only a hundred yards or so' to somewhere, rather than a hundred metres or so.

Most food is sold in metric weights (g and kg) but the imperial weights of pounds (lb: 1lb = 453g) and ounces (oz: 1oz = 28g) are often displayed too. The weather – a frequent topic of conversation – is also an issue: while most forecasts predict temperatures in centigrade (C), many people continue to think in terms of fahrenheit (F; see temperature chart on p14 for conversions).

● **Time** During the winter the whole of Britain is on Greenwich Meantime (GMT). The clocks move one hour forward on the last Sunday in March, remaining on British Summer Time (BST) until the last Sunday in October.

● **Smoking** Smoking in enclosed public places is banned. The ban relates not only to pubs and restaurants, but also to B&Bs, hostels and hotels. These latter have the right to designate one or more bedrooms where the occupants can smoke, but the ban is in force in all enclosed areas open to the public – even in a private home such as a B&B. Should you be foolhardy enough to light up in a no-smoking area, which includes pretty well any indoor public place, you could be fined £50, but it's the owners of the premises who suffer most if they fail to stop you, with a potential fine of £2500.

● **Telephones** The international access code for Britain is +44, followed by the area code minus the first 0, and then the number you require. To call a number with the same area code as the landline phone you are calling from you can omit the area code. It's cheaper to phone at weekends and after 6pm and before 8am on weekdays. **Mobile phone reception** is better than you think. Even in the Lakes you're often actually quite close to a town and on high ground where a weak signal can often be picked up. It's said the Vodafone network works best across rural northern England followed by O2 or EE.

● **Internet access** See p27.

● **Emergency services** For police, ambulance, fire and mountain rescue dial ☎ 999 (or the EU standard number ☎ 112).

PLANNING YOUR WALK

the cost of staying in a hostel, once breakfast has been added on, is in many instances not that much cheaper (from £17-27 for YHA members) than staying in a B&B, especially if you're walking with someone.

Bed and breakfast

Bed and Breakfasts (B&Bs) are a great British institution and many of those along the Coast to Coast are absolutely charming, with buildings often three or four hundred years old. Older owners often treat you as surrogates for their long-departed offspring and enjoy nothing more than looking after you.

As the name suggests, they provide you with a bed in a private room, and breakfast – a hearty, British-style cooked one unless you specify otherwise beforehand – though they range in style enormously. Most B&Bs on the route have **en suite rooms** – which usually mean there's a bathroom attached to the room. Where a room is advertised as having **private facilities**, it means that the bathroom is not directly connected to the room though the nearby bathroom is reserved solely for the use of the room's occupants. **Shared facilities** mean that you share a bathroom with other guests. With private/shared facilities there may be a bath, which is what most walkers prefer at the end of a long day. These rooms usually contain either a double bed (known as a **double room**), or two single beds (known as a **twin room**). **Family rooms** are for three or more people. Solo trekkers should take note: single rooms are not so easy to find so you'll often end up occupying a double room, for which you'll have to pay a single occupancy supplement (see below). **Smoking** is banned in all enclosed places open to the public in England but places to stay are able to designate rooms for smokers, so do check this if it's important to you.

Some B&Bs provide an **evening meal**; if not, there's often a pub or restaurant nearby and, if it's far, the owner may give you a lift to and from it.

B&B rates and booking B&Bs in this guide start at around £30 per person for the most basic accommodation to well over £50 for the most luxurious en suite places in a popular tourist haunt like Grasmere. Most charge around £30-35 per person. A typical **single occupancy supplement** is between £10 and £20. An evening meal (usually around £10-20) is sometimes provided, but you'll need to book in advance. Packed lunches are often available too for around £5-6.

Some B&Bs have their own website and offer online/email booking but for the majority you will need to phone. Most places ask for a **deposit** (about 50%) which is generally non-refundable if you cancel at short notice. Some places may charge 100% if the booking is for one night only. Always let the owner know as soon as possible if you have to cancel your booking so they can offer the bed to someone else.

Larger places take credit or debit cards. Most smaller B&Bs accept only cheques by post or payments by bank transfer for the deposit; the balance can be settled with cash or a cheque.

Guesthouses, hotels, pubs and inns

A guesthouse offers bed and breakfast but should have a better class of décor and more facilities such as offering evening meals and a lounge for guests. All of which make guesthouses sound very much hotels, of course – except, unlike a hotel, they are unlikely to offer room service.

Pubs and inns may also offer bed and breakfast accommodation and tariffs are no more than in a regular B&B. However, you need to be prepared for a noisier environment, especially if your room is above the bar.

Hotels do usually cost more, however, and some might be a little displeased by a bunch of muddy trekkers turning up. That said, most places on the walk, particularly in the quieter towns and villages, are used to seeing trekkers, make a good living from them and welcome them warmly. Prices in hotels and pubs start at around £35 per person.

Airbnb

The rise and rise of Airbnb (🖳 www.airbnb.co.uk) has seen private homes and apartments opened up to overnight travellers on an informal basis. While accommodation is primarily based in cities, the concept is spreading to tourist hotspots in more rural areas, but do check thoroughly what you are getting and the precise location. While the first couple of options listed may be in the area you're after, others may be far too far afield for walkers. At its best, this is a great way to meet local people in a relatively unstructured environment, but be aware that these places are not registered B&Bs, so standards may vary, yet prices may not necessarily be any lower than the norm.

FOOD AND DRINK

Breakfast

Stay in a B&B/guesthouse/hotel and you'll be filled to the gills each morning with a cooked English breakfast. This can consist of a bowl of cereal followed by a plateful of eggs, bacon, sausages, mushrooms, tomatoes, and possibly baked beans or black pudding, with toast and butter, and all washed down with coffee, tea and/or juice. Enormously satisfying the first time you try it, by the fourth or fifth morning you may start to prefer the lighter continental breakfast or porridge, which most establishments now offer. Alternatively, and especially if you're planning an early start, you might like to request a packed lunch instead of this filling breakfast and just have a cup of coffee before you leave.

The youth hostels mentioned in this guide offer breakfast; usually it's a good meal but they charge an additional £6 or so.

> ❑ **Is a full English breakfast healthy?**
> You've paid for the bed, it's understandable you want the breakfast too, and enough breakfast to fuel you down the trail all the way to lunch. But is the traditional 'FEB' the way to go? At the beginning of the day it's complex carbohydrates you want, not a stomach full of fat and salt. Slow-release carbs keep you going till lunchtime, don't put your gall bladder on action stations and contain negligible fat. Ask for a big bowl of **porridge**, ideally cooked with milk and a little salt and if you do go fried, keep off offal-packed sausages, hope the bacon and tomatoes are grilled not fried, and refuse fried bread and black pudding altogether. (Black pudding is a sausage of oats soaked in blood, in case you didn't know, and a constituent of a 'Full *Yorkshire* breakfast').

Lunch

Your B&B host or youth hostel can usually provide a packed lunch at an additional cost, though of course there's nothing to stop you preparing your own. There are some fantastic locally made cheeses and pickles that can be picked up along the way, as well as some wonderful bakers still making bread in the traditional manner (the bakeries in Kirkby Stephen and Reeth spring to mind). Alternatively, stop in a pub.

At least four of the stages in this book are devoid of eateries or shops so **read ahead** about the next day's walk to make sure you never go hungry.

Cream teas

Never miss a chance to avail yourself of the treats on offer in the tearooms and farmhouses of Cumbria and Yorkshire. Nothing relaxes and revives like a decent pot of tea, and the opportunity to accompany it with a scone served with jam and cream, or a cake or two, is one that should not be passed up.

Evening meals

If your B&B doesn't do an evening meal you may find that, in many villages, the pub is the only place to eat out. **Pubs** are as much a feature of this walk as moorland, churches and views, and in some cases the pub is as much a tourist attraction as the finest ruined abbey. Most of them have become highly attuned to the needs of walkers and offer both lunch and evening meals (with often a few regional dishes and usually a couple of vegetarian options), some locally brewed beers, a garden to relax in on hot days and a roaring fire to huddle around on cold ones. The standard of the food varies widely, though portions are usually large, which is often just about all walkers care about at the end of a long day.

That other great British culinary tradition and a favourite of Wainwright's in the bigger towns is the **fish 'n' chip shop** which will deep fry your dinner and then slather it in a layer of mushy peas and brown sauce. Larger towns also have Chinese and Indian **takeaways**; a welcome change from too much pub food and usually the only places still serving food late in the evenings, usually until at least 11pm.

© Bryn Thomas

Catering for yourself

The list of village shops (often combined with a post office) along the route grows sadly shorter with each edition but those that manage to remain in business have a pretty good selection of foods and your diet will depend on what you can find there. A couple of these small stores sell camping gas stove cartridges (which you can also pick up in the bigger towns such as Grasmere, Kirkby Stephen and Richmond). Part 4 goes into greater detail about what can be found where.

The Patterdale Village Store & Post Office is the perfect example of a well run business that serves not only the needs of the community but those of serious walkers and campers. You'll find everything from a pork rib sandwich to a new pair of hiking socks here.

Drinking water

There may be plenty of ways of perishing on the Coast to Coast trail but thirst won't be one of them. Be careful, though, for on a hot day in some of the remoter parts of the Lake District after a steep climb or two you'll quickly dehydrate, which is at best highly unpleasant. Always carry some water with you and in hot weather aim to drink **three or four litres** per day, supplemented by rehydration tablets such as Nuun.

Out of the hills, don't be tempted by the water in the streams you come across in lowland areas where the chemicals from the pesticides and fertilisers used on the farms may become concentrated. It's a lot safer to fill up from taps or high mountain pools and becks. Remember, what makes you ill can't be seen by the naked eye so filling up from a peat-stained tarn or fellside beck will probably be much less polluted than a dribbling brook in somewhere like the intensively farmed Vale of Mowbray.

MONEY

Banks are very few and far between on the Coast to Coast path. There's one in Shap open just a few hours a week, a couple in Kirkby Stephen, and Richmond has branches of all the major banks, but apart from in these places there's nothing. **Post offices**, however, provide a very useful service. Most banks in Britain have agreements with the post office allowing customers to make cash withdrawals using their debit card at post offices throughout the country. To find branches and check their services contact the Post Office (☎ 0345-611 2970, ⌨ www.postoffice.co.uk/branch-finder). Some post offices also play host to the village **cashpoint/ATM**. Usually you can withdraw cash for free but some may still be privately operated and charge £1.25-1.85 per withdrawal.

Another way of getting cash is to use the **cashback** system: find a store that will accept a debit card and ask them to advance cash against the card. A number of the local village stores as well as some pubs will do this, though you'll usually have to spend a minimum of £5 with them first. It pays to ask.

As not all local stores, pubs or B&Bs accept credit/debit cards, it's essential to carry plenty of cash (reckon on £200 per person). A **chequebook** could prove useful as a back-up.

INTERNET ACCESS

Most places to stay offer **wi-fi** free to visitors. Some B&Bs and hotels provide an internet-enabled **computer** in the guest lounge free of charge while the bigger youth hostels do so for around £4 an hour. Otherwise, where present and open, the local **library** is the place to find internet access.

OTHER SERVICES

Many small villages have a **post office** that doubles as the local store and bank (see Money, above), and nearby you'll usually find a **phone box**, though be warned, to combat vandalism some only accept cards, taking a £1 connection fee which is charged whether you get an answer or not. Otherwise 60p is the minimum fee to make a cash call; no change is given. Be aware that if you're phoning a mobile from a call box, your £1 will last for less than a minute.

There are **outdoor equipment shops** and **pharmacies** in the larger towns of Grasmere, Kirkby Stephen and Richmond and **tourist information centres** at Kirkby Stephen, Ullswater (near Patterdale), Reeth and Richmond.

WALKING COMPANIES

It's possible to turn up with your boots and backpack at St Bees and just start walking without planning much other than your accommodation (about which, see the box on p21). The following companies, however, are in the business of making your holiday as stress-free and enjoyable as possible.

Baggage carriers

There are several baggage-carrying companies serving the Coast to Coast route. With all these services you can usually book up to around 8pm the previous evening, though it can be cheaper if you book in advance. All baggage forwarders will give an estimated latest time by which you can expect your bags to be delivered, usually 4.30pm. These companies also offer **self-guided holidays** (see opposite), long-term car parking and passenger bus services using their baggage vans along the Coast to Coast route.

These last two services have two important consequences for trekkers. Firstly, it means that, should you want to skip a walking stage, you can ride with your luggage on their **passenger bus service** to the next stage. Secondly, you can use Kirkby Stephen (Coast to Coast Packhorse), Richmond (Sherpa Van) or Kirkby Malham (Brigantes) as your base, getting a lift in their van to St Bees, and another back to their base at the end of the walk back from Robin Hood's Bay. However, seating is often limited so you must book well in advance.

You can leave your car at the **secure parking** at their base, which is better than the alternative of leaving it in St Bees and travelling all the way back from the east coast to pick it up again. Or you can buy a return train ticket from your home to one place which may be cheaper and quicker than having to buy one ticket to St Bees, and another from Robin Hood's Bay.

● **Sherpa Van** (baggage line ☎ 01748 826917, 🖥 www.sherpavan.com, also see Sherpa Expeditions on p30 & p31), based at 29 The Green, Richmond, is a national organisation that runs a baggage-delivery service from April to mid-October for many of Britain's other walking and cycling trails as well as the Coast to Coast. They charge from £8 a bag and will transfer (or effectively, store) your excess baggage left at St Bees and deliver it to Robin Hood's Bay for £25.

They also operate two daily **passenger bus services**: in the mornings between Richmond (leaving at 7.30am), Kirkby Stephen and St Bees (arriving 10am); and in the afternoon from Robin Hoods Bay (leaving at 4.30pm) to Richmond (arriving at 6.15pm). Each journey between Richmond and either coast is £22. Furthermore, they have secure **parking** in Richmond (£3 per day) and can also arrange parking in St Bees and Kirkby Stephen.

● **Coast to Coast Packhorse** (☎ 017683 71777, 🖳 www.c2cpackhorse.co.uk; see also below; early Apr-Sep) based near Kirkby Stephen receives regular recommendations from our readers and also shifts the baggage for many other Coast to Coast operators. Having paid for baggage transfers (from £7.50 per stage or £103 for up to 16 transfers) Packhorse customers are welcome to ride on the minibus with their bags, at no extra cost, should the need arise. Non-baggage customers are also welcome to hop on and off as the Packhorse passes through, paying only the appropriate fee for the distance on this **daily westbound bus service** along the route.

One van departs Kirkby Stephen at 8.30am, arriving at St Bees around 10.15am, before travelling via the pick-up points back to Kirkby Stephen. A second bus also leaves Kirkby Stephen at 8.30am, stopping at the drop-off points before reaching Robin Hood's Bay at 3.30pm, departing at 4pm for the direct trip back to Kirkby Stephen, arriving around 6.15pm. In other words, the buses stop at the various drop-off points only when travelling from west to east. The cost of travelling directly from Kirkby Stephen to St Bees or Robin Hood's Bay to Kirkby Stephen is £28 per person.

They also have a **secure parking** lot in Kirkby Stephen, where you can leave a car for the duration of the walk for £3.95 per day.

● **Brigantes Walking Holidays and Baggage Carriers** (☎ 01756 770402, 🖳 www.brigantesenglishwalks.com; see also below) run a family operated baggage courier service with locally based drivers covering the whole of the north of England.

For baggage transfer they charge from £8 per person per day. They have a secure parking facility in Kirkby Malham with transport provided to the start of the walk, and back from the end.

Self-guided holidays
Self-guided means that the company will organise accommodation, baggage transfer (some contracting out the work to other companies), transport to and from the walk and various maps and advice, but leave you on your own to actually walk the path and cover lunch and dinner. In addition to these, don't forget the specialist Coast to Coast websites (see box p48) that can also book accommodation and provide details of the walk.
● **Absolute Escapes** (☎ 0131 240 1210, 🖳 www.absoluteescapes.com) Edinburgh
● **Alpine Exploratory** (☎ 0131 247 6702, 🖳 www.alpineexploratory.com) Settle, Yorkshire Dales
● **AMS Outdoors** (☎ 0141 812 7370, 🖳 www.ams-outdoors.com) Erskine, Renfrewshire
● **Brigantes Walking Holidays** (☎ 01756 770402, 🖳 www.brigantesenglish walks.com) Skipton, North Yorkshire
● **British and Irish Walks** (☎ 01242 254353, 🖳 www.britishandirishwalks .com) Cheltenham, Gloucestershire
● **Coast to Coast Packhorse** (☎ 017683 71777, 🖳 www.c2cpackhorse.co.uk) Kirkby Stephen, Cumbria

- **Contours Walking Holidays** (☎ 01629 821900, 🖥 www.contours.co.uk) Wirksworth, Derbyshire
- **Discovery Travel** (☎ 01904 632226, 🖥 www.discoverytravel.co.uk) York
- **Explore Britain** (☎ 01740 650900, 🖥 www.explorebritain.com) Ferryhill, north of Richmond, County Durham
- **Footpath Holidays** (☎ 01985 840049, 🖥 www.footpath-holidays.com) Warminster, Wiltshire
- **Freedom Walking Holidays** (☎ 07733 885390, 🖥 www.freedomwalking holidays.co.uk) Goring-on-Thames, Berkshire
- **Load Off Your Back** (☎ 01707 331133, 🖥 www.loadoffyourback.co.uk) Part of Ramblers Worldwide Holidays
- **Macs Adventure** (☎ 0141 530 8886, 🖥 www.macsadventure.com) Glasgow
- **Mickledore** (☎ 017687 72335, 🖥 www.mickledore.co.uk) Keswick, Cumbria
- **Northwestwalks** (☎ 01257 424889, 🖥 www.northwestwalks.co.uk) Wigan
- **Sherpa Expeditions** (☎ 020 8875 5070, 🖥 www.sherpaexpeditions.com) Richmond, Yorkshire, and London
- **Walk the Trail** (☎ 01326 567252, 🖥 www.walkthetrail.co.uk) Helston Cornwall
- **The Walking Holiday Company** (☎ 01600 713008, 🖥 www.thewalkingholi daycompany.co.uk) Monmouth
- **Wandering Aengus Treks** (☎ 016974 78443, 🖥 www.watreks.com) Fellside, Cumbria

Group/guided walking tours

If you don't trust your navigational skills or simply prefer the company of other walkers as well as an experienced guide, the following companies will be of interest. Packages nearly always include all meals, accommodation, transport arrangements, minibus back-up and baggage transfer.

Look very carefully at each company's website before booking as each has its own speciality and it's important to choose one that's suitable for you.

- **Alpine Exploratory** (see p29) Offers private guided trips.
- **Badger Adventures** (☎ 01900 516167, 🖥 www.badgeradventures.co.uk) A family business based in the Lake District offering 16 days walking, fully guid-ed with trained guide. No hidden costs and a vehicle on the trip all the way to provide support as required.
- **Cumbria Tourist Guides** (☎ 0755 764 5078, 🖥 www.cumbriatourist guides.org) Has fully qualified Blue Badge Guides who lead walks along the path. Can arrange a personalised itinerary for individuals travelling on their own or groups of any size.
- **Footpath Holidays** (see above) Runs guided walking tours along the trail in three 4- to 6-day sections from individual bases (one in the Lake District, one

in the Yorkshire Dales, and one in the North York Moors) so avoiding the hassle of daily packing. Guests can book one section or all three to complete the whole trail. Can tailor-make walks if required.

● **HF Holidays** HF Holidays (☎ 0345 470 7558, 🖳 www.hfholidays.co.uk) A reliable and frequently recommended Hertfordshire and Cumbria-based company that runs 15-day Coast to Coast treks.

● **Northwestwalks** (see opposite) operates around half-a-dozen 15-day guided holidays – and occasionally one 19-day guided holiday – a year. Has an excellent reputation and also leads guided holidays along half the route as well as offering tailor-made guided holidays for private groups.

● **Ramblers Worldwide Holidays** (☎ 01707 386800, 🖳 www.ramblersholi days.co.uk) This walking specialist offers the western part of the Coast to Coast from St Bees to Kirkby Stephen (7 days) and the eastern part from Kirkby Stephen to Robin Hood's Bay (8 days), as well as guided walks in the Lakes.

● **Sherpa Expeditions** (see opposite) A long-running, experienced company that operates five 15-day and one 18-day Coast to Coast treks a year.

WALKING WITH A DOG (see also p257)

The Coast to Coast is a dog-friendly path, though it's extremely important that dog owners behave in a responsible manner. Dogs should always be kept on leads while on the footpath to avoid disturbing wildlife, livestock and other walkers. Dog excrement should be cleaned up and not left to decorate the boots of others; take a pooper scooper or plastic bags if you're walking with a dog.

It's particularly important to **keep your dog on a lead** when crossing fields with livestock in them, especially around calving or lambing time which can be as early as February or as late as the end of May. Most farmers would prefer it if you did not bring your dog at all at this time.

In addition, in certain areas on the Coast to Coast trail (particularly east of Shap near Oddendale and around Sunbiggin Tarn, as well as on the North York Moors) there are notices ordering owners to keep their dogs on a lead to protect endangered ground-nesting birds between March and July; dogs can frighten them off and possibly cause them to desert their nests.

Remember when planning and booking your accommodation that you'll need to check if your dog will be welcome. Youth hostels do not permit them unless they're for assistance. Places that accept dogs in the accommodation are identified in the route guide by the symbol 🐾 : some charge an extra £5-10 for a dog.

Note, too, that your dog needs to be extremely fit to complete the Coast to Coast path. You may not believe it when you watch it haring around the fields, but they do have a finite amount of energy, so make sure your dog is up to the task of walking for 10-20 miles a day (indeed often much more, considering how far some dogs wander).

For general information about long-distance walking with a dog see p257.

Budgeting

England is not a cheap place to go travelling and, while the north may be one of the less expensive regions, the towns and villages in the Lakes especially can get all the business they can handle and charge accordingly. You may think before you set out that you're going to keep your budget to a minimum by camping every night and cooking your own food, but it's a rare trekker who sticks to this. Besides, the B&Bs and pubs on the route are amongst the Coast to Coast's major attractions and it would be a pity not to sample their hospitality from time to time.

If the only expenses of this walk were accommodation and food, budgeting would be a piece of cake. Unfortunately, in addition to these there are all the little **extras** that push up the cost of your trip: for example beer, cream teas, internet use, buses or taxis, baggage carriers, laundry, souvenirs. It's surprising how much these add up!

CAMPING

You can survive on less than £15 per person per day if you use the cheapest campsites, don't visit a pub, avoid all the museums and tourist attractions in the towns, forage for or cook all your own food from staple ingredients ... and generally have a pretty miserable time of it. Even then, unforeseen expenses will probably nudge your daily budget up. Include the occasional pint, and perhaps a pub meal every now and then, and the figure will be nearer £20 per day.

HOSTELS, BUNKHOUSES AND CAMPING BARNS

The charge for staying in a **hostel** is £15-27 per night. Whack on another £6 for breakfast and £9-12 for an evening meal, though you can use their self-catering facilities for both, and there's also lunch (packed lunches about £5.50) to consider. This means that, overall, it will cost £30-40 per day, or £45-50 to live in a little more comfort, enjoy the odd beer and go out for the occasional meal.

There are a few basic **camping barns** along the Coast to Coast. They vary in quality and price (expect to pay around £10-20).

B&BS, GUESTHOUSES AND HOTELS

B&B prices start at around £30 per person per night but can be up to twice this. Add on the cost of food for lunch and dinner and you should reckon on about £50 minimum per day. Staying in a guesthouse or hotel will cost more. Remember that there is often a supplement of £10-20 for single occupancy of a double or twin room and you may even have to pay the full price of the room.

Itineraries

Most people tackle the Coast to Coast from west to east, mainly because this allows them to walk 'with the weather at their back' (most of the time the winds blow off the Atlantic from the south-west). It's also usual for people to attempt the walk in one go, though there's much to be said for breaking it up and not crawling into Robin Hood's Bay in an Ibuprofen-induced daze.

Part 4 of this book has been written from west to east, but there is of course nothing to stop you from tackling it in the opposite direction (see below). To help plan your walk look at the **planning maps** (see opposite inside back cover) and the **table of village/town facilities** (on pp36-7), which gives a run-down on the essential information you'll need regarding accommodation possibilities and services at the time of writing. You could follow one of the **suggested itineraries** (see boxes pp34-5) which are based on preferred type of accommodation and walking speeds. There's also a list of recommended linear **day and weekend walks** on pp38-9 which cover the best of the Coast to Coast path, all of which are well served by public transport or the Packhorse/Sherpa van. The services table is on pp52-5 and **public transport map** on p52.

Once you have an idea of your approach turn to Part 4 for detailed information on accommodation, places to eat and other services in each village and town on the route. Also in Part 4 you will find summaries of the route to accompany the detailed trail maps.

WHICH DIRECTION?

There are a number of advantages in tackling the path in a west to east direction, not least the fact that the prevailing winds will, more often than not, be behind you. If you are walking alone but wouldn't mind some company now and again you'll find that most of the other Coast to Coast walkers are heading in your direction, too. However, there is also something to be said for leaving the Lake District – many people's favourite part of the British Isles, let alone the path – until the end of the walk.

SUGGESTED ITINERARIES

The itineraries in the boxes on these pages are based on different accommodation types – camping (not including wild camping which opens your options right out), hostels/bunkhouses/camping barns, and B&Bs – with each one divided into three alternatives depending on your walking speed (relaxed, medium and fast). They are only suggestions so feel free to adapt them. Don't forget to **add your travelling time** before and after the walk.

PLANNING YOUR WALK

SIDE TRIPS

The Coast to Coast path is long enough and few walkers will be tempted to make side trips. However, Wainwright's series of guides to Lakeland fells describes other walks around the Lake District in further detail and it may be worth making time for an ascent of some of the hills in the area as they give an entirely different perspective of the Lakeland landscape. Old favourites include Great Gable, Striding Edge on Helvellyn, High Street and England's highest mountain Scafell Pike (3209ft/978m).

STAYING IN HOSTELS/CAMPING BARNS/BUNKHOUSES

Night	Relaxed pace Place	Approx Distance miles/km	Medium pace Place	Approx Distance miles/km	Fast pace Place	Approx Distance miles/km
0	St Bees		St Bees		St Bees	
1	Sandwith	3/5	Sandwith	3/5	Ennerdale	20/32
2	Ennerdale Br*	12/19.5	Ennerdale	15.5/25	Grasmere	20.5/33
3	Black Sail YH	8.5/13.5	Borrowdale§	10.5/17	Shap	23.5/38
4	Borrowdale§	5.5/9	Grasmere	10/16	K. Stephen	20.5/33
5	Grasmere	10/16	Patterdale	10/16	Reeth [Dales]	29/47
6	Patterdale	10/16	Shap	15.5/25	East Applegarth	10/16
7	Shap	15.5/25	K. Stephen	20.5/33	Osmotherley	28.5/46¶
8	Orton*	8/13	Keld	13/21	Blakey Ridge*	20.5/33
9	K. Stephen	13/21	Reeth [Grinton]	12.5/20	Grosmont*	13.5/22
10	Keld	13/21	East Applegarth	9.5/15	R. Hood's Bay	15.5/25
11	Reeth [Dales]	12.5/20	Danby Wiske*	16.5/26.5¶		
12	East Applegarth	10/16	Osmotherley	12/19.5		
13	Danby Wiske*	16.5/26.5¶	Clay Bank Top†*	11/18		
14	Osmotherley	12/19.5	Glaisdale*	19/30.5		
15	Clay Bank Top†*	11/18	R. Hood's Bay	19/30.5		
16	Blakey Ridge*	9/14.5				
17	Glaisdale*	10/16	* No camping barns, bunkhouses or hostels but			
18	Littlebeck*	7/11.5	alternative accommodation is available			
19	R. Hood's Bay	12/19.5	§ Borrowdale = Longthwaite, Rosthwaite & Stonethwaite			

† Clay Bank Top = Urra, Chop Gate & Gt Broughton

¶ The A1 (M) roadworks diversion (see p205) currently adds 1 mile (1.6km) to this

Note: some of the above are seasonal so check in advance

❏ Next time ...

I will discipline myself to take more time on the trail and to savour the experience of the walking. The metronomic, almost trance-like state that can occur when all you need to do is put one foot in front of the other is rarely achieved when you're focussing on getting to the end. Too often I arrived at my destination by 3pm or even 2pm and although this means more time relaxing in the pub it also means I could have taken more time on the hills, perhaps sitting quietly enjoying a view or taking time to divert from the path to explore the landscape. **Stuart Greig**

CAMPING (Note: campsites may be seasonal)

	Relaxed pace		Medium pace		Fast pace	
Night	**Place**	**Approx Distance** miles/km	**Place**	**Approx Distance** miles/km	**Place**	**Approx Distance** miles/km
0	St Bees		St Bees		St Bees	
1	Cleator*	11/18	Ennerdale Br*	14/22.5	Ennerdale Br*	14/22.5
2	Ennerdale Br*	7/11	Borrowdale§	15/24	Borrowdale§	15/24
3	Seatoller	13/21	Grasmere*	9/14.5	Patterdale	16/26
4	Grasmere*	11/18	Patterdale	8.5/13.5	Shap	15.5/25
5	Patterdale	7.5/12	Shap	15.5/25	K. Stephen	20.5/33
6	Shap	15.5/25	Kirkby Stephen	20.5/33	Reeth	28/45
7	Orton	8/13	Keld	13/21	Colburn	17/27¶
8	Kirkby Stephen	13/21	Reeth	11/18	Ingleby Cross	20/32
9	Keld	13/21	East Applegarth	8/13	Blakey Ridge	20.5/33
10	Reeth	11/18	Danby Wiske*	17.5/28¶	Grosmont	13.5/22
11	East Applegarth	8/13	Osmotherley	12/19.5	R. Hood's Bay	15.5/25
12	Brompton-o-S	8.5/13.5	Blakey Ridge	20.5/33		
13	Danby Wiske*	8.5/13.5¶	Grosmont	13.5/22		
14	Ingleby Cross	9/14.5	R. Hood's Bay	15.5/25		
15	Clay Bank Top†*	11.5/17.5				
16	Blakey Ridge	9/14.5	*Basic camping available*			
17	Grosmont	14/22.5	§ *Borrowdale = Longthwaite, Rosthwaite, Stonethwaite*			
18	High Hawsker	10/16	† *Clay Bank Top = Urra, Chop Gate & Gt Broughton*			
19	R. Hood's Bay	5.5/9	¶ *Plus 1 mile (1.6km) for A1 (M) roadworks (see p205)*			

STAYING IN B&Bs

	Relaxed pace		Medium pace		Fast pace	
Night	**Place**	**Approx Distance** miles/km	**Place**	**Approx Distance** miles/km	**Place**	**Approx Distance** miles/km
0	St Bees		St Bees		St Bees	
1	Cleator	11/18	Ennerdale Br	14/22.5	Ennerdale Br	14/22.5
2	Ennerdale Br	5/8	Borrowdale§	15/24	Borrowdale§	15/24
3	Seatoller	14/22.5	Grasmere	9/14.5	Patterdale	17/27
4	Grasmere	10.5/17	Patterdale	8.5/13.5	Shap	15.5/25
5	Patterdale	7.5/12	Shap	15.5/25	K. Stephen	20.5/33
6	Shap	15.5/25	K. Stephen	20.5/33	Reeth	28/45
7	Orton	8/13	Keld	13/21	Colburn	17/27¶
8	K. Stephen	13/21	Reeth	11/18	Ingleby Cross	20/32
9	Keld	13/21	Richmond	10.5/17	Blakey Ridge	20.5/33
10	Reeth	11/18	Danby Wiske	14/22.5¶	Littlebeck	17.5/28
11	Richmond	10.5/17	Osmotherley	12/19.5	R. Hood's Bay	12/19.5
12	Danby Wiske	14/22.5¶	Clay Bank Top†	11/18		
13	Ingleby Cross	9/14.5	Blakey Ridge	8.5/13.5		
14	Clay Bank Top†	12/19.5	Grosmont	13.5/22		
15	Blakey Ridge	8.5/13.5	R. Hood's Bay	15.5/25		
16	Glaisdale	10/16				
17	Littlebeck	7/11.5	§/†/¶ *See notes above*			
18	R. Hood's Bay	12/19.5				

PLANNING YOUR WALK

VILLAGE AND

Place name (Places in brackets are a short walk off the Coast to Coast path)	Distance from previous place approx miles/km	Cash Machine/ ATM	Post Office	Tourist Information Centre/Point (TIC/TIP)
St Bees		✔	✔	TIP
Sandwith	4.5/7.2			
Moor Row	3.5/5.6			
Cleator	1/1.6			
Ennerdale Bridge	6/9.6 (via Dent)			
Seatoller	14/22.5			
Borrowdale	2/3.2 (to Rosthwaite)			
(Longthwaite, Rosthwaite, Stonethwaite)				
Grasmere	9/14.5 (from Rosthwaite)	✔	✔	
Patterdale	7.5/12 (not Helvellyn routes)	✔**	✔	TIC (at Glenridding)
Shap	15.5/25	✔**	✔	
(Orton)	8/12.9		✔	
Kirkby Stephen	20.5/33 (from Shap)	✔	✔	TIC
Keld	13/21 (not Green route)			
(Thwaite)	2/3.2 (from Keld)			
(Muker)	3.5/5.6 (from Keld)			
(Gunnerside)	2.5/4 (from Muker)			
Reeth	4/6.4 (from Gunnerside)	✔	✔	TIC/NPC*
	11/18 (from Keld on high route)			
Marrick	3.5/5.6			
Richmond	10.5/16.9	✔	✔	TIC
Colburn	3/4.8			
Catterick Bridge	2/3.2⁋			
(Brompton-on-Swale)	0.5/0.8			
Danby Wiske	7.5/12.1			
Oaktree Hill	2.5/4			
Ingleby Cross/Arncliffe	8/12.9		✔	
(Osmotherley)	3/4.8 (from Ingleby Cross)		✔	
Clay Bank Top†	12/19.3			
Blakey Ridge	8.5/13.7			
Glaisdale	10/16.1		✔	
Egton Bridge	2/3.2			
Grosmont	2/3.2	✔**	✔	NPC*
Littlebeck	3.5/5.6			
High Hawsker	7.5/12			
Robin Hood's Bay	4.5/7.2	✔**	✔	

TOTAL DISTANCE 189.5 miles (305km) – see p18
* NPC = National Park Centre   ✔** cashback available (no ATM)
⁋ The A1 (M) roadworks diversion (see p205) currently adds 1 mile (1.6km) to this

TOWN FACILITIES

Eating Place ✔=one; ✔✔=two; ✔✔✔=three+	Food Store	Campsite (approx miles off the path)	Hostels Y (YHA) H-B (IndHostel or Bunkhouse) B (Barn)	B&B-style accommodation ✔=one; ✔✔=two; ✔✔✔=three+	Place name (Places in brackets are a short walk off the Coast to Coast path)
✔✔✔	✔	✔		✔✔✔	**St Bees**
			B		**Sandwith**
✔				✔	**Moor Row**
✔	✔			✔✔✔	**Cleator**
✔✔		✔(1.5)	B(5)/H-B(1.5)/ Y(5)	✔✔✔	**Ennerdale Bridge**
✔		✔	Y(1.5)	✔✔	**Seatoller**
✔✔✔	✔	✔	Y/B	✔✔✔	**Borrowdale**
	(basics)			(Longthwaite, Rosthwaite, Stonethwaite)	
✔✔✔	✔		Y/H-B	✔✔✔	**Grasmere**
✔✔	✔	✔	Y/H-B	✔✔✔	**Patterdale**
✔✔✔	✔	✔	H-B	✔✔✔	**Shap**
✔	✔	✔		✔✔✔	**(Orton)**
✔✔✔	✔	✔	H-B	✔✔✔	**Kirkby Stephen**
✔✔		✔	H-B	✔✔✔	**Keld**
✔				✔	**(Thwaite)**
✔	✔			✔✔✔	**(Muker)**
✔✔				✔	**(Gunnerside)**
✔✔✔	✔	✔	Y/H-B	✔✔✔	**Reeth**
		✔		✔	**Marrick**
✔✔✔	✔	✔(3)	H-B(3)	✔✔✔	**Richmond**
✔		✔		✔	**Colburn**
✔		✔		✔	**Catterick Bridge**
		✔	B		**(Brompton-on-Swale)**
✔		✔		✔✔✔	**Danby Wiske**
		✔	H-B	✔	**Oaktree Hill**
✔		✔		✔✔✔	**Ingleby Cross/Arncliffe**
✔✔✔	✔	✔	Y	✔✔✔	**(Osmotherley)**
✔		✔(3.5)		✔✔✔	**†Clay Bank Top**
✔		✔		✔✔	**Blakey Ridge**
✔	✔			✔✔✔	**Glaisdale**
✔✔✔				✔✔✔	**Egton Bridge**
✔✔	✔	✔		✔✔✔	**Grosmont**
		✔		✔	**Littlebeck**
✔		✔		✔✔✔	**High Hawsker**
✔✔✔	✔	✔	Y	✔✔✔	**Robin Hood's Bay**

DISTANCE Distances are between places directly on the Coast to Coast path
† Clay Bank Top This refers to Urra, Chop Gate & Great Broughton

PLANNING YOUR WALK

❑ DAY WALKS

The best day loops and weekend walks on the Coast to Coast

The following suggested trails are for those who don't want to tackle the entire path in one go or just want to get a flavour of the challenge before committing themselves.

You won't go thirsty on the Esk Valley Glaisdale to Grosmont day walk.
© Jim Manthorpe

In our opinion they include the best parts of the Coast to Coast path, and are all described in more detail in Part 4.

Day walks bring you back to your starting point, either along other routes not mapped in this book or in some cases it is possible to use public transport.

There is good public transport (see pp52-5) to the start and end points on the suggested weekend walk but no direct service between Reeth and Kirkby Stephen. However, if there are two of you, you can shuttle with two cars, or a car and bike as many walkers do.

St Bees to Sandwith   5 miles/8km (pp93-8)
Get a flavour of the walk by completing the first 2.5 per cent of it! Set out from St Bees and strike off along the red rock sea cliffs; you can be back in St Bees that night, either by walking from Sandwith or taking the bus.

Around Ennerdale Water   11 miles/18km (pp104-13)
he first truly gorgeous stretch of the Coast to Coast passes along the south shore of Ennerdale Water to the River Liza. You can carry on to Black Sail along an easy track, then take a walk back along the northern access track.

Borrowdale to Grasmere and back   15 miles/24km (pp119-29)
Grasmere for lunch? In good weather it's a great training walk and you'll be able to pin down the Greenup Edge crossing to boot. Warm yourself up on the long climb to the Edge and we recommend you take the regular valley route down to Grasmere. Rest up, revive yourself in the fleece-wearing capital of the UK, and then take the haul back with the sun to Borrowdale. We don't recommend the high route via Helm Crag unless you're really on form.

Grasmere to Grasmere   8 miles/13km (pp122-9)
A very popular day trip for the more active visitor to Grasmere. It's up to you which direction you take; probably reversing the Coast to Coast by tackling the acute climb up to Helm Crag is best. At the junction at the top of Easedale (Wpt 30, p122) you come down the valley. A great day out but tougher than you think.

Grasmere to Patterdale and back   16½ miles/26.5km (pp129-39)
A pretty hefty proposition and another great training walk through the heart of the Lakes. The walk takes you up to Helvellyn summit and along Striding Edge, lunch at the pub and then back either up the valley or along St Sunday Crag (same distance but more climbing on the latter) and back down the other side of Tongue Gill. With very little overlapping, it's easily one of the best days out in the Lakes.

Patterdale to Kidsty Pike and back   13 miles/21km (pp137-42)
Take a 6½ mile walk to the 784-metre (2572ft) summit of Kidsty Pike on the eastern edge of the Lakes and the highest point on the original Coast to Coast route (though Helvellyn and St Sunday are much higher).

Have a sandwich and a look around then walk right back down again to Patterdale for a slap-up meal in the pub. It's a stiff old climb up to Angle Tarn but from there on the gradients just blend in with the surroundings and the views all the way up and down are well worth the effort. Another Lakeland classic that will have you fired up for the real thing.

Kirkby Stephen to Nine Standards and back   12 miles/19.5km (pp160-9)
An easy climb to the mysterious stone cones atop Nine Standards Rigg. From the top you might try a southward link towards Rigg Beck and the Green Route back to town, adding a mile or two, but that can involve some messy bog-trotting.

Keld to Reeth   12½ miles/20km (pp176-90)
Whether you take the high route via a string of evocative mine ruins between breezy moors, or the lowland amble past the hamlets of Upper Swaledale, you're sure to find something you like. If you want to return to Keld you can either take a bus or, with a bit of forward planning, can cycle-shuttle back to the car.

Lord Stones Café to Clay Bank Top and back   7½ miles/12km (pp224-7)
On some days a rather too popular run with Teeside dog walkers but the gradients will all be good training for the big day.

The Esk Valley: Glaisdale to Grosmont   4 miles/6.5km (see pp238-43)
Not so much a trek as an easy pub crawl, this path takes you along the Esk Valley following the course of the river through woodland and along country tracks, via pretty Egton Bridge. Grosmont, at the end of the trail, has steam trains to Pickering or Whitby or buses and regular trains to Scarborough, Whitby, and even the beginning of the trail. There are also buses back to Glaisdale.

Little Beck Wood excursion   4½ miles/7km (pp244-7)
A shady afternoon's round trip to Falling Foss waterfall and the adjacent tea room through the lovely Little Beck Wood.

Whitby to Robin Hood's Bay   7 miles/11.5km (pp250-5)
Not on the Coast to Coast until the last few miles but a stirring cliff-top tramp nonetheless, ending at the hallowed slipway below the Bay Hotel. You won't be the first to pretend you've just finished the entire Coast to Coast, but no one need know. Take the regular bus service back to Whitby, which is a fun place too.

❑ WEEKEND WALKS
In addition to the walk described below, any number of the day walks can be combined into a two-day trek, particularly in the Lake District.

Kirkby Stephen to Reeth   28 miles/45km (pp160-90)
Anyone who manages to scramble over the Pennines and negotiate the boggy ground down to the old mining village of Keld deserves a reward of some sort, and picturesque Swaledale is just that. As an encore, take Wainwright's high route over the moors to Reeth or the less demanding stroll down the dale, passing through or near the villages of Muker, Gunnerside and Thwaite to end up in Reeth.

PLANNING YOUR WALK

What to take

Not ending up schlepping over the fells like an overloaded mule with a migraine takes experience and some measure of discipline. **Taking too much** is a mistake made by first-time travellers of all types, an understandable response to not knowing what to expect and not wanting to be caught short.

By UK standards the Coast to Coast is a long walk but it's not an expedition into the unknown. Experienced independent hill walkers trim their gear to the essentials because they've learned that an unnecessarily heavy pack can exacerbate injuries and put excess strain on the already hard-pressed feet. Note that if you need to buy all the gear listed, keep an eye out for the ever-more frequent online **sales** at outdoor gear shops; time it right and you could get it all half price.

TRAVELLING LIGHT

Organised tours apart, baggage-forwarding services tempt walkers to partially miss the point of long-distance walking: the satisfaction of striding away from

---

❏ **Next time I do the C2C...**

Next time we do the coast to coast we will make sure that we have booked into B&Bs that have baths! It's incredible how hard it is to stand up in a shower after a day's walking and also it is good to soak your muscles.

Parts of the walk are very remote and it is therefore important to make sure you have plenty of cash and/or your cheque book. Very few places accept cash cards and it is easy to get caught out. Likewise we would suggest that you take plenty of Compeed plasters for your possible blisters and pain killers as they are hard to get hold of once you get going on the walk and if you have a similar experience to ours then you'll go through plenty!

Be prepared for all weathers no matter what time of year you are walking. We experienced five days of horrendous weather in the Lakes at the end of July. A pair of gloves and a woolly hat are essential, along with a trusty compass for the top of mountains when you can't see beyond your arm!

Walking poles are a must for all ages – they saved our knees. In our experience they worked for us for a number of reasons from taking some of the weight off our feet, to clearing pathways, supporting our leaps across fast flowing streams and warning off angry looking cattle! Invest in a camel pack (at least two litres). By having easy access to water it means that you don't get dehydrated. Take inner soles to cushion feet as they came into their own, especially on the middle section of the walk when it is very flat and your feet take a pounding.

Birkdale Farm B&B in Keld is a find. It is the best accommodation we had the pleasure of staying in en route and if we knew this prior to our walk, we may well have stayed there for more than one night. The accommodation is a converted barn and completely self sufficient with a great open fire and a whole stash of logs!

Noelle Cox & Chris Foster

---

one coast knowing that you're carrying everything you need to get to the other. But if you've chosen to carry it all you must be ruthless in your packing choices.

HOW TO CARRY IT

Today's rucksacks are hi-tech affairs that make load-carrying as tolerable as can be expected. Don't get hung up on anti-sweat features; unless you use a wheelbarrow your back will always sweat a bit. It's better to ensure there is thick padding and a **good range of adjustment**. In addition to hip belts (allied with some sort of stiff back frame/plate), use an unelasticated **cross-chest strap** to keep the pack snug; it makes a real difference.

If camping you'll need a pack of at least 60 or 70 litres' capacity. Staying in hostels 40 litres should be ample, and for those eating out and staying in B&Bs a 20- to 30-litre pack should suffice; you could even get away with a daypack.

Few backpacks these days claim to be waterproof; use a waterproof **liner** or the elasticated backpack cover like a shower cap that comes with some packs. It's also handy to **compartmentalise** the contents into smaller bags so you know what is where. Take a few (degradable) **plastic bags** for wet things, rubbish etc; they're always useful. Finally, pack intelligently with the most frequently used things readily accessible.

FOOTWEAR

Boots

A good pair of boots is vital. Scrimp on other gear if you must – you'll only use waterproofs some days but you'll be walking every mile on every day. Expect to spend up to £150 on quality, three-season footwear which is light, breathable and waterproof, and has ankle support as well as flexible but thick **soles** to insulate your own pulverised soles. Don't buy by looks or price and avoid buying online until you've been to a shop and tried on an identical pair (and even this can backfire on you). Go to a big outdoor shop on a quiet weekday and spend an hour trying on everything they have in stock that appeals to you.

With modern fabric **breaking in** boots is a thing of the past but arriving in St Bees with an untried pair of boots is courting disaster. You must try them out beforehand, first round the house or office, and then on a full day's walk or two. An old and trusted pair of boots can be resoled and transformed with shock-absorbing after-market **insoles**. Some of these can be thermally moulded to your foot in the shop, but the less expensive examples are also well worth the investment, even if the need for replacement by the end of the walk is likely. Some walkers wisely carry old trusted boots in their luggage in case their new footwear turns on them – though this can be quite a heavy tactic, of course. Blisters are possible even with a much-loved boot if you walk long and hard enough; refer to p83 for blister-avoidance strategies.

Boots might be considered over the top for the Coast to Coast; much of the walking is on easy paths and some experienced walkers have turned to trail shoes. They won't last as long as boots, be as tough or crucially, have the height

PLANNING YOUR WALK

to keep your socks dry in the bogs and streams; but the rewards of nimbleness and greater comfort can transform your walk, just as bad footwear can cast a shadow over it.

Socks

As with all outdoor gear, the humble sock has not escaped the technological revolution (with prices to match) so invest in two non-cotton pairs designed for walking. Although cushioning is desirable, avoid anything too thick which will reduce stability. As well as the obvious olfactory benefits, frequent washing will maintain the socks' springiness.

CLOTHES

Tops

The proven system of **layering** is a good principle to follow. A quick-drying synthetic (or the less odiferous merino wool) **base layer** transports sweat away from your skin; the mid-layer, typically a **fleece** or woollen jumper, keeps you warm; and when needed, an outer 'shell' or **jacket** protects you from the wind and rain.

Maintaining a comfortable temperature in all conditions is the key. This means not **overheating** just as much as it means keeping warm. Both can pre-

---

❑ Next time...

Take our time. It's a holiday. Forget about the keen types who set off before 8am – let them go. Plan most days at 10-14 miles, that gives plenty of time.

Expect to feel tired, especially on days 2-4. It isn't Pennine Way-tough, but it isn't an easy stroll either.

Stay in B&Bs, especially farms. Last time, except for the terrific Langstrath, the pubs and hotels were a bit disappointing while the B&Bs were all good to great.

See the eagle in Riggindale again. We saw it for a few seconds last time, fabulous.

Do the high routes, weather permitting – Helm Crag and St Sunday Crag are fantastic on clear days. Helvellyn next time?

If we've time, have a rest day in Kirkby Stephen as well as in Richmond. It's welcome after the Lakes. (And there's a launderette!).

Take the Swale route from Keld to Reeth. The mines are interesting but bleak; everyone said the river is beautiful ... but then, lots of them wished they'd done the high-level route.

Spend longer in the Swaledale Museum in Reeth, and stay overnight in their lovely quirky cottage. Then stock up in the Reeth Bakery.

Take a lightweight camera, binoculars, a notebook. Make notes at least every evening – it's easy to forget the details, the days merge into one another. Take more notice of the small things: wild flowers, how the dry-stone walls change, curlews. The big things are dramatic, but the small ones are fascinating.

Make sure boots are 100% waterproof. A tiny damp spot on a Sunday stroll in Cheshire is trench foot on Nine Standards Rigg.

Think about going east to west. The Lakes are the highlight but they're hard work at the start. They'd be a great climax starting from the east, when we're more walking-fit. As for the rain-in-your-face argument ... what rain?!

David Bull

maturely tire you: trudging out of Patterdale on a warm day will soon have you down to your base layer, but any exposed and prolonged descent, or rest on an unsheltered summit like Kidsty Pike with a strong wind blowing will soon chill you. Although tedious, the smart hiker is forever fiddling with zips and managing their layers and headwear to maintain an optimal level of comfort.

Avoid cotton; as well as being slow to dry, when soaked it saps away body heat but not the moisture – and you'll often be wet from sweat if not rain. Take a change of **base layers** (including underwear), a **fleece** suited to the season, and the best **breathable waterproof** you can afford. **Soft shells** are an alternative to walking in rustling nylon waterproofs when it's windy but not raining.

It's useful to have a **spare set of clothing** so you're able to get changed should you arrive chilled at your destination, but choose **quick-drying clothes** as washing them reduces your payload. Once indoors your body heat will quickly dry out a synthetic fleece and nylon leggings. However, always make sure you have a **dry base layer** in case you or someone you're with goes down with hypothermia. This is why a quality waterproof is important.

Leg wear

Your legs are doing all the work and don't generally get cold so your trousers can be light which will also mean quick-drying. Although they lack useful pockets, many walkers find leg-hugging cycling polyester **leggings** very comfortable (eg Ron Hill Tracksters). Poly-cotton or microfibre trousers are excellent. Denim jeans are cotton and a disaster when wet.

If the weather's good, **shorts** are very agreeable to walk in, leaving a light pair of trousers clean for the evenings. It also means your lower legs get muddy and not the trousers. On the other hand **waterproof trousers** would only suit people who really feel the cold; most others will find them unnecessary and awkward to put on and wear; quick drying or minimal legwear is better. For Lakeland stream crossings and Pennine peat bogs, **gaiters** are a great idea; they also stop irritating pebbles dropping into your footwear. You don't have to wear them all the time.

Headwear and other clothing

Your head is both exposed to the sun and loses most of your body heat so, for warmth, carry a woolly beany that won't blow away and for UV protection a peaked cap; a bandana or microfibre 'buff' makes a good back-up or sweat band too. Between them they'll conserve body heat or reduce the chances of dehydration. **Gloves** are a good idea in wintry conditions (carry a spare pair in winter).

TOILETRIES

Besides **toothpaste**/brush, **liquid soap** can also be used for shaving and washing clothes, although a ziplock bag of **detergent** is better if you're laundering regularly. Carry **toilet paper** and a lightweight **trowel** to bury the results out on the fells (see pp78-9).

Less obvious items include **ear plugs**, **sun screen**, **moisturiser**; **insect repellent** if camping and possibly a means of **water purification**.

FIRST-AID KIT

Apart from aching limbs your most likely ailments will be blisters so a first-aid kit can be minimal. **Ibuprofen** and **paracetamol** help numb pain – although rest, of course, is the only real cure. '**Compeed**', or '**Second Skin**' all treat blisters. An **elastic knee support** is a good precaution for a weak knee as are walking poles (see box p40). A tube of Nuun tablets can flavour water and restore lost minerals on the march, and a few sachets of Dioralyte or Rehydrat powders will quickly remedy more serious dehydration. Other items worth considering are: **plasters** for minor cuts; a small selection of different-sized **sterile dressings** for wounds; **porous adhesive tape**; **antiseptic wipes**; **antiseptic cream**; **safety pins**; **tweezers**; and **scissors**.

GENERAL ITEMS

Essential

Carry a **compass**, **whistle** and **mobile phone** as well as at least a one-litre **water bottle** or bag; an LED **headtorch**; **emergency snacks**, a **penknife** and a **watch**.

Useful

If you're not carrying a proper bivvy bag or tent, a compact foil **space blanket** is a good idea in the cooler seasons. Many people take a **camera**, **batteries** and **sunglasses**. A **book** is a good way to pass the evenings, especially in mid-summer wild camps. A **vacuum flask**, for hot drinks or soup, is recommended if walking in a cooler season. Studies have shown that nothing improves a hilltop view on a chilly day like a hot cup of tea or soup.

SLEEPING BAG & CAMPING GEAR

If you're camping or planning to stay in camping barns you'll need a sleeping bag. Many bunkhouses now offer bedding, some at a nominal cost. All youth hostels provide bedding and insist you use it.

A **two-season bag** will do for indoor use, but if you can afford it or anticipate outdoor use, go warmer. The choice over a **synthetic** or **down** filling is a debate without end. Year by year less expensive synthetic-filled bags (typically under £100) approach down's enviable qualities of good compressibility while expanding or 'lofting' fully once unpacked to create maximum warmth. But get a down bag wet (always a risk in the UK) and it clogs up and loses all its thermal qualities; and drying down bags takes half a day at the launderette.

If committed to the exposure of wild camping you'll need a **tent** you can rely on; light but able to withstand the rain and wind. In campsites you may just get away with a cheap tent. Otherwise, a good one-man tent suited to the wilds can cost under £120 and weigh just 1.5kg, with a sub-2kg two-man example costing around £250. An inflatable **sleeping mat** is worth many times its weight.

As for **cooking**, is it really worth the bother on the Coast to Coast? The extra weight and hassle in buying provisions is only viable when shared by a group of three or more; otherwise get down the pub and help support the local economy.

MONEY

Cash machines (ATMs) are infrequent along the Coast to Coast path, with none east of Richmond (but you can get cashback in Grosmont and Robin Hood's Bay). Furthermore, some of them do not work with foreign cards. Banks are even rarer, with only Shap, Kirkby Stephen and Richmond boasting any. Not everybody accepts **debit** or **credit cards** as payment either – though many B&Bs and restaurants now do. As a result, you should always carry plenty of cash with you, just to be on the safe side. A **cheque book** from a British bank is useful in those places where credit cards are not accepted. See also the table of village and town facilities on pp36-7. Crime on the trail is thankfully rare though it can't hurt to carry your money in a **moneybelt**; note, however, that the small loss of comfort you may feel at having a belt wrapped around your midriff will be overshadowed by the discomfort of having to hand over sweaty notes to B&B owners – so maybe keep your cash in a small plastic bag inside the pouch.

MAPS

The hand-drawn maps in this edition cover the trail at a scale of just under 1:20,000: one mile equals 3¹/₈ths of an inch (1km = 5cm). At this generous scale, combined with the notes and tips written on the maps, and the waypoints, they should be enough to stop you losing your way as long as you don't stray too far off the route. That said, a supplementary map of the region – ie one with contours – can prove invaluable should you need to abandon the path and find the quickest route off high ground in bad weather. It also helps you to identify local features and landmarks and devise possible side trips.

Unfortunately, the two Outdoor Leisure strip maps produced by the **Ordnance Survey** (🖳 www.ordnancesurvey.co.uk) that covered the entire trail at a scale of 1:27,777 went out of print in 2002, and although it may still be possible to get second-hand copies these are increasingly rare (and cost a premium – usually upwards from £30 each – if you can find them); look for sheets OL33 covering the trail from St Bees to Keld and OL34 covering it from Keld to Robin Hood's Bay. The good news is that electronic copies are available online and could of course be printed off. Have a look at 🖳 www.walkingplaces .co.uk/c2c/osmaps.htm.

In their place the Ordnance Survey now have the Explorer series of maps at a scale of 1:25,000 but in order to cover the whole trail you will need eight maps. The trouble here, of course, is one of weight and expense and also, **they don't always show the path** and are sometimes out of date with details like plantations. The details are: 303 (for St Bees); Outdoor Leisure (OL) 4 for the western Lake District; OL5 for the eastern Lake District; OL19 for the upper Eden Valley (Kirkby Stephen); OL30 for Swaledale; Explorer Series 304 (though very occasionally it dips south into 302) for Richmond and the Vale of Mowbray; OL26 for the western North York Moors; and OL27 for the eastern half to Robin Hood's Bay. While it may be extravagant to buy all of these maps, members of Ramblers (see box p48) can borrow up to 10 maps for free from their library, paying only for return postage.

PLANNING YOUR WALK

We say again that with a bit of nous many readers manage with the maps in this book, but if any two of the above OS maps are worth getting they are the **OL4 and OL5** covering the Lake District where the weather can be bad, the waymarking is worse and the consequences of losing the path vexing in the extreme. By a stroke of luck both these double-side sheets can be neatly cut in

❑ Digital mapping

There are numerous software packages now available that provide Ordnance Survey (OS) maps for a PC, smartphone, tablet or GPS. Maps are supplied by direct download over the Internet. The maps are then loaded into an application, also available by download, from where you can view them, print them and create routes on them.

Digital maps are normally purchased for an area such as a National Park, but the Coast to Coast walk is available as a distinct product from some vendors. When compared to the eight OS Explorer maps that are needed to cover the walk, they are very competitively priced. Once you own the electronic version of the map you can print any section of the map you like, as many times as you like.

The real value of the digital maps though, is the ability to draw a route directly onto the map from your computer or smartphone. The map, or the appropriate sections of it, can then be printed with the route marked on it, so you no longer need the full versions of the OS maps. Additionally, the route can be viewed directly on the smartphone or uploaded to a GPS device, providing you with the whole C2C route in your hand at all times while walking. If your smartphone has a GPS chip, you will be able to see your position overlaid onto the digital map on your phone.

Many websites now have free routes you can download for the more popular digital mapping products. Anything from day walks around the Lakes to complete Long Distance Paths like the Coast to Coast. It is important to ensure any digital mapping software on your smartphone uses pre-downloaded maps, stored on your device and doesn't need to download them on-the-fly, as this will be impossible in the hills.

Taking OS quality maps with you on the hills has never been so easy. Most modern smartphones have a GPS receiver built in to them and almost every device with built-in GPS functionality now has some mapping software available for it. One of the most popular manufacturers of dedicated handheld GPS devices is Garmin, who have an extensive range of map-on-screen devices. Prices vary from around £100 to £600.

Smartphones and GPS devices should complement, not replace, the traditional method of navigation (a map and compass) as any electronic device is susceptible to problems and, if nothing else, battery failure. Remember, too, that battery life will be significantly reduced, compared to normal usage, when you are using the built-in GPS and running the screen for long periods.

Memory Map (❑ www.memory-map.co.uk) currently sell OS 1:25,000 mapping covering the whole of the UK for £50.

Anquet (❑ www.anquet.com) has the Coast to Coast Path available for £27.45 using OS 1:25,000 mapping. They also have a range of Harvey maps.

For a subscription of £7.99 for one month or £17.95 for a year (on their current offer) **Ordnance Survey** (❑ www.ordnancesurvey.co.uk) will let you download and then use their UK maps (1:25,000 scale) on a mobile or tablet without a data connection for a specific period.

Harvey (❑ www.harveymaps.co.uk) sell their Coast to Coast Path maps (1:40,000 scale) as a download for £25.99 for use on any device.

Stuart Greig (❑ http://lonewalker.net)

half while still retaining the full extent of the path from west to east. The alternatives to OS are the strip maps produced by either **Footprint** (💻 www.stir lingsurveys.co.uk) or **Harvey Maps** (💻 www.harveymaps.co.uk), both of which cover the trail over two maps at a scale of around 1:50,000 and 1:40,000 respectively. The problem is that, like our maps, they only cover a narrow strip either side of the trail and consequently give limited opportunities for exploring further afield. Weighing 45g each, Footprint's maps are waterproof, have a useful cumulative mile count and cost around £6.95; Harvey's waterproof maps are £13.95 each and weigh 60g.

RECOMMENDED READING

Most of the following books can be found in the tourist information centres; the centre at Richmond has a particularly good supply of books about the path and the places en route. As well as stocking many of the titles listed below, the tourist offices also have a number of books about the towns and villages en route, usually printed by small, local publishers.

Guidebooks, travelogues and DVDs

We have to mention here Wainwright's original *A Coast to Coast Walk (Wainwright Pictorial Guides*, 2010), a veritable work of art and now reprinted by local publisher, Frances Lincoln. For the coffee table *Coast to Coast with Wainwright* (also Frances Lincoln, 2009) marries Wainwright's original text with photos by Derry Brabbs; it makes a great souvenir of the walk as does *The Coast to Coast Walk* (2012) by Karen Frenkel, another beautiful photo collection from the Frances Lincoln stable. *Ancient Feet* (Matador, 2008) by Alan Nolan, is a humourous tale of five friends in their sixties tackling the path. Returning with the Wainwright theme, Hunter Davies's *Wainwright: The Biography* (Orion Press) is an absorbing account of this complex man.

Towards the end of each year Doreen Whitehead produces the latest edition of her long-running publication *Coast to Coast Bed & Breakfast Accommodation Guide* (£5). See 💻 www.coasttocoastguides.co.uk.

It's possible you saw *Coast to Coast with Julia Bradbury* (DVD; Acorn Media, 2009, 165 mins), the five-part BBC show broadcast twice in 2009 and part of a 'Wainwright Walks' series. Julia Bradbury makes an engaging presenter and approaches the task with gusto, interviewing characters along the way (including writer Alan Nolan, see *Ancient Feet* above). Unfortunately, the production hit terrible weather in the Lakes which dampened the impression of that part of the walk; many of the aerial shots were filmed in much better conditions. Rumours circulated on the web and along the trail about body doubles standing in on long shots while she got choppered to the summits looking fresh as a daisy, and whether she walked the entire route. The reality of television as well as of filming outdoors makes the former likely (though she may well have done the walk on another occasion) and watching the parts in quick succession you can't help thinking that it's more fun to walk than to watch. Nevertheless, to have the Coast to Coast featured on mainstream TV at all is something of a coup

❑ SOURCES OF FURTHER INFORMATION

Online trail information

🖥 **www.coast2coast.co.uk** Run by Sherpa Van, this site is crammed full of information and has an online shop for books and maps as well as a popular accommodation-booking and luggage-transfer service (see p28). They also have a busy Coast to Coast forum, where trekkers share their experiences and others post questions, although it does suffer from a level of flippancy by the 'seen-it-all' regulars who dominate the board. Scrutinise at length before enquiring; it's probably been asked before.

🖥 **www.coasttocoastguides.co.uk** Richmond-based organisation and another excellent website with books and maps for sale and a thorough accommodation guide based on Doreen Whitehead's booklet (see p47).

🖥 **www.walkingplaces.co.uk/c2c** An extensive and cleanly designed website that's not trying too hard to do everything or sell you something. Run by Coast to Coast enthusiast, there are some excellent resources here that you won't find anywhere else, as well as a tolerant and supportive Coast to Coast forum. The site also hosts blogs (many with lots of photos) by recent walkers, that make interesting reading. There's also a map downloads section; make a donation if you use it.

🖥 **www.wainwright.org.uk** The website of the Wainwright Society, dedicated to 'keeping alive the fellwalking traditions promoted by AW', has a section on the trail.

Tourist information organisations

● **Tourist information centres (TICs)** TICs are based in towns throughout Britain and provide all manner of locally specific information and an accommodation-booking service. There are four centres relevant to the Coast to Coast path: **Ullswater/Glenridding** (near Patterdale, p139), **Kirkby Stephen** (p162), **Reeth** (p188) and **Richmond** (p200).

● **Yorkshire Tourist Board** (🖥 www.yorkshire.com) The tourist board oversees all the local tourist information centres in the county. It's a good place to find general information about the county as well as on outdoor activities and local events. They can also help with arranging holidays and accommodation.

● **Cumbria Tourist Board** (🖥 www.golakes.co.uk) Performing much the same role as the Yorkshire board above but, of course, for the county encompassing the Lake District.

Organisations for walkers

● **Backpackers' Club** (🖥 www.backpackersclub.co.uk) A club aimed at people who are involved or interested in lightweight camping through walking, cycling, skiing and canoeing. They produce a quarterly magazine, provide members with a comprehensive advisory and information service on all aspects of backpacking, organise weekend trips and also publish a farm-pitch directory. Membership is £15/20/8.50 per year for an individual/family/anyone under 18 or over 65.

● **The Long Distance Walkers' Association** (🖥 www.ldwa.org.uk) Membership includes a journal (*Strider*) three times per year with details of challenge events and local group walks as well as articles on the subject. Information on over 730 paths is presented in their *UK Trailwalkers' Handbook*, published by Cicerone. Membership is £13.

● **Ramblers** (🖥 www.ramblers.org.uk) A charity that looks after the interests of walkers throughout Britain and promotes walking for health. Membership costs £33/44 individual/joint and includes their quarterly *Walk* magazine.

for British long-distance paths and has further enshrined the popularity of the trail. The DVD contains no 'special features' of any significance.

Finally, 2014 saw the release of *Downhill* (DVD; Crisis Films, 98 mins), a Britflick about a group of former schoolfriends reuniting to tackle both the Coast to Coast and their collected midlife crises. It is perhaps best enjoyed after your trip, as you try to spot the locations they've used during for their footage of the trail and those inevitable 'Hey that's the same chair I sat in!' moments when the action moves into the local pubs.

If you're a seasoned long-distance walker, or even new to the game and like what you see, check out the other titles in the Trailblazer series; see p268.

Flora and fauna field guides

Collins *Bird Guide* with its beautiful illustrations of British and European birds continues to be the favourite field guide of both ornithologists and laymen alike. For a guide to the flora you'll encounter on the Coast to Coast path, *The Wild Flower Key* (Warne) by Francis Rose and Clare O'Reilly, is arranged to make it easy to identify unfamiliar flowers. Another in the Collins Gem series, *Wild Flowers*, is more pocket-sized and thus more suitable for walkers.

There are also several field guide apps for smart phones and tablets, including those that can aid in identifying birds by their song as well as by their appearance.

Getting to and from the Coast to Coast path

Both St Bees and Robin Hood's Bay are quite difficult to reach on public transport. For this reason, many people who are using the baggage carrier companies (see pp28-9) opt to start and finish at their bases (Kirkby Stephen, Richmond or Kirkby Malham) where they have car parking facilities and offer their own transport links to St Bees and Robin Hood's Bay

If you want to make your own way to **St Bees**, it's best to take a train to Carlisle or Barrow-in-Furness, and then take the train to St Bees. Alternatively take a bus from Carlisle to Whitehaven (Stagecoach No 300, 301 & No 600; see box p54) and then walk, bus or train the 4½ miles south from Whitehaven.

For **Robin Hood's Bay**, Arriva's No X93 Middlesbrough to Scarborough bus service operates daily (see box p55); all these towns are well connected by rail.

NATIONAL TRANSPORT

All train **timetable and fare information** can be found at National Rail Enquiries (☎ 03457 484950, 24hrs; 🖳 www.nationalrail.co.uk). Alternatively, and to book tickets, you can look on the websites of the train companies concerned: **Virgin Trains** (🖳 www.virgintrains.co.uk), **Virgin East Coast** (🖳 www.virgintrainseastcoast.com), **Northern Rail** (🖳 www.northernrail.org) and

Trans-Pennine Express (🖳 www.tpexpress.co.uk). Timetables and tickets are also available on 🖳 www.thetrainline.com and 🖳 www.qjump.co.uk. You are advised to book in advance – it may well save you a small fortune. If your journey involves changes, it's worth checking which train company operates each leg of the journey – you may find you can save money by buying separate tickets for each train company rather than one through ticket for your whole journey.

Coach travel is generally cheaper (though with the excellent advance-purchase train fares that is not always true) but takes longer. The principal coach (long-distance bus) operator in Britain is **National Express** (☎ 08717 81 81 81,

---

❑ GETTING TO BRITAIN

● **By air** Manchester Airport (🖳 www.manchesterairport.co.uk) remains the nearest major international airport to St Bees. Trans-Pennine Express (see p51) operates services from Manchester Airport to Barrow-in-Furness and Northern Rail (see p51) can take you from there to St Bees.

Leeds Bradford Airport (🖳 www.leedsbradfordairport.co.uk) is convenient for Kirkby Stephen and has flights to many European destinations. Durham Tees Valley Airport (www.durhamteesvalleyairport.com) is 7 miles/11km outside Darlington and useful for Richmond; it also rivals Newcastle (🖳 www.newcastleairport.com) as the nearest airport to Robin Hood's Bay – though with journeys from either airport to Robin Hood's Bay taking at least four hours, neither can be considered convenient for the Coast to Coast's eastern end. Nevertheless, though the services to and from these airports increase year on year, for most foreign visitors one of the London airports remains the most likely entry point to the country.

A number of **budget airlines** (easyJet 🖳 www.easyjet.com, jet2 🖳 www.jet2 .com and Ryanair 🖳 www.ryanair.com) fly from many of Europe's major cities to Manchester and the London terminals (Stansted, Luton, Gatwick and Heathrow). See p51 & p56 for details about Getting to St Bees, Kirkby Stephen or Robin Hood's Bay from London.

● **From Europe by train** Eurostar (🖳 www.eurostar.com) operates a high-speed passenger service via the Channel Tunnel between Paris, Brussels (and some other cities) and London St Pancras International – convenient for both the trains for Carlisle (which leave from nearby Euston) and to the north-east coast (which leave from neighbouring King's Cross). For more information about rail services from Europe contact your national rail operator, or Railteam (🖳 www.railteam.eu).

● **From Europe by coach** Eurolines (🖳 www.eurolines.com) have a huge network of long-distance coach services connecting over 600 cities in 36 European countries to London. Check carefully, however: once such expenses as food for the journey are taken into consideration, it often does not work out that much cheaper than taking a flight, particularly when compared to the prices of some of the budget airlines.

● **From Europe by ferry (with or without a car)** Numerous ferry companies operate routes between the major North Sea and Channel ports of mainland Europe and the ports on Britain's eastern and southern coasts as well as from Ireland to ports in both Wales and England. For further information see websites like 🖳 www.directferries.com.

● **From Europe by car** Eurotunnel (🖳 www.eurotunnel.com) operates the shuttle train service for vehicles via the Channel Tunnel between Calais and Folkestone taking one hour between the motorway in France and the motorway in Britain.

24 hrs, 🖥 www.nationalexpress.com). **Megabus** (🖥 uk.megabus.com) has a more limited service though may be cheaper.

Getting to St Bees

● **Train** Carlisle and Barrow-in-Furness are the main access points for St Bees. Virgin's London Euston to Glasgow service calls at Carlisle; trains operate approximately hourly during the day and the journey takes $3^1/4$-4 hours. Virgin's Birmingham New St to Edinburgh/Glasgow service stops in Carlisle hourly.

Trans-Pennine Express operates a service from Manchester Airport/ Manchester Piccadilly to Barrow-in-Furness (Mon-Sat 4/day, Sun 1/day). They also operate a service from Manchester Airport/Manchester Piccadilly to Glasgow/ Edinburgh via Carlisle (Mon-Sat 15/day, Sun 9/day).

Northern Rail (see p49) operates a service from Carlisle to Barrow-in-Furness via Whitehaven and St Bees (Mon-Sat 10/day). On Sunday the service only goes from Carlisle to Whitehaven (4/day), just over four miles up the road from St Bees.

● **Coach/bus** Whitehaven is the closest place to St Bees that National Express services operate to; stops on the once daily 571 London to Whitehaven service include Grasmere, and Kendal for bus services to Kirkby Stephen. From Whitehaven take a train (see above) to St Bees.

Alternatively, National Express has services to Carlisle from several towns and cities in Britain. Services that stop at least once a day in Carlisle include: 592 London to Aberdeen; 590 London to Glasgow; 538 Birmingham to Aberdeen; 532/539 Birmingham to Edinburgh and 532 Plymouth to Edinburgh.

From Carlisle take a train (see above) to St Bees, or a bus to Whitehaven (Stagecoach No 300, 301 & No 600; see box p54).

● **Car** You can of course drive to St Bees and leave your car (for a fee) at a B&B there. The nearest motorway is the M6 to Carlisle which joins the M1 just outside Coventry. From the south, leave the M1 at junction 36 (the Southern Lakes turn-off), then take the A590 till it meets the A5092; this then meets the A595 (to Whitehaven) and turn off just before Egremont.

Getting to Robin Hood's Bay

● **Train** Robin Hood's Bay is, if anything, even harder to reach than St Bees. The nearest rail station is at Whitby: East Coast's London King's Cross to Newcastle/Edinburgh/Glasgow service calls at Darlington, change here for Middlesbrough (Northern Rail service), then change at Middlesbrough for a train to Whitby (see box p52). From London to Whitby takes 5-6 hours. From Whitby Arriva's No X93 (see box p55) bus takes 20 minutes to Robin Hood's Bay.

A better way, involving only one change of train, is to get off the East Coast train at York and take one of TransPennine Express's trains to Scarborough and then take Arriva's No X93 (see box p55) bus to the Bay. The bus journey is longer (approximately 40 minutes) but the train journey is only around three hours in total.

(cont'd on p56)

LOCAL PUBLIC TRANSPORT SERVICES

Public transport is limited along the Coast to Coast path. While most places do have some sort of bus service, these services may be irregular and often just two or three times per day. Usually the choice of destination is limited too, often the nearest big town.

To check the current bus timetables, contact **traveline** (☎ 0871 200 2233; ☐ www.traveline.info), which has public transport information for the whole of the UK. This is usually easier than contacting the operator directly as many bus services are run by more than one operator. From the Cumbria County Council website (☐ www.cumbria.gov.uk/buses) you can search details of buses, trains and ferries in the county. For information about services in North Yorkshire visit ☐ www.dalesbus.org or ☐ www.northyorks.gov.uk.

Notes
● Service details were as accurate as possible at the time of writing but it is essential to check before travel
● Services on Bank Holiday Mondays are usually the same as Sunday services; services that operate Monday to Saturday generally don't operate on Bank Holiday Mondays
● Services generally operate at the same frequency in both directions
● Be aware that where routes are serviced by more than one operator (usually during the peak season), the different operators may not accept each other's tickets.
● In rural areas where there are no fixed bus stops it is usually possible to 'hail and ride' a passing bus though it is important to stand where visibility is good and also somewhere where it would be safe for the driver to stop
● See pp28-9 for details of **Packhorse's** and **Sherpa Van's** services along this route.

RAIL SERVICES & OPERATORS
Northern Rail Ltd (☎ 0845 000 0125 Mon-Sat 8am-8pm, Sun 9am-5pm, ☐ www.northernrail.org)
See p51 & p56 for details of the services to Carlisle for St Bees, to Whitby (for Robin Hood's Bay) and to Kirkby Stephen
● Middlesbrough to Whitby (Esk Valley Railway) via Glaisdale, Egton & Grosmont, Mon-Sun 4/day.

North York Moors Railway (enquiries ☎ 01751 472508, option 1 for talking timetable, ☐ www.nymr.co.uk)
● Grosmont to Pickering/Whitby via Goathland, Newtondale Halt & Levisham, daily Mar-Oct plus in holiday periods such as Christmas/New Year and February half-term, weekends only at other times; 6-9/day depending on the time of year.

See pp54-5 for BUS SERVICES

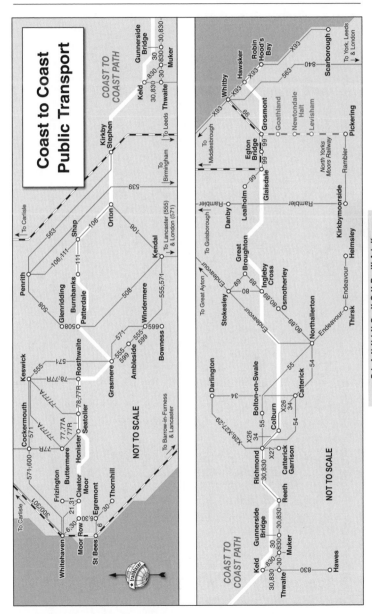

Coast to Coast
Public Transport

COAST TO
COAST PATH

BUS SERVICES & OPERATORS – CUMBRIA

SEE p53 FOR MAP

Route No	From	To	Via	Frequency	Operator
6	Whitehaven	Seascale	St Bees & Egremont	Mon-Fri 2/day	Reays
21	Frizington	Frizington	Circular route via Cleator Moor & Whitehaven	Mon-Sat 1-2/hr	Reays
30	Whitehaven	Thornhill	Egremont	Mon-Sat 1-2/hr, Sun 1/hr	Stagecoach
31	Whitehaven	Frizington	Cleator Moor	Mon-Sat 1-2/hr to 7pm	Stagecoach
32	Whitehaven	Cleator	Cleator Moor	Mon-Sat 1/hr to 6pm	Stagecoach
77/77A	Keswick	Keswick	Circular route via Buttermere, Honister slate mine & Seatoller	Easter-Oct 4/day	*Honister Rambler*, Stagecoach
77R	Cockermouth	Keswick	B'mere, Honister, Seatoller & Rosthwaite	late Jul-early Sep daily 2/day	Reays
78	Keswick	Seatoller	Rosthwaite	Daily 7/day	*Borrowdale Rambler*, Stagecoach
106	Penrith	Kendal	Shap & Orton	Mon-Fri 1/day	Stagecoach
111	Penrith	Burnbanks Village		Thurs only 1/day	Fellrunner Village Bus
300/301	Whitehaven	Carlisle		Mon-Sat hourly, Sun 5/day	Stagecoach
508	Penrith	Patterdale Hotel	Glenridding	Mon-Sat 5/day, Sun 3/day	Stagecoach
555	Keswick	Lancaster	Grasmere, Ambleside, Windermere & Kendal	Mon-Sat 1/hr, Sun 6/day	Stagecoach
563	Penrith	Kirkby Stephen		Mon-Fri 4/day, Sat 2/day	Grand Prix Coaches
599	Ambleside	Bowness	Windermere	Mon-Sun 1/hr	*Open-top Lakeland Experience*, Stagecoach
600	Carlisle	Whitehaven	Cockermouth	Mon-Sat 6/day	Stagecoach

Contacts

Fellrunner Village Bus (☎ 017688 81956)

Grand Prix Coaches (☎ 017683 41328 Mon-Fri 9am-5pm, 🖳 www.grandprixservices.co.uk)

Reays (☎ 016973 49999, 🖳 www.reays.co.uk)

Stagecoach (Traveline ☎ 0871 200 2233, 🖳 www.stagecoachbus.com)

BUS SERVICES & OPERATORS – NORTH YORKSHIRE

SEE p53 FOR MAP

Route No	From	To	Via	Frequency	Operator
Rambler	Darlington	Pickering	Danby	Jul-Sep Sun/Bank Hol 1-2/day	Moorsbus
Endeavour	Saltburn	Helmsley	Stokesley, North Allerton	Jul-Sep Sun/Bank Hol 1-2/day	Moorsbus
X26/X27	Catterick Garrison	Darlington	Richmond	Mon-Sat 2/hr, Sun 1/hr	Arriva North East
29	Darlington	Richmond		Mon-Sat 7/day	Dales & District
30	Keld	Richmond	Thwaite, Muker, Gunnerside Bridge & Reeth	Mon-Sat 4/day	Little White Bus
30	Reeth	Richmond		Mon-Sat 6/day	Dales & District
34	Richmond	Darlington	Brompton-on-Swale & Catterick	Mon-Sat 4/day	Dales & District
54	Richmond	Northallerton	Catterick Bridge	Mon-Sat 4/day	Dales & District
55	Richmond	Northallerton	Brompton-on-Swale & Bolton-on-Swale	Mon-Sat 3/day	Dales & District
80	Stokesley	Northallerton	Ingleby Cross & Osmotherley	Mon-Sat 4/day	Abbotts of Leeming
89	Stokesley	Northallerton	Great Broughton, Ingleby Cross & Osmotherley	Mon-Sat 4/day	Abbotts of Leeming
X93	Scarborough	M'brough	Robin Hood's Bay, Hawsker Village & Whitby	Mon-Sat 1/hr, Sun 7/day	Arriva North East
99	Whitby	Lealholm	Grosmont, Egton Bdge, Glaisdale	Mon-Sat 4/day	Coastal & Country
830	Hawes	Richmond	Thwaite, Keld, Muker, Gunnerside & Reeth	May-Sep, Sun 1/day	Arriva North East
840	Leeds	Whitby	York	Mon-Sat 5/day, Sun 1-2/day	Yorkshire Coastliner

Abbotts of Leeming (☎ 01677 424987)
Arriva North East (⌨ www.arrivabus.co.uk)
Coastal & Country (☎ 01947 602922, ⌨ www.coastalandcountry.co.uk)
Dales & District (☎ 01677 425203, ⌨ www.procterscoaches.com)
Little White Bus (☎ 01969 667400, ⌨ www.littlewhitebus.co.uk)
Moorsbus (☎ 01751 477216, ⌨ www.moorsbus.org)
Stagecoach (Traveline ☎ 0871 200 2233, ⌨ www.stagecoachbus.com)
Yorkshire Coastliner (☎ 01653 692556, ⌨ www.yorkbus.co.uk)

PLANNING YOUR WALK

NATIONAL TRANSPORT (cont'd from p51)

Getting to Robin Hood's Bay (cont'd)

● **Coach/bus** National Express operates direct services (426) to Middlesbrough. From there Arriva's No X93 service (Middlesbrough to Scarborough) calls in at Whitby and Robin Hood's Bay.

● **Car** It's not entirely straightforward to get to Robin Hood's Bay by car either, though compared to public transport it is at least the simplest. From London head up to Doncaster on the M1/A1(M), then the M18/A19 to York. From there you can head north-east to Scarborough on the A64, then follow the A171 heading towards Whitby, turning off on the B1447 for Robin Hood's Bay. Coming from Manchester take the M62 north-east to Leeds, then the A64 all the way to Scarborough, from where you pick up the A171 as outlined above.

Getting to Kirkby Stephen

● **Train** Kirkby Stephen is a stop on the Carlisle to Settle line. Coming from London (Kings Cross) either take an East Coast train from King's Cross to Leeds (2¼ hours) and then catch a Northern Rail train to Kirkby Stephen (Mon-Sat 7/day, Sun 4/day; 1¾ hours), or take a Virgin train to Carlisle (3¼ hours) from London Euston and then a Northern rail train to Kirkby Stephen (Mon-Sat 7/day, Sun 4/day; 50 mins).

● **Coach/bus** National Express runs to Penrith (588/539 London to Inverness/Bournemouth to Edinburgh), from where you can get Grand Prix Coaches' No 563 service to Kirkby Stephen (see box p54).

● **Car** The A685 runs through the town and the trans-Pennine A66 (which shadows the Coast to Coast path to the north) crosses the A685 just four miles north of the town. The nearest motorway, the M6, is 22 miles west of the A66 interchange. See pp28-9 for information about long stay parking facilities operated by the baggage carrier companies.

PLANNING YOUR WALK

THE ENVIRONMENT & NATURE

Conserving the Coast to Coast path

With a population of over 64 million Britain is an overcrowded island, and England is the most densely populated part of it. As such, the English countryside has suffered a great deal of pressure from both over-population and the activities of an ever more industrialised world. Thankfully, there is some enlightened legislation to protect the surviving pockets of forest and heathland.

Apart from these, it is interesting to note just how much man has altered the land that he lives on. Whilst the aesthetic costs of such intrusions are open to debate, what is certain is the loss of biodiversity that has resulted. The last wild boar was shot near the Coast to Coast trail a few centuries ago; add to that the extinction of bear, wolf and beaver (now being reintroduced in selected pockets in Scotland and Dorset) as well as, far more recently, a number of other species lost or severely depleted over the decades and you get an idea of just how much of an influence man has over the land, and how that influence is all too often used negatively.

There is good news, however. In these enlightened times when environmental issues are quite rightly given more precedence, many endangered species, such as the otter, have increased in number thanks to the active work of voluntary conservation bodies. There are other reasons to be optimistic. The environment is no longer the least important issue in party politics and this reflects the opinions of everyday people who are concerned about issues such as conservation on both a global and local scale.

GOVERNMENT AGENCIES AND SCHEMES

Natural England
Natural England is responsible for enhancing biodiversity, landscape and wildlife in rural, urban, coastal and marine areas; promoting access, recreation and public well-being; and contributing to the way natural resources are managed. One of its roles is to identify, establish and manage: national trails, national parks, areas of outstanding natural beauty (AONBs), national nature reserves (NNRs), sites of

special scientific interest (SSSIs), and special areas of conservation (SACs) and to enforce regulations relating to these sites.

The highest level of landscape protection is the designation of land as a **national park** which recognises the national importance of an area in terms of landscape, biodiversity and as a recreational resource. At the time of writing there were ten national parks in England. Three of these are bisected by the Coast to Coast path: Lake District, Yorkshire Dales and North York Moors national park). This designation does not signify national ownership and these are not uninhabited wildernesses, making conservation a knife-edged balance between protecting the environment and the rights and livelihoods of those living in the parks.

The second level of protection is **area of outstanding natural beauty** (AONB). The only AONB passed on the Coast to Coast trail covers the very southern extremity of the North Pennines as you pass Nine Standards Rigg and before you enter the Yorkshire Dales. The primary objective for an AONB is conservation of the natural beauty of a landscape. As there is no statutory administrative framework for their management, this is the responsibility of the local authority within whose boundaries they fall. Some AONBs, including the North Pennines, have also been designated **geoparks** (🖳 www.europeangeo parks.org), a European Union initiative originally set up as a socio-economic project to help the development and management of deprived areas which nevertheless benefited from a rich geological heritage, defined as both unique and important. The concept has since moved on, with today's geoparks designed to raise awareness of an area and to educate the general public.

National nature reserves (NNRs) are places where the priority is protection of the wildlife habitats and geological formations. There are currently 224 (including Smardale in Cumbria) in England and they are either owned or managed by Natural England or by approved organisations such as wildlife trusts.

Local nature reserves (LNRs) are places with wildlife or geological features that are of special interest to local inhabitants; there are nine in Cumbria and 17 in North Yorkshire.

Sites of Special Scientific Interest (SSSIs) range in size from little pockets protecting wild flower meadows, important nesting sites or special geological features, to vast swathes of upland, moorland and wetland. SSSIs, of which there are currently 4130 in England, are a particularly important designation as they have some legal standing. They are managed in partnership with the owners and occupiers of the land who must give written notice before initiating any operations likely to damage the site and who cannot proceed without consent from Natural England. Many SSSIs are also either a NNR or a LNR.

Special Area of Conservation (SAC) is an international designation which came into being as a result of the 1992 Earth Summit in Rio de Janeiro, Brazil. This European-wide network of sites is designed to promote the conservation of habitats, wild animals and plants, both on land and at sea. Every land SAC is also an SSSI.

❑ **Government agencies and other bodies**
● **Department for Environment, Food and Rural Affairs** (🖳 www.gov.uk/defra)
Government ministry responsible for sustainable development in the countryside.
● **Natural England** (🖳 www.naturalengland.org.uk) See p57.
● **English Heritage** (🖳 www.english-heritage.org.uk) Organisation with a central aim of ensuring that the historic environment of England is properly maintained. English Heritage is the name of the charity arm of the public body, Historic England.
● **Forestry Commission** (🖳 www.forestry.gov.uk) Government department for establishing and managing forests for a variety of uses.
● **National Association of Areas of Outstanding Natural Beauty** (🖳 www.land scapesforlife.org.uk); for further information on the North Pennines AONB visit 🖳 www.northpennines.org.uk.
● **Lake District National Park Authority** (🖳 www.lakedistrict.gov.uk); **Yorkshire Dales National Park Authority** (🖳 www.yorkshiredales.org.uk); **North York Moors National Park Authority** (🖳 www.northyorkmoors.org.uk). The government authorities charged with managing the respective areas. None of these has much in the way of specific Coast to Coast trail information on their websites, though they might be worth contacting to find out the latest developments to the path.

CAMPAIGNING AND CONSERVATION ORGANISATIONS

These voluntary organisations started the conservation movement in the mid-19th century and are still at the forefront of developments. Independent of government but reliant on public support, they can concentrate their resources either on acquiring land which can then be managed purely for conservation purposes, or on influencing political decision-makers by lobbying and campaigning.

Managers and owners of land include well-known bodies such as the RSPB, the NT and the CPRE. The **Royal Society for the Protection of Birds** (RSPB; 🖳 www.rspb.org.uk), has over 150 nature reserves and more than a million members. There are two reserves on the Coast to Coast path, both of great significance. St Bees Head, at the very start of the trail, is the largest seabird colony in north-west England, home in spring and summer to guillemots, kittiwakes, fulmars and razorbills; while Haweswater, at the eastern end of the Lake District, is England's only golden eagle territory.

The **National Trust** (NT; 🖳 www.nationaltrust.org.uk) is a charity with over three million members which aims to protect, through ownership, threatened coastline, countryside, historic houses, castles and gardens, and archaeological remains for everyone to enjoy. On the Coast to Coast trail, the NT's properties are concentrated in the Lakes where they look after such beauty spots as Ennerdale, supposedly England's wildest valley; parts of Ullswater; and 4925 hectares (12,170 acres) of Grasmere and Great Langdale including, curiously, the bed of Grasmere Lake, Johnny Wood and Bay Ness (see Map 93).

Often overlapping the work of National Trust, **English Heritage** (🖳 www.english-heritage.org.uk) looks after and advises the government on historic buildings and places. It has recently split into a new charity that retains the name English Heritage and a non-departmental public body, Historic England.

THE ENVIRONMENT AND NATURE

❑ **Campaigning and conservation organisations**
● **Royal Society for the Protection of Birds** (RSPB; 🖳 www.rspb.org.uk) See p60.
● **National Trust** (NT; 🖳 www.nationaltrust.org.uk) See p60.
● **Campaign to Protect Rural England** (CPRE; 🖳 www.cpre.org.uk) See p60.
● The umbrella organisation for the 47 wildlife trusts in the UK is **The Wildlife Trusts** (🖳 www.wildlifetrusts.org). Two relevant to the Coast to Coast path are **Cumbria Wildlife Trust** (🖳 www.cumbriawildlifetrust.org.uk) and **Yorkshire Wildlife Trust** (🖳 www.ywt.org.uk).
● **Woodland Trust** (🖳 www.woodlandtrust.org.uk) Restores woodland throughout Britain for its amenity, wildlife and landscape value.

The **Campaign to Protect Rural England** (CPRE; 🖳 www.cpre.org.uk) exists to promote the beauty and diversity of rural England by encouraging the sustainable use of land and other natural resources in both town and country.

A huge increase in public interest and support of these and many other conservation/campaigning groups since the 1980s indicates that people are more conscious of environmental issues and believe that it cannot be left to our political representatives to take care of them for us without our voice. We are becoming the most powerful lobbying group of all, an informed electorate.

BEYOND CONSERVATION

Pressures on the countryside grow year on year. Western society, whether directly or indirectly, makes constant demands for more oil, more roads, more houses, more cars. At the same time awareness of environmental issues increases, as does the knowledge that our unsustainable approach to life cannot continue. Some governments appear more willing to adopt sustainable ideals, others less so.

Yet even the most environmentally progressive of governments are some way off perfect. It's all very positive to classify parts of the countryside as National Parks and Areas of Outstanding Natural Beauty but it will be of little use if we continue to pollute the wider environment, the seas and skies. For a brighter future we need to adopt that sustainable approach to life. It would not be difficult and the rewards would be great.

The individual can play his or her part. Walkers in particular appreciate the value of wild areas and should take this attitude back home with them. This is not just about recycling the odd green bottle or two and walking to the corner shop rather than driving, but about lobbying for more environmentally sensitive policies in local and national government.

The first step to a sustainable way of living is in appreciating and respecting this beautiful, complex world we live in and realising that every one of us plays an important role within the great web. The natural world is not a separate entity. We are all part of it and should strive to safeguard it rather than work against it. So many of us live in a way that seems far removed from the real world, cocooned in centrally heated houses and upholstered cars. Rediscovering our place within the natural world is both uplifting on a personal level and important regarding our outlook and approach to life.

Flora and fauna

The beauty of walking from one side of England to the other is that on the way you pass through just about every kind of habitat this country has to offer. From woodland and grassland to heathland, bog and beach, the variety of habitats is surpassed only by the number of species of flower, tree and animal that each supports.

The following is not in any way a comprehensive guide – if it were, you would not have room for anything else in your rucksack – but merely a brief guide to the more commonly seen flora and fauna of the trail, together with some of the rarer and more spectacular species.

MAMMALS

The Coast to Coast path is alive with all manner of native species and the wide variety of habitats encountered on the way means that the wildlife is varied too. Unfortunately, most of these creatures are shy and many are nocturnal, and walkers can consider themselves extremely lucky if during their trek they see more than three or four species.

One creature that you will see everywhere along the walk, from the cliffs at St Bees to the fields outside Robin Hood's Bay, is the **rabbit** (*Oryctolagus cuniculus*). Timid by nature, most of the time you'll have to make do with nothing more than a brief and distant glimpse of their white tails as they stampede for the nearest warren at the first sound of your footfall. Because they are so numerous, however, the laws of probability dictate that you will at some stage get close enough to observe them without being spotted; trying to take a decent photo of one of them, however, is a different matter.

If you're lucky you may also come across **hares**, often mistaken for rabbits but much larger, more elongated and with longer back legs and ears.

Rabbits used to form one of the main elements in the diet of the **fox** (*Vulpes vulpes*), one of the more adaptable of Britain's native species. Famous as the scourge of chicken coops, their reputation as indiscriminate killers is actually unjustified: though they will if left undisturbed kill all the chickens in a coop in what appears to be a mindless and frenzied attack, foxes will actually eat all their victims, carrying off and storing the carcasses in underground burrows for them and their families to eat at a later date. These days, however, you are far more likely to see foxes in towns, where they survive mostly on the scraps and leftovers of the human population, rather than in the country. While generally considered nocturnal, it's not unusual to encounter a fox during the day too, often lounging in the sun near its den.

One creature that is strictly nocturnal, however, is the **bat**, of which there are 17 species in Britain, all protected by law. Your best chance of spotting one is just after dusk while there's still enough light in the sky to make out their flitting forms as they fly along hedgerows, over rivers and streams and around

Red squirrels

© Bryn Thomas

street lamps in their quest for moths and insects. The most common species in Britain is the pipistrelle (*Pipistrellus pipistrellus*).

The Lakes offer one of the few chances in England to see the rare **red squirrel** (*Sciurus vulgaris*), particularly around Patterdale and Haweswater. While elsewhere in the country these small, tufty-eared natives have been usurped by their larger cousins from North America, the **grey squirrel** (*Sciurus carolinensis*), in the Lakes the red squirrel maintains a precarious foothold.

Patterdale offers walkers on the Coast to Coast their best chance of seeing the **badger** (*Meles meles*). Relatively common throughout the British Isles, these nocturnal mammals with their distinctive black-and-white-striped muzzles are sociable animals that live in large underground burrows called setts, appearing after sunset to root for worms and slugs.

One creature which you almost certainly won't encounter, though they are said to exist in the Lakes, is the **pine marten** (*Martes martes*). Extremely rare in England since being virtually wiped out during the 19th century for their pelts and their reputation as vermin, there are said to be a few in the valley of Ennerdale, though the last positive identification was in 2011. In addition to the above, keep a look out for other fairly common but little-seen species such as the carnivorous **stoat** (*Mustela erminea*), its smaller cousin the **weasel** (*Mustela nivalis*), the **hedgehog** (*Erinaceus europaeus*) – these days, alas, most commonly seen as roadkill – and a number of species of **voles**, **mice** and **shrews**.

One of Britain's rarest creatures, the **otter** (*Lutra lutra*), is enjoying something of a renaissance thanks to concerted conservation efforts. Though more common in the south-west, otters are still present in the north of England. At home both in salt and freshwater, they are a good indicator of a healthy unpolluted environment. Don't come to the north expecting otter sightings every day though. If you see one at all you should consider yourself *extremely* fortunate, for they remain rare and very elusive. There are said to be some in Swaledale and their numbers are growing. A surprisingly large number of trekkers encounter deer on their walk. Mostly this will be the **roe deer** (*Capreolus capreolus*), a small native species that likes to inhabit woodland, though some can also be seen grazing in fields. As with most creatures, your best chance of seeing one is very early in the morning, with sightings particularly common in Ennerdale, the upper end of Swaledale and the Vale of Mowbray.

Britain's largest native land mammal, the **red deer** (*Cervus elaphus*), is rarely seen on the walk though it does exist in small pockets around the Lakes.

BIRDS

The Coast to Coast is without doubt an ornithologist's dream. The seaside cliffs, woods, moorland and hedgerows encountered on the path provide homes for a wealth of different species including the golden eagle, Britain's rarest and most majestic bird, and even a flock of parrots.

The red sandstone cliffs above St Bees (see p94) have been owned by the RSPB since 1973 and dotted along the trail are viewpoints where you can gaze down at the nesting seabirds. This is in fact the only colony of cliff-nesting seabirds in north-west England to which birds return year after year to lay their eggs and hatch chicks.

The most common of the seabirds is the **guillemot** (*Uria aalge*), with an estimated minimum of 5000 crowding onto the cliff's open ledges, including the rare **black guillemot** (*Cepphus grylle*); indeed, the cliffs are believed to be the only place where this rare sub-species nests in England. **Razorbills** (*Alca torda*), a close relative of the guillemot, are also present, as are **puffins** (*Fratercula arctica*), though their numbers seldom rise above two dozen or so.

GUILLEMOT
L: 450MM/18"

Kittiwakes (*Rissa tridactyla*), **fulmars** (*Fulmarus glacialis*), **gulls** (family *Larus*) and their collective nemesis, **peregrine falcons** (*Falco peregrinus*), may be seen on these cliffs too, the falcons preying on the other birds by plummeting onto them from above and catching them on the wing. A little further inland **ravens** (*Corvus corax*) can be seen in the fields that edge the cliffs.

Away from the coast, the rarest species in England is the **golden eagle** (*Aquila chrysaetos*), a pair of which had set up an eyrie near the Coast to Coast trail, on the way down to Haweswater Reservoir from Kidsty Pike. Enthusiastic twitchers could be seen peering up the valley most hours of the day, and there was also a 24hr guard keeping watch to protect it from the predations of the egg collectors. This was the only pair of breeding golden eagles in England. However, the female has now disappeared but it is hoped another can be attracted down from Scotland for the lone male.

BLACK GUILLEMOT
L: 350MM/13.5"

GOLDEN EAGLE
L: 910MM/36"

The first wild **ospreys** (*Pandion haliaetus*) to breed in England for centuries are also present in the Lakes, though not near the trail. Other birds of prey include **kestrel** (*Falco tinnunculus*), **buzzard** (*Buteo buteo*), **barn owl** (*Tyto alba*) and **short-eared owl** (*Asio flammeus*).

One of the most common birds seen on the path, particularly in the latter half of the walk, is the **pheasant** (*Phasianus colchicus*). Ubiquitous on the moors, the male is distinctive thanks to his beautiful long, barred tail feathers, brown body and glossy green-black head with red head-sides, while the female is a dull brown. Another way to distinguish them is by the distinctive strangu-

THE ENVIRONMENT AND NATURE

LAPWING/PEEWIT
L: 320MM/12.5"

lated hacking sound they make, together with the loud flapping of wings as they fly off. Another reasonably common sight on the moors of Yorkshire is the **lapwing** (*Vanellus vanellus*), also known as the peewit. Black and white with iridescent green upper parts and approximately the size of a pigeon or tern, the lapwing's most distinctive characteristic is the male's tumbling, diving, swooping flight pattern when disturbed, believed to be either a display to attract a female or an attempt to distract predators from its nest, which is built on the ground. Less common but still seen by most walkers is the **curlew** (*Numenius arquata*), another bird that, like the lapwing, is associated with coastal and open fields, moors and bogs.

With feathers uniformly streaked grey and brown, the easiest way to identify this bird is by its thin elongated, downward curling beak. Both the lapwing and the curlew are actually wading birds that nest on the moors in the spring, but which winter by the coast.

Other birds that make their nest on open moorland and in fields include the **redshank** (*Tringa totanus*), **golden plover** (*Pluvialis apricaria*), **snipe** (*Gallinago gallinago*), **dunlin** (*Calidris alpina*) and **ring ouzel** (*Turdus torquatus*).

CURLEW
L: 600MM/24"

Somewhat ironically, these birds have benefited from the careful management of the moors which is mainly done to protect the populations of game birds such as **black grouse** (*Tetrao tetrix*).

In the deciduous woodland areas on the trail, look out for **treecreepers** (*Certhia familiaris*), **tits** (family *Paridae*, including blue, coal, long-tailed and great), **nuthatches** (*Sitta europaea*), **pied flycatchers** (*Ficedula hypoleuca*) and **redstarts** (*Phoenicurus phoenicurus*), while in the conifers watch out for **crossbills** (*Loxia curvirostra*) and **siskins** (*Carduelis spinus*).

Finally, for something completely different, in Kirkby Stephen there are ten or so '**homing parrots**': macaws let out by their owner to fly around the town during the day, before returning home each night.

BLACK GROUSE
L: 580MM/23"

THE ENVIRONMENT AND NATURE

REPTILES

The **adder** is the only common snake in the north of England, and the only poisonous one of the three species in Britain. They pose very little risk to walkers – indeed, you should consider yourself extremely lucky to see one, providing you're a safe distance away. They only bite if provoked, preferring to hide instead. The venom is designed to kill small mammals such as mice, voles and shrews, so deaths in humans are very rare, but a bite can be extremely unpleasant and occasionally dangerous to children or the elderly. You are most likely to encounter them in spring when they come out of hibernation and during the summer when pregnant females warm themselves in the sun. They are easily identified by the striking zigzag pattern on their back. Should you be lucky enough to encounter one, enjoy it but leave it undisturbed.

Gorse
Ulex europaeus

FLOWERS

Spring is the time to come and see the spectacular displays of colour on the Coast to Coast path. Alternatively, arrive in August and you'll see the heathers carpeting the moors in a blaze of purple flowers.

The coastal meadows

The coastline is a harsh environment subjected to strong, salt-laced winds. One plant that does survive in such conditions, and which will probably be the first you'll encounter on the path, is **gorse** (*Ulex europaeus*) with its sharp-thorned bright yellow, heavily scented flowers. Accompanying it are such cliff-top specialists as the pink-flowering **thrift** (*Armeria maritima*) and white **sea campion** (*Silene maritima*) and **fennel** (*Foeniculum vulgare*), a member of the carrot family which grows to over a metre high.

Thrift (Sea Pink)
Armeria maritima

Woodland and hedgerows

From March to May **bluebells** (*Hyacinthoides non-scripta*) proliferate in the woods along the Coast to Coast, providing a wonderful spectacle. Little Beck (see p244) and Clain (see p222) woods are particularly notable for these displays. The white **wood anemone** (*Anemone nemorosa*) and the yellow **primrose**

Sea Campion
Silene maritima

THE ENVIRONMENT AND NATURE

66 Flora and fauna

Dog Rose
Rosa canina

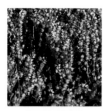

Forget-me-not
Myosotis arvensis

Heather (Ling)
Calluna vulgaris

THE ENVIRONMENT AND NATURE

(*Primula vulgaris*) also flower early in spring. **Red campion** (*Silene dioica*), which flowers from late April, can be found in hedge banks along with **rosebay willowherb** (*Epilobium angustifolium*) which also has the name fireweed due to its habit of colonising burnt areas.

In scrubland and on woodland edges you'll find **bramble** (*Rubus fruticosus*), a common vigorous shrub, responsible for many a ripped jacket thanks to its sharp thorns and prickles. **Blackberry** fruits ripen from late summer into autumn. Fairly common in scrubland and on woodland edges is the **dog rose** (*Rosa canina*) which has a large pink flower, the fruits of which are used to make rose-hip syrup.

Other flowering plants common in wooded areas and in hedgerows include the tall **foxglove** (*Digitalis purpurea*) with its trumpet-like flowers, **forget-me-not** (*Myosotis arvensis*) with tiny, delicate blue flowers and **cow parsley** (*Anthriscus sylvestris*), a tall member of the carrot family with a large globe of white flowers which often covers roadside verges and hedge banks.

Heathland and scrubland

There are three species of heather. The most dominant one is **ling** (*Calluna vulgaris*), with tiny flowers on delicate upright stems. The other two species are **bell heather** (*Erica cinerea*), with deep purple bell-shaped flowers, and **cross-leaved heath** (*Erica tetralix*) with similarly shaped flowers of a lighter pink, almost white colour. Cross-leaved heath prefers wet and boggy ground. As a result, it usually grows away from bell heather which prefers well-drained soils.

Heather is an incredibly versatile plant which is put to many uses. It provides fodder for livestock, fuel for

Bell Heather
Erica cinerea

Foxglove
Digitalis purpurea

Bluebell
Hyacinthoides non-scripta

Common Dog Violet
Viola riviniana

Heartsease (Wild Pansy)
Viola tricolor

Common Vetch
Vicia sativa

Lousewort
Pedicularis sylvatica

Primrose
Primula vulgaris

Ox-eye Daisy
Leucanthemum vulgare

Rowan (tree)
Sorbus aucuparia

Common Hawthorn
Crataegus monogyna

Red Campion
Silene dioica

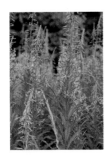

Rosebay Willowherb
Epilobium angustifolium

Yarrow
Achillea millefolium

Hogweed
Heracleum sphondylium

THE ENVIRONMENT AND NATURE

Bird's-foot trefoil
Lotus corniculatus

Germander Speedwell
Veronica chamaedrys

Tormentil
Potentilla erecta

Early Purple Orchid
Orchis mascula

fires, an orange dye and material for bedding, thatching, basketwork and brooms. It is still sometimes used in place of hops to flavour beer, and the flower heads can be brewed to make good tea. It is also incredibly hardy and thrives on the denuded hills, preventing other species from flourishing. Indeed, at times, highland cattle are brought to certain areas of the moors to graze on the heather, allowing other species a chance to grow.

Not a flower but worthy of mention is the less attractive species, **bracken** (*Pteridium aquilinum*), a vigorous non-native fern that has invaded many heathland areas to the detriment of native species.

Grassland

There is much overlap between the hedge/woodland-edge habitat and that of pastures and meadows. You will come across **common bird's-foot trefoil** (*Lotus corniculatus*), **Germander speedwell** (*Veronica chamaedrys*), **tufted** and **bush vetch** (*Vicia cracca* and *V. sepium*) and **meadow vetchling** (*Lathyrus pratensis*) in both.

Often the only species you will see in heavily grazed pastures are the most resilient. Of the thistles, the three most common species are **creeping thistle**, **spear thistle** and **marsh thistle** (*Cirsium arvense, C. vulgare* and *C. palustre*). Among them you may find **common ragwort** (*Senecio jacobaea*), **yarrow** (*Achillea millefolium*), **sheep's** and **common sorrel** (*Rumex acetosella* and *R. acetosa*), and **white** and **red clover** (*Trifolium repens* and *T. pratense*).

Other widespread grassland species include **harebell** (*Campanula rotundifolia*), delicate yellow **tormentil** (*Potentilla erecta*) which will often spread up onto the lower slopes of mountains along with **devil's-bit scabious** (*Succisa pratensis*). Also keep an eye out for orchids such as the **fragrant orchid** (*Gymnadenia conopsea*) and **early purple orchid** (*Orchis mascula*).

TREES

It seems incredible that, before man and his axe got to work, most of the bleak, empty moors and windswept Lakeland fells were actually covered by trees. Overgrazing of land by sheep and, to a lesser extent, deer, which eat the young shoots of trees, has ensured that the ancient forests have never returned. These days, the biggest areas of tree cover are the ghastly pine plantations of Ennerdale and other places in the Lakes. Yet

Ramsons (Wild Garlic)
Allium ursinum

Meadow Buttercup
Ranunculis acris

Marsh Marigold (Kingcup)
Caltha palustris

Meadow Cranesbill
Geranium pratense

Water Avens
Geum rivale

Scarlet Pimpernel
Anagallis arvensis

Harebell
Campanula rotundifolia

Herb-Robert
Geranium robertianum

Cotton Grass
Eriophorum angustifolium

Common Ragwort
Senecio jacobaea

Hemp-nettle
Galeopsis speciosa

Cowslip
Primula veris

THE ENVIRONMENT AND NATURE

there are still small patches of indigenous woodland on the Coast to Coast path. Perhaps the most interesting are the Atlantic Oakwoods at Borrowdale, including Johnny Wood (see map p117) on the way to Longthwaite. The woods are cared for by the National Trust and are actually correctly known as temperate rainforest, the moist Atlantic climate creating a landscape of boulders covered by liverworts and ferns, under **oaks** (*Quercus petraea*) dripping in moss and lichen.

There are other areas of woodland in the Lakes, including Easedale Woods on the way into Grasmere and Glenamara Park, just before Patterdale, which has some truly spectacular mature trees. One interesting thing about oak trees is that they support more kinds of insects than any other tree in Britain and some of these insects affect the oak in interesting ways. The eggs of the gall-fly, for example, cause growths on the leaves, known, appropriately enough, as galls. Each of these contains a single insect. Other kinds of gall-flies lay eggs in stalks or flowers, leading to flower galls – growths the size of currants.

Oak woodland is a diverse habitat and not exclusively made up of oak. Other trees that flourish in oak woodland include **downy birch** (*Betula pubescens*), its relative the **silver birch** (*Betula pendula)*, **holly** (*Ilex aquifolium*), and **hazel** (*Corylus avellana*) which has traditionally been used for coppicing (where small trees are grown for periodic cutting). Further east there are some examples of limestone woodland. **Ash** (*Fraxinus excelsior*) and oak dominate, along with **wych elm** (*Ulmus glabra*), **sycamore** (*Acer*) and **yew** (*Taxus*). **Hawthorn** (*Crataegus monogyna*) also grows on the path, usually in isolated pockets on pasture. These species are known as pioneer species and play a vital role in the ecosystem by improving the soil. It is these pioneers, particularly the **rowan** (*Sorbus aucuparia*) and hawthorn, that you will see growing all alone on inaccessible crags and ravines. Without interference from man, these pioneers would eventually be succeeded by longer-living species such as oak. In wet, marshy areas and along rivers and streams you are more likely to find **alder** (*Alnus glutinosa*).

Colour photos (following pages)

● **Opposite**: Paragliding over Cringle Moor near the Alex Falconer Memorial Seat.

● **p72 Top**: The view over Buttermere from near Grey Knotts, on the way to Honister. **Middle left:** Wordsworth's Dove Cottage (see p128) in Grasmere. **Middle right**: Local sculptor Colin Telfer's 'Coast to Coast' figure stands at the seven-mile mark (see p99). **Bottom**: Strolling into Seatoller (p114).

● **p73 Main picture**: The precarious Striding Edge (p133), as viewed from near the top of Helvellyn, England's third highest peak. **Top left**: Red squirrels still thrive in the Lake District (and beyond!). This fellow was spotted near Shap. **Middle**: The Great West Door at the church at St Bees (p88) dates back to Norman times. **Bottom left**: The ruins of the abbey (p146) at Shap. **Bottom right**: Two Coast to Coast spectators near Grasmere.

● **p74 Top**: The church at Muker (p185) in exquisite Swaledale. **Bottom**: Taking a break outside the post office at Reeth.

● **p75 Top**: Pausing near the Bloworth Crossing, on the way to Blakey Ridge on the North York Moors. **Bottom left**: View from above Scandal Beck towards Smardale Gill Viaduct **Bottom right**: The lofty ruins of Richmond Castle (p202) as seen from the River Swale.

MINIMUM IMPACT & OUTDOOR SAFETY

3

Minimum impact walking

In this world in which people live their lives at an increasingly frenetic pace, many of us living in overcrowded cities and working in jobs that offer little free time, the great outdoors is becoming an essential means of escape. Walking in the countryside is a wonderful means of relaxation and gives people the time to think. However, as the popularity of the countryside increases so do the problems that this pressure brings. It is important for visitors to remember that the countryside is the home and workplace of many others.

By following a few simple guidelines while walking the Coast to Coast path you can have a positive impact, not just on your own well-being but also on local communities and the environment, thereby becoming part of the solution.

ENVIRONMENTAL IMPACT

A walking holiday in itself is an environmentally friendly approach to tourism. The following are some ideas on how you can go a few steps further in helping to minimise your impact on the environment while walking the Coast to Coast path.

Use public transport whenever possible

Public transport along the Coast to Coast trail is not bad, with just about everywhere served by at least one bus or train a day. Public transport is always preferable to using private cars as it benefits everyone: visitors, locals and the environment.

Never leave litter

'Pack it in, pack it out'. Leaving litter is antisocial so carry a degradable plastic bag for all your rubbish, organic or otherwise and even other people's too, and pop it in a bin in the next village. Better still, reduce the litter you take with you by getting rid of packaging in advance.

(Opposite) Top left: The North York Moors Railway at Grosmont (see p242). **Top right**: Skipping over the stepping stones at charming Egton Bridge. **Bottom left**: A welcome sight for weary walkers: Robin Hood's Bay (p252). **Bottom right**: The Hermitage (p244), in Little Beck Wood.

Support local businesses
© Bryn Thomas

● **Is it OK if it's biodegradable?** Not really. Apple cores, banana skins, orange peel and the like are unsightly, encourage flies, ants and wasps, and ruin a picnic spot for others; they can also take months to decompose. In high-use areas such as the Coast to Coast path either bury them or take them away with you.

Buy local

Look and ask for local produce to buy and eat. Not only does this cut down on the amount of pollution and congestion that the transportation of food creates, so-called 'food miles', it also ensures that you are supporting local farmers and producers.

Erosion

● **Stay on the main trail** The effect of your footsteps may seem minuscule but when they're multiplied by several thousand walkers each year they become rather more significant. Avoid taking shortcuts, widening the trail or taking more than one path, especially across hay meadows and ploughed fields. This is particularly true on parts of the Coast to Coast with the boggy Pennine stage now divided into three trails to be used for four months a year (see p166), so reducing erosion on any one trail.

● **Consider walking out of season** Maximum disturbance by walkers coincides with the time of year when nature wants to do most of its growth and repair. In high-use areas, like that along much of the Coast to Coast path, the trail is often prevented from recovering.

Walking at less busy times eases this pressure while also generating year-round income for the local economy. Not only that, but it may make the walk a more relaxing experience with fewer people on the path and less competition for accommodation.

Respect all flora and fauna

Care for all wildlife you come across along the path; it has as much right to be there as you. Tempting as it may be to pick wild flowers, leave them so the next people who pass can enjoy them too. Don't break branches off trees.

If you come across wildlife keep your distance and don't watch for too long. Your presence can cause considerable stress, particularly if the adults are with young, or in winter when the weather is harsh and food is scarce. Young animals are rarely abandoned. If you come across young birds keep away so that their mother can return.

The code of the outdoor loo

'Going' in the outdoors is a lost art worth reclaiming, for your sake and everyone else's. As more and more people discover the joys of the outdoors this is becoming an important issue. In some parts of the world where visitor pressure is higher than in Britain, walkers and climbers are required to pack out their excrement. This might one day be necessary here. Human excrement is not only offensive to our senses but, more importantly, can infect water sources.

● **Where to go** Wherever possible **use a toilet**. Public toilets are marked on the trail maps in this guide and you'll also find facilities in pubs, cafés and campsites along the path. If you do have to go outdoors, avoid ruins which can otherwise be welcome shelter for other walkers, as well as sites of historic or archaeological interest, and choose a place that is at least **30 metres away from running water**. Use a stick or trowel to **dig a small hole** about 15cm (6") deep to bury your excrement. It decomposes quicker when in contact with the top layer of soil or leaf mould. Stirring loose soil into your deposit speeds up decomposition. Do not squash it under rocks as this slows down the composting process. If you have to use rocks to cover it make sure they are not in contact with your faeces.

● **Toilet paper and tampons** Toilet paper takes a long time to decompose whether buried or not. It is easily dug up by animals and may then blow into water sources or onto the path.

The best method for dealing with it is to **pack it out**. Put the used paper inside a paper bag which you then place inside a plastic bag. Then simply empty the contents of the paper bag at the next toilet you come across and throw the bag away. If this is too much bother, light your used toilet paper and watch it burn until the flames are out, you don't want to start a wild fire. Pack out **tampons** and **sanitary towels**; they take years to decompose and may also be dug up and scattered about by animals.

Wild camping

Wild camping is not encouraged within the national parks which make up the majority of the walk. This is a shame since wild camping is much more fulfilling than camping on a designated site. Living in the outdoors without any facilities provides a valuable lesson in simple, sustainable living where the results of all your actions, from going to the loo to washing your plates, can be seen.

If you do wild camp always ask the landowner for permission. In most cases this is, of course, completely impractical so don't camp on farmland at all, but out on the uncultivated moors or in forests, and follow these suggestions:

● **Be discreet** Camp alone or in small groups, spend only one night in each place, pitch your tent late and leave early.

● **Never light a fire** Accidental fire is a great fear for farmers and foresters. Never make a camp fire; take matches and cigarette butts out with you to dispose of safely. The deep burn caused by camp fires, no matter how small, damages turf which can take years to recover. Cook on a camp stove instead.

● **Don't use soap or detergent** There is no need to use soap; even biodegradable soaps and detergents pollute streams. You won't be away from a shower for more than a couple of days. Wash up without detergent; use a plastic or metal scourer, or failing that, a handful of fine pebbles or some bracken or grass.

● **Leave no trace** Endeavour to leave no sign of having been there: no moved boulders, ripped up vegetation or dug drainage ditches. Make a final check of your campsite before departing; pick up any litter leaving the place in the same state you found it in, or better.

❑ The Countryside Code

Respect other people
● Consider the local community and other people enjoying the outdoors
● Leave gates and property as you find them and follow paths unless wider access is available

Protect the natural environment
● Leave no trace of your visit and take your litter home
● Keep dogs under effective control

Enjoy the outdoors
● Plan ahead and be prepared
● Follow advice and local signs

There's more on each point at
🖳 www.naturalengland.org.uk/
ourwork/enjoying/countrysidecode

ACCESS

Britain is a crowded island with few places where you can wander as you please. Most of the land is a patchwork of fields and agricultural land and the terrain through which the Coast to Coast path marches is no different. However, there are countless public rights of way, in addition to the Coast to Coast path, that criss-cross the land.

This is fine, but what happens if you feel a little more adventurous and want to explore the moorland, woodland and hills that can also be found near the walk?

Right to roam

The Countryside & Rights of Way Act 2000 (CRoW), or 'Right to Roam' as dubbed by walkers, came into effect in 2005 after a long campaign to allow greater public access to areas of countryside in England and Wales deemed to be uncultivated open country; this essentially means moorland, heathland, downland and upland areas. Some land is covered by restrictions (ie high-impact activities such as driving a vehicle, cycling, horse-riding are not permitted) and some land is excluded (such as gardens, parks and cultivated land). Full details are given on 🖳 www.naturalengland.org.uk.

With more freedom in the countryside comes a need for more responsibility from the walker. Remember that wild open country is still the workplace of farmers and home to all sorts of wildlife. Have respect for both and avoid disturbing domestic and wild animals.

The Countryside Code

The Countryside Code seems like common sense but sadly some people still appear to have no understanding of how to treat the countryside they walk in. The Countryside Code is revised from time to time (a major revision took place after the CRoW Act (see above). The following is an expanded version, launched under the logo 'Respect, Protect and Enjoy':
● **Be safe** The Coast to Coast path is pretty much hazard free but you're responsible for your own safety so follow the simple guidelines outlined on pp81-5.
● **Leave all gates as you found them** Normally a farmer leaves gates closed to keep livestock in but may sometimes leave them open to allow livestock access to food or water. Leave them as you find them and if there is a sign, follow the instructions.
● **Leave livestock, crops and machinery alone** Help farmers by not interfering with their means of livelihood.
● **Take your litter home**

● **Keep your dog under control** See
p31. During lambing time they should
not be taken with you at all.

● **Enjoy the countryside and respect
its life and work** Access to the countryside depends on being sensitive to
the needs and wishes of those who live
and work there.

Being courteous and friendly to
those you meet will ensure a healthy
future for all based on partnership and
co-operation.

● **Keep to paths across farmland**

> ❏ **Lambing**
> Lambing takes place from mid-
> March to mid-May when dogs
> should not be taken along the path.
> Even a dog secured on a lead can dis-
> turb a pregnant ewe.
>
> If you see a lamb or ewe that
> appears to be in distress contact the
> nearest farmer.
>
> Also, be aware of cows with
> calves.

Stick to the official path across arable or pasture land. Minimise erosion by not
cutting corners or widening the path.

● **Use gates and stiles to cross fences, hedges and walls** The Coast to Coast
path is well supplied with stiles where it crosses field boundaries. On some of
the side trips you may find the paths less accommodating. If you have to climb
over a gate because you can't open it always do so at the hinged end.

● **Guard against all risk of fire** See p79.

● **Help keep all water clean** Leaving litter and going to the toilet near a water
source can pollute people's water supplies. See p78-9 for more guidelines.

● **Take special care on country roads** Drivers often drive dangerously fast on
narrow winding lanes. To be safe, walk on the right facing the oncoming traffic
and carry a torch or wear highly visible clothing when it's getting dark.

● **Protect wildlife, plants and trees** Care for and respect all wildlife you come
across along the Coast to Coast path. Don't pick plants, break trees or scare wild
animals. If you come across young birds that appear to have been abandoned
leave them alone.

● **Make no unnecessary noise** Enjoy the peace and solitude of the outdoors by
staying in small groups and acting unobtrusively.

Outdoor safety

AVOIDANCE OF HAZARDS

With good planning and preparation most hazards can be avoided. This information is just as important for those out on a day walk as for those walking the
entire Coast to Coast path. Always make sure you have suitable **clothing** (see
pp42-3) to keep warm and dry, whatever the conditions, and a change of inner
clothes. Carrying plenty of food and water is vital too.

The **emergency signal** is six blasts on the whistle or six flashes with a
torch, best done when you think someone might see or hear them.

Safety on the Coast to Coast path

Sadly every year people are injured while walking the Coast to Coast path. The most dangerous section is the Lake District, where the visitor numbers, elevation, lack of signage and the sometimes extreme weather all combine to imperil walkers. Locally based mountain-rescue teams are staffed by volunteers who are ready 24 hours a day 365 days of the year.

© Bryn Thomas

In an emergency phone ☎ 999 and the police will activate the service. Rescue teams rely on donations (the Patterdale's running costs are estimated to be £40,000 a year). There is another rescue team based at Kirkby Stephen.

All rescue teams should be treated as very much the last resort, however, and it's vital you take every precaution to ensure your own safety:

● Avoid walking on your own if possible, particularly on the Lakeland fells.
● Make sure that somebody knows your plans for every day that you're on the trail. This could be a friend or relative whom you have promised to call every night, or the place you plan to stay in at the end of each day's walk. That way, if you fail to turn up or call that evening, they can raise the alarm.
● If the weather closes in suddenly and mist descends while you're on the trail, particularly on the moors or fells, and you become uncertain of the correct trail, do not be tempted to continue. Just wait where you are and you'll find that mist often clears, at least for long enough to allow you to get your bearings. If you're still uncertain, and the weather does not look like improving, return the way you came to the nearest point of civilisation.
● Fill up with water at every opportunity and carry some high-energy snacks.
● Always carry a torch, compass, map, whistle, mobile phone and wet-weather gear with you.
● Wear sturdy boots or shoes, not trainers.
● Be extra vigilant if walking with children.

Dealing with an accident
● Use basic first aid to treat the injury to the best of your ability.
● Work out exactly where you are. If possible leave someone with the casualty while others go to get help. If there are only two people, you have a dilemma. If you decide to get help leave all spare clothing and food with the casualty.
● In an emergency dial ☎ 999 (or the EU standard number ☎ 112). Don't assume your mobile won't work up on the fells.

WEATHER FORECASTS

The Coast to Coast suffers from enormously unpredictable weather so it's wise to try to find out what the weather is going to be like before you set off for the day, especially if heading for high routes in the Lakes. Many hostels and tourist information centres will have pinned up somewhere a summary of the weather forecast.

The **Mountain Weather Information Service** (🖳 www.mwis.org.uk) gives detailed online forecasts for the upland regions of Britain including the Lake District and Yorkshire Dales. Online weather forecasts are also available at 🖳 www.bbc.co.uk/weather or 🖳 www.metoffice.gov.uk/public/weather/forecast.

Pay close attention to the forecast and consider altering your plans accordingly. That said, even if a fine sunny day is forecast, always assume the worst and pack some wet-weather gear.

© Chris Scott

BLISTERS

It's essential to try out new boots before embarking on your long trek. Make sure they're comfortable and once on the move try to avoid getting them wet on the inside and remove small stones or twigs that get in the boot. Air and massage your feet at lunchtime, keep them clean, and change your socks regularly. As soon as you start to feel any hot spots developing, stop and apply a few strips of low-friction zinc oxide tape. Leave it on until the foot is pain free or the tape starts to come off. As you're walking continuously the chances are it won't get better, but it won't get worse so quickly. If you know you have problems apply the tape pre-emptively. If you've left it too late and a blister has developed you should apply a plaster such as Compeed (or the slightly cheaper clone now made by Boots). Many walkers have Compeed to thank for enabling them to complete their walk; they can last for up to two days even when wet and work with a combination of good adhesive, a gel pad and a slippery outer surface. Popping a blister reduces the pressure but can lead to infection. If the skin is broken keep the area clean with antiseptic and cover with a non-adhesive dressing material held in place with tape.

Blister-avoiding strategies include rubbing the prone area with Vaseline or wearing a thin and a thick sock as well as adjusting the tension of your laces. All are ways of reducing rubbing and foot movement against the inside of the boot.

HYPOTHERMIA

Also known as exposure, hypothermia occurs when the body can't generate enough heat to maintain its normal temperature, usually as a result of being wet, cold, unprotected from the wind, tired and hungry. It's usually more of a problem in upland areas such as in the Lakes and on the moors.

Hypothermia is easily avoided by wearing suitable clothing, carrying and consuming enough food and drink, being aware of the weather conditions and checking the morale of your companions. Early signs to watch for are feeling cold and tired with involuntary shivering. Find some shelter as soon as possible and warm the victim up with a hot drink and some chocolate or other high-energy food. If possible give them another warm layer of clothing and allow them to rest until feeling better.

If allowed to worsen, erratic behaviour, slurring of speech and poor co-ordination will become apparent and the victim can very soon progress into unconsciousness, followed by coma and death. Quickly get the victim out of wind and rain, improvising a shelter if necessary.

Rapid restoration of bodily warmth is essential and best achieved by bare-skin contact: someone should get into the same sleeping bag as the patient, both having stripped to the bare essentials, placing any spare clothing under or over them to build up heat. Send or call urgently for help.

HYPERTHERMIA

Not an ailment that you would normally associate with the north of England, hyperthermia (heat exhaustion and heatstroke) is a serious problem nonetheless.

Symptoms of **heat exhaustion** include thirst, fatigue, giddiness, a rapid pulse, raised body temperature, low urine output and, if not treated, delirium and finally a coma. The best cure is to drink plenty of water.

Heatstroke is another matter altogether, and even more serious. A high body temperature and an absence of sweating are early indications, followed by symptoms similar to hypothermia (see above) such as a lack of co-ordination, convulsions and coma.

Death will follow if treatment is not given instantly. Sponge the victim down, wrap them in wet towels, fan them, and get help immediately.

SUNBURN

It can happen, even in northern England and even on overcast days. The only surefire way to avoid it is to stay wrapped up or smother yourself in sunscreen (with a minimum factor of 15) and apply it regularly throughout the day. Don't forget your lips, nose and the back of your neck.

COLLAPSE OF MORALE

This is not something that can be quickly treated with medication, but is probably the biggest cause of abandoned attempts on the Coast to Coast walk. Weather and injury which add up to exhaustion might be presumed to be the most common culprit but, as we know, plenty manage the walk in monsoonal conditions and hobble into Robin Hood's Bay with a great experience behind them. Others though, can suddenly think: 'what's the point, I'm not enjoying this'.

What it all boils down to is this: knowing your limitations and addressing your motivation; matching expectations with your companions; avoiding putting yourself under stress and being flexible rather than insisting on hammering out every last mile without repetition, hesitation or deviation. You can add having good equipment to that list too.

Above all, settle on a **realistic schedule** with at least one, if not two, rest day(s) over the full trek. Even then, it's amazing how sore muscles and feet can recover overnight, especially if you can at least start the day in sunshine. Don't assume a rest day has to be in a town like Kirkby Stephen or Richmond. A big room in a lone moorland farmhouse or even two nights in a holiday cottage with a telly or a fat book may suit those who find the bigger towns an intrusion on the spirit of the walk.

© Henry Stedman

It's not fashionable to admit it, but not every day on the Coast to Coast will necessarily be a winner. It's one reason why many people go on to do the walk again and again; the first time is often looked back on as an eye-opening reconnaissance (see the boxes on p40 & p42).

Perhaps the best way to avoid the risk of getting fed up is not to tackle the full 190 miles in one go. Wainwright certainly didn't (but then he was in his sixties). Thirteen days non-stop on the trail, come rain or shine, really is a bit much for most people (a schedule which at first glance the thirteen stages of this book may seem to encourage). Some days end up as nothing more than forced marches or gritty lessons in pain management because, for many, our prized vacation time is treated as an extension of our busy work life where we must make the most of every minute, 24/7. Here at Trailblazer we propose: turn on, tune in, and slow down.

❑ **Norse names** We have the Vikings to thank for many names in the north of England. Unless otherwise stated the following are derived from Old Norse words.

Place names		**Landscape features**	
Borrowdale	Valley of the fort	Beck	Stream
Ennerdale	Valley of the River Ehen	Dale	Valley
Glaisdale	Valley of the River Glas	Fell	Mountain
Grasmere	Grass lake (Old English)	Force/ Foss	Waterfall
Grosmont	Big hill (Old French)	Garth	Enclosure
Grisedale	(Gris dalr) Valley of pigs	Ghyll/Gill	Ravine
Keld	Spring (of water)	Hause	Narrow neck of land
Kirkby	Village with church	Mere	Lake/ pond (Old English)
Marrick	Horse ridge	Ness	Headland
Marske	Marsh	Pike	Peak
Patterdale	Patrick's Valley	Rigg	Ridge
Richmond	Strong hill	Scar	Bare rocky cliff or crag
	(Old French: Riche monte)	Tarn	Lake
River Rothay	Trout river	Thwaite	Clearing or meadow
St Sunday Crag	St Dominic's Crag (Celtic)		

MINIMUM IMPACT & OUTDOOR SAFETY

4 ROUTE GUIDE & MAPS

Using this guide

The route is described from west to east and divided into 13 stages. Though each of these roughly corresponds to a day's walk between centres of accommodation, it's not necessarily the best way to structure *your* trek. There are enough places to stay – barring a couple of stretches – for you to pretty much divide the walk up however you want. This is even more true if you're prepared to camp, in which case you can pitch your tent virtually anywhere, as long as you follow the guidelines on p79.

On pp34-5 are tables to help you plan an **itinerary**. To provide further help, **practical information** is presented on the trail maps, including waypoints (WPT) and walking times, places to stay, camp and eat, as well as shops from which to buy provisions. Further **service details** are given in the text under the entry for each settlement. See box pp91-3 for **navigation trouble spots**. For **map profiles** and cumulative **distance chart** see the colour pages at the end of the book.

TRAIL MAPS   [for map key see inside back cover]
Scale and walking times
The trail maps are to a scale of 1:20,000 (1cm = 200m; $3^1/8$ inches = one mile). Each full size map covers about two miles but that's a very rough estimate owing to variety of terrain.

Walking times are given along the side of each map; the arrow shows the direction to which the time refers. Black triangles indicate the points between which the times have been taken. These times are merely a tool to help you plan and are not there to judge your walking ability. After a couple of days you'll know how fast you walk compared with the time bars and can plan your days more accurately as a result. **See note on walking times in the box on p87**.

Up or down?
The trail is shown as a dashed line. An arrow across the trail indicates the slope; two arrows show that it is steep. Note that the arrow points towards the higher part of the trail. If, for example, you are walking from A (at 80m) to B (at 200m) and the trail between the two is short and steep it would be shown thus: A — — — >> — — – B. Reversed arrow heads indicate a downward gradient. Note that the *arrow points uphill*, the opposite of what OS maps use on steep roads.

❏ **Important note – walking times**
Unless otherwise specified, **all times in this book refer only to the time spent walking**. You will need to add 20-30% to allow for rests, photography, checking the map, drinking water etc. When planning the day's hike count on 5-7 hours' actual walking.

Other features
The numbered **GPS waypoints** refer to the list on pp259-63. Other features are marked on the map when they are pertinent to navigation.

Accommodation
Accommodation marked on the map is either on or within easy reach of the path. Many B&B proprietors based a mile or two off the trail will offer to collect walkers from the nearest point on the trail and take them back next morning.

Details of each place are given in the accompanying text. The number of **rooms** of each type is given at the beginning of each entry, ie: **S** = Single, **T** = Twin room, **D** = Double room, **Tr** = Triple room and **Qd** = Quad. Note that many of the triple/quad rooms have a double bed and one/two single beds thus in a group of three or four, two people would have to share the double bed but it also means the room can be used as a double or twin.

Your room will either have **en suite** (bath or shower) facilities, or a **private** or **shared** bathroom or shower room just outside the bedroom.

Rates quoted for B&B-style accommodation are **per person (pp)** based on two people sharing a room for a one-night stay; rates are usually discounted for longer stays. Where a single room **(sgl)** is available the rate for that is quoted if different from the rate per person. The rate for single occupancy **(sgl occ)** of a double/twin may be higher, and the per person rate for three/four sharing a triple/quad may be lower. At some places the only option is a **room rate**; this will be the same whether one or two people (or more if permissible) use the room. See p24 for more information on rates.

The text also indicates whether the premises have: **wi-fi** (WI-FI); if a bath (☛) is available either as part of en suite facilities, or in a separate bathroom – for those who prefer a relaxed soak at the end of the day; if a **packed lunch** (Ⓛ) can be prepared, subject to prior arrangement; and if **dogs** (🐾 – see also p31 and p257) are welcome, again subject to prior arrangement, either in at least one room or at campsites. The policy on charging for dogs varies; some places make an additional charge per day or per stay, while others may require a refundable deposit against any potential damage or mess.

ST BEES   see map p89
Situated close to the county's westernmost point, the ancient village of St Bees makes a fine starting point to your walk. Sleepy for the most part – except for the rowdy Friday nights when the workers from Sellafield come to let off some steam – St Bees has just enough facilities and services to set you on your way. The village is agricultural in origin; many of the buildings along the main street were once farms dating back to the 17th century and, on Outrigg, there's even an ancient **pinfold** – a circular, stone-walled enclosure once used to house stray livestock recovered from the surrounding hills. The livestock would

remain in the pinfold until the farmer could afford to pay a fine to retrieve them.

The town's main sight is its distinctive red sandstone **Priory Church**, once part of a thriving 12th-century Benedictine priory dedicated to the saints Bega (see box below) and Mary. Original Norman features include the impressively elaborate Great West Door and, standing opposite, the curious carved Dragon Stone, a door lintel also from the 12th century. The church is believed to stand on a site that had been holy to Christians for centuries prior to the monastery's foundation and has seen over eight hundred years of unbroken worship since then. Not even the dissolution of the monasteries ordered by Henry VIII in 1538, which led to the closure of this and every other priory you'll come across on the Coast to Coast path, could stop the site from being used by the villagers as their main centre of worship even though Henry's commissioners had removed the lead from the roof and for much of the 16th century the whole building was left open to the elements. Restoration began in the early 17th century, with a major overhaul of the building taking place in the 19th. Thankfully, however, the architects preserved much of the church's sturdy Norman character.

As with quite a few of the larger churches on the route, there's a table just inside the door with various pamphlets on the history of both the church and the village. Don't miss the glass case in the southern aisle displaying a shroud and a lock of woman's hair unearthed in the excavation of a 14th-century grave; and the graveyard to the north of the church, where you'll find the shaft of a stone cross from the 10th century (in other words, older than every other part of the church), with its Celtic decorations still visible.

Incidentally, **St Bees School** across the road from the church is one of the most venerable in Cumbria, having been founded by **Edmund Grindal** on his deathbed in 1583. Grindal rose to become Archbishop of Canterbury during the reign of Elizabeth I and his birthplace, on the junction of Finkle St and Cross St, is the oldest surviving house in St Bees. The school itself, the alma mater of Rowan Atkinson amongst other luminaries, is currently in financial difficulty owing to falling pupil numbers and may soon be forced to close.

Services

There's a well-stocked **post office** and **shop** (☎ 01946 822343, ⌨ www.stbees-post office.co.uk; post office Mon-Fri 9am-5.30pm, Sat 9am-12.30pm, shop Mon-Sat 6.30am-8pm, Sun 6.30am-8pm) with a decent selection of groceries, including delicious hot pies, wine and beer, Coast to Coast maps, T-shirts (£4.99) and souvenirs.

❑ Who was St Bees?

The statue of **St Bega** on Station Rd.

St Bees is actually a corruption of St Bega, an Irish princess who fled her native country sometime between the 6th and 9th centuries to avoid an arranged marriage with a Norwegian prince. Landing on England's north-west coast, so the story goes, St Bega lived as a hermit and became renowned for the good deeds she carried out. And that's about it really, or at least it would be, if it wasn't for the legends that have grown up over the centuries. In the most famous of these, St Bega approached the local landlord, Lord Egremont, for some land for a convent she wished to found.

Egremont promised St Bega all the land covered by snow the next day; which, as it was to be midsummer's day, was not as generous an offer as it first appeared. Miraculously, however, snow did fall that day and St Bega was able to build her convent, around which the village was founded.

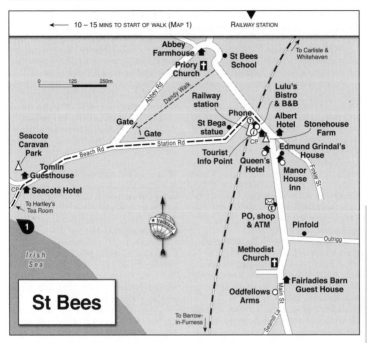

Abbey Farmhouse
Priory Church
St Bees School
To Carlisle & Whitehaven
Lulu's Bistro & B&B
Railway station
Phone
Albert Hotel
Stonehouse Farm
Gate
St Bega statue
Edmund Grindal's House
Seacote Caravan Park
Beach Rd
Station Rd
Gate
Tourist Info Point
Queen's Hotel
Manor House Inn
Tomlin Guesthouse
Seacote Hotel
To Hartley's Tea Room
Irish Sea
St Bees
Finkle St
PO, shop & ATM
Pinfold
Outrigg
Methodist Church
Fairladies Barn Guest House
Oddfellows Arms
Main St
Seamill La
To Barrow-in-Furness

ROUTE GUIDE AND MAPS

It's also the home of the local Link **cash machine** (£1.75 fee), the last on the trail before Grasmere; though note that **neither it nor the one at Grasmere takes foreign cards**. There's a **tourist information point** by the train station but it has limited information; a better bet is St Bees' website (💻 www.stbees.org.uk). There's also a **public phone**.

Two things the town lacks are an outdoor shop and a pharmacy, but a 10-minute train ride north to Whitehaven will deliver you alongside a huge Tesco as well as both a Millets and a Boots on King St, ten minutes' walk into town. Alternatively you have to wait until you reach Grasmere.

Where to stay

On the front behind the RNLI lifeboat station and owned by the adjacent hotel (see p90) are the serried cabins of *Seacote Caravan Park* (Map 1, p95; ☎ 01946

822777, 💻 www.seacote.com; 🐕 £3 ; WI-FI free but only available in the hotel). You can camp for £10-18 depending on the size of your tent. They recommend booking in peak season though they will try to accommodate Coast to Coast walkers. **Camping** (£5pp) is also available in the back garden of the central *Stonehouse Farm* (☎ 01946 822224, 💻 www.stonehousefarm.net; 1S/3D/1T/3Tr; all en suite; ➖; 🐕£5; Ⓛ £6; WI-FI), where you can fall asleep to the hiss of the barn owl. A long-established and reliable **B&B**, Stonehouse is situated just 30 metres from the station and is the only working farm within St Bees. Stonehouse's en suite rooms are located in its Georgian farmhouse, while the dairy next door has been converted into a spacious family cottage. On the other side of the farmhouse is an even older cottage (dating back to 1660). B&B costs £35pp (£40/50 for a single/single occupancy). They accept most credit cards (but not Amex). Breakfast is available for campers (around £7). **Long-term parking** (£2 per night) is also available.

Abbey Farmhouse (☎ 01946 823534; 💻 www.abbeyfarm-stbees.co.uk; 1S/2D/1T; en suite or private facilities; ▼; WI-FI; Ⓛ £6) is a sumptuous place just around the corner from the church. B&B is from £40pp (£45 single) and they also have long-stay parking facilities for £2 a night, donated to charity. They offer a free bottle of wine to guests who have just finished the Coast to Coast.

Recommended by readers for its cosy rooms, good breakfast and welcoming staff is ***Lulu's Bistro & Wine Bar*** (☎ 01946 822600, 💻 www.lulusbistro.co.uk; 4D; en suite; ▼; WI-FI; Ⓛ £7.50). B&B costs from £41pp (sgl occ £55); £30pp (sgl occ £50) with a continental breakfast.

Further up Main St the 17th-century ***Queen's Hotel*** (☎ 01946 822287; 💻 www.marstonspubs.co.uk/queenshotelcumbria; 3S/4D/3D or T/2T/1Qd; all en suite; ▼; WI-FI) charges £45-55 for a single, £35pp for two sharing or £80 for the quad room.

Manor House Inn (☎ 01946 820587, 💻 www.manorhousestbees.co.uk; 3D/3T/1F; all en suite; ▼ in one of the doubles; 🐕£10; WI-FI; Ⓛ £5.95) is another impressive-looking St Bees hotel with B&B from £37.50pp (sgl/sgl occ £60; £85 in the family room).

Albert Hotel (☎ 01946 822345, 💻 www.alberthotel-stbees.co.uk; 1 Finkle St; 2S/2D/3T; some en suite; others share facilities; Ⓛ £4) has B&B for £32.50-45pp single, £35pp in the double/twin. There are great views from some of the rooms.

Up at the top of Main St, ***Fairladies Barn Guest House*** (☎ 01946 822718, 💻 www.fairladiesbarn.co.uk; 1S/3D/2T/2Tr; all en suite; WI-FI; Ⓛ £7) is a cut above the rest; a large, restored 17th-century sandstone barn with varied and charming rooms. The most popular is the unusually shaped studio room under the roof at the end of the barn; this is used as a triple. B&B costs £32.50pp or £30 in the triple, single occupancy is £45.

Tomlin Guest House (☎ 01946 822284, 💻 iwhitehead44@yahoo.co.uk; 1D/2D or T/1Tr; one en suite, others share facilities; 🐕; WI-FI; Ⓛ £5.50) is on Beach Rd, a short walk from Mile Zero (see Map 1, p95) and is a friendly little place charging £28-30pp, single occupancy £40. Off-street parking is £2 per night.

The massive complex by the beach car park is ***Seacote Hotel*** (☎ 01946 822300, 💻 www.seacote.com/Hotel/; 🐕 in the villas; 7S/27D/25T/4Qd; all en suite; ▼; WI-FI). B&B costs £37.50pp, £50/60 for a single/single occupancy and £105 for four in a quad room; breakfast is £8.50pp.

Where to eat and drink

If it's just a snack you want, the pies in the **village shop** are excellent. You can buy provisions here and also in Hartley's Beach Shop & Tea Room (see below).

Manor House Inn (see Where to stay; food served daily noon-2pm & 5.30-8.45pm) is a reliable place with a comprehensive menu and a Sunday lunch from £8.95. They also have the ***Coast to Coast*** bar (daily noon to around 1am) so how can you resist a swift pint here?

The waiting room at the railway station has been reborn as ***Lulu's Bistro & Wine Bar*** (see Where to stay; Tue-Sat 6pm to late; in the main season if the weather is good they may be open all day). Sharing platters (seafood, charcuterie, nachos or oriental) range from £11 to £26 for 2-4 people. Other interesting choices include Thai beef salad (£14.95), moules frites (£13.45) and barbary duck with sloe gin (£17.95).

Queen's Hotel (see Where to stay; food served Easter to Oct daily noon-2pm & 5-9pm) has a good-value menu and a bar known for its real ales (such as the Jennings Bitter) and malt whiskies. If it's a Sunday you have one other option, up the hill at 92 Main St, where a reasonable Sunday lunch is served at ***Oddfellows Arms*** (☎ 01946 822317; food served Sun noon-4pm).

For sea views, cream teas and excellent ice-cream made on the premises, call in at ***Hartley's Beach Shop & Tea Room*** (Map 1, p95; ☎ 01946 820175; daily summer 8am-8pm, winter to 5pm) on the foreshore, just a short walk before Mile Zero. They also sell provisions, books and maps.

At nearby *Seacote Hotel* (see Where to stay) there's a bar serving pub grub noon-8.30pm.

Transport (see also pp52-5)
Trains (Mon-Sat) from St Bees go north to Carlisle and south to Barrow-in-Furness; see p51.

The No 6 **bus** (Mon-Fri) runs twice daily from Whitehaven to Seascale via St Bees and Egremont.

❑ HOW NOT TO LOSE YOUR WAY

Although it improves incrementally, the Coast to Coast path is the least well sign-posted of Britain's popular long-distance trails. Principally this is because it's not been officially designated a 'National Trail' with all the funding benefits that involves such as consistent and effective signage or slabs over bogs that the less popular Pennine Way got years ago. The trail also passes through the Lake District where the national park authorities have elected not to sully the upland trails with signposts. (On our last research trip we counted three signposts in total in the Lakes – all of them on the way to Seatoller from Honister Pass and well away from anywhere where people might actually get lost!) All this, combined with occasions of low visibility, may in places give problems with navigation. The minute you step out of the Lake District National Park signage by local authorities, local landowners or well-wishers, improves in places, all the way across the Pennines into Yorkshire. Here, among other signs, the North Yorkshire County Council's yellow waymark discs are used towards the North Yorkshire Moors and the North Sea. Elsewhere, wooden 'Coast to Coast' fingerposts point the way – though not always accurately.

In 2012 the Wainwright Society announced agreements had been made to mark fingerposts at public road crossings with a special C2C logo featuring Wainwright's 'AW' monogram. In 2015 we spotted very few of these so the value seems more pro-motional than navigational, to celebrate the fortieth anniversary of the original guide-book's publication.

Consistency aside, what is actually needed are *additional* marker posts and direc-tional waymarks across the trouble spots listed below, as well as a few other places. In many places supportive farmers have taken it upon themselves to fulfill this task.

A few tips

Our advice is to **study the book's maps closely** and read through the entire day's stage before you start it, making a note of possible tricky spots (we have made a list of these to help you – see pp92-3). Once on the move it's easy to get distracted, be it blindly following others who may be on some other walk or simply following the obvious trail while engrossed in a natter, and so you end up missing an obscure but crucial turn off. It's a nuisance, but the C2C being what it is, you'll have to consult the book frequently to keep on track.

Keep this book readily accessible come rain or shine; at times you'll be referring to it several times an hour. A large pocket will do in the dry, but overall a waterproof **map case** on a neck string works best. In pelting rain you'll probably want to get your head down and press on, but the book's maps may still need frequent attention.

This guidebook's maps depict only a narrow strip along the trail. Depending on your experience in reading maps as well as the location of the accommodation you may use, getting the **Ordnance Survey sheets OL4, OL5 and OL19** covering the Lake District and the Pennines might be worthwhile. Even then, a **compass** helps on the occasions when you're not sure the path you're following is heading in the same direction as the one you think you're on according to the book.

(cont'd overleaf)

❏ HOW NOT TO LOSE YOUR WAY *(cont'd from p91)*

Trailblazer tracklog and GPS waypoints

The absolute bombproof way of not getting lost on the Coast to Coast is to refer to a **GPS tracklog**, displayed as a continuous line on either a GPS unit or a smartphone running GPS. Ground-based mobile location signals aren't the same and anyway, don't cover remote areas or even some lakeland valleys. The C2C requires a GPS satellite signal which on a smartphone eats battery power. Clearly you won't depend on a tracklog every step of the way, so save the batteries on either unit by merely activating them when in need. To download the GPS tracklog on which this edition's maps are based, see the Trailblazer website. In addition, **GPS waypoints** are listed on pp259-63 and are also downloadable from the website. They can be imported into a device or simply manually keyed from the back of the book into a GPS or plotted on an OS map to pin down a location.

Common navigational trouble spots

These are the well-known trouble spots on the Coast to Coast path. The list may well be rendered obsolete by improvements in waymarking and signage, and in some cases, drainage – or by simply making use of the book's GPS data. On our maps we've also highlighted the places where people frequently get lost with a **warning triangle** to emphasise the need for vigilance; note them well. That's not to say that you won't get lost elsewhere, but we think in most places you'll recognise your error within less than a mile.

● **Stanley Pond** (Maps 3 & 4) Just after the rail tunnel the route is often waterlogged, causing walkers to detour to the south, get disoriented and so take the wrong route into the woods. At the woods (WPT 004) head north-east up the field to the tunnel, as the map suggests.

● **Dent Hill** (Maps 5 & 6) This shouldn't be a problem as long as you remember to look out for the signpost (to 'Dent Fell') to your left (and often half obscured by the trees) taking you off the forestry trail. A few metres away a second signpost points you rightwards, straight up the hill. As you leave the trees you join a wall and cross over a stile, the wall taking you virtually to Dent's summit before stones across some boggy patches help keep you on the right path. Continue in the same direction to the water tanks, where a right turn brings you to the tall ladder stile leading to Raven Crag hill. If the weather/visibility are terrible on your Dent Hill day, consider taking the quiet road from Black How Farm to Ennerdale Bridge.

● **Leaving Black Sail Hut** (WPT 021 and 022) (Map 12) Take the higher, more northerly **and barely visible** path even though the majority of walkers – including many C2Cers foolish enough to have a different guidebook – will take the obvious path heading southeast to Great Gable. Don't worry about striking out alone; after a few metres the path is obvious and you'll see the others below you negotiating the boggy ground while you skip merrily over and above the drumlins. And when you hit Loft Beck, it's you who'll find it straightforward finding the trail that climbs alongside it – for your path will lead you straight onto it after you've crossed the beck – while those who took the lower path will have to ford Tongue Beck before they can even think about tackling the climb.

● **Top of Loft Beck** (Map 12) Clear as a bell in good conditions, in poor visibility some lose their way here and OS maps aren't much help. If you miss the massive, beck-top cairn (WPT 022) and arrive at the fence in the bogs, just follow it east and south to the stile (WPT 023), then carry on towards Grey Knotts (Map 13).

● **Greenup Edge** (Map 16) The 'edge' is actually a broad col preceded by bogs crossed by an indistinct path marked by hard-to-see cairns on low outcrops. Even in perfect visibility hitting the right fence post and nearby twin cairns (WPT 029) takes some luck as other, more prominent fenceposts along the col's rim can lure you astray. Aim resolutely for the southern side of the col at a point where a track begins to ascend to Low White Stones to the south. Or, do as many do and hit the Edge early to avoid the mired cairned path, then follow it southeast to WPT 029. Having located the twin cairns, the route down to the next key junction at the top of Easedale is clearer.

● **Boredale Hause** (Map 25) Several converging paths can make this grassy junction confusing; take the most used one bending right (ie south-east) then south to Angle Tarn.

● **High Street** (Map 27) From Angle Tarn to The Knott is these days a single, clear path and short of a white-out, it's hard to think what the problem is at High Street other than simply missing the flattened trackside cairn before the col. It marks another clear track running north-east to Kidsty Pike, the route's high point.

● **South of Oddendale** (Map 36) Some experience a brief route-finding wobble here even though there are poles and good landmarks. Leave the main track for WPT 061 at the southern corner of the strip plantation, then head up to the wall-like rim of limestone and use the 'two trees' landmark (WPT 062).

● **Sunbiggin Tarn** (Maps 39 & 40) Locate the clear path off the road curving south of the tarn and over a footbridge (WPT 067), then at the southern edge of a walled pen aim uphill for the reservoir head on a hilltop, just over a minor road.

● **Nine Standards routes** (Maps 45, 46 & 47) In very thick mist seeing the mysterious cairns (WPT 082) before they see you can be tricky as can continuing from there south past the trig point to the key Red and Blue route junction (WPT 085, half a mile away) while avoiding bogs on the way. But the real problems lie further on; see p169 for more details and help with wayfinding. If you get to this junction, the Blue route has posts leading to Whitsundalebeck valley; the Red route has less frequent landmarks and great care is required to find the right path – especially as there is no actual 'path'. This ruined section is in dire need of Pennine-Way-like paving. The lower Green route is easier to follow and much less of a mire.

● **Graystone Hills** (Maps 91 & 92) Even in clear weather, the loss of the useful poles that used to mark the way when crossing this final stretch of moorland make this a tricky stretch, even though you can see the cars on the nearby A171. Then once off the moor, getting the 500m from WPT 144 to the start of the rocky/muddy trail may take some intuition. Watch your orientation closely or use GPS.

ROUTE GUIDE AND MAPS

STAGE 1: ST BEES TO ENNERDALE BRIDGE   MAPS 1-7

Introduction

There is a lot of variety in this **14-mile (22.5km, 6¼hr)** stage, beginning with a cliff-top walk along the Irish Sea and ending (weather permitting) with a high-level view from Dent Hill across to the brooding western fells of the Lake District.

Most will find this first day a bit of a struggle, particularly the haul up and over Dent Hill into Ennerdale Bridge (where there are few places to stay). If you think this may include you, pace yourself while you have a choice and consider stopping near Cleator or Egremont, both a mile or two off the path, before continuing on the second day to the youth hostels at High Gillerthwaite or even Black Sail. In a couple of days you may be glad you did.

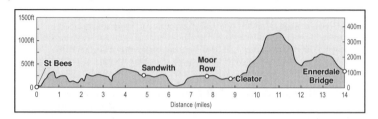

The route

As far as we and most other walkers are concerned, '**Mile Zero**' (WPT 001) on the path is at the Coast to Coast monument by the RNLI hut facing the Irish Sea. To get to Mile Zero follow Beach Rd to the shore, baptise your boots in the surf and take a photo by the sign with its new steel adornment showing the entire C2C elevation profile. Some walkers even collect a small pebble as a keepsake to drop into the North Sea at the end of the walk. Suitably initiated, turn north-west, steel yourself for the adventure about to unfold, and climb up the steep path to the clifftop. You're now on the Coast to Coast path, with a fence on one side and what becomes a 300ft (90m) drop on the other.

The cliffs themselves are made of red St Bees sandstone, used in the construction of many of the buildings in the vicinity since medieval times and part of a broad sedimentary bed which you'll encounter again in the Vale of Eden on the far side of the Lakes.

The first notable landmark is the cleft of **Fleswick Bay** (Map 2) composed of a secluded pebble beach surrounded by red sandstone cliffs with some unusually weathered boulders on the shore.

This bay marks the dividing line between the constituent parts of St Bees Head: **South Head**, which you've been on up to now, and **North Head** (Map 2), which you now climb up to from the bay. Two features distinguish this latter part of St Bees Head: the three **RSPB observation points**, to the left of the path, which allow you to safely peer over the cliffs and observe the seabirds nesting there (including puffins, terns and England's only colony of black guillemots); and **St Bees Lighthouse**, a little way inland from the path but clearly visible since South Head.

If you're already puffed out, ***Tarn Flatt Hall*** (Map 2; ☎ 01946 692162, 🖥 www.tarnflattfarm.co.uk; dogs OK if sole occupancy only), a basic **camping barn**, is best reached by turning off the path here towards the lighthouse and continuing east for ¼ mile/400m. It sleeps 12 and costs £8.50pp. The barn comes with electric lighting (no power sockets), a slab to put your camping stove on and a wood-burning fire, with wood available from the farm. Showers cost 50p. Booking is recommended and should be done through the website; however, if you have queries you can phone. Parking (long- and short-stay) is also available.

After the lighthouse the path continues to the tip of **North Head** before curving east along the coast and eventually turning inland at **Birkham's Quarry**.

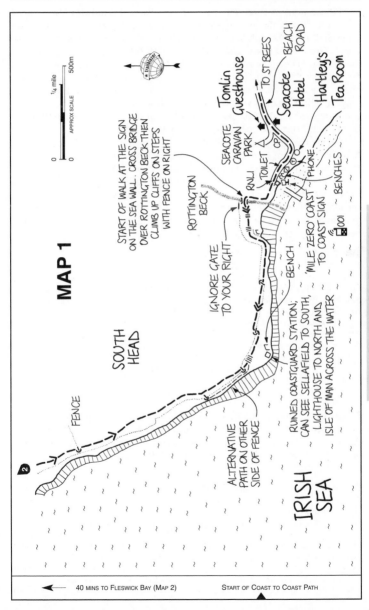

MAP 1

SOUTH HEAD

FENCE

START OF WALK AT THE SIGN ON THE SEA WALL. CROSS BRIDGE OVER ROTTINGTON BECK THEN CLIMB UP CLIFFS ON STEPS WITH FENCE ON RIGHT

IGNORE GATE TO YOUR RIGHT

ROTTINGTON BECK

SEACOTE CARAVAN PARK

Tomlin Guesthouse

TO ST BEES

BEACH ROAD

Seacote Hotel

Hartley's Tea Room

TOILET

RNLI

PHONE

BENCHES

BENCH

'MILE ZERO' COAST TO COAST SIGN

RUINED COASTGUARD STATION; CAN SEE SELLAFIELD TO SOUTH, LIGHTHOUSE TO NORTH AND ISLE OF MAN ACROSS THE WATER

ALTERNATIVE PATH ON OTHER SIDE OF FENCE

IRISH SEA

APPROX SCALE

¼ mile

0   500m

40 MINS TO FLESWICK BAY (MAP 2)

START OF COAST TO COAST PATH

ROUTE GUIDE AND MAPS

Fifteen minutes later you arrive in the village of **Sandwith** (pronounced 'Sanith'). This is the first settlement of note on the trail; it's almost five miles/8km along the path from St Bees (though only two miles/3km as the crow flies!). *Grovewood House B&B* (Map 3; ☎ 01946 63482; 🖳 www.grovewood house.com; 1D or T en suite with whirlpool bath ➤; WI-FI; continental breakfast; £55pp, £75 sgl occ) offers self-contained accommodation with a kitchenette. The owners are happy to meet people at St Bees station and take their luggage which means you can arrive in St Bees and then set off on the walk unencumbered for the first stage. The village pub, the *Dog and Partridge* (☎ 01946 592177) is now open daily and also does **food**.

Taking the road past the pub, the path crosses Byerstead Rd and, just over half a mile (0.8km) later, the B5345 linking Whitehaven to St Bees. From the tunnel beneath the railway line (Map 3) at the foot of the hill, the trail crosses waterlogged fields around what was **Stanley Pond** (with possible navigation issues; see box p92) and a small stream (**Scalegill Beck**; Map 4), before passing underneath a disused railway. We, however, advise you to take the steps on your right up the side of the tunnel onto the disused railway track; take a left here and follow the 'track' to Moor Row.

MOOR ROW   MAP 4, p99

Moor Row lacks the village-green charm of Sandwith but does have *Su Ellen's Baker's Shop* (☎ 07749 485492, Tue-Fri 8am-4pm, Sat 8am-1pm) which does takeaway pasties, pies and snacks. For accommodation, *Jasmine House* (☎ 01946 815795, 🖳 www.jasminehousebandb.com; 1S/2D/2D or T or Tr; all en suite; ➤; WI-FI; Ⓛ £7 if ordered the night before) does B&B from £32.50pp (sgl £39, three in room £90). The owner, Jean, is very welcoming to Coast to Coasters and offers transport to and back

from the nearest pub for supper, making this a great first night if you don't feel quite ready for the long haul over Dent Hill to Ennerdale. If staying more than one night then the owners will happily provide free transfers between St Bees and/or Ennerdale – making this a worthy base for the first couple of nights on the trail.

The No 30 **bus** (Mon-Sat) passes through on its route between Whitehaven and Thornhill; see pp52-5 for further details.

Following the uncomfortably narrow and busy road south out of Moor Row (signposted to Egremont), you're relieved to get off it soon and head into a field. A series of kissing gates follows as you cross the dismantled railway once more on your way towards Cleator, arriving alongside St Leonard's Church.

CLEATOR   MAP 5, p101

As with Moor Row before it, it's clear that Wordsworth's lyrical ballads never reached out to immortalise the grim, pebbledashed, terraces of Cleator. Remnants of 12th-century masonry in the **church** (St Leonard's) attest to the village's venerability, but the abiding impression dates from a 19th-century iron-ore mining boom when Irish migrants flooded into the area

(as the many Celtic house names suggest). The mining collapsed in the latter half of the 19th century and the nearby settlements followed suit; a familiar story repeated across west Cumbria. It's ameliorated today by the ongoing decommissioning of the ageing Sellafield nuclear plant, offering work to the 10,000 who want it.

(cont'd on p100)

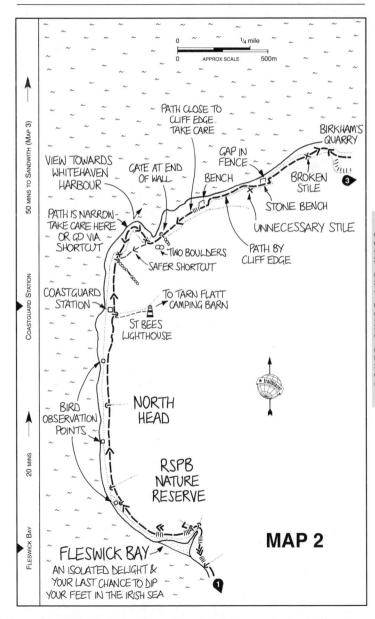

PATH CLOSE TO
CLIFF EDGE.
TAKE CARE

BIRKHAM'S
QUARRY

GAP IN
FENCE

VIEW TOWARDS
WHITEHAVEN
HARBOUR

GATE AT END
OF WALL

BENCH

BROKEN
STILE

STONE BENCH

PATH IS NARROW-
TAKE CARE HERE
OR GO VIA
SHORTCUT

UNNECESSARY STILE

TWO BOULDERS

PATH BY
CLIFF EDGE

SAFER SHORTCUT

COASTGUARD
STATION

TO TARN FLATT
CAMPING BARN

ST BEES
LIGHTHOUSE

BIRD
OBSERVATION
POINTS

NORTH
HEAD

RSPB
NATURE
RESERVE

MAP 2

FLESWICK BAY
AN ISOLATED DELIGHT &
YOUR LAST CHANCE TO DIP
YOUR FEET IN THE IRISH SEA

50 MINS TO SANDWITH (MAP 3)

COASTGUARD STATION

20 MINS

FLESWICK BAY

0   ¼ mile
APPROX SCALE
0   500m

ROUTE GUIDE AND MAPS

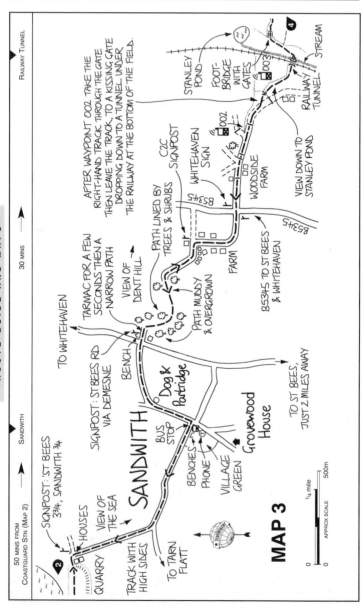

MAP 3

50 MINS FROM COASTGUARD STN (Map 2) — SANDWITH — 30 MINS — RAILWAY TUNNEL

APPROX SCALE
0   ¼ mile
0   500m

2

SIGNPOST: 'ST BEES 3¾, SANDWITH ¾'

HOUSES

VIEW OF THE SEA

QUARRY

TRACK WITH HIGH SIDES

TO TARN FLATT

TO WHITEHAVEN

SIGNPOST: ST BEES RD VIA DEMESNE

BENCH

SANDWITH

Dog & Partridge

BUS STOP

BENCHES
PHONE
VILLAGE GREEN

Grovewood House

TO ST BEES, JUST 2 MILES AWAY

TARMAC FOR A FEW SECONDS THEN A NARROW PATH

VIEW OF DENT HILL

PATH MUDDY & OVERGROWN

PATH LINED BY TREES & SHRUBS

C2C SIGNPOST

WHITEHAVEN SIGN

B5345

FARM

B5345 TO ST BEES & WHITEHAVEN

WOODSIDE FARM

VIEW DOWN TO STANLEY POND

B5345

002

AFTER WAYPOINT 002 TAKE THE RIGHT-HAND TRACK THROUGH THE GATE THEN LEAVE THE TRACK, TO A KISSING GATE DROPPING DOWN TO A TUNNEL UNDER THE RAILWAY AT THE BOTTOM OF THE FIELD.

STANLEY POND

FOOT-BRIDGE WITH GATES

RAILWAY TUNNEL

STREAM

003

4

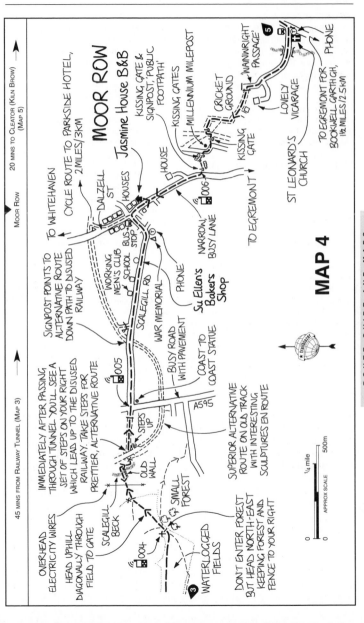

MOOR ROW

Jasmine House B&B

CYCLE ROUTE TO PARKSIDE HOTEL, 2 MILES/3KM

TO WHITEHAVEN

DALZELL ST

HOUSES

HOUSE

KISSING GATE & SIGNPOST, 'PUBLIC FOOTPATH'

KISSING GATES

MILLENNIUM MILEPOST

'WAINWRIGHT PASSAGE'

CRICKET GROUND

KISSING GATE

LOVELY VICARAGE

ST LEONARD'S CHURCH

PHONE

TO EGREMONT FOR BOOKWELL GARTH GH, 1½ MILES/2.5KM

TO EGREMONT

NARROW, BUSY LANE

Su Ellen's Baker's Shop

WAR MEMORIAL

PHONE

SCALEGILL RD

SCHOOL

BUS STOP

WORKING MEN'S CLUB

SIGNPOST POINTS TO ALTERNATIVE ROUTE DOWN PATH TO DISUSED RAILWAY

IMMEDIATELY AFTER PASSING THROUGH TUNNEL YOU'LL SEE A SET OF STEPS ON YOUR RIGHT WHICH LEAD UP TO THE DISUSED RAILWAY. TAKE STEPS FOR PRETTIER, ALTERNATIVE ROUTE

OVERHEAD ELECTRICITY WIRES

HEAD UPHILL DIAGONALLY THROUGH FIELD TO GATE

SCALEGILL BECK

OLD WALL

SMALL FOREST

WATERLOGGED FIELDS

DON'T ENTER FOREST BUT HEAD NORTH-EAST KEEPING FOREST AND FENCE TO YOUR RIGHT

SUPERIOR ALTERNATIVE ROUTE ON OLD TRACK WITH INTERESTING SCULPTURES EN ROUTE

STEPS UP

BUSY ROAD WITH PAVEMENT

COAST TO COAST STATUE

A595

MAP 4

¼ mile

500m

0

APPROX SCALE

CLEATOR (*cont'd from p96*) Note that **Cleator Stores** (☎ 01946 810038; summer Mon-Fri 5.30am-6.30pm, Sat 8am-1pm, Sun 8.30am-12.30pm) is now the **last decent store** until Grasmere, although you can get basics in Borrowdale (see p118). Otherwise, **Cleator Moor**, the regional hub with many grand 19th-century edifices, some once painted by Lowry, is a mile to the north, with an ATM, corner shops and several junk-food outlets. There's also an ATM at Egremont.

Stagecoach's **bus** No 32 (Mon-Sat) shuttles between Whitehaven and Cleator, or there's also the No 31/31A which travels between Whitehaven and Frizington via Cleator Moor; see pp52-5.

Where to stay and eat

Nine miles along the Coast to Coast path from St Bees, Cleator can make a good first day destination after a weary first walk.

Set in the former council offices, ***Ennerdale Country House Hotel*** (☎ 01946 813907, 🖳 www.bespokehotels.com/ennerdalehotel; 2S/14D/8T/4Tr/2 suites; 🐾 £10; all en suite; ☕; ⓁŁ12.95; WI-FI; open all year) is pitched at visiting nuclear executives, weddings and conferences, with rooms starting at about £40 per person. It could be worth a look as it's closest to the path. Food is served daily (2-9pm) in both the restaurant and the bar. Less than half a

mile further up the road, ***Grove Court Hotel*** (☎ 01946 810503, 🖳 www.grovecourthotel.co.uk; 2T/8D/2Tr/1Qd; all en suite; 🐾 by prior arrangement £10; WI-FI; open all year; Ⓛ £4.95) is a slightly classier version of the same, with rooms from £34.50pp in the twins and doubles, £69 in the triples and £89 in the quad (sgl occ £59). Meals are available (11.45am-1.45pm, 6.30pm-8.45pm); booking recommended, particularly for Monday's steak night.

Under new ownership, two miles north of Cleator along the A5086 is the ***Parkside Hotel*** (☎ 01946 811001, 🖳 www.theparksidehotel.co.uk; 2D/4T or D or Tr; all en suite; WI-FI). Refurbished, it's well priced at £42.50-47.50pp, (sgl occ £75-85). Meals won't cost the earth and the bar is open daily. It's a dreary roadside schlep up from Cleator to the Parkside Hotel so it's better to get a bus or follow the quieter cycleway directly from Moor Row (Map 4) north-east for two miles via Cleator Moor to the hotel.

As an alternative to Cleator, **Egremont** is only 1¹/2 miles/2.5km to the south and has ***Bookwell Garth Guest House*** (☎ 01946 820271, 16 Bookwell; 5S/6T/1Tr; shared shower facilities; 🐾; Ⓛ); B&B from £30pp. They also have a large car park.

Several **bus** services stop in Egremont including the No 30 (daily) and No 6 (Mon-Fri); see pp52-5.

From Cleator it's possible to take the road route north and east to Ennerdale Bridge, so avoiding Dent Hill, either off the A5086 or at Black How Farm just before you enter the Dent-side plantation. Either way is said to be not too bad for traffic, though unless the weather is positively treacherous, or you're intent on saving energy, take the high route. It would be a shame to miss the summit of **Dent Hill** (Map 5) and the trickling tranquillity of Nannycatch Beck that lies hidden away at its foot. The long and sweaty climb to Dent Hill summit takes about an hour from Cleator. At the top there could be views to the Lakeland fells ahead and the sea behind, with the gigantic plant of Sellafield to the south-west and, on a good day, the silhouette of the Isle of Man and Galloway (Scotland) across the Solway Firth.

After the hilltop the Coast to Coast path signpost points left to the tall stile from where you contour and then descend Raven Crag hill (Map 6). Although very steep, it's become the *de facto* path now, contrary to Wainwright's original instructions. Maybe he had a point – when we say steep we mean it; poles may help and irate readers still write in and complain about the gradient down Raven

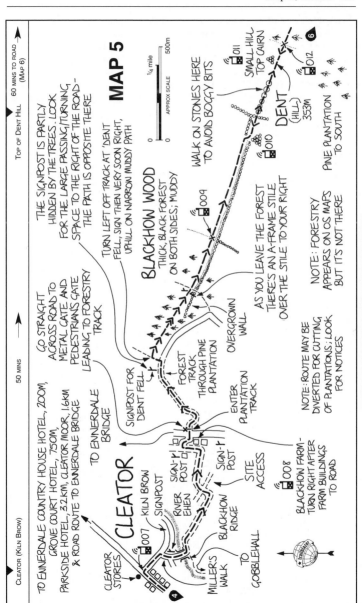

MAP 5

CLEATOR

CLEATOR STORES

TO ENNERDALE COUNTRY HOUSE HOTEL, 2KM, GROVE COURT HOTEL, 750M, PARKSIDE HOTEL, 3.2KM, CLEATOR MOOR, 1.6KM & ROAD ROUTE TO ENNERDALE BRIDGE

TO ENNERDALE BRIDGE

KILN BROW SIGNPOST

RIVER EHEN

SIGN-POST

SIGN-POST

SITE ACCESS

BLACKHOW RIDGE

MILLER'S WALK

TO COBBLEHALL

BLACKHOW FARM - TURN RIGHT AFTER FARM BUILDINGS TO ROAD

SIGNPOST FOR DENT FELL

ENTER PLANTATION TRACK

FOREST TRACK THROUGH PINE PLANTATION

OVERGROWN WALL

NOTE: ROUTE MAY BE DIVERTED FOR CUTTING OF PLANTATIONS; LOOK FOR NOTICES

AS YOU LEAVE THE FOREST THERE'S AN A-FRAME STILE OVER THE STILE TO YOUR RIGHT

NOTE: FORESTRY APPEARS ON OS MAPS BUT IT'S NOT THERE

BLACKHOW WOOD THICK, BLACK FOREST ON BOTH SIDES; MUDDY

TURN LEFT OFF TRACK AT 'DENT FELL' SIGN THEN VERY SOON RIGHT, UPHILL ON NARROW MUDDY PATH

THE SIGNPOST IS PARTLY HIDDEN BY THE TREES. LOOK FOR THE LARGE PASSING/TURNING SPACE TO THE RIGHT OF THE ROAD - THE PATH IS OPPOSITE THERE

GO STRAIGHT ACROSS ROAD TO METAL GATE AND PEDESTRIANS GATE LEADING TO FORESTRY TRACK

WALK ON STONES HERE TO AVOID BOGGY BITS

DENT (HILL) 353M

PINE PLANTATION TO SOUTH

SMALL HILL TOP CAIRN

¼ mile

0   APPROX SCALE   500m

007

008

009

010

011

012

4

6

ROUTE GUIDE AND MAPS

Crag hill but trust us, it's a lot quicker, good for the quads and more scenic.

From Nannycatch, head due north along the pretty beck, following the course of the water to the road into Ennerdale Bridge. Here you'll find *Low Cock How Farm* (Bradley's Riding Centre; Map 6; ☎ 01946 861354, 🖥 www.walk-rest-ride.co.uk; 4D or T; shared bathrooms; 🐕; Ⓛ £5), a riding centre with B&B from £35pp, a well-equipped 10-berth **bunkhouse** for £20pp as well as **camping** for £10pp. There are shower and cooking facilities for campers. Breakfast (for bunkhouse/campers) costs £5 booked the night before. Evening meals are not available but anyone can order a home delivery; there are three menus to choose from.

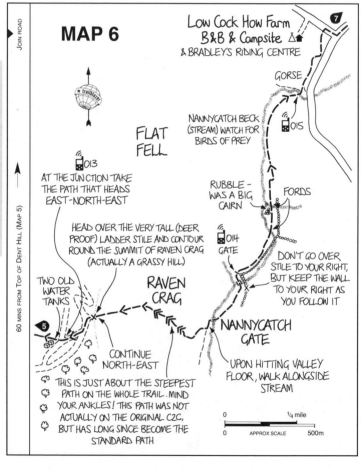

ROUTE GUIDE AND MAPS · 60 MINS FROM TOP OF DENT HILL (MAP 5) · JOIN ROAD

MAP 6

Low Cock How Farm
B&B & Campsite △🏠
& BRADLEY'S RIDING CENTRE

GORSE

★ trailblazer

FLAT FELL

NANNYCATCH BECK
(STREAM) WATCH FOR
BIRDS OF PREY

📱 015

📱 013
AT THE JUNCTION TAKE
THE PATH THAT HEADS
EAST-NORTH-EAST

RUBBLE –
WAS A BIG
CAIRN

FORDS

HEAD OVER THE VERY TALL (DEER
PROOF) LADDER STILE AND CONTOUR
ROUND THE SUMMIT OF RAVEN CRAG
(ACTUALLY A GRASSY HILL)

📱 014
GATE

DON'T GO OVER
STILE TO YOUR RIGHT,
BUT KEEP THE WALL
TO YOUR RIGHT AS
YOU FOLLOW IT

TWO OLD
WATER
TANKS

RAVEN
CRAG

NANNYCATCH
GATE

CONTINUE
NORTH-EAST

UPON HITTING VALLEY
FLOOR, WALK ALONGSIDE
STREAM

THIS IS JUST ABOUT THE STEEPEST
PATH ON THE WHOLE TRAIL. MIND
YOUR ANKLES! THIS PATH WAS NOT
ACTUALLY ON THE ORIGINAL C2C,
BUT HAS LONG SINCE BECOME THE
STANDARD PATH

0   ¼ mile
0   APPROX SCALE   500m

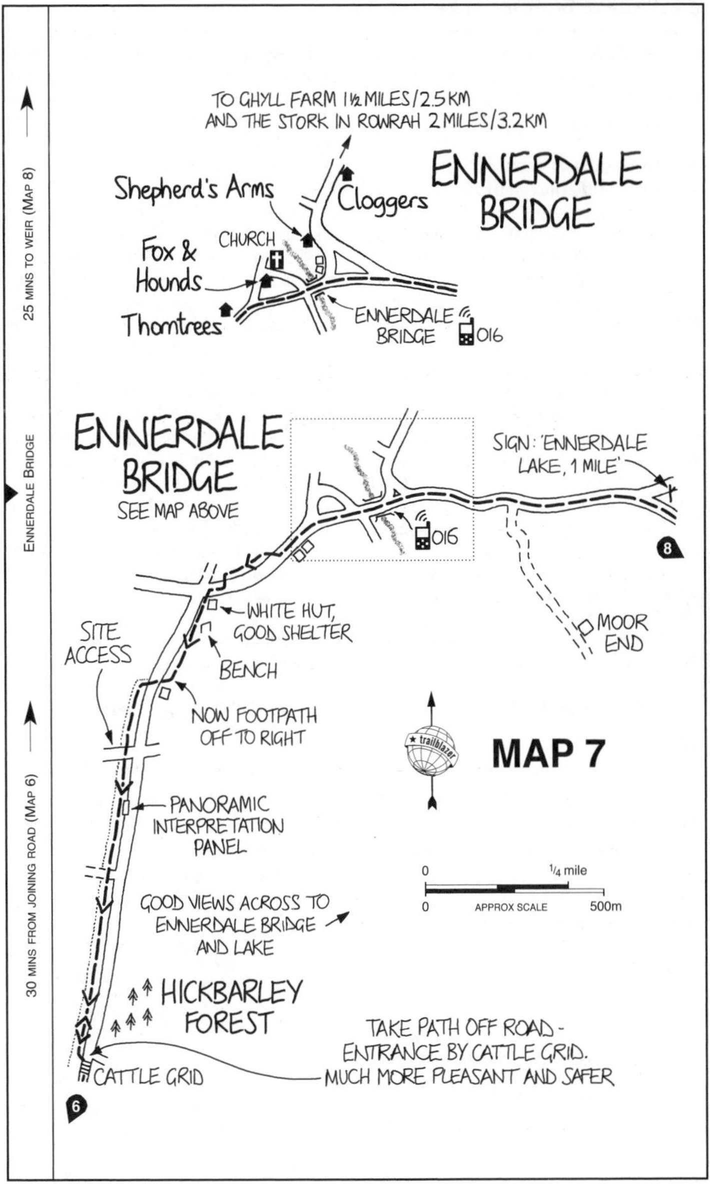

TO GHYLL FARM 1½ MILES/2.5 KM
AND THE STORK IN ROWRAH 2 MILES/3.2 KM

ENNERDALE BRIDGE

Shepherd's Arms

Cloggers

CHURCH

Fox & Hounds

Thorntrees

ENNERDALE BRIDGE 016

ENNERDALE BRIDGE
SEE MAP ABOVE

SIGN: 'ENNERDALE LAKE, 1 MILE'

016

8

MOOR END

SITE ACCESS

WHITE HUT, GOOD SHELTER

BENCH

NOW FOOTPATH OFF TO RIGHT

PANORAMIC INTERPRETATION PANEL

MAP 7

GOOD VIEWS ACROSS TO ENNERDALE BRIDGE AND LAKE

0   ¼ mile
0   APPROX SCALE   500m

HICKBARLEY FOREST

CATTLE GRID

TAKE PATH OFF ROAD -
ENTRANCE BY CATTLE GRID.
MUCH MORE PLEASANT AND SAFER

6

25 MINS TO WEIR (MAP 8)

ENNERDALE BRIDGE

30 MINS FROM JOINING ROAD (MAP 6)

ROUTE GUIDE AND MAPS

ENNERDALE BRIDGE   MAP 7, p103

Ennerdale Bridge is the first of the self-consciously pretty Lakeland villages, occupying a wonderful location spanning the River Ehen in one of Britain's least-developed valleys.

Where to stay and eat

The *Fox and Hounds* (☎ 01946 861373, 🖳 www.foxandhoundsinn.org; 2D/1T; all en suite; ✆; 🐾 £5; WI-FI; ⓛ £6) is run by the community and we've had several very good reports of the **food** (daily noon-2pm & 5.30-9pm), the service and the beer here. **B&B** is £45pp. You can **camp** for £5 per tent; there are no facilities but campers can use the toilet in the pub when it's open. Breakfast for campers is £8.

Thorntrees B&B (☎ 01946 862549; 🖳 www.thorntreesennerdale.co.uk; 3D/3T en suite or private facilities; ✆; WI-FI; ⓛ £6) is on the trail as you enter the village. B&B is from £42.50pp in a double, £45pp in a twin and £60 sgl occ. It's a recommended place; they do an excellent breakfast.

Cloggers (☎ 01946 862487; 1D or T; private facilities; ✆) is good value with B&B from £35pp (sgl occ £45).

In the centre of the village *Shepherd's Arms Hotel* (☎ 01946 861249, 🖳 www .shepherdsarms.com; 2D or T/2T/4D; all en suite; ✆; 🐾; WI-FI; ⓛ £3.50-6.50) offers B&B for £47pp (sgl occ £57, £111 for three sharing a room. **Food** is served daily Apr-Oct noon-9pm, Oct-Apr noon-2pm & 6-9pm. Mains are from around £9.99.

A mile and a half away from Ennerdale Bridge near **Kirkland** is *Ghyll Farm B&B* (☎ 01946 861330. 🖳 www.ghyllfarm.co .uk; 2D or T, 1Tr en suite; WI-FI; ⓛ £5.50). B&B is up to £45pp, with single occupancy costing £60. To get there, head for Kirkland, half a mile after you leave the village of Ennerdale Bridge take the (first) right turn down a single track road. There are signs at the junction but look for the remains of an old barn and a timber footpath signpost; follow the single track road for a further half-mile where there's a sign for the farm and it's a further half mile to the top of the hill.

The Stork Hotel (☎ 01946 861213, 🖳 www.storkhotel.co.uk; 2S/2D/2D or T; all en suite with good showers; WI-FI; ⓛ £2.50-4.50) is two miles away in **Rowrah** but they will pick up Coast to Coasters who book in advance. B&B starts at £37.50pp, £40 in a single. They do **food** (daily 6.30-9pm, Fri & Sun noon-2pm) with mains from £8 and portions generous.

STAGE 2: ENNERDALE BRIDGE TO BORROWDALE   MAPS 7-14

Introduction

As with any day in the Lakes, the enjoyment of this **15-mile (24km, 6½hr** via low route) stage depends largely on the weather. And be warned you are heading towards the spot which records the highest rainfall in England; the wryly named **Sprinkling Tarn** just south of Seathwaite receives an average of 185 inches (a phenomenal 4.7m) of rain a year. Lakeland is known for its wash-outs (eg December 2015) but in 2009 well over 200 inches fell, helped by no less

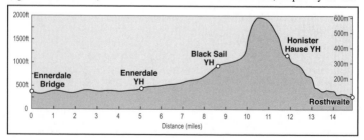

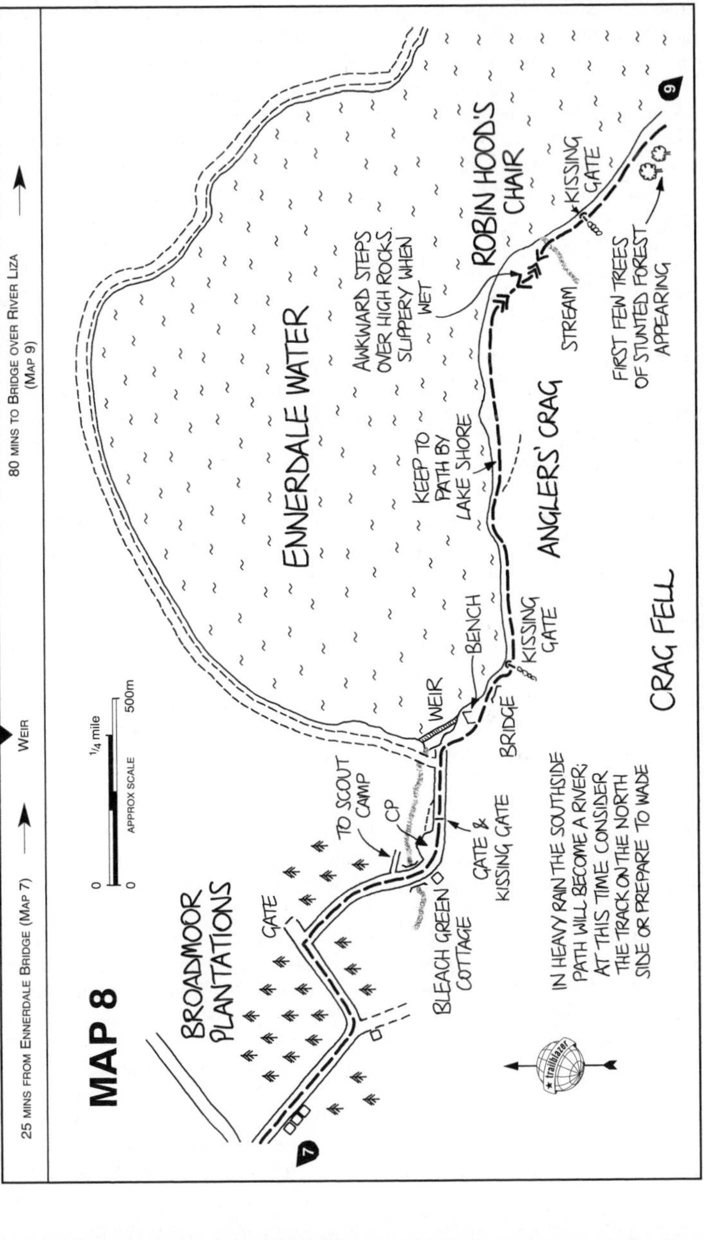
25 MINS FROM ENNERDALE BRIDGE (MAP 7)
WEIR
80 MINS TO BRIDGE OVER RIVER LIZA (MAP 9)
MAP 8
7
9
BROADMOOR PLANTATIONS
GATE
BLEACH GREEN COTTAGE
GATE & KISSING GATE
TO SCOUT CAMP
CP
0
0
1/4 mile
500m
APPROX SCALE
WEIR
BRIDGE
BENCH
KISSING GATE
ENNERDALE WATER
KEEP TO PATH BY LAKE SHORE
ANGLERS' CRAG
CRAG FELL
AWKWARD STEPS OVER HIGH ROCKS. SLIPPERY WHEN WET
ROBIN HOOD'S CHAIR
STREAM
KISSING GATE
FIRST FEW TREES OF STUNTED FOREST APPEARING
IN HEAVY RAIN THE SOUTHSIDE PATH WILL BECOME A RIVER; AT THIS TIME CONSIDER THE TRACK ON THE NORTH SIDE OR PREPARE TO WADE
trailblazer

than 12.4 inches (315mm) falling at Seathwaite Farm in one 24-hour period in late November, setting a new record for the British Isles since records began nearly 300 years ago. Indeed if it's raining horizontally with waterfalls running off the crags, chances are the path along the **southern edge of Ennerdale Water** will be one long stream with occasional fords rising halfway up your shins. Unless you like splashing about in such weather the access track along the north shore may be preferable. Beyond the lake's end, in clear conditions even the high route via Red Pike can get busy, but be warned it's a fair old climb and you can still enjoy great views down to Buttermere from the top of Loft Beck or Grey Knotts on the standard route. If the weather is closing in, it would be foolhardy to attempt the fell-top alternative. It's a long walk from Ennerdale Bridge, your first real stage in the Lakes, although you can rearrange this day at any of the four hostels spaced out along the route.

The route

The stage's first half involves a walk along the southern side of **Ennerdale Water** and though it's not quite the dreamy lakeside stroll you may have imagined, navigation couldn't be simpler. At one point the path rises over the outcrop of **Robin Hood's Chair** (Map 8; take the easier right route at the top of the crag) to enter mossy light woodland as you near the eastern extremity of the lake.

  Low Gillerthwaite Field Centre (Map 10; ☎ 01946 861229, 🖳 www.lgfc .org.uk; 🐾 OK but must be kept on a lead) has **camping** for £5pp; **bunkhouse** accommodation (40 beds: 2x4 beds, 1x8, 1x10, 1x14) is available from £15.50pp. There is a kitchen, a drying room and two lounges with open wood fires as well as shower and toilet facilities; campers also have access to shower/washing facilities and a basic cooking area. Note that if a school group is in residence (which is not unusual) you may not be allowed to stay so call ahead. Frozen ready meals (lasagne/cottage pie around £4.75-5.50) are now available though it's best to ring ahead to make sure they are in stock and defrosted – the nearest shop is 10 miles away; beers can also be organised – again, make sure you ring ahead for this. Breakfast can be ordered in advance from the YHA next door.

  Up the track a bit *YHA Ennerdale* (Map 10; ☎ 0845 371 9116, 🖳 www.yha.org.uk/hostel/ennerdale; 24 beds, 3x4 beds, 2x6 beds; beds £15-27, 4-bed rooms £49-79; Ⓛ £5.50), at High Gillerthwaite is a small hostel that's open from the week before Easter to the end of October. Meals are available, though these should be booked in advance. The hostel is licensed and has a slick self-catering kitchen and cosy lounge. The hostel generates its own hydro-powered electricity. The hostel reception opens at 5pm but hot drinks are available all day. Next door, *Ennerdale Camping Barn* (aka *High Gillerthwaite Camping Barn*; bookings ☎ 0800 0191700, arrival ☎ 01946 861237, 🖳 www.yha.org.uk/barn/ high-gillerthwaite-camping-barn; 14 beds) is managed by the YHA. Beds here are £12pp; there's electric lighting but no plug sockets, and a cooking area though no cooking facilities so you'll either need a stove or have to pop next door for a meal. Camping is also available for about £8pp and dogs are welcome on the campsite though not in the hostel. Just beyond the camping barn is the start of the alternative trail up to Red Pike, High Stile and Hay Stacks (see p110).

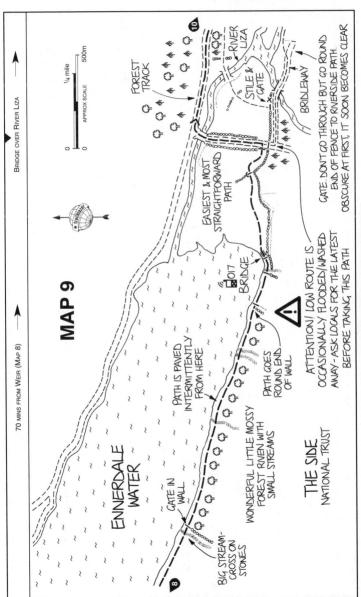

BRIDGE OVER RIVER LIZA

70 MINS FROM WEIR (MAP 8)

MAP 9

APPROX SCALE
0 500m
0 ¼ mile

ENNERDALE WATER

10

RIVER LIZA

FOREST TRACK

STILE & GATE

BRIDLEWAY

GATE. DON'T GO THROUGH BUT GO ROUND END OF FENCE TO RIVERSIDE PATH. OBSCURE AT FIRST, IT SOON BECOMES CLEAR

EASIEST & MOST STRAIGHTFORWARD PATH

1017 BRIDGE

ATTENTION! LOW ROUTE IS OCCASIONALLY FLOODED/WASHED AWAY - ASK LOCALS FOR THE LATEST BEFORE TAKING THIS PATH

PATH GOES ROUND END OF WALL

THE SIDE
NATIONAL TRUST

PATH IS PAVED INTERMITTENTLY FROM HERE

WONDERFUL LITTLE MOSSY FOREST RIVEN WITH SMALL STREAMS

GATE IN WALL

BIG STREAM- CROSS ON STONES

8

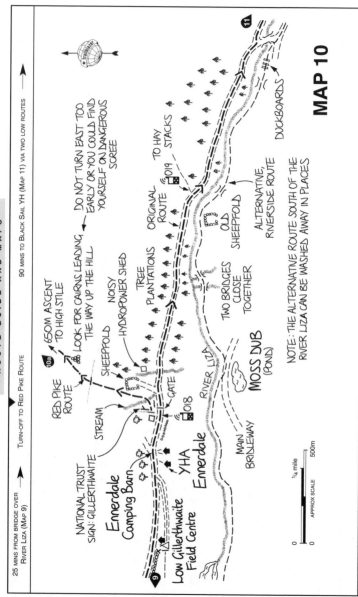

MAP 10

RED PIKE ROUTE

650M ASCENT TO HIGH STILE

10a

LOOK FOR CAIRNS LEADING THE WAY UP THE HILL

DO NOT TURN EAST TOO EARLY OR YOU COULD FIND YOURSELF ON DANGEROUS SCREE

NOISY HYDROPOWER SHED

SHEEPFOLD

TREE PLANTATIONS

STREAM

NATIONAL TRUST SIGN: GILLERTHWAITE

Ennerdale Camping Barn

GATE

018

TO HAY STACKS

019

ORIGINAL ROUTE

OLD SHEEPFOLD

YHA Ennerdale

Low Gillerthwaite Field Centre

RIVER LIZA

MOSS DUB (POND)

TWO BRIDGES CLOSE TOGETHER

ALTERNATIVE, RIVERSIDE ROUTE

MAIN BRIDLEWAY

NOTE: THE ALTERNATIVE ROUTE SOUTH OF THE RIVER LIZA CAN BE WASHED AWAY IN PLACES

DUCKBOARDS

9

11

¼ mile

500m

APPROX SCALE

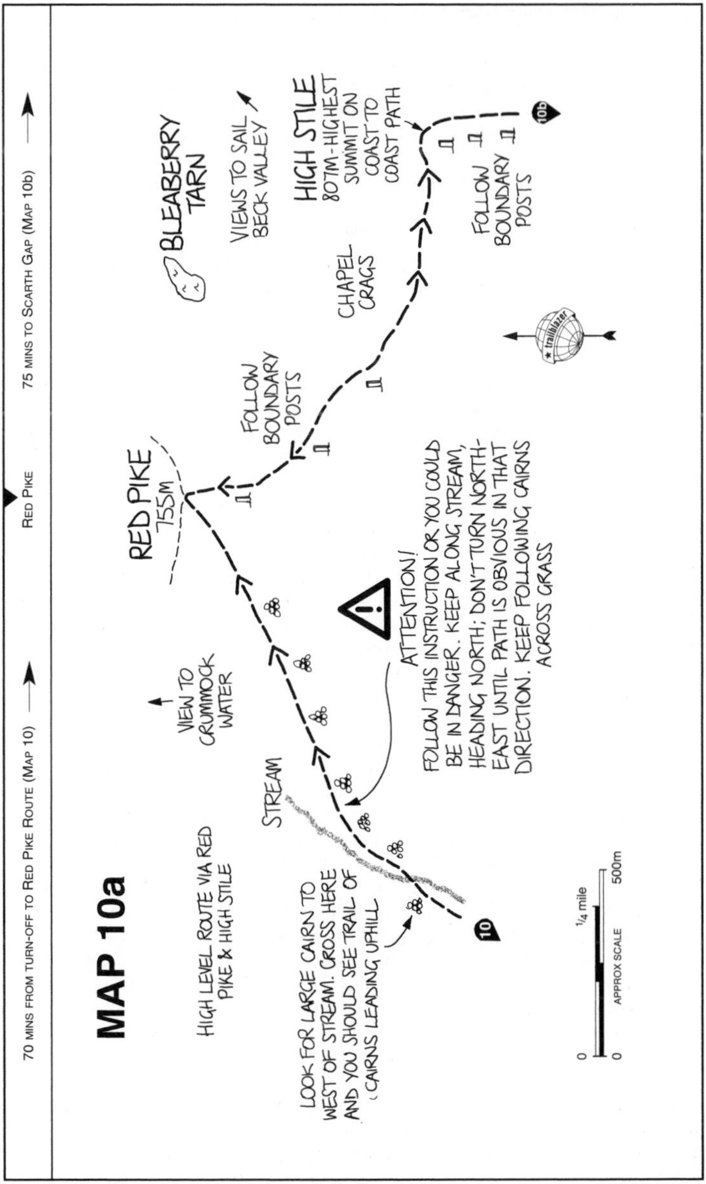
70 MINS FROM TURN-OFF TO RED PIKE ROUTE (MAP 10) →
RED PIKE
75 MINS TO SCARTH GAP (MAP 10b) →
MAP 10a
HIGH LEVEL ROUTE VIA RED PIKE & HIGH STILE
LOOK FOR LARGE CAIRN TO WEST OF STREAM. CROSS HERE AND YOU SHOULD SEE TRAIL OF CAIRNS LEADING UPHILL
STREAM
VIEW TO CRUMMOCK WATER
ATTENTION!
FOLLOW THIS INSTRUCTION OR YOU COULD BE IN DANGER. KEEP ALONG STREAM, HEADING NORTH; DON'T TURN NORTH-EAST UNTIL PATH IS OBVIOUS IN THAT DIRECTION. KEEP FOLLOWING CAIRNS ACROSS GRASS
RED PIKE 755M
FOLLOW BOUNDARY POSTS
BLEABERRY TARN
VIEWS TO SAIL BECK VALLEY
CHAPEL CRAGS
HIGH STILE 807M - HIGHEST SUMMIT ON COAST TO COAST PATH
FOLLOW BOUNDARY POSTS
10
10b
trailblazer
APPROX SCALE
0
1/4 mile
0
500m

The Red Pike, High Stile & Hay Stacks route
Maps 10, 10a, 10b & 12

'All I ask for, at the end, is a last, long resting place by the side of Innominate Tarn, on Haystacks where the water gently laps the gravelly shore and the heather blooms and Pillar and Gable keep unfailing watch. A quiet place, a lonely place. I shall go to it, for the last time, and be carried: someone who knew me in life will take me there and empty me out of a little box and leave me there alone. And if you, dear reader, should get a bit of grit in your boot as you are crossing Haystacks in the years to come, please treat it with respect. It might be me'.   **Alfred Wainwright** *Memoirs of an Ex-Fellwanderer*

In his *Coast to Coast* guide Wainwright describes this route as suitable only for 'very strong and experienced fellwalkers' in clear weather. While we don't think the group of people who can do this walk is quite as exclusive as Wainwright suggests, we certainly agree that the weather needs to be clear, if only because the views possible at the top – in particular across Buttermere to the north and to Great Gable and Pillar in the south – benefit from it. (If the weather takes a significant turn for the worse up there, you can drop down from Scarth Gap on steps to the Black Sail hostel; see Map 10b.) There are no technically difficult parts, though there are some steep ascents and particularly descents which will hammer the knees, and route finding on the way up to Red Pike can be tricky. This alternative route should add about **1½ miles (2.5km, 1¾hrs)** to this stage, all in all making it a pretty tough day so early in the walk.

The high-level route takes in a number of summits, including Red Pike (755m), High Stile (807m), High Crag (744m) and Hay Stacks (597m), the lowest but the most interesting. The place where some err from the path is on the initial climb up to Red Pike where it's tempting to branch off eastwards too early: make sure that, having crossed the stream, you continue north-east (following cairns) until you're firmly on the grassy upper reaches of Red Pike (Map 10a). There are *just* enough cairns to show the way, though if in doubt, your motto should be: head up the slope rather than along it.

Having gained the ridge the path becomes clear and you'll find yourself ticking off one peak after another as you make your way to **Innominate Tarn** (Map 12). From there, Wainwright recommends ignoring the obvious path that continues in an easterly direction to the north of **Blackbeck Tarn**, instead continuing in a south-easterly direction to an unmarked reunion with the low route near the top of **Loft Beck**. Though you'll struggle to follow any clear path in the ground, this trail is marked on Map 12. However, it's said that few trekkers actually manage to successfully rejoin the low route and instead forge their own path to **Honister Quarries**. If you wish to try, the best tactic from Innominate Tarn is to aim for the **Brandreth Fence** to the south and continue along it until you come to a reunion with the regular route at the gate in the fence (WPT 023). Otherwise, the easiest solution is to continue on the clear trail to Blackbeck, from where you can follow the wide track down to Honister (see p116). Just make sure you don't start to descend to Buttermere.

Continuing on the low route up the valley, just over 90 minutes after joining the forest track you emerge at the head of Ennerdale and the isolated bothy that is now *YHA Black Sail* (Maps 11/12; ☎ 0845 371 9680, 🖥 www.yha.org.uk/hostel/black-sail; 16 beds: 2x4 beds, 1x8 beds; beds £30pp; fully open Mar-Oct).

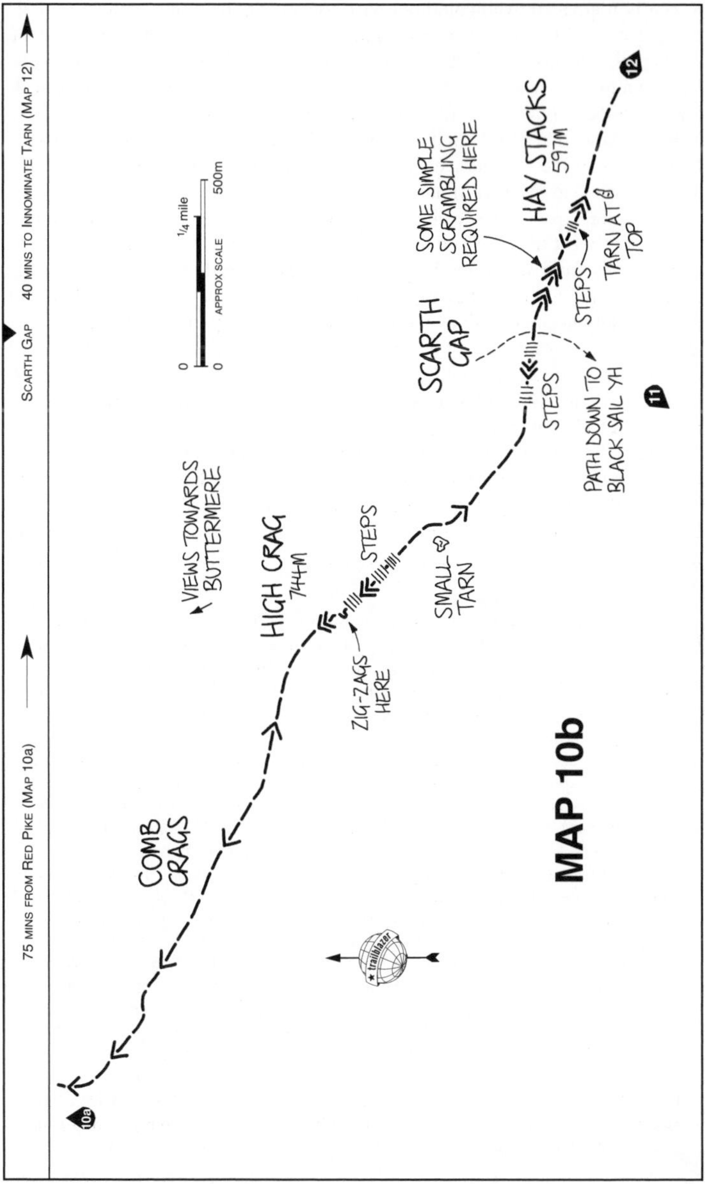
75 MINS FROM RED PIKE (MAP 10a)
SCARTH GAP
40 MINS TO INNOMINATE TARN (MAP 12)
MAP 10b
10a
COMB CRAGS
HIGH CRAG
744M
VIEWS TOWARDS BUTTERMERE
ZIG-ZAGS HERE
STEPS
SMALL TARN
STEPS
SCARTH GAP
PATH DOWN TO BLACK SAIL YH
11
SOME SIMPLE SCRAMBLING REQUIRED HERE
STEPS
TARN AT TOP
HAY STACKS
597M
12
0
1/4 mile
0
APPROX SCALE
500m
trailblazer

Recently renovated, who could not wish to wake up here one sunny morning? Breakfast, packed lunches and evening meals are served (these need to be booked in advance) and the hostel is licensed; credit cards aren't accepted. Having a torch is recommended. The hostel is left open during the day, providing welcome shelter from rain and the chance to make a cup of tea in the kitchen. Note that Black Sail is beyond the reach of the baggage carriers. Incidentally, if the weather clears, just before the hostel are some steps leading up to Scarth Gap (Map 10b) on the high route (see p110).

From the hostel things can get a little tricky. You need to follow the correct path east to meet the climb up the side of **Loft Beck** and from there the path to Grey Knotts from where the long descent to Honister Hause and Borrowdale begins. Armed with this advice, in fine weather the way is crystal clear, but unfortunately such conditions are infrequent in these parts, particularly in the afternoon when most attempt the climb. At the top of Loft Beck follow Map 12 carefully to negotiate this section and have a compass or GPS at hand. At worst, at the top of the Beck blunder north over the boggy saddle to the Brandreth Fence and follow it east (right) to the gate at WPT 023.

From the gate/stile at **Brandreth Fence**, an initially indistinct path rises to contour around the western face of Brandreth and **Grey Knotts** (Map 13), with occasional cairns along the way. The working Hopper Quarry can be seen in the distance to the north. The path soon joins the larger track (WPT 025) coming

❑ Honister Slate Mine

The story of mining at Honister began 400 million years ago when volcanic ash, combined with water and subsequent compression, formed the fine-grained rock now called slate. When the glaciers of the last Ice Age retreated up Gatesgarthdale they exposed three parallel veins of slate along the steep sides of the valley and sporadic mining may have taken place before the Roman era. Certainly by the early 1700s slate was being quarried here on an industrial scale and, as well as the disused tramway you walk down, there were roads and aerial ropeways to take the slate to the road. The workers who split and finished the slate lived in barracks in Honister during the week; the adjacent youth hostel is a former quarry workers' building. After closing in the 1980s, the mine (along with the nearby quarry) re-opened in 1997 and has since developed into a slick, tourist-oriented facility backed by small-scale mining operations.

The **Visitors Centre** (☎ 01768 777230, 🖳 www.honister.com; daily 9am-5pm) is well worth a look. There are guided tours into the mine daily at 10.30am, 12.30pm and 3.30pm for £12.50, 2pm at peak times too. For those with energy to spare they've also set up a *via ferrata*. Common in the Dolomites of northern Italy, a via ferrata, or 'iron way', is essentially a series of fixed iron ropes, ladders and other climbing aids to help non-climbers reach places that would otherwise be inaccessible. The one at Honister, for which a guide is compulsory, takes climbers through the quarry up to Fleetwith Pike on what they claim is the old miners' route to work. The cost is from £35, including equipment hire. Book via the website. The **shop** is full of slate-based souvenirs, from great slabs that have been fashioned into coffee tables, to smaller chippings sold by the bagful. Some of the stuff is lovely but think twice before leaving with a full-size slate coffee table on your back; it's still a long way to Robin Hood's Bay. Something small such as a Coast to Coast coaster may be more appropriate.

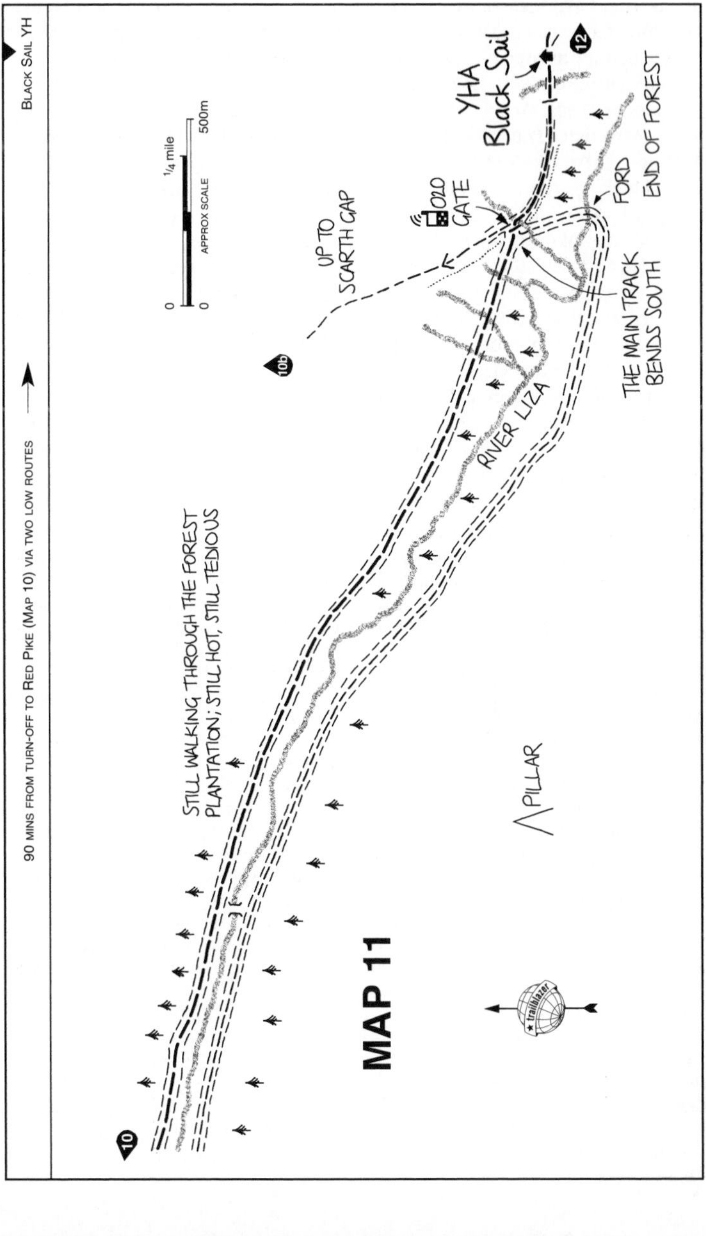

Black Sail YH

90 MINS FROM TURN-OFF TO RED PIKE (MAP 10) VIA TWO LOW ROUTES

MAP 11

STILL WALKING THROUGH THE FOREST
PLANTATION; STILL HOT, STILL TEDIOUS

RIVER LIZA

Pillar

10

10b

UP TO SCARTH GAP

COLD GATE

YHA
Black Sail

12

FORD
END OF FOREST

THE MAIN TRACK
BENDS SOUTH

APPROX SCALE

¼ mile

500m

trailblazer

ROUTE GUIDE AND MAPS

down from Brandreth and Great Gable and drops gently to the **Drum House**, now little more than a massive pile of stones and slate. The path's arrow-straight course betrays its previous incarnation as a quarry tramway; the Drum House's original purpose was to house the cable that operated the tramway that ran to the cutting sheds. At the bottom of the steep and rather precarious tramway track is **Honister Hause**, and the hullabaloo surrounding **Honister Slate Mine Visitor Centre** (see p112) at the crest of the notoriously steep Honister Pass road which many a caravanner has regretted tackling. *YHA Honister Hause* (Map 13; ☎ 01768 777267; for bookings call Borrowdale – see p118, 🖥 www.yha.org.uk/hostel/honister-hause; 26 beds: 3x2 beds, 5x4 beds; beds £7-25, rooms £47-69; fully open Mar-Oct) is next door, serves meals (currently £8.50 for three courses) and is licensed. Credit cards are accepted. One of our readers rated it as the best hostel on the whole trail and they're certainly friendly and the food is good. Stagecoach's No 77 **bus** runs from here to Seatoller (8 minutes) and to Keswick (40 minutes) and the 77A goes via Buttermere to Keswick (60 mins); see pp52-5 for details.

From Honister the Coast to Coast path parallels the B5289 to Little Gatesgarthdale. Down in the valley the path loops back on itself to join the road at **Seatoller**, although for a nifty short cut avoiding this village and saving you half a mile, see Map 14.

SEATOLLER   MAP 14, p117

The National Trust village of Seatoller has a couple of B&Bs, an outdoor activity centre, a public phone, post box and bus stop.

Stagecoach's 78 **bus** service calls here daily. The 77/77A also calls here between Easter & Oct; see pp52-5 for details.

Where to stay and eat

You're now well and truly among the vallybound Lakeland honeypots with prices which can suddenly make hostelling seem not such a bad idea after all. In the village centre *Seatoller House* (☎ 01768 777218, 🖥 www.seatollerhouse.co.uk; 1D/3T or D/4Tr/2Qd; all en suite with private facilities; ▼; 🐾; WI-FI; Ⓛ £5-6; Mar-Nov) is a 300-year-old building that's been a guesthouse for over a century. The rate is £50-55pp (sgl occ £60-65) for B&B; add £22.50 a four-course dinner (fixed menu) served at 7pm every day except Tuesday.

Right opposite, *Seatoller Farm* (☎ 01768 777232, 🖥 www.seatollerfarm.co.uk; 2D/1T; all en suite; ▼; Ⓛ from £3;

Mar-Nov) is a working National Trust hill farm that charges £40pp (sgl occ £60-65). They also allow **camping** (£7pp including use of a shower; late Mar-Oct). Breakfast may be available for campers by prior arrangement for £6.

Just outside the village, *Glaramara House* (01768 777222, www.glaramara house.co.uk; 22S/20T or D; WI-FI; 🐾 £5; Ⓛ £6) is a hotel and outdoor activity centre. Despite the slightly institutional atmosphere it's a great place to stay with good food and it's well set up for walkers and there are lots of single rooms. Facilities include a spacious residents' lounge with log fires, bar, and drying room. Prices start at £45 per person for B&B with an additional £8 en-suite premium charge. Ten of the twin rooms are en suite. Home made **food** is good value at £23 for a three-course meal, using local and seasonal ingredients. Non-residents can use the hotel during the day for teas and coffees.

From Seatoller the trail wends its way through **Johnny Wood** (see p68), joining the short cut mentioned above and passing the YHA hostel into Borrowdale (Map 14, p117).

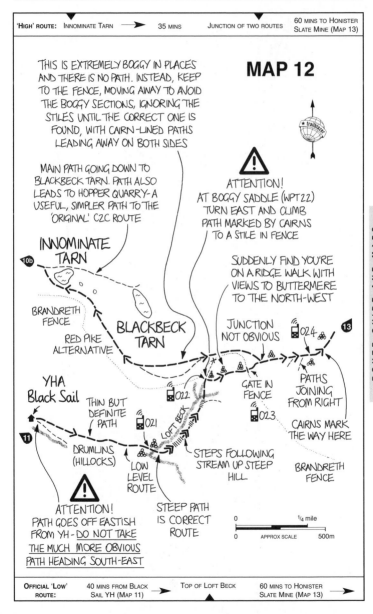

MAP 12

THIS IS EXTREMELY BOGGY IN PLACES AND THERE IS NO PATH. INSTEAD, KEEP TO THE FENCE, MOVING AWAY TO AVOID THE BOGGY SECTIONS, IGNORING THE STILES UNTIL THE CORRECT ONE IS FOUND, WITH CAIRN-LINED PATHS LEADING AWAY ON BOTH SIDES

MAIN PATH GOING DOWN TO BLACKBECK TARN. PATH ALSO LEADS TO HOPPER QUARRY - A USEFUL, SIMPLER PATH TO THE 'ORIGINAL' C2C ROUTE

⚠ ATTENTION!
AT BOGGY SADDLE (WPT 22) TURN EAST AND CLIMB PATH MARKED BY CAIRNS TO A STILE IN FENCE

SUDDENLY FIND YOU'RE ON A RIDGE WALK WITH VIEWS TO BUTTERMERE TO THE NORTH-WEST

INNOMINATE TARN

10b

BRANDRETH FENCE

RED PIKE ALTERNATIVE

BLACKBECK TARN

JUNCTION NOT OBVIOUS

024
13

YHA Black Sail

THIN BUT DEFINITE PATH

022

GATE IN FENCE

PATHS JOINING FROM RIGHT

CAIRNS MARK THE WAY HERE

11

021

LOFT BECK

023

DRUMLINS (HILLOCKS)

LOW LEVEL ROUTE

STEPS FOLLOWING STREAM UP STEEP HILL

BRANDRETH FENCE

⚠ ATTENTION!
PATH GOES OFF EASTISH FROM YH - <u>DO NOT TAKE THE MUCH MORE OBVIOUS PATH HEADING SOUTH-EAST</u>

STEEP PATH IS CORRECT ROUTE

0 · · · · 1/4 mile
0 · · · · 500m
APPROX SCALE

ROUTE GUIDE AND MAPS

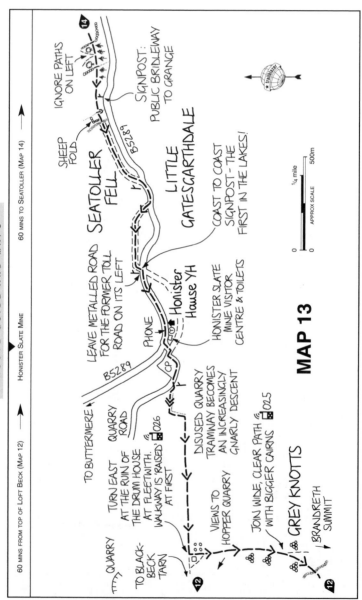

MAP 13

IGNORE PATHS ON LEFT

SIGNPOST: PUBLIC BRIDLEWAY TO GRANGE

SHEEP FOLD

SEATOLLER FELL

B5289

LITTLE GATESGARTHDALE

COAST TO COAST SIGNPOST – THE FIRST IN THE LAKES!

LEAVE METALLED ROAD FOR THE FORMER TOLL ROAD ON ITS LEFT

Honister House YH

PHONE

HONISTER SLATE MINE VISITOR CENTRE & TOILETS

TO BUTTERMERE

QUARRY ROAD

B5289

CP

QUARRY

TURN EAST AT THE RUIN OF THE DRUM HOUSE AT FLEETWITH. WALKWAY IS RAISED AT FIRST

026

DISUSED QUARRY TRAMWAY BECOMES AN INCREASINGLY GNARLY DESCENT

TO BLACK-BECK TARN

VIEWS TO HOPPER QUARRY

JOIN WIDE, CLEAR PATH WITH BIGGER CAIRNS

025

GREY KNOTTS

BRANDRETH SUMMIT

12

12

14

APPROX SCALE

0   ¼ mile

0   500m

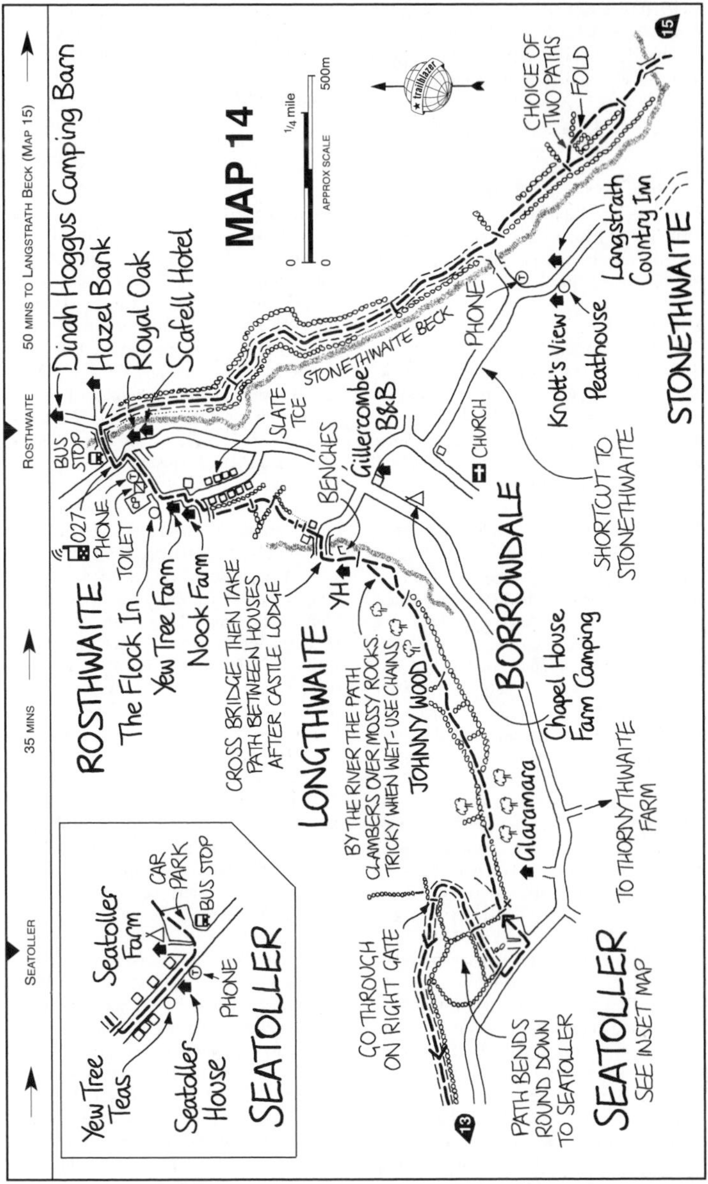
MAP 14
SEATOLLER
35 MINS
ROSTHWAITE
50 MINS TO LANGSTRATH BECK (MAP 15)
APPROX SCALE
0
1/4 mile
0
500m
trailblazer
Yew Tree Teas
Seatoller House
Seatoller Farm
CAR PARK
BUS STOP
PHONE
SEATOLLER
ROSTHWAITE
The Flock In
Yew Tree Farm
Nook Farm
027
PHONE
TOILET
BUS STOP
Dinah Hoggus Camping Barn
Hazel Bank
Royal Oak
Scafell Hotel
SLATE TCE
STONETHWAITE BECK
CROSS BRIDGE THEN TAKE PATH BETWEEN HOUSES AFTER CASTLE LODGE
LONGTHWAITE
YH
BENCHES
Gillercombe B&B
CHURCH
PHONE
BY THE RIVER THE PATH CLAMBERS OVER MOSSY ROCKS. TRICKY WHEN WET - USE CHAINS
JOHNNY WOOD
BORROWDALE
Chapel House Farm Camping
SHORTCUT TO STONETHWAITE
Knott's View
Peathouse
Longstrath Country Inn
STONETHWAITE
CHOICE OF TWO PATHS
FOLD
15
Glaramara
TO THORNYTHWAITE FARM
GO THROUGH ON RIGHT GATE
PATH BENDS ROUND DOWN TO SEATOLLER
SEATOLLER
SEE INSET MAP
13

BORROWDALE   MAP 14, p117

Borrowdale is made up of three separate settlements: Longthwaite, Rosthwaite and Stonethwaite. Small, picturesque and composed largely of slate-roofed, whitewashed stone farm cottages, these are the iconic Lake District hamlets that tourists from around the world flock to see.

Stagecoach's No 78 **bus**, known as the Borrowdale Rambler, runs between Seatoller and Keswick (from where buses run to other destinations in Cumbria) via Rosthwaite; see pp52-5.

Longthwaite

The first building you come to in Borrowdale is **YHA Borrowdale** (☎ 0845 371 9624, ⌨ www.yha.org.uk/hostel/bor rowdale; 86 beds in 2-, 3-, 4-, 6-bedded rooms; WI-FI), a spacious and well-run lodge with a laundry and drying room. As with all YHA hostels the prices vary from season to season but typically in summer a bed in a dorm is around £18-21, while you can also book the whole room, with twin-bed rooms around £39 in summer, four-berth rooms around £49 and six-berth rooms around £69; add £5.25 per person for breakfast. Credit cards are accepted and you can also **camp** here in the summer holidays and May bank holidays for £12. There are also three **camping pods** for around £49 in summer. The hostel also boasts an alcohol licence and spirited catering well worth crossing the fells for – indeed its dinners, at £7.50 for mains, and £11.95 for three courses are the best value in the valley. You don't have to be sleeping here to eat here – but do call in before you let them know you're coming!

Longthwaite also plays host to **Gillercombe B&B** (☎ 01768 777602; 1S/1D/2T; shared facilities; ✆; ⓛ £6; Mar-Oct). The friendly owner, Rachel Dunckley, is a mine of useful local information and local gossip, and her B&B offers a comfortable and convenient place to stay right in the heart of Borrowdale. B&B rates are £38pp. However, it is essential to book well in advance to stay here.

A hop and a skip down the road is **Chapel House Farm Campsite** (☎ 01768 777256, ⌨ www.chapelhousefarmcamp site.co.uk; 🐾; Mar-Oct) where you can

pitch in a roadside field for £6pp. Facilities are basic – a clean and simple toilet and shower block (50p for 4-minute shower).

Rosthwaite

The biggest settlement of the three is Rosthwaite to the north. Stagecoach's No 78 bus calls here. On the way into town there are two National Trust farms offering B&B. The first is **Nook Farm** (☎ 01768 777677, ⌨ www.nookfarmborrowdale.co .uk; 1D with en suite shower/1T with private bathroom; WI-FI; ⓛ £5-6; Feb-Nov), a 16th-century farmhouse with lovely open fires – the perfect treat after a rainy day's walk. B&B costs £35pp (sgl occ £50-70).

Round the corner and under new ownership – though still providing a first rate service for walkers – **Yew Tree Farm** (☎ 01768 777237, ⌨ www.borrowdaleherd wick.co.uk; 1D/1T; en suite; WI-FI; ⓛ £5-7; Feb-mid Nov) charges from £42.50pp (sgl occ £65). As well as selling their own produce, they also run a tearoom **The Flock In** (Feb-mid Nov daily 10am-5pm, variable in winter), opposite, where the tea is served in pints or half pints. Most of their dishes are home made, many using produce from the farm though presumably not the chewy Ewe's Poo Cookies (£1.50)! Particularly recommended is the Herdwick Stew served with a brown bun and you can try Borrowdale teabread and cheese here, too.

The Royal Oak Hotel (☎ 01768 777214, ⌨ www.royaloakhotel.co.uk; 2S/ 2T/3D/4Tr/1Qd; all with private facilities; ✆; 🐾 free; WI-FI), is a fine family-run place which once hosted the poet William Wordsworth. They normally accept bookings only on a dinner, bed and breakfast basis; rates are £64-68pp; single/single occupancy is £64/£79 by prior arrangement. Add £4 for Friday and Saturday night bookings and Sundays before Bank Holidays. The majority of rooms are in the main hotel but some are in a converted barn across the farmyard. The owner is a keen walker and walkers get a warm welcome.

Next door is **Scafell Hotel** (☎ 01768 777208, ⌨ www.scafell.co.uk; 3S/10D/7T/ 3Tr; all en suite; 🐾 £6; ⓛ £6-10; WI-FI on ground floor only), a large place which has served as a coaching inn since 1850, with some rooms furnished with antiques. B&B costs £60-90pp and dinner B&B is £75-110pp. The menu is extensive and the **food** good. The restaurant is open daily 6.30-9pm but booking is essential. Their *Riverside Bar* (generally open daily noon-9pm) has cheaper bar meals (£8-15.95) including burgers, steak and local trout.

On the Coast to Coast path leading over the river out of the village, *Hazel Bank Country House* (☎ 01768 777248, 🖥 www.hazelbankhotel.co.uk; 7D or T; all with private facilities; 🛏; WI-FI; ⓛ £5.75), is a very comfortable hotel set in extensive grounds. B&B is £70-78pp; single occupancy is £95-103. Dinner is an extra £22-26 or £29 if you're not staying here. In peak season there may be a two-night minimum if staying over a Saturday night.

Nearby is *Dinah Hoggus Camping Barn* (☎ 01768 777689, 🖥 www.lakeland campingbarns.co.uk; shower available) is a very simple but attractively rustic place sleeping 12 people. They charge £10pp (bring your own sleeping bag; mattresses provided); booking is essential.

Stonethwaite
Just under a mile (about 1.6km) to the south and away from the relative clamour of Rosthwaite, Stonethwaite nestles in its own little world at the end of a road running parallel to the beck that shares its name.

Although frequently rained upon, it's among the prettiest of the Lakeland hamlets with an attractive little church.

As for lodgings, *Knotts View* (☎ 01768 777604; 2D/1T/1D or T; shared facilities; ⓛ £6) charges from £37pp (sgl occ £40) for B&B. The building is 450 years old and, with its low ceilings, it feels like it. Under the same ownership is the *Peathouse Tea & Coffee Shop* (Easter-Nov; flexible opening hours) next door. Incidentally, if you're not familiar with the nature of peat, by the time you get to Greenup Edge tomorrow you'll be an expert.

Best of all has long been *The Langstrath Country Inn* (☎ 01768 777239, 🖥 www.thelangstrath.com; 3D/5D or T; all en suite; 🛏; Mar-Nov Tue-Sun, WI-FI), though this place really divides trekkers these days, with opinions split between those who think it's the best restaurant on the whole trail – and those who think it's actually a little overpriced. Their menu (Mar-Nov Tue-Sun noon-2.30pm 2.30-4pm soups and sandwiches only; & 6-9pm; bar Tue-Sun noon-10.30pm) includes such locally sourced dishes as slow-roasted Rosthwaite Herdwick lamb. Mains cost £13.25-17.95. The rooms are undoubtedly worthy of praise: B&B costs £50-64pp (sgl occ £70-84) but in general they don't accept advance bookings for single-night stays on a Friday or Saturday.

STAGE 3: BORROWDALE TO GRASMERE   MAPS 14-18

Introduction
In good weather this **9-mile (14.5km, 4-5½hr high route)** stage is a Lakeland classic, a straightforward climb up past Lining Crag to Greenup Edge, followed by the high-level ridge walk we recommend (see p123) or a less adventurous

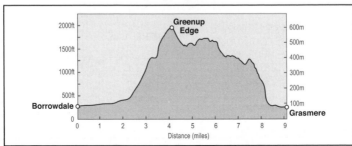

and slightly shorter plod down the valley to the edge of Grasmere. Wainwright combines this stage with the next one to Patterdale, adding up to at least a 17-mile (27.5km) hike, and a few walkers do just that. Sticking to the valley routes as Wainwright did, it's not too demanding. If doing so, we recommend you take at least one of the high-level options on either stage; this is the Lake District after all. Taking on the high routes in one long day – not least via Helvellyn and Striding Edge which will add **two miles and up to two hours** – may leave you a little drained for the 15½-miler from Patterdale to Shap which follows and along which there are no easy gradients.

The route

The stage begins with a level amble through the fields alongside **Stonethwaite Beck** (Maps 14 and 15), with **Eagle Crag** a looming presence across the water. It looks massive but by the time you get to Greenup Edge you'll be looking *down* on Eagle Crag. At Stonethwaite you join **Greenup Gill** (Map 15), one long torrent of white water and waterfalls when we came through, with views back down to Borrowdale growing more impressive with every upward step. The path's gradient picks up a notch past Eagle Crag, drops into a basin of

50 MINS FROM ROSTHWAITE (MAP 14) → LANGSTRATH BECK → 70 MINS TO LINING CRAG (MAP 16)

14

CROSS STREAM ON STONES

BRIDGE TO RIGHT OF PATH TO FOOT OF EAGLE CRAG WHICH LOOMS ABOVE

SHEEP FOLDS

START OF STEPS AGAIN. FORD STREAM ON STONES

MAP 15

LANGSTRATH BECK

FOLD

WATERFALL

CAIRN

GO THROUGH GAP IN WALL

BOULDER-MEMORIAL TO GORDON HALLWORTH

AFTER RAIN STONETHWAITE BECK IS ONE CONTINUOUS TORRENT OF WHITE WATER WITH OCCASIONAL WATERFALLS

TWIN WATERFALLS

EAGLE CRAG c525M

WATER-FALL

0 ¼ mile
0 APPROX SCALE 500m

GREENUP GILL 16

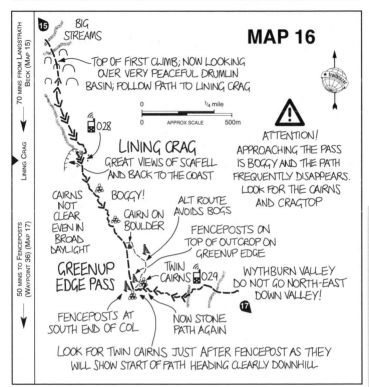

MAP 16

15 · BIG STREAMS

TOP OF FIRST CLIMB; NOW LOOKING OVER VERY PEACEFUL DRUMLIN BASIN; FOLLOW PATH TO LINING CRAG

028

0 — 1/4 mile

0 — APPROX SCALE — 500m

ATTENTION!
APPROACHING THE PASS IS BOGGY AND THE PATH FREQUENTLY DISAPPEARS. LOOK FOR THE CAIRNS AND CRAGTOP

LINING CRAG
GREAT VIEWS OF SCAFELL AND BACK TO THE COAST

BOGGY!

CAIRNS NOT CLEAR EVEN IN BROAD DAYLIGHT

CAIRN ON BOULDER

ALT ROUTE AVOIDS BOGS

FENCEPOSTS ON TOP OF OUTCROP ON GREENUP EDGE

GREENUP EDGE PASS

TWIN CAIRNS · 029

WYTHBURN VALLEY DO NOT GO NORTH-EAST DOWN VALLEY!

17

FENCEPOSTS AT SOUTH END OF COL

NOW STONE PATH AGAIN

LOOK FOR TWIN CAIRNS JUST AFTER FENCEPOST AS THEY WILL SHOW START OF PATH HEADING CLEARLY DOWNHILL

70 MINS FROM LANGSTRATH BECK (MAP 15)

LINING CRAG

50 MINS TO FENCEPOSTS (WAYPOINT 36) (MAP 17)

ROUTE GUIDE AND MAPS

drumlins (mounds created by glacial action) and a stepped climb up onto the top of **Lining Crag** (Map 16) from where, weather permitting, views reach over towards Scafell Pike, England's highest summit at 3210ft (978m).

Look to the south and you'll also make out the beginning of the path to the broad col of **Greenup Edge**. This next section is where some lose their way, the boggy ground and indistinct cairns obscuring the correct direction even in ideal conditions. As you near the col look out for the old fence posts which once stretched up and over to Low White Stones, the hill south of the col; see box p92. If you see one on an outcrop, aim to the south of it to a less conspicuous fence post at ground level and, a few metres further on, the key twin **cairns** (WPT 029) from where the descent from the Edge commences across the head of **Wythburn Valley**. You cross the upper basin of **Wythburn** on clearer tracks to the 'gateposts' on Map 17 (WPT 030) marking its neighbour, **Far Easedale**. From here you choose the valley route or the more demanding high route which most hikers take these days, along with casually clad day trippers out of Grasmere who commonly combine both into a loop.

ROUTE GUIDE AND MAPS

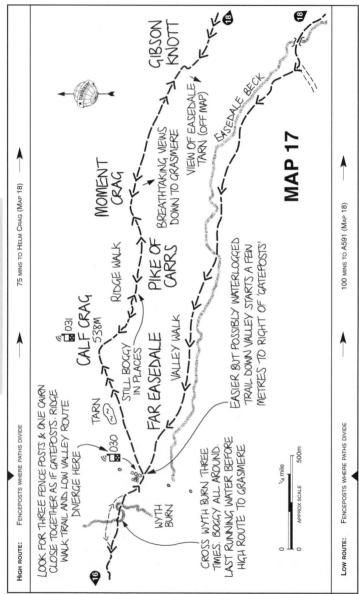

HIGH ROUTE: FENCEPOSTS WHERE PATHS DIVIDE   →   75 MINS TO HELM CRAG (MAP 18)   →

LOOK FOR THREE FENCE POSTS & ONE CAIRN CLOSE TOGETHER AS IF GATEPOSTS. RIDGE WALK TRAIL AND LOW VALLEY ROUTE DIVERGE HERE

GIBSON KNOTT

18

18

MOMENT CRAG

BREATHTAKING VIEWS DOWN TO GRASMERE

VIEW OF EASEDALE TARN (OFF MAP)

EASEDALE BECK

MAP 17

RIDGE WALK

PIKE OF CARRS

CALF CRAG
538M

031

TARN

STILL BOGGY IN PLACES

FAR EASEDALE

VALLEY WALK

030

EASIER BUT POSSIBLY WATERLOGGED TRAIL DOWN VALLEY STARTS A FEW METRES TO RIGHT OF 'GATEPOSTS'

WYTH BURN

CROSS WYTH BURN THREE TIMES. BOGGY ALL AROUND. LAST RUNNING WATER BEFORE HIGH ROUTE TO GRASMERE

16

APPROX SCALE

0   ¼ mile
0   500m

LOW ROUTE: FENCEPOSTS WHERE PATHS DIVIDE   →   100 MINS TO A591 (MAP 18)   →

The ridge-walk alternative to Grasmere via Helm Crag
Map 17 & Map 18

The high-level route takes in **Calf Crag**, **Gibson Knott** and **Helm Crag** amongst others. The ground is often saturated but the climbs up to the various summits take only a few minutes and give some great viewpoints down to Easedale Gill and Easedale Tarn glistening below. It's a long hard walk with rocky steps and bogs; allow at least 90 minutes from the 'gateposts' to Lancrigg Woods. That is the price of surveying Castle, Lang and Silver Hows (hills) behind you to the south-west, and Helvellyn and Great Rigg beyond. By the time you've reached Helm Crag overlooking the following stage, the steep descent to the north-western outskirts of Grasmere may well finish you off!

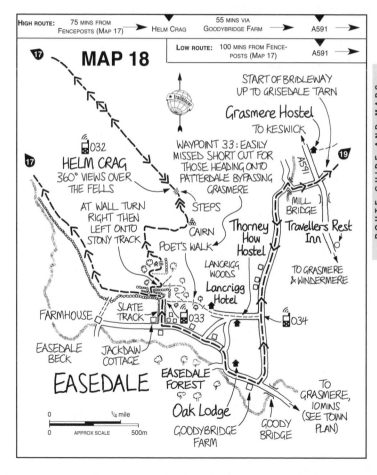

HIGH ROUTE: 75 MINS FROM FENCEPOSTS (MAP 17) → HELM CRAG — 55 MINS VIA GOODYBRIDGE FARM → A591 →

LOW ROUTE: 100 MINS FROM FENCE-POSTS (MAP 17) → A591 →

MAP 18

17

★ trailblazer

☐032
HELM CRAG
360° VIEWS OVER
THE FELLS

17

AT WALL TURN
RIGHT THEN
LEFT ONTO
STONY TRACK

STEPS

CAIRN

POET'S WALK

START OF BRIDLEWAY
UP TO GRISEDALE TARN

Grasmere Hostel
TO KESWICK

WAYPOINT 33: EASILY
MISSED SHORT CUT FOR
THOSE HEADING ONTO
PATTERDALE BYPASSING
GRASMERE

19

MILL
BRIDGE

Thorney
How
Hostel

Travellers Rest
Inn

TO GRASMERE
& WINDERMERE

LANCRIGG
WOODS

Lancrigg
Hotel

FARMHOUSE

SLATE
TRACK

☐033

☐034

EASEDALE
BECK

JACKDAW
COTTAGE

EASEDALE

EASEDALE
FOREST

Oak Lodge

GOODYBRIDGE
FARM

GOODY
BRIDGE

TO
GRASMERE,
10 MINS
(SEE TOWN
PLAN)

0 — 1/4 mile
0   APPROX SCALE   500m

ROUTE GUIDE AND MAPS

Whichever route you take, when you reach the bottom and Easedale it's worth a diversion through **Lancrigg Woods** along the **Poet's Walk** (Map 18), a tranquil delight that may soothe sore feet. It comes as no surprise to find that the Lakeland poets enjoyed it; indeed, they planted many of the trees that grow in the woods. Along the way is an inscription, in Latin, describing how Wordsworth's sister Dorothy would sit at this spot while her brother walked up and down composing verses. The path crosses the croquet lawn of Lancrigg Hotel (see below) and a minute later, Thorney How Hostel. Here at the road the trail continues north-east for the climb over to Patterdale. To the south a 20-minute walk leads to Grasmere, the Lake District's busiest tourist village.

EASEDALE   MAP 18, p123
Picturesque Easedale has a few places to stay and eat right on the path if you aren't diverting into Grasmere.

Where to stay and eat
Right on the route, *Thorney How Independent Hostel* (Map 18; ☎ 015394 35597, 🖳 www.thorneyhow.co.uk; 50 beds in 2- to 6-bed dorms sharing shower facilities; also 1D/1Qd/1F all en suite; dorm bed from £18.50, private double from £30pp inc breakfast; WI-FI) offers **hostel-style accommodation** as well as a **bunkhouse**. There's a *café* and *bar* (open daily around 3.30-11pm) and they offer dinner, B&B deals. If you make it clear you are walking the Coast to Coast they will allow single-night stays at weekends and in peak periods. The bunkhouse sleeps 16 and prices start from £18.

On the A591 north of Grasmere near where the path crosses it, there's the plush *Grasmere Independent Hostel* (☎ 015394 35055, 🖳 grasmereindependenthostel.co .uk; 24 beds – 1Tr, 1Qd, 1x5 beds, 2x6 beds; internet access & WI-FI) complete with kitchen, laundry, lounge and even a Nordic sauna (£4). Each room has its own shower and contains no more than six beds; £22-23pp. However, since the hostel focuses on groups, individuals cannot book more than six weeks in advance and a minimum 2-night stay is required at the weekend.

Oak Lodge (☎ 015394 35527, 🖳 www.oaklodge.homecall.co.uk; 2D/1D or T; all en suite; ➡; Ⓛ from £3) is on Easedale Rd. It's a very smart little establishment in a wonderful location next to tranquil Easedale Forest. B&B is from £36pp (sgl occ £45-70).

If you stick to the path via Poet's Walk you'll walk right past *Lancrigg Vegetarian Country House Hotel* (☎ 015394 35317, 🖳 www.lancrigg.co.uk; 8D/2D or T/1 suite; all en suite; ➡; 🐾£15; WI-FI; Ⓛ £7.50), a large country house with parts dating back to the 17th century. The ambience is rather more conventional 'genteel' than 'vegetarian' in any alternative sense, but in Grasmere £115-135pp (sgl occ plus 20%) for DB&B (£75-120pp, sgl occ £90-110 for B&B) is actually not so bad. Like so many fancy Grasmere hotels it's not really a walkers' place but we have no reservations about the food, with the vegetarian restaurant (daily 1-3pm & 6.30-8pm, to 7.30pm in winter) open to non residents.

On the A591 not far from the Grasmere Hostel, is a pub, the *Traveller's Rest Inn* (☎ 015394 35604, 🖳 www.lake districtinns.co.uk/travellers_welcome.cfm; 7D/2T; all en suite; 🐾£15). B&B ranges from £25pp to £60pp. Food is served Feb-Oct daily all day in the main season, other times noon-2pm & 5-9.30pm) and includes hearty portions of mainly local dishes.

❑ **Important note – walking times**
Unless otherwise specified, **all times in this book refer only to time spent walking**. You will need to add 20-30% to allow for rests, photography, checking the map, drinking water etc. When planning the day's hike count on 5-7 hours' actual walking.

GRASMERE   see map p127

Wordsworth called this valley 'the fairest place on earth' and his association with Grasmere has done so much to popularise the place that on some days you might wish you'd not paused here in your wandering o'er the hills and vales. Fleece-clad hordes stream in all summer to mill about or grab a lunch, but looking out to the glorious hills surrounding the village, you can see why. And with facilities and services that include discount hiking outlets, a cash machine, internet access and more than one shop, it can all add up to a worthwhile stopover.

Though Wordsworth lived in Grasmere for only nine years, the period was a productive one and he wrote many of his best-known works here. (All together now: '*I wandered lonely as a cloud...*') His cottage is the main sight in the village and his grave is in the grounds of St Oswald's Church (see p129), one of the more peaceful spots in Grasmere's often overcrowded centre.

More spacious than the preceding valley settlements, to the west the large farmhouses and grand homes share the undulating land with forests of mature deciduous trees and flocks of dozy sheep and through the busy jumble of buildings in the centre flows the River Rothay, a tranquil haven for ducks and other waterfowl; to the south lies brooding Grasmere Lake, flanked by steep, forested hills.

Services

There's a free **cash machine** at the **Co-op** (Mon-Sun 7am-10pm), which also provides a cashback service and is the best place to stock up on provisions. Note that it does not accept foreign cards.

Although there's a chance it may have been forced to close by the time you read this, the **post office** (Mon-Wed & Fri 9am-5pm, Thur & Sat 9am-12.30pm) also has a **cash machine** but with a £1.85 withdrawal charge. However, unless yours is one of the few banks that does not have an agreement with the post office (see p27) you can withdraw cash from the counter at no charge.

Grasmere has an excellent bookshop, **Sam Read Bookseller** (☎ 015394 35374, 🖳 www.samreadbooks.co.uk; open daily 9am-6pm or 5pm in winter; closed some weeks in Jan) that has been trading since 1887. There's a surprisingly wide range of books in this tardis of a shop and when you've found something to read you can pick up a coffee from the shop next door.

Close to the Co-op is a **pharmacy** (Mon-Fri 9am-5.30pm, Sat 9am-1pm) if your Compeed supply is running perilously low. There are numerous **outdoors shops** dotted around the town centre.

Where to stay

This is our selection of places to stay in Grasmere; you'll find plenty more on somewhere like 🖳 www.grasmere.com. Being Grasmere, with all the tourist business it can handle, B&Bs will be very reluctant to accept a one-night-only booking on summer weekends. Either stay for two nights or try to avoid the high-season weekends. Single occupancy may well mean paying the full room rate.

Hostels The surviving *YHA Grasmere Butharlyp Howe* (☎ 0845 371 9319, 🖳 www.yha.org.uk/hostel/grasmere-butharlyp-howe; 80 beds, 2-/4-/6-/8-bed rooms; beds start at £10; WI-FI in lounges; open all year) is in the most central location and has internet access, an alcohol licence, a smart self-catering kitchen and attractive grounds. The meals are good here too. Credit cards are accepted; 24hr access is possible once you've checked in and there is a drying room, laundry facilities and a very small shop. However, because it's also the largest of the hostels in the area it tends to attract school groups, making the independent hostels far more preferable on these days. You can also camp here for £9.

B&Bs *Silver Lea* (☎ 015394 35657, 🖳 www.silverlea.com; 2T/2D; all en suite; ☞; WI-FI; (Ⓛ); Apr-Jun & Sep), on Easedale Rd, is a charming ivy-clad slate cottage, surprisingly bright inside. B&B for a one-night stay is from £52.50pp (sgl occ £85); this must be paid at the time of booking.

Nearby, *Glenthorne* (☎ 015394 35389, 🖳 www.glenthorne.org; 7S/14T/5D; most en suite, other rooms share facilities; ☞;

WI-FI; Ⓛ £5; Feb-Nov) is a Victorian, Quaker country house (though folk of any creed can stay) next to another of Wordsworth's old houses, Allan Bank. Though the place feels like a hostel when you first walk in – perhaps owing to the wonderfully informal atmosphere – the rooms are fine. Overriding everything, however, is the hospitality here, with trays of cakes and tea laid out for guests at 4.30pm. One of the rooms (twin en suite) is available for people with dogs. Evening meals (7pm) must be booked in advance; all they ask is a few seconds silence before eating. There is a voluntary 15-minute prayer meeting in the mornings. B&B/DB&B is £47.99-53.99/£67-74.74pp for a one-night stay and yes, they do offer porridge for breakfast – presumably Quaker Oats – though it may be necessary to request it in summer.

Heidi's Grasmere Lodge (☎ 015394 35248, 🖳 www.heidisgrasmerelodge.co.uk; 6D; all en suite; WI-FI, 🐾), above Heidi's of Grasmere (see Where to eat) is right in the middle of town. It's very clean and as quaint as a doll's house. B&B here is from £39.50-65pp (sgl occ £71) but at weekends in high season they often insist on a two-night minimum stay if booking in advance.

Beck Allans (☎ 015394 35563, 🖳 www.beckallans.com; 4D/1D or T; all en suite; 🐾; WI-FI) is a guesthouse overlooking the Rothay. B&B rates are £45.50pp (sgl occ from £65). They can dry wet clothes or boots and will make packed lunches but you may prefer to assemble your own from the shops in the village. Note that they have a minimum 2- to 3-night stay policy at weekends.

Lake View Country House (☎ 015394 35384, 🖳 www.lakeview-grasmere.com; 2D/1D or Tr/1T or Tr; all en suite; 🐾; 🐕 £6.50; WI-FI; Ⓛ) is, as its name suggests, one of the few places to stay from where you can actually see the lake (from the first floor). It's a lovely place near the centre of Grasmere but quietly tucked away at the end of a lane. B&B costs £52.50-62pp in high season (sgl occ £96-119 with discount for cost of breakfast, three in Tr £36pp). If

booking in advance stays of two nights are likely to be required except in winter. There's direct access to the lakeshore which could be useful for people with dogs; though if your dog is a terrier you might need to keep it on a short leash as there's a badger sett in the garden!

If you can't get a bed in town, try the B&Bs on Keswick Rd, the best of which is *Chestnut Villa* (☎ 015394 35218, 🖳 www.chestnutvilla.com; 1T/6D; all en suite; 🐾; WI-FI; Ⓛ £7) charging £42.50-47.50pp for B&B (sgl occ £65).

South of Grasmere, 150m beyond Dove Cottage is *How Foot Lodge* (☎ 015394 35366, 🖳 howfootlodge.co.uk; 4D/2T all en suite; 🐾, 🐕 by arrangement; WI-FI) though there is a limit on one-night stays in the summer; B&B starts from £38.50pp (sgl occ £72).

Hotels *Moss Grove Organic* (☎ 015394 35251, 🖳 www.mossgrove.com; 10D/1D or T; all en suite; 🐾; 🐕 £20; WI-FI) is a smashing place whose strict green ethos extends beyond the kitchen to their accommodation, with some of the beds made from reclaimed timber sitting atop oak floors from sustainable forests. All this, and yet the building still retains its original Victorian charm. The prices, however, do reflect the quality, with B&B costing from £49.50pp (Sun-Thur in the winter and in the cheaper executive rooms) up to £127.50pp on a Friday or Saturday (sgl occ £84-112.50). One reader wrote saying it was worth it for the luxurious bed alone (they stayed in Room 5). Breakfast is organic; there is no restaurant or bar though it is possible to buy bottles of organic wine and beer. If booking in advance stays of two nights are likely to be required if it includes a Saturday night.

Red Lion Hotel (☎ 015394 35456, 🖳 www.grasmereredlionhotel.co.uk; 5S/44D or T; all en suite; 🐾; 🐕 £10; WI-FI) *is* the centre of town; it's been recommended by some readers and it's pleasant enough though lacks a little of the charm of some of the other places around here. B&B costs around £65-87.50pp (sgl £30-52.50) but special packages are sometimes available.

Dale Lodge Hotel (☎ 015394 35300, 🖥 www.dalelodgehotel.co.uk; 1T/15D; all en suite; ✆; 🐾 £25 per stay; WI-FI) is a huge, rambling place. An old-fashioned-looking pile on the outside, inside it is all polished floorboards and original tilework and really rather chic, with each bedroom individually decorated. The three acres of sprawling gardens are another attraction, as is its location in the heart of town. The attached bar, Tweedies (see Where to eat), is also recommended. B&B costs from £50pp (sgl occ £100).

The Wordsworth Hotel (☎ 015394 35592, 🖥 www.thewordsworthhotel.co.uk; 35D or T/4 suites; all en suite; ✆; 🐾 £20;

WI-FI) was formerly the smartest address in the centre of town, a large attractive hotel with facilities including pool, sauna, Jacuzzi and cocktail bar. B&B costs £69-139, from £70 for a single. Advance bookings for a one-night stay on a Saturday may not be accepted.

Bridge House Hotel (☎ 015394 35425, 🖥 www.bridgehousegrasmere.co.uk; 9D/9D or T; all en suite; ✆; 🐾 £10 per stay; WI-FI in most areas) is another large place near the river, with two acres of gorgeous grounds. Rates for dinner B&B are £57.50-66pp (sgl occ around £100). They accept one-night bookings only if it's quiet which, in summer, is unlikely.

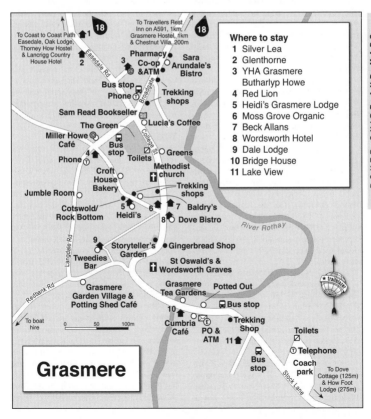

Where to stay
1 Silver Lea
2 Glenthorne
3 YHA Grasmere Butharlyp Howe
4 Red Lion
5 Heidi's Grasmere Lodge
6 Moss Grove Organic
7 Beck Allans
8 Wordsworth Hotel
9 Dale Lodge
10 Bridge House
11 Lake View

ROUTE GUIDE AND MAPS

Where to eat and drink

As you'd expect for a major tourist centre like Grasmere, cafés and restaurants are plentiful throughout the village.

For excellent Fair Trade coffee there's *Lucia's Takeaway Coffee Shop* (Fri-Wed 9am-5pm), beside the bookshop. The banana bread (£1.50) they occasionally have on sale is delicious. *Heidi's* (daily 10am-6pm) does a good cream tea as well as light lunches and welcomes dogs with well-behaved owners. *Baldry's* (☐ www .baldryscottage.co.uk), across the road, is another genteel tearoom, open daily from 10am to '4.30-ish'.

A number of other cafés vie for position near the bridge, including *Grasmere Tea Gardens* (☎ 015394 35590; daily 9.30am-5pm), overlooking the river, and the contemporary *Potted Out* (☎ 015394 35572; ☐ www.pottedout.co.uk; daily 11am-8.30pm), an Italian bistro with pizzas from £8.50.

At the Grasmere Garden Village there's the *Potting Shed Café* (Mon-Sat 9.30am-5.30pm; Sun 11am-4.45pm). Related to Potted Out (above) it has a cheaper, more traditional menu, eg fish & chips (£9.25).

At *The Dove Bistro* (Mon-Sat noon-2pm & 6-9pm, Sun noon-9pm; afternoon tea served noon-5pm), part of Wordsworth Hotel (see Where to stay) you can try crispy lamb belly medallions with pearl barley risotto (£17.50). On the same street is *Greens* (☎ 01539 435790; ☐ greensgras mere.com; Fri-Wed 9.30am to 5pm), a contemporary eatery specialising in good traditional food. The shepherd's pie is particularly good.

Miller Howe Café (☎ 015394 35234, ☐ millerhowecafe.co.uk; spring & autumn daily 9am-6pm, to 7pm in summer, 5pm in winter) has a long menu with some imaginative dishes – eg homity pie (a cheddar cheese, potato, garlic and onion pie, served with jacket potato, butter and salad) costs £8.95.

On Broadgate, *Sara Arundale's Bistro* (☎ 015394 35266, ☐ www.restaurantin grasmere.co.uk; May-Nov Tue-Sun 10.30am-4pm & 6-9pm; days/hours vary at other times) has also been recommended.

There's a fancy menu at *Tweedies Bar* (daily noon-11pm or midnight; food served Mon-Sat noon-3pm & 6-9pm, Sun noon-3.30pm & 6.30-9pm) in Dale Lodge Hotel (see Where to stay). Try Cumbrian pig – confit pork belly, mini braised shoulder and hock pie, loin, black pudding, bubble and squeak and pork scratchings for £18.50. On most Fridays and Saturdays there is live music. The same menu is also available in *Lodge Restaurant* (Mon-Sat 6-9pm, Sun 6.30-9pm) though in a more formal setting.

Best of all is *The Jumble Room* (☎ 015394 35188, ☐ www.thejumbleroom .co.uk; Wed-Sun 5.30-9.30pm but check in advance particularly in Dec-Jan; booking advisable) on Langdale Rd. The decor looks less of a jumble with each passing year but this quirky little place still gets rave reviews. The menu changes frequently and includes dishes from all four corners of the globe with a few extra corners you never knew about. Their Thriller of Manila, a delicious melange of pan-seared seafood, chicken, vegetables, noodles and peanuts, is currently on the menu for £17.

What to see

Dove Cottage William Wordsworth lived for less than ten years in beautiful Dove Cottage (☎ 015394 35544, ☐ www.words worth.org.uk; Mar-Oct daily 9.30am-5pm, Nov-late Dec & Feb 9.30am-4pm; £7.75, children £4.50; student/YHA member discounts available), about 500m walk southeast from The Green, just off the A591, yet its importance in both his development as a poet and his life was enormous. Many of his best-loved and most powerful works were written here and this was his first home with his wife Mary Hutchinson and where three of his children were born.

Today all but the first room is furnished entirely with items owned by the poet, though some have come from other Wordsworth properties. Guides show visitors around the cottage, pointing out such items as Wordsworth's famous **suitcase** (where he's carefully sewn his name inside but didn't leave enough room for the final 'h' tucked up in the corner); a letter of introduction – a precursor to the modern-day passport – penned by the French authorities, and which has been stamped on the back by the border guards of a host of European countries; and the **Royal Warrant** of 1843 in which he was bestowed with the honour of being Queen Victoria's poet laureate. It was an honour he accepted grudgingly, having already turned down the position twice, and one that he never truly fulfilled; indeed, from his acceptance of the post to his death in 1850, Wordsworth wrote precisely no official poems as poet laureate, the first (and so far only) poet laureate to do so.

The cottage is, by the standards of the Lake District, relatively large, containing eight rooms rather than the more typical three or four, thus betraying its origins as a 17th-century pub. One of Wordsworth's frequent visitors at the cottage was that other well-known literary figure (and opium fiend) Thomas de Quincey. De Quincey declared the house to be a fortuitous one for writers and when the Wordsworths vacated it in 1808 the de Quinceys moved in, thus continuing the literary connections of the place.

The **museum** next door contains original manuscripts by both Wordsworth and de Quincey and stages frequent special exhibitions.

Other sights Before you leave, you may like to pay a visit to **Wordsworth's family grave** around the back of **St Oswald's**, a 13th-century church named after the 7th-century king of Northumbria who preached on this site. Wordsworth's prayer-book is on display in the church.

Standing by the side entrance to the church grounds is the 150-year-old **Gingerbread Shop** (☎ 015394 35428, 🖳 www.grasmeregingerbread.co.uk), a tiny 'factory' that, incredibly, used to be the local school. It is said that Wordsworth taught here occasionally.

Opposite is the **Storyteller's Garden** (🖳 www.taffythomas.co.uk) which hosts several events throughout the year – see the website for details. Around the village centre are a number of **galleries** displaying works by local artists.

Make sure, too, that you check out Lancrigg Woods and the Poet's Walk (Map 18, p123), the start of which you walked past on your way into Grasmere.

Transport (see also pp52-5)
From Easter to October Stagecoach's open-top No 599 **bus** service travels regularly via Ambleside (15 mins) and the train station and Bowness Pier at Windermere (25 mins), from where in the evening a few buses go on to Kendal. Their No 555 goes from Keswick to Lancaster via Ambleside, Windermere and Kendal (Grasmere to Lancaster takes 1hr 50mins). Buses leave from The Green.

For other destinations, Grasmere **Taxis** can be reached on ☎ 015394 35506.

STAGE 4: GRASMERE TO PATTERDALE   MAPS 18-25

Introduction

Ignoring the alternative routes for the moment, this is the shortest of our stages. Short, but no less sweet for it's another classic hike along which walkers can enjoy some great views back to Grasmere and, once over the pass, down across Grisedale to Patterdale, another gorgeous valley with the lake of Ullswater twinkling away to the north.

The most direct routes avoiding Striding Edge are a mere **8½ miles (13.5km, 3-4hrs)** and deliver a simple walk up to **Grisedale Pass (Hause)** and either down the valley or – more satisfyingly – up along the ridge of St Sunday Crag. The longer route ascends the 950-metre bulk of Helvellyn, returning to the valley via the stirringly named Striding Edge ridge walk; an additional dis-

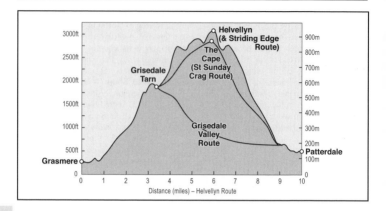

Distance (miles) – Helvellyn Route

tance of around **two miles** and a considerable amount of climbing and at times, exposure. Both the high routes are described on pp133-6. You can delay your choice on which path to take until Grisedale Tarn, where the three paths go their separate ways.

The route

First of all you need to reach the heights of Grisedale Tarn, which involves a climb up a bridleway running off the A591 reached by walking up the A591 to the bridleway from Grasmere or, as we've mapped it (Map 18, p123) picking up the original Coast to Coast path near Thorney How Youth Hostel.

At a footbridge or ford the bridleway divides at the foot of **Great Tongue** (Map 19) into a steeper route alongside **Little Tongue Gill** or a mildly steadier gradient to the east of Great Tongue along Tongue Gill which is slabbed for part of its length. Of course you're still climbing to the same elevation where the two paths rejoin.

Soon you arrive at the pretty mountain lake of **Grisedale Tarn** (Map 20) with the trail zigzagging up **Dollywaggon Pike** towards Helvellyn. Keeping to the easier path down Grisedale valley, the descent is as uncomplicated as the ascent, with the **Brothers' Parting Stone** just below the tarn (so-called because it's said that here in 1800 Wordsworth last met with his brother John, who died at sea a few years later). Just under a mile further on by Ruthwaite Beck, **Ruthwaite Lodge**, a climbers' hut, is usually locked up.

The path continues down the valley and briefly joins a tarmac road (Map 24) where the Helvellyn/Striding Edge route comes in. You then leave the road to the right to enter the National Trust's **Glenamara Park** (and where the St Sunday Crag route converges), with some wonderful views over Patterdale and beyond to Ullswater (Norse for 'Water with a Bend').

All being well, you'll drop onto the road by the Patterdale Hotel about two hours after leaving Grisedale Tarn.

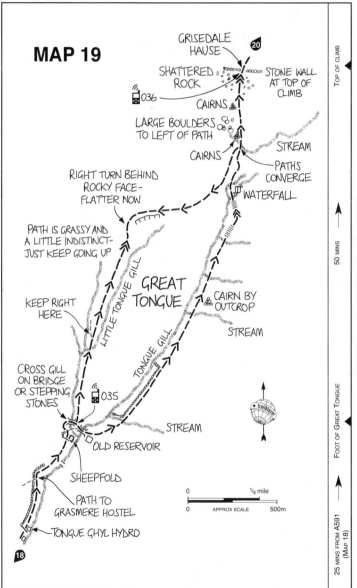

MAP 19

GRISEDALE HAUSE

20

SHATTERED ROCK

STONE WALL AT TOP OF CLIMB

📱036

CAIRNS

LARGE BOULDERS TO LEFT OF PATH

CAIRNS

STREAM

PATHS CONVERGE

RIGHT TURN BEHIND ROCKY FACE- FLATTER NOW

WATERFALL

PATH IS GRASSY AND A LITTLE INDISTINCT- JUST KEEP GOING UP

LITTLE TONGUE GILL

GREAT TONGUE

CAIRN BY OUTCROP

KEEP RIGHT HERE

STREAM

CROSS GILL ON BRIDGE OR STEPPING STONES

TONGUE GILL

📱035

STREAM

OLD RESERVOIR

SHEEPFOLD

PATH TO GRASMERE HOSTEL

TONGUE GHYL HYDRO

18

0   ¼ mile

0   500m
APPROX SCALE

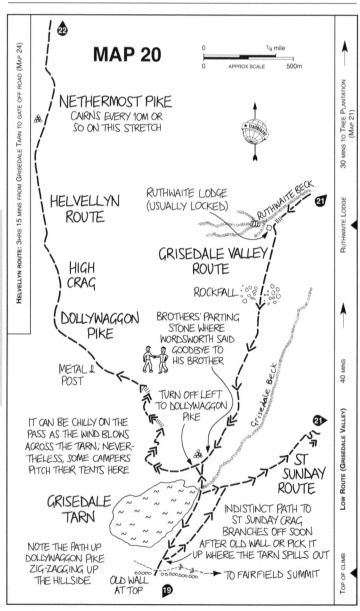

MAP 20

0   ¼ mile

0   APPROX SCALE   500m

HELVELLYN ROUTE: 3HRS 15 MINS FROM GRISEDALE TARN TO GATE OFF ROAD (MAP 24)

22

★ trailblaze

NETHERMOST PIKE
CAIRNS EVERY 10M OR
SO ON THIS STRETCH

**HELVELLYN
ROUTE**

RUTHWAITE LODGE
(USUALLY LOCKED)

RUTHWAITE BECK

21

**HIGH
CRAG**

**GRISEDALE VALLEY
ROUTE**

ROCKFALL

**DOLLYWAGGON
PIKE**

BROTHERS' PARTING
STONE WHERE
WORDSWORTH SAID
GOODBYE TO
HIS BROTHER

Grisedale Beck

METAL
POST

TURN OFF LEFT
TO DOLLYWAGGON
PIKE

IT CAN BE CHILLY ON THE
PASS AS THE WIND BLOWS
ACROSS THE TARN; NEVER-
THELESS, SOME CAMPERS
PITCH THEIR TENTS HERE

21

**ST
SUNDAY
ROUTE**

**GRISEDALE
TARN**

INDISTINCT PATH TO
ST SUNDAY CRAG
BRANCHES OFF SOON
AFTER OLD WALL OR PICK IT
UP WHERE THE TARN SPILLS OUT

NOTE THE PATH UP
DOLLYWAGGON PIKE
ZIG-ZAGGING UP
THE HILLSIDE

OLD WALL
AT TOP

TO FAIRFIELD SUMMIT

19

30 MINS TO TREE PLANTATION (MAP 21)

RUTHWAITE LODGE

40 MINS

LOW ROUTE (GRISEDALE VALLEY)

TOP OF CLIMB

The high-level options: Helvellyn & Striding Edge; St Sunday Crag
If weather conditions allow, one of these two high-level routes should be seri-
ously considered. After all, it would be a shame on this, the penultimate stage
in the Lake District, if you didn't try to climb as many peaks as possible.

Helvellyn & Striding Edge   **Map 20, Maps 22-24 pp134-5**
IMPORTANT NOTE! Since the descent via Striding Edge is precarious and,
given the sheer drops on either side, **can be very dangerous indeed** even in

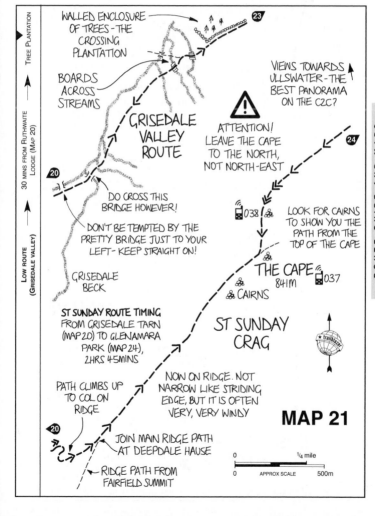

TREE PLANTATION

30 MINS FROM RUTHWAITE LODGE (MAP 20)

LOW ROUTE (GRISEDALE VALLEY)

ROUTE GUIDE AND MAPS

WALLED ENCLOSURE OF TREES - THE CROSSING PLANTATION

BOARDS ACROSS STREAMS

VIEWS TOWARDS ULLSWATER - THE BEST PANORAMA ON THE C2C?

GRISEDALE VALLEY ROUTE

⚠ ATTENTION! LEAVE THE CAPE TO THE NORTH, NOT NORTH-EAST

038

LOOK FOR CAIRNS TO SHOW YOU THE PATH FROM THE TOP OF THE CAPE

DO CROSS THIS BRIDGE HOWEVER!

DON'T BE TEMPTED BY THE PRETTY BRIDGE JUST TO YOUR LEFT - KEEP STRAIGHT ON!

GRISEDALE BECK

THE CAPE 841M
037

CAIRNS

ST SUNDAY ROUTE TIMING
FROM GRISEDALE TARN (MAP 20) TO GLENAMARA PARK (MAP 24), 2HRS 45MINS

ST SUNDAY CRAG

trailblazer

PATH CLIMBS UP TO COL ON RIDGE

NOW ON RIDGE. NOT NARROW LIKE STRIDING EDGE, BUT IT IS OFTEN VERY, VERY WINDY

MAP 21

JOIN MAIN RIDGE PATH AT DEEPDALE HAUSE

RIDGE PATH FROM FAIRFIELD SUMMIT

0   ¼ mile
0   APPROX SCALE   500m

ROUTE GUIDE AND MAPS

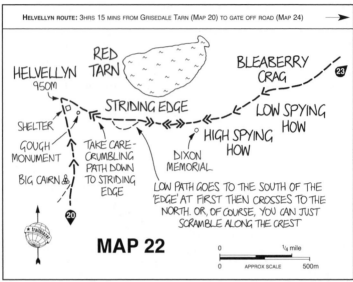

MAP 22

RED TARN

HELVELLYN 950M

STRIDING EDGE

BLEABERRY CRAG

LOW SPYING HOW

HIGH SPYING HOW

SHELTER

GOUGH MONUMENT

TAKE CARE - CRUMBLING PATH DOWN TO STRIDING EDGE

DIXON MEMORIAL

BIG CAIRN

LOW PATH GOES TO THE SOUTH OF THE 'EDGE' AT FIRST THEN CROSSES TO THE NORTH. OR, OF COURSE, YOU CAN JUST SCRAMBLE ALONG THE CREST

23

20

0   1/4 mile
0   APPROX SCALE   500m

HELVELLYN ROUTE: 3HRS 15 MINS FROM GRISEDALE TARN (MAP 20) TO GATE OFF ROAD (MAP 24) ➡

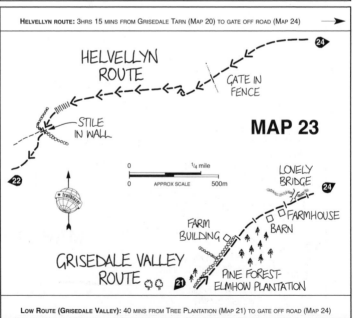

MAP 23

HELVELLYN ROUTE

GATE IN FENCE

24

STILE IN WALL

22

0   1/4 mile
0   APPROX SCALE   500m

LOVELY BRIDGE

24

FARMHOUSE

BARN

FARM BUILDING

GRISEDALE VALLEY ROUTE

21

PINE FOREST - ELMHOW PLANTATION

LOW ROUTE (GRISEDALE VALLEY): 40 MINS FROM TREE PLANTATION (MAP 21) TO GATE OFF ROAD (MAP 24)

calm weather with little wind, this route is only for people experienced in such conditions and certainly not for anyone who suffers at all from vertigo.

Of the two high-level options, **Helvellyn**, at 950m (3113ft) the third highest peak in England after Scafell Pike and Scafell, is understandably the more popular. The climb is arduous and, having reached the top, you then face a nerve-tingling drop on a crumbing slope above Red Tarn, followed by a knife-edge walk along Striding Edge ridge to reach the trail dropping to Patterdale. A memorial plaque to Robert Dixon who was killed here in 1858 whilst following his fox hounds during a hunt does little to calm the nerves – and there are many more recent victims of this vertiginous trail. But with a steady head and light winds the sense of achievement is ample reward for your efforts.

Wainwright waxes lyrical about this side trip, describing the notorious Striding Edge as the 'best quarter mile between St Bees and Robin Hood's Bay'. He visited Helvellyn on his first trip to the Lakes in 1930, and it was this trip that

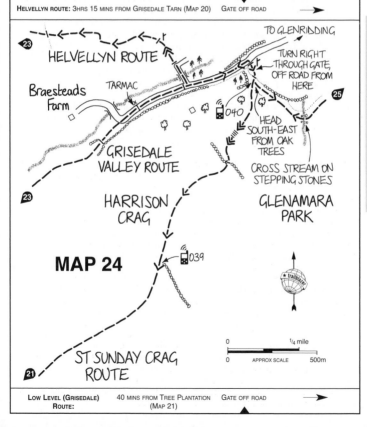

HELVELLYN ROUTE: 3HRS 15 MINS FROM GRISEDALE TARN (MAP 20)   GATE OFF ROAD

TO GLENRIDDING

HELVELLYN ROUTE

TURN RIGHT THROUGH GATE, OFF ROAD FROM HERE

TARMAC

Braesteads Farm

040

HEAD SOUTH-EAST FROM OAK TREES

GRISEDALE VALLEY ROUTE

CROSS STREAM ON STEPPING STONES

HARRISON CRAG

GLENAMARA PARK

MAP 24

039

trailblazer

ST SUNDAY CRAG ROUTE

0   1/4 mile
0   APPROX SCALE   500m

LOW LEVEL (GRISEDALE) ROUTE: 40 MINS FROM TREE PLANTATION (MAP 21)   GATE OFF ROAD

ROUTE GUIDE AND MAPS

inspired his passion for the Lakes. He approached the peak from the opposite direction to that given here and he edged along it 'in agonies of apprehension'.

This route takes about 3hrs 15mins from Grisedale Tarn to Patterdale, though that assumes you take the lower path just below the knife-edge crest of Striding Edge which can be traversed in as little as 20 minutes. However, with the inevitable waiting that needs to be done to let people coming the other way go by (at least at weekends), expect it all to add up to four hours from the tarn. You won't regret the extra time – it is truly exhilarating.

St Sunday Crag   Maps 20-21 pp132-3, Map 24 p135

It's said that better views, if fewer thrills, lie in wait on the south side of the valley along St Sunday Crag. Indeed, for many people these are the best views on the entire route, particularly those towards Ullswater. What's more, the effort required to climb up to St Sunday Crag is, by the standards of the lakes, fairly negligible, a steady plod away from the Tarn followed by a reasonably steady descent, at least until the sudden drop into Glenamara Park. It takes about **2hrs, 45 mins** (walking time only) from Grisedale Tarn to Glenamara Park.

Soon after leaving Grisedale Tarn, you'll see a trail rising away from the lake, presently joined by the usual path from the tarn's mouth. You join the ridge at Deepdale Hause, where the path from Fairfield summit feeds in from the right, and soon arrive at the high point known as **The Cape** (841m/2759ft). All along you've fine views of the next stage; a ramp rising steadily past briefly glimpsed Angle Tarn to Kidsty Pike and the unseen depths of Haweswater beyond.

From The Cape make sure you walk briefly north and not east for Gavel Pike. Then at a cairn (WPT 038) the path continues north-east before dropping off the ridge and tumbling down to Glenamara Park, where you meet up with the low-level route and enter Patterdale.

PATTERDALE   MAP 25, p137

Patterdale is little more than a meandering collection of houses strung along the A592. Normally valleys this beautiful would be full of souvenir shops and tearooms. But Patterdale, while not exactly undiscovered, is mercifully free of the 'Lakeland Babylon' found in Grasmere. The valley is also something of a **wildlife** haven, including a population of red squirrels – some of the last remaining in England.

The **fountain of St Patrick** (Patterdale is a corruption of St Patrick's Dale) is an ornate Victorian construction set in a bank by the side of the road just outside Glenridding, and is said to mark the spot where the saint baptised the locals.

All your needs will be comprehensively met at **Patterdale Village Store** (summer daily 8.30am-6pm, winter to 5.30pm and to noon on Wed & Sun; 🖳 www.patterdalevillagestore.co.uk). Gillian and Tom run one of

the best-provisioned village stores along the route – including gifts and souvenirs for owners of that lovable terrier breed, the Patterdale, named after the valley.

The shop includes a **post office** (Mon 8.30am-5.30pm, Tue 8.30am-3.30pm, Wed & Thur 8.30am to noon), a large variety of hot and cold sandwiches including bacon rolls fit to choke a hog, delicious BBQ pork rib sandwiches as well as a lavish array of groceries for those camping, staying in the hostel or just unable to resist temptation. There are also hats, gloves, knee supports, maps and Coast to Coast path souvenirs and even copies of this book.

Both the shop and the post office have **cashback** facilities and outside is a walkers' **message board** plus reams of information on local lodgings, bus times, phone numbers and so on.

You'll be lucky to get a mobile signal in Patterdale.

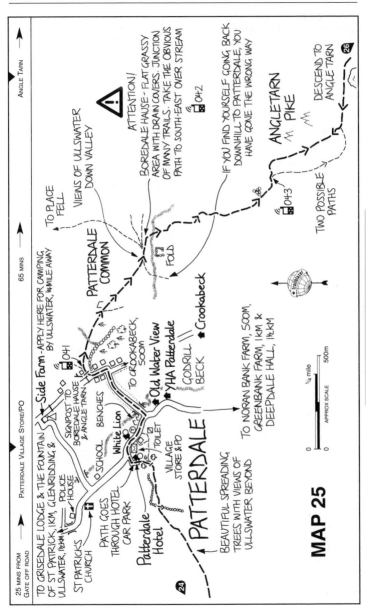

TO GRISEDALE LODGE & THE FOUNTAIN
- APPLY HERE FOR CAMPING,
BY ULLSWATER, ¼MILE AWAY

TO ST PATRICK, 1KM, GLENRIDDING &
ULLSWATER, 1½KM

Side Farm

POLICE
HOUSE

SIGNPOST TO
BOREDALE HAUSE
& ANGLE TARN

TO PLACE
FELL

VIEWS OF ULLSWATER
DOWN VALLEY

ST PATRICKS CHURCH

SCHOOL

BENCHES

White Lion

041

TO CROOKABECK,
SOOM

PATTERDALE COMMON

ATTENTION!
BOREDALE HAUSE - FLAT GRASSY
AREA WITH DRAIN COVERS. JUNCTION
OF MANY TRAILS. TAKE THE OBVIOUS
PATH TO SOUTH-EAST OVER STREAM

042

PATH GOES
THROUGH HOTEL
CAR PARK

Patterdale
Hotel

VILLAGE
STORE & PO

TOILET

Old Water View
YHA Patterdale

GODRILL
BECK

Crookabeck

FOLD

IF YOU FIND YOURSELF GOING BACK
DOWNHILL TO PATTERDALE, YOU
HAVE GONE THE WRONG WAY

043

ANGLETARN
PIKE

TO NORAN BANK FARM, SOOM,
GREENBANK FARM, 1KM &
DEEPDALE HALL, 1½KM

TWO POSSIBLE
PATHS

DESCEND TO
ANGLE TARN

26

PATTERDALE

BEAUTIFUL SPREADING
TREES WITH VIEWS OF
ULLSWATER BEYOND

24

MAP 25

APPROX SCALE

¼ mile

500m

trailblazer

Where to stay and eat

There's a range of **accommodation** in Patterdale, though this being the Lakes, booking ahead is vital if you don't want to end up sleeping in a ditch with a red squirrel for a duvet. Remember, the next stage to Shap is commonly agreed to be the toughest on the Coast to Coast walk, so you'll want to be on form. If you run out of luck in Patterdale, there's more accommodation in Glenridding (see box p139); it's listed on the **community website** 🖳 www.patterdale.org, or outside the shop.

For **campers**, across Goldrill Beck is *Side Farm* (☎ 01768 482337, ☎ 07796 128897; 🖳 www.patterdale.org/Side%20 Farm.htm; £8pp; 🐕 kept on lead; Easter to Oct). Genuine Coast to Coast walkers will always be accepted (sometimes even if the sign says they're full) but in general they do not take advance bookings. The site has toilets, hot showers and laundry facilities. It actually lies a little way beyond the farm on the edge of the lake but they insist you check in at the farm first. However, considering they have a **tearoom** (Easter to Oct, school holidays daily 10.30am-5pm; hours vary at other times), it's a great place to recuperate before pitching your tent. Indeed, in summer one reader recommends getting here before 4pm or you may struggle to find a flat pitch for your tent. And just in case you thought you'd heard the last of him, it's said our old friend Wordsworth was a regular visitor to Side Farm.

At the other end of the village, *YHA Patterdale* (☎ 0845 371 9337, 🖳 www.yha .org.uk/hostel/patterdale; 77 beds, 1x single, 4 x 2-bed/6 x 8-beds/2x10-bed rooms; beds £15-21; WI-FI) is on the main road. The 1970s' building may not win any design awards, but inside has been refitted comfortably and, unusually, the building is open all day; reception opens at 5pm. Meals and packed lunches are available as well as supper (order before 6pm, 3 courses for £8.50). The hostel is licensed and there is a drying room and laundry facilities. Credit cards are accepted. They also offer camping at £9pp; dogs allowed in the campground.

At Noran Bank Farm (see p139) you'll find *Shepherd's Crook Bunkhouse* (☎ 01768 482327, 🖳 www.patterdale.org/Nor anbank.htm; 🐕 £4; Ⓛ £6) with two rooms; one has a double bunk bed and en suite shower, the other sleeps six and has separate shower facilities. It's open all year and is a very reasonable £15-20pp, £5 supplement for single occupancy of the double bunk-bed room. There is a fully equipped kitchen and a DIY breakfast costs £6.

Just before the YHA hostel, *Old Water View Country Inn* (☎ 01768 482175, 🖳 www.oldwaterview.co.uk; 2D/4T or Tr; all en suite; 📶; WI-FI; Ⓛ £2.75) is a wonderful place and a favourite of Wainwright's. The current owner is a mine of information and is the guy to speak to about shortcuts along High St to Shap. There's comfortable accommodation and good food here: several readers have recommended it for both. B&B costs £49pp (sgl occ £98). Food is available all day 8am-11pm and the bar which serves the local brew, Tirril, on draft is also open those times. There's a beer garden and you can also get essentials such as plasters as well as components for a packed lunch.

Very close to the path and the focus of the village is the 19th-century *White Lion* pub (☎ 01768 482214, 🖳 www.the-white lion.com; 1S/1S or D/ 2D/3T; all with private facilities; 🐕 £5; Ⓛ £4.95). B&B starts at £37pp (sgl occ £47) and they do bar meals (daily noon-9pm) too. The extensive menu includes steaks, curry and fish & chips; whatever dish you choose, it will be big! They also do breakfasts (Apr-Sep from 9am; £7.95) for non-residents as long as they have requested this the night before.

The smartest and most expensive lodgings in the village are at *Patterdale Hotel* (☎ 01768 482440, 🖳 www.patterdale hotel.co.uk; 4S/10T/39D/4Qd; all en suite; 📶; WI-FI). Part of a chain, it's an enormous establishment and their reluctance to accept bookings for anything less than two-night stays may deter C2Cers; however, they are happy to take one-night bookings if there is a vacancy near the time. Unravelling the tariff takes a degree in metaphysics, but during the week expect to pay £147-202pp for dinner B&B for two nights (£99-127pp for two nights at weekends). **Food** is served daily 8am-8.30pm; the bar serves hot food and snacks daily noon-5pm & 6.30-8.30pm.

There are other B&Bs further south along the road beyond the YHA hostel. Less than a mile south of the path, *Noran Bank Farm* (see Shepherd's Crook Bunkhouse p138; 1Tr with private bathroom; ☞; 🐾 £4; Ⓛ £6; Mar-Oct) is a whitewashed 16th-century farmhouse. Rates are £30pp (sgl occ £35). A minimum stay of two nights is required on bank holiday weekends.

Nearby is another old farmhouse, *Greenbank Farm* (☎ 01768 482292, ☐ www.coast2coast.co.uk/greenbankfarm; 1S/1D/1Qd; shared shower facilities; wi-fi; Ⓛ £5; Mar-Oct) a working sheep farm charging £24.50pp and £13.50 for an evening meal (book in advance). They also have a static caravan where up to four people can sleep for £20pp including breakfast.

Just after Greenbank Farm is *Deepdale Hall* (☎ 01768 482369, ☐ www.deepdale hall.co.uk; 1D/1Tr; en suite with private facilities; ☞; wi-fi; Ⓛ £8; Mar-Nov) with

B&B from £45-50pp (sgl occ £65).

Grisedale Lodge (☎ 01768 482155, ☐ www.grisedalelodge.co.uk; 1D/2D or T; all with private facilities; ☞; wi-fi; Ⓛ from £6) is set halfway between Patterdale and Glenridding villages, close to the shores of Ullswater. It's a lovely location and by all accounts a lovely B&B too, with swish rooms and large breakfasts. B&B costs £42.50pp (sgl occ £55).

Crookabeck B&B (☎ 07747 587635, ☐ www.crookabeck.com; 1T/1F; en suite; wi-fi; Ⓛ £5) offers self-contained accommodation with its own lounge, superb views, Sky TV, sink and fridge (no cooking facilities). A cooked breakfast is brought up to the room. B&B costs from £45pp (sgl occ £60).

Transport (see also pp52-5)
Stagecoach's **bus** No 508 (Patterdale Bus) travels to Penrith railway station and operates year-round, five times a day Monday to Saturday, and three times a day on Sunday, via Glenridding.

❑ Ullswater and Glenridding

I wandered lonely as a cloud,
That floats on high o'er vales and hills,
When all at once I saw a crowd,
A host of golden daffodils,
Beside the lake, beneath the trees,
Fluttering and dancing in the breeze.
William Wordsworth, *Daffodils*

It is said that Wordsworth was inspired to write these words after a trip to Ullswater. Certainly it's a beautiful lake and unlike neighbouring Grasmere and Haweswater there's plenty to do *on* the water too.

There is a **tourist information centre** (☎ 017684 82414, ☐ ullswater tic@lake-district.gov.uk) in the main car park in Glenridding; it is open daily 9.30am-5.30pm March until the end of October and at weekends only (roughly 9.30am-3.30pm, though phone first to check) the rest of the year.

Boats (motorboats) can be hired (see ☐ www.lakelandboathire.co.uk) though don't try to emulate Donald Campbell, who broke the 200mph water speed record on Ullswater in 1955.

For something more sedate, hire a rowing boat, or you can take a cruise on a **steamer** (☎ 017684 82229; ☐ www.ullswater-steamers.co.uk). There have been steamers on the lake since 1859 and two of the five boats currently in service, *Lady of the Lake* and *Raven*, have been operating since the late 19th century with the former believed to be the oldest working passenger vessel in the world. Services operate year-round (3-9/day) to Howton, Pooley Bridge and back.

For further details of accommodation, activities and events around Ullswater see ☐ www.ullswater.co.uk.

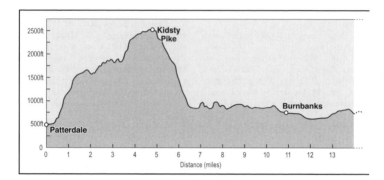

STAGE 5: PATTERDALE TO SHAP   MAPS 25-34

Introduction

Today is the day you leave the Lake District and it is true that, as a rule, once the Lakes are behind you the wayfinding becomes easier and the gradients kinder. But the crags, knotts, pikes and fells that have been your high-level chums for the past few days won't let you go without a struggle.

Be prepared to feel very tired at the end of this **15½-mile (25km, 6½hr)** stage from Patterdale to Shap. The long climb up to Kidsty Pike, the trickily steep descent down to Haweswater (see box below) and the undulating stage above the lake's shore add up to well over **1300 metres** (4400ft) of ascent. Together it all conspires to make the seemingly harmless spin down over field and farmland to Shap enough to curse the very name of Wainwright.

With no accommodation directly on the route nor, indeed, any shops, tearooms or pubs, you have little choice but to grit your teeth and knuckle down.

❑ Haweswater Reservoir

What is now one of Cumbria's largest bodies of water was once a small and fairly unassuming lake stuck on the eastern edge of the national park. In 1929, however, a bill was passed authorising the use of Haweswater as a reservoir to serve the needs of the population of Manchester. A concrete dam, 470m wide and 35m high, was constructed at the northern edge of the lake, raising the depth of the lake by over 30m and increasing the surface area to four miles long by half a mile wide (6km by 1km).

This project was not without its opponents, many protested at the loss of the settlements such as Mardale Green on Haweswater's eastern shore (near the pier). Before the village was flooded, coffins were removed from the graveyard and buried elsewhere and the 18th-century Holy Trinity Church was pulled down. Some of the windows from this church are now in the reservoir tower. Even today, during times of drought when the water level is low, the walls of Mardale emerge from the reservoir.

Despite man's interference the lake is still something of a wildlife haven. Swimming in the waters are wild brown trout, char, gwyniad and perch, while **Riggindale** is an RSPB haven, with wheatear, raven, ring ouzel and peregrine.

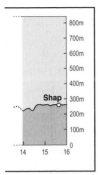

To shorten the day, a few walkers now take a 1¼ mile (2km) detour to Bampton (see p144). Otherwise, consider camping at Angle Tarn having come over from Grasmere and stocked up at the Patterdale village store. You won't find many more truly wild places like this in the days to come and at all other times the baggage van can carry the camping gear.

The route

You'll have spotted the ramp rising up from the far side of Patterdale. After much huffing and puffing it drops you down to the grassy platform known as **Boredale Hause** where the right way is (for once!) actually the most obvious continuing south-east, by one trail or another, to the scalloped shoreline of Angle Tarn. The gradient levels off for a while until another haul leads up around The Knott and soon the hard-to-miss turn-off that brings you with rather less effort than you might expect to **Kidsty Pike**, at a modest 784m (2572ft) the high point on the original Coast to Coast route.

From the top, looking west, you can see the Pillar looking down onto Ennerdale Water from all those days ago, Scafell Pike, Helvellyn and St Sunday from the previous stage. To the south lie unknown lands including the deep cleft of Riggindale in whose crags is said to be the eyrie of England's last **golden eagle**.

R O U T E   G U I D E   A N D   M A P S

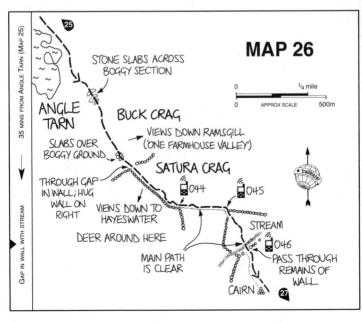

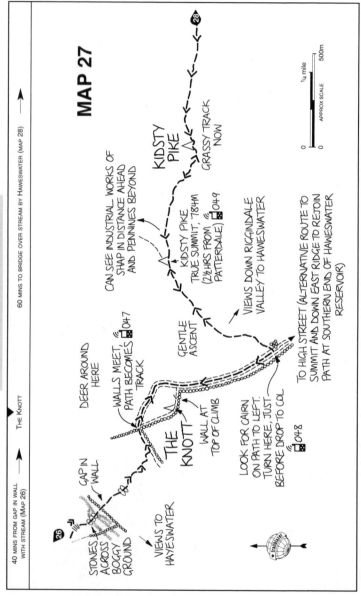

40 MINS FROM GAP IN WALL WITH STREAM (MAP 26) →

THE KNOTT

60 MINS TO BRIDGE OVER STREAM BY HAWESWATER (MAP 28) →

MAP 27

STONES ACROSS BOGGY GROUND

GAP IN WALL

VIEWS TO HAYESWATER

DEER AROUND HERE

WALLS MEET, PATH BECOMES TRACK 📷047

THE KNOTT

WALL AT TOP OF CLIMB

LOOK FOR CAIRN ON PATH TO LEFT. TURN HERE, JUST BEFORE DROP TO COL 📷048

GENTLE ASCENT

TO HIGH STREET (ALTERNATIVE ROUTE TO SUMMIT AND DOWN EAST RIDGE TO REJOIN PATH AT SOUTHERN END OF HAWESWATER RESERVOIR)

CAN SEE INDUSTRIAL WORKS OF SHAP IN DISTANCE AHEAD AND PENNINES BEYOND

KIDSTY PIKE TRUE SUMMIT, 784M (2½ HRS FROM PATTERDALE) 📷049

KIDSTY PIKE

VIEWS DOWN RIGGINDALE VALLEY TO HAWESWATER

GRASSY TRACK NOW

¼ mile

APPROX SCALE

0   500m

0

The biggest descent on the walk now follows – at times you'll need your hands – to the very shores of Haweswater reservoir, but a lakeside amble while spinning your dainty parasol is sadly not on the cards. Instead you're soon panting like a hippo on a treadmill high above the shore, measuring each streaming gill until the dammed waters terminate at the wooded glade along Haweswater Beck.

The 'model' village of **Burnbanks** (Map 30) is little more than a huddle of 18 houses at the head of the reservoir. There's an infrequent (Thu only) bus service (No 111) to Bampton, Penrith and the outside world (see pp52-5). You can **camp** at *Aragon* (☎ 01931 713629, 🖥 chizzer@homecall.co.uk; 🐾) for £7pp (showers £1). Booking appreciated. Follow the trail from Burnbanks for five minutes and turn left where the path crosses the lane at Naddle Bridge. It's a quiet riverside spot with beautiful woodland all around. Look out for red squirrels.

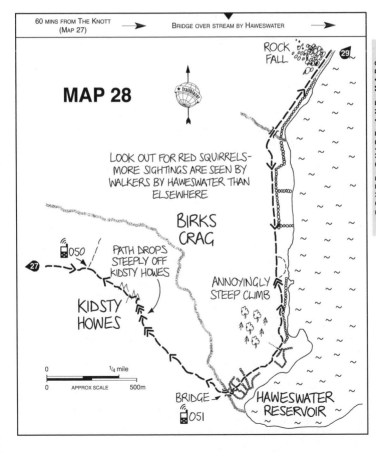

60 MINS FROM THE KNOTT (MAP 27) →

BRIDGE OVER STREAM BY HAWESWATER →

ROCK FALL

29

MAP 28

trailblazer

LOOK OUT FOR RED SQUIRRELS-
MORE SIGHTINGS ARE SEEN BY
WALKERS BY HAWESWATER THAN
ELSEWHERE

BIRKS CRAG

050

PATH DROPS
STEEPLY OFF
KIDSTY HOWES

27

ANNOYINGLY
STEEP CLIMB

KIDSTY HOWES

0   ¼ mile

0   APPROX SCALE   500m

BRIDGE
051

HAWESWATER
RESERVOIR

ROUTE GUIDE AND MAPS

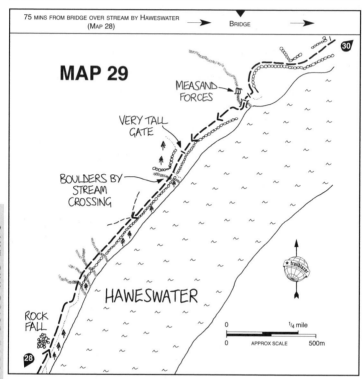

MAP 29

MEASAND
FORCES

VERY TALL
GATE

BOULDERS BY
STREAM
CROSSING

HAWESWATER

ROCK
FALL

30

28

0   ¼ mile

0   APPROX SCALE   500m

ROUTE GUIDE AND MAPS

BAMPTON   **OFF MAP 30, p145**

For a B&B that seems to supply your every need, there's *Bampton Village Store* (☎ 01931-713351, 💻 www.bvs-bandb.co.uk; 1T/1F sleeps 4, both en suite; 🍺, WI-FI). B&B is from £40pp (£47.50 sgl occ). Their **tearoom** does sandwiches and home-made cakes. The **store** is open Mon & Thur 8am-1pm, Tue, Wed, Fri & Sat 8am-5pm, Sun 9am-4pm. There's **internet access** (£1/15mins) plus a **post office** (Mon 9am-1pm, Tue & Wed 9am-noon).

Another splendid option is *Howgate Foot* (☎ 01931 713454, 💻 www.howgate foot.co.uk; 1D; WI-FI; 🐾 but must stay in the old stable; Ⓛ £5) offering lovely accommodation in a converted barn with a bedroom, shower room, and upstairs a lounge with wood burner. Best of all, they

are happy to meet you at Burnbanks and drop you off again there next morning; no charge for pick up. They'll also run you to the pub and back in the evening (see below), or you can opt to have dinner there if you book in advance (£20). Rates are £47.50pp, though single trekkers will have to pay the full £95 room rate.

In **Bampton Grange**, about 10 minutes' walk east of Bampton, the equally recommended *Crown and Mitre* (☎ 01931 713225; 💻 www.crownandmitre.com; 2S/4D/2T; all en suite; 🍺; 🐾; WI-FI; Ⓛ) charges £42.50-50pp (sgl occ £50) for B&B. **Food** is available daily 6-9pm. Incidentally, the 1987 cult film *Withnail & I* was filmed in the area and the telephone box from which Withnail calls his agent in London is actually a stone's throw from the Inn, in which one

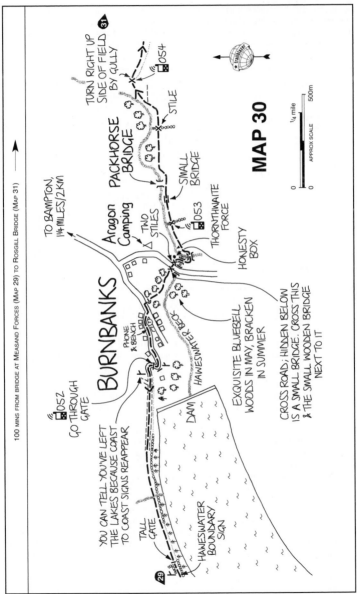

100 MINS FROM BRIDGE AT MEASAND FORCES (MAP 29) TO ROSGILL BRIDGE (MAP 31)

TO BAMPTON, 1¼ MILES/2 KM

TURN RIGHT UP SIDE OF FIELD BY GULLY

31

OS4

STILE

PACKHORSE BRIDGE

SMALL BRIDGE

THORNTHWAITE FORCE

OS3

HONESTY BOX

Aragon Camping

TWO STILES

BURNBANKS

PHONE & BEACH

HAWESWATER BECK

OS2 GO THROUGH GATE

YOU CAN TELL YOU'VE LEFT THE LAKES BECAUSE COAST TO COAST SIGNS REAPPEAR

TALL GATE

HAWESWATER BOUNDARY SIGN

29

DAM

EXQUISITE BLUEBELL WOODS IN MAY, BRACKEN IN SUMMER

CROSS ROAD; HIDDEN BELOW IS A SMALL BRIDGE. CROSS THIS & THE SMALL WOODEN BRIDGE NEXT TO IT

MAP 30

APPROX SCALE

¼ mile

500m

trailblazer

would be right to expect nothing less than the finest wines available to humanity. (The famously decrepit cottage of 'Crow Crag' is actually a derelict farmhouse called Sleddale Hall, situated by a reservoir three miles south-west of Shap – off Map 34).

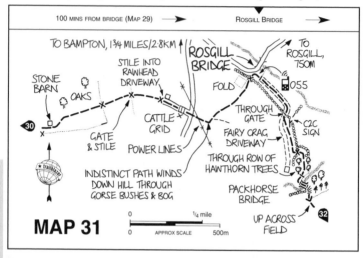

Back on the trail it now feels a relief to be walking on the level, soft grass for miles at a time and, free of the national park's edicts, helpful 'Coast to Coast' signposts reappear too. Wall follows stile follows field follows stile until, towards the end of the stage, you descend on **Shap Abbey** (see box below and Map 32), an atmospheric ruin set in a peaceful spot by the River Lowther. It's just regrettable that, by the time you get there, you'll probably be somewhat of a ruin yourself, your thoughts having long ago turned from holy orders to hors d'oeuvres following a hot bath. From the abbey, all that remains is to tick off the road or parallel paths presaging your triumphant entry into **Shap**.

❑ Shap Abbey

Shap Abbey (see Map 32) has the distinction of being the last abbey to be founded in England, in 1199. It was built by the French Premonstratensian order founded by St Norbert at Prémontré in Northern France, who were also known as the White Canons after the colour of their habits. The abbey was also the last to be dissolved by Henry VIII, in 1540. Presumably Henry's henchmen would have had plenty of practice in plundering monasteries by this time, which is perhaps why the abbey is today in such a ruinous state. The best-preserved section is the **western belltower**, built around 1500.

Since its demise, the abbey has had to suffer the commonplace indignity of having some of its most carved stonework purloined by the locals for use in their own buildings. The cottage by the abbey clearly used some in its construction, albeit to good effect, while Shap's 17th-century market hall is built largely from abbey stone. Even some of the local stone walls contain abbey stones.

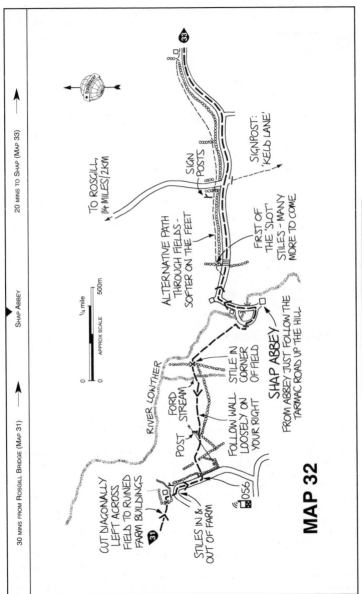

33

TO ROSGILL, 1¼ MILES/2KM

SIGN POSTS

SIGNPOST: 'KELD LANE'

ALTERNATIVE PATH THROUGH FIELDS - SOFTER ON THE FEET

FIRST OF THE 'SLOT' STILES - MANY MORE TO COME

¼ mile

500m

APPROX SCALE

0

0

RIVER LOWTHER

STILE IN CORNER OF FIELD

POST

FORD STREAM

FOLLOW WALL LOOSELY ON YOUR RIGHT

SHAP ABBEY
FROM ABBEY JUST FOLLOW THE TARMAC ROAD UP THE HILL.

056

CUT DIAGONALLY LEFT ACROSS FIELD TO RUINED FARM BUILDINGS

31

STILES IN & OUT OF FARM

MAP 32

ROUTE GUIDE AND MAPS

SHAP 30 MINS TO SIGNPOST TO ODDENDALE
(MAP 34)

New Ing
Lodge

The Hermitage 057

Phone

Bus stops

Co-op

Shap
Chippy

0   100m

Abbey
Coffee
Shop

Fire
station

Market
Square

School Bus stop

Market Hall

Memorial Hall

Crown Inn

Toilets Swimming
pool

Library &
internet

Bus stop

Newsagent
& PO

To Kings Arms, 50m,
Greyhound, 500m,
& Brookfield, 1km

MAP 33 Shap

SHAP   **MAP 33**

Shap is a long, narrow village lining a wide
street, the former A6, once the north-west's
main route to Scotland and still the highest
main road in the country as it passes over
the Howgill Fells. The road used to supply
Shap's traders with enough passing trade to
make a living and the village prospered.
But then they built the M6 and, like the
motel in *Psycho*, things have been pretty
quiet since, bar the presence of a couple of
quarries and cement factories. That said,
you have to admire the sense of community in Shap – spend half an hour in the café
(the main hub of Shap during the day) and
you'll notice pretty much everyone knows
everyone else – and many of them actively
volunteer with various schemes to make
Shap that little bit better. It's really quite
inspiring.

There are some attractive features in
town, including a 17th-century **market hall**
built with masonry from the **abbey** (see box
p146), but overall the place is not exactly
Las Vegas on New Year's Eve. However,
now you're out of the Lakes you don't have
to fight over the great accommodation, plus
there's a chippy, a Co-op, three pubs, a post
office and even an outdoor heated (seasonal) **swimming pool** – at over 900ft above
sea level (274m), it's England's highest!

There's a **newsagent** (Mon-Fri 5am-
5.30pm, Sat 5am-7pm, Sun 8am-noon) at
the southern end of town which now hosts
the **post office** (Mon-Thur 9am-12.30pm &
1.30-5.30pm; Fri 9am-12.30pm; Sat 9am-
noon). The decent-sized **Co-op** (daily 8am-
10pm) boasts the town's ATM. They also
do cashback at the till. The **library** (Mon
11am-2pm, Tue 2-5pm, Fri 2-7pm, Sat
10am-noon) in the Old Courthouse has
internet access. The village has its own
website (www.shapcumbria.co.uk).

Where to stay

Being out of the Lakes, many B&B owners
need to make more of an effort to attract
custom, and with most of their guests being
Coast to Coasters, it's something that is
appreciated by many of our readers. There's
none of that 'two nights minimum stay at
weekends' malarkey or overpricing you've
put up with on previous days.

As you come into town *The Hermitage*
(☎ 01931 716671; www.coast2coast.co
.uk/thehermitage; 2T/1D/ 1Tr; mostly en
suite; ; WI-FI; from £3.50) is on your
right and has been recommended by readers. The beautiful house itself is over 300
years old but the rooms come with all mod
cons. B&B costs £40pp; evening meals
available by prior arrangement.

Over the road *New Ing Lodge* (☎
01931 716719, www.newinglodge.co
.uk; 3D/2T/1Tr/1Qd; some en suite with
; most rooms share showers; dogs £5
though not allowed in the dorm; WI-FI;
£6) offers a variety of accommodation.
B&B costs £30-37.50 (sgl £40). Under the
same roof there are also two notably spacious mixed **dorms** (six in one room, eight
in the other) for £17pp. There is a large

camping space (£8pp). Evening **meals** (two courses for about £13) and breakfast (£4-8) are available if requested in advance; there is also a very basic 'kitchen' which can be used by people staying in a dorm. The eggs from the free-roaming chickens are delicious, by the way.

Right at the southern end of town, few begrudge the walk to ***Brookfield House*** (Map 34; ☎ 01931 716397, 🖥 www.brook fieldshap.co.uk; 1S/3D or T/1S or D; all with private facilities; 🛁; WI-FI; Ⓛ £6.50; Mar-Nov) which has become a legend among Coast to Coasters and is frequently cited as the best stay on the entire walk. Nothing is too much trouble for Margaret, who charges £40pp (sgl £40-55). They have a bar, lounge and drying facilities and will do a wash for a small charge; the breakfasts and packed lunches are the talk of the walk.

The Greyhound Hotel (Map 34; ☎ 01931 716474, 🖥 www.greyhoundshap.co .uk; 2S/7D or T/2D/1Qd; all en suite; 🛁; 🐾; WI-FI) dates back to 1680. B&B costs £50, or £45-60pp in the doubles/twin. ***The King's Arms*** (Map 34; ☎ 01931 716277, 🖥 www.kingsarmsatshap.co.uk; 1D/2T/3Tr/ 1Qd, all with private facilities; 🛁; WI-FI; Ⓛ £4.95) charges £37.50pp (sgl occ £45, around £30pp for 3/4 people in a room).

Where to eat and drink
The ***Greyhound Hotel*** (see Where to stay; daily noon-9pm) is reputed to be the best place to eat. The menu consists of mainly local dishes including steak and ale pie (£10.95), braised Lakeland lamb Henry (£14.95) or a double bacon cheeseburger (£9.95). Unfortunately, the Greyhound's location is over a mile from The Hermitage or New Ing Lodge at the top end of town.

The ***King's Arms*** (see Where to stay; food served Sat noon-3pm, Sun noon-2pm, daily 5-8.30pm) keeps things simple by charging £6.95 for most of the main meals. ***The Crown Inn*** also does pub grub. Good value bar meals are served in summer (noon-3pm, 5-9pm) for around £7-10.

The revamped ***Shap Chippy*** (☎ 01931 716060; 🖥 www.shapchippy.co.uk; Tue-Sat noon-1.30pm, Tues-Sun 4.30-8pm), resplendent in its smart new blue livery, does excellent fish and chips either to take away or eat in, in their restaurant here.

A little further south is ***Abbey Coffee Shop*** (☎ 01931 716238, Tue-Sat 8.30am-4.30pm) which is good for cakes and sandwiches but usually closed by the time Coast to Coasters hobble into town – which is a shame, as it's a lovely, friendly place to rest your bunions for a while and enjoy the chatter and gossip from the locals.

Transport   (see also pp52-5)
Bus No 106 calls here en route between Kendal and Penrith. The buses leave from Shap's Market Square and take 30 minutes to reach Penrith, 12 minutes to Orton (see p152) and 45 minutes to Kendal.

STAGE 6: SHAP TO KIRKBY STEPHEN   MAPS 34-43

Introduction
Those who struggled over the previous stages may be less than delighted to learn that, at **20½ miles (33km, 7hrs)**, today's hike across the **Westmoreland plateau** is even longer. But the good news is that prolonged gradients and rocky sole-mashing trails have been replaced by grassy strolls across the well-drained limestone bedrock, making it something of a 'recovery day' and, with your fitness now improving, rather satisfying in its own right. Before you unrolls a steady, undulating transit over field and moorland as you flank the enigmatic Howgill Fells to the south and approach the peat-sodden ridge they call the Pennines.

If you're not convinced a fine day's walk lies ahead, there's a chance to break it in two by taking the short diversion into Orton, only eight miles from Shap. It's coming across 'lost' villages like Orton that is part of the appeal of the Coast to Coast walk. Stranded far from well-established tourist trails (and, until 2016, most of these villages were outside of a national park too, though many have now been incorporated within the newly enlarged Yorkshire Dales National Park), they're simply what they are; places where people live but in a manner and locale that for most of us is long past. It's then that it dawns on you that, away from the coach-tour honeypots, the forgotten corners of rural England are full of these charming places, scraping by with a shop, a pub, a church and maybe even a bus. This stage is also replete with **prehistoric sites**, though it's fair to say that none of them will make your jaw drop in amazement; unforewarned you'd probably pass by none the wiser but still cheered by a surprisingly great day aboard the Coast to Coast path.

The route

With over 20 miles to cover, you leave Shap to cross first the railway then the motorway which funnel through north-west England. They are soon forgotten as you skirt the hidden, walled village of **Oddendale** (Map 35) and cross the new boundary of the Yorkshire Dales National Park, extended in 2016. (You'll leave the national park just before Kirkby Stephen, and won't re-enter it until past Nine

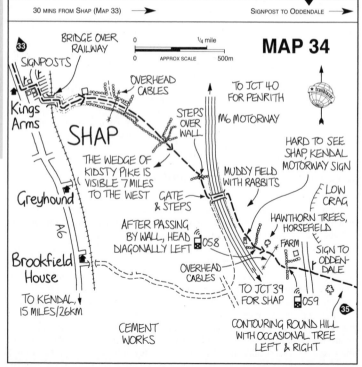

30 MINS FROM SHAP (MAP 33) ⟶   SIGNPOST TO ODDENDALE ⟶

MAP 34

33 BRIDGE OVER RAILWAY

0   ¼ mile
0   APPROX SCALE   500m

SIGNPOSTS

Kings Arms

SHAP

OVERHEAD CABLES

STEPS OVER WALL

TO JCT 40 FOR PENRITH

M6 MOTORWAY

★ trailblaze

THE WEDGE OF KIDSTY PIKE IS VISIBLE 7 MILES TO THE WEST

Greyhound

GATE & STEPS

MUDDY FIELD WITH RABBITS

HARD TO SEE SHAP, KENDAL MOTORWAY SIGN

LOW CRAG

A6

AFTER PASSING BY WALL, HEAD DIAGONALLY LEFT

058

HAWTHORN TREES, HORSEFIELD

FARM

SIGN TO ODDEN-DALE

Brookfield House

OVERHEAD CABLES

TO JCT 39 FOR SHAP

059

TO KENDAL, 15 MILES/26KM

CEMENT WORKS

CONTOURING ROUND HILL WITH OCCASIONAL TREE LEFT & RIGHT

35

ROUTE GUIDE AND MAPS

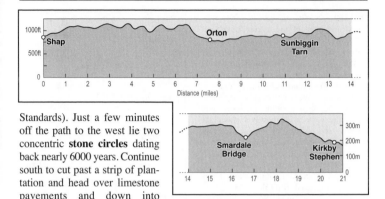

Standards). Just a few minutes off the path to the west lie two concentric **stone circles** dating back nearly 6000 years. Continue south to cut past a strip of plantation and head over limestone pavements and down into Lyvennet Beck. Now you turn north-east, passing **Robin Hood's Grave** (Map 37), a large cairn in a shallow fold in the moor and certainly not the grave of the man who gives his name to the bay that is the ultimate destination on this path.

Eventually, with the Howgills bubbling up ahead, the trail drops down to a road and follows it south to the B6260, before leaving the tarmac to drop left down again past a well-preserved **limekiln** above Broadfell Farm. Those bound for Orton, whose churchtower has been clearly visible since the brow of the hill, should continue down through the farm from here; the rest march resolutely on to join the farm's driveway and continue east round Orton Scar.

R O U T E   G U I D E   A N D   M A P S

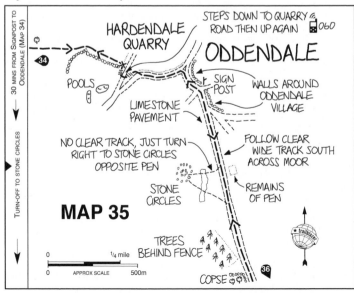

30 MINS FROM SIGNPOST TO ODDENDALE (MAP 34)

TURN-OFF TO STONE CIRCLES

34

HARDENDALE QUARRY

POOLS

LIMESTONE PAVEMENT

NO CLEAR TRACK, JUST TURN RIGHT TO STONE CIRCLES OPPOSITE PEN

STONE CIRCLES

MAP 35

STEPS DOWN TO QUARRY ROAD THEN UP AGAIN 📱060

ODDENDALE

SIGN POST

WALLS AROUND ODDENDALE VILLAGE

FOLLOW CLEAR WIDE TRACK SOUTH ACROSS MOOR

REMAINS OF PEN

TREES BEHIND FENCE

COPSE

36

0   ¼ mile
0   APPROX SCALE   500m

★ trailblazer

ORTON

Orton is typical of the quaint 'unknown' villages in which the Coast to Coast specialises, but one with a couple of surprises in store for walkers. For one thing there's the **church** dating back to 1293 below which are the remains of some **pillories** or stocks once used to punish wrongdoers. Perhaps they were spending too much time round the back of **Kennedy's chocolate factory** (see p154). Popping in here you may think you've been transported to a chocolaterie in some upmarket Parisian suburb but no, this is Orton, east Cumbria.

The well-stocked **village shop** (Mon-Sat 8am-6pm; **post office** hours Mon, Tues & Fri 9am-1pm, 2-5pm, Wed & Sat 9am-noon, closed Thur) is nearby, in rude health we're pleased to report and with enough provisions to restock your travelling larder. Stagecoach's **Bus** No 106 (Kendal to Penrith and vice versa) stops in the village; see pp52-5 for details.

Where to stay and eat

Recommended time and again by Coast to Coasters, **Barn House** (☎ 015396 24259, 🖳 www.thebarnhouseorton.co.uk; 1D/2T; all en suite; ➖; ⓛ £7; WI-FI) on the southern side of the village on Raisbeck Rd has just three rooms but each is supremely comfortable, with Judith and Peter serving scones and jam on arrival. B&B starts at £41pp (£51 for sgl occ).

The George Hotel (☎ 015396 26046, 🖳 www.thegeorgehotelorton.co.uk; 1S/3D/3T/1Qd; most en suite, others share bathroom; ➖; ⓛ £6.50) is in the centre of town. B&B costs £40pp (sgl £35, sgl occ £35-50). They have a drying room but also provide a laundry service (£5, £6 to dry). They now offer **camping** space for 4-5 tents in part of the beer garden for £5 per pitch, which is reasonable, though the cost of using the bathroom/➖ is £6, which is less so. *New House Farm* (off Map 38; ☎ 015396 24324) offers **camping** (£8pp; £1 for a shower; 🐾; ⓛ available) with very basic facilities – perhaps they've now upgraded their showers. The farm is best reached from Knott Lane (Map 38). Follow Knott Lane south to the T-junction. Turn left and

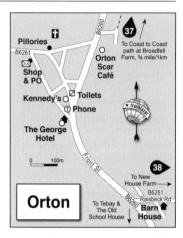

continue for five minutes. It's on the right.

About three miles south of Orton, in **Tebay** there's the commodious *Old School House* (☎ 015396 24286, 🖳 theoldschool tebay.co.uk; 1S/2D/1Tr/1 6-bed room; all en suite; 🐾 £5; WI-FI; ⓛ £5.50) charges £35pp for B&B. Since they are a little way out they are happy to pick walkers up if arranged at the time of booking. Also if requested in advance they can provide an evening meal (around £15) and do laundry & ironing for a small charge. Another place recommended by a reader is *Primrose Cottage* (☎ 01539 624791, 🖳 primrosecottagecumbria.co.uk; 2D/1T; ➖, WI-FI) a very smart B&B with flat-screen TVs in every room; rates are £35pp in the twin, £37.50pp in the double (single occupancy from £45). They will also pick you up from Orton at the end of your walk, and drop you off again the next day (£2.50 each way). They also have their own holiday flat (1D; £40pp; 🐾£10) with its own lounge and wet room.

Orton Scar Café (☎ 015396 24421; 🖳 www.silveryard.co.uk; Mon-Sat 9am-5pm, Sun 10am-4pm in summer; WI-FI) is a lovely place on the edge of the village. You can sit inside or out and they serve gourmet sandwiches, pies, stews and hot filled buns all made from locally-sourced ingredients. You could make yourself an excellent picnic from the deli. For pub grub there's *The*

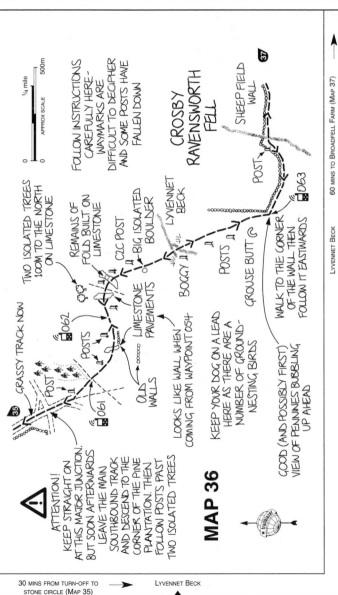

MAP 36

ATTENTION!
KEEP STRAIGHT ON
AT THIS MAJOR JUNCTION.
BUT SOON AFTERWARDS
LEAVE THE MAIN
SOUTHBOUND TRACK
AND DESCEND TO THE
CORNER OF THE PINE
PLANTATION. THEN
FOLLOW POSTS PAST
TWO ISOLATED TREES

35 GRASSY TRACK NOW

POST

061

POSTS

062

OLD WALLS

LIMESTONE PAVEMENTS

LOOKS LIKE WALL WHEN
COMING FROM WAYPOINT 054

KEEP YOUR DOG ON A LEAD
HERE AS THERE ARE A
NUMBER OF GROUND-
NESTING BIRDS

GOOD (AND POSSIBLY FIRST)
VIEW OF PENNINES BUBBLING
UP AHEAD

TWO ISOLATED TREES
100M TO THE NORTH
ON LIMESTONE

REMAINS OF
FOLD BUILT ON
LIMESTONE

C2C POST

BIG ISOLATED
BOULDER

LYVENNET
BECK

BOGGY

POSTS

GROUSE BUTT

WALK TO THE CORNER
OF THE WALL THEN
FOLLOW IT EASTWARDS

FOLLOW INSTRUCTIONS
CAREFULLY HERE-
WAYMARKS ARE
DIFFICULT TO DECIPHER
AND SOME POSTS HAVE
FALLEN DOWN

CROSBY
RAVENSWORTH
FELL

SHEEP FIELD
WALL

POST

37

063

APPROX SCALE
0   ¼ mile
0   500m

30 MINS FROM TURN-OFF TO
STONE CIRCLE (MAP 35) ➤ LYVENNET BECK

LYVENNET BECK 60 MINS TO BROADFELL FARM (MAP 37)

George Hotel (daily noon-2.30pm & 6-8.30pm; evenings only on Mon & Tue in winter). There are 12" pizzas from £7.50. You can't leave Orton without sampling the chocolate at *Kennedy's* (🖳 www.kennedys chocolates.co.uk; Mon-Sat 9am-5pm; Sun

11am-5pm; café shuts 30 mins earlier) in their coffee house and ice-cream parlour. For a chocoholic overdose, their chocolate cake washed down with a hot chocolate ought to hit the mark – followed by a Coast to Coast souvenir chocolate bar (£4.95), of course!

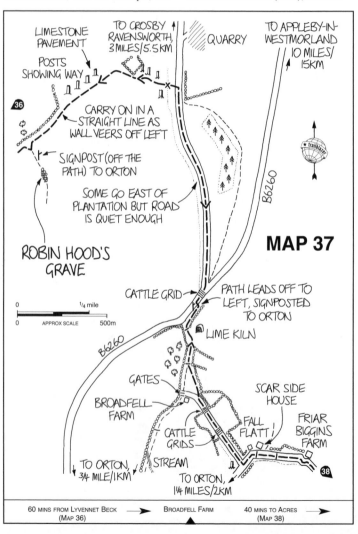

LIMESTONE PAVEMENT

POSTS SHOWING WAY

TO CROSBY RAVENSWORTH, 3 MILES/5.5KM

QUARRY

TO APPLEBY-IN-WESTMORLAND 10 MILES/15KM

36

CARRY ON IN A STRAIGHT LINE AS WALL VEERS OFF LEFT

SIGNPOST (OFF THE PATH) TO ORTON

SOME GO EAST OF PLANTATION BUT ROAD IS QUIET ENOUGH

ROBIN HOOD'S GRAVE

B6260

★ trailblazer

MAP 37

0 ¼ mile

0 APPROX SCALE 500m

B6260

CATTLE GRID

PATH LEADS OFF TO LEFT, SIGNPOSTED TO ORTON

LIME KILN

GATES

BROADFELL FARM

CATTLE GRIDS

SCAR SIDE HOUSE

FALL FLATT

FRIAR BIGGINS FARM

38

TO ORTON, 3/4 MILE/1KM

STREAM

TO ORTON, 1¼ MILES/2KM

60 MINS FROM LYVENNET BECK ⟶ (MAP 36) BROADFELL FARM 40 MINS TO ACRES ⟶ (MAP 38)

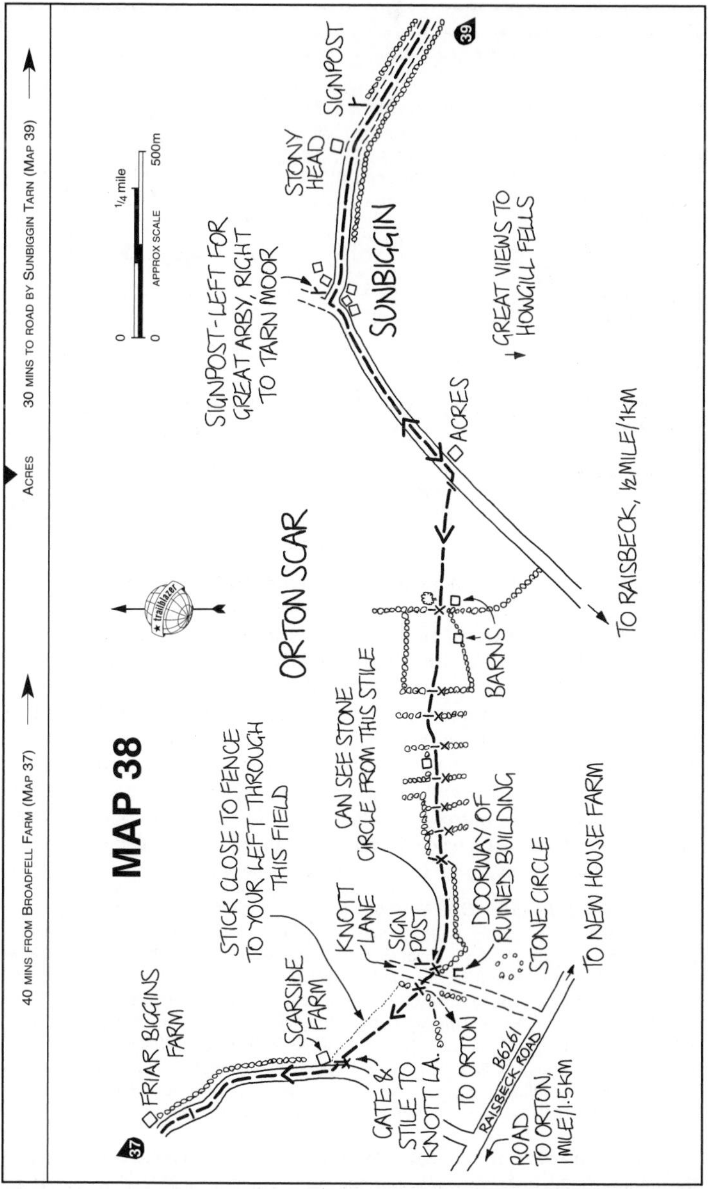

40 mins from Broadfell Farm (Map 37)
Acres
30 mins to road by Sunbiggin Tarn (Map 39)
MAP 38
0
0
1/4 mile
500m
APPROX SCALE
trailblazer
ORTON SCAR
SIGNPOST-LEFT FOR GREAT ARBY, RIGHT TO TARN MOOR
STONY HEAD
SIGNPOST
SUNBIGGIN
GREAT VIEWS TO HOWGILL FELLS
ACRES
TO RAISBECK, ½MILE/1KM
BARNS
CAN SEE STONE CIRCLE FROM THIS STILE
STICK CLOSE TO FENCE TO YOUR LEFT THROUGH THIS FIELD
KNOTT LANE
SIGN POST
DOORWAY OF RUINED BUILDING
STONE CIRCLE
TO NEW HOUSE FARM
SCARSIDE FARM
FRIAR BIGGINS FARM
GATE & STILE TO KNOTT LA.
TO ORTON
B6261
RAISBECK ROAD
ROAD TO ORTON, 1 MILE/1.5KM
37
39

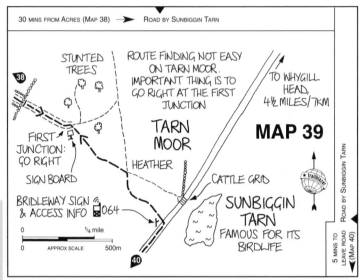

There's a second and more impressive **stone circle** (Map 38) a mile to the east of Orton on the Coast to Coast path. It can be reached, for those who didn't take the Orton detour, via a driveable track running east from Broadfell Farm (Map 37). (Those who *did* visit Orton can rejoin this track at the stone circle by taking the Raisbeck road east and heading up Knott Lane).

After this, the trail continues east across walled fields and on to **Tarn Moor** (Map 39). All being well you'll emerge from the moor on a back road alongside **Sunbiggin Tarn**, an important bird sanctuary. Here you turn briefly south and then cut directly east across the heather-clad moor; you'll have seen the sign boards indicating the course, a path the Coast to Coast shares with the Dales Way. You reach another lane on the far side of the moor. (For the accommodation options at Newbiggin-on-Lune follow this lane south).

NEWBIGGIN-ON-LUNE OFF MAP 40
About a mile and a quarter south of the point where the path crosses a lane after Ravenstonedale Moor you'll find this little village nestling at the foot of Howgill fells.

Well established *Tranna Hill* (☎ 01539 623227, 🖥 www.trannahill.co.uk; 1D/1T/ 1D or T or F; WI-FI; ⓛ £5) has a cosy lounge with a woodburning stove. B&B starts at £34pp (£48 sgl occ); for supper,

lifts are available to and from the pub.

To the north of the village is *Brownber Hall Country House* (☎ 015396 23208, 🖥 www.brownberhall.co.uk; 3S/5D/1T/1Tr; all en suite or with private facilities; 🐾 by prior arrangement £5 per room; ⓛ £5; WI-FI) where B&B is from £40-45 per person. They don't do evening meals but can arrange lifts to somewhere that does, by prior arrangement. However, they are licensed.

To continue on the Coast to Coast don't follow the lane but cross it, head past the underground reservoir and continue east. Tracking a thread of dry-stone

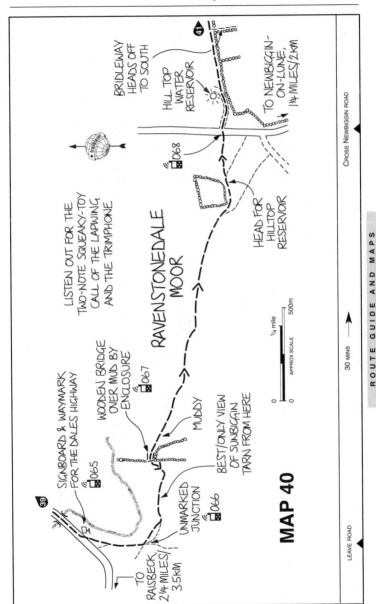

LISTEN OUT FOR THE TWO-NOTE SQUEAKY-TOY CALL OF THE LAPWING AND THE TRIMPHONE

BRIDLEWAY HEADS OFF TO SOUTH

HILL TOP WATER RESERVOIR

TO NEWBIGGIN-ON-LUNE, 1¼ MILES/2KM

RAVENSTONEDALE MOOR

📷068

HEAD FOR HILLTOP RESERVOIR

SIGNBOARD & WAYMARK FOR THE DALES HIGHWAY

📷065

WOODEN BRIDGE OVER MUD BY ENCLOSURE

📷067

MUDDY

BEST/ONLY VIEW OF SUNBIGGIN TARN FROM HERE

UNMARKED JUNCTION

📷066

MAP 40

TO RAISBECK, 2¼ MILES/3.5KM

APPROX SCALE
0 — ¼ mile
0 — 500m

30 MINS

LEAVE ROAD

CROSS NEWBIGGIN ROAD

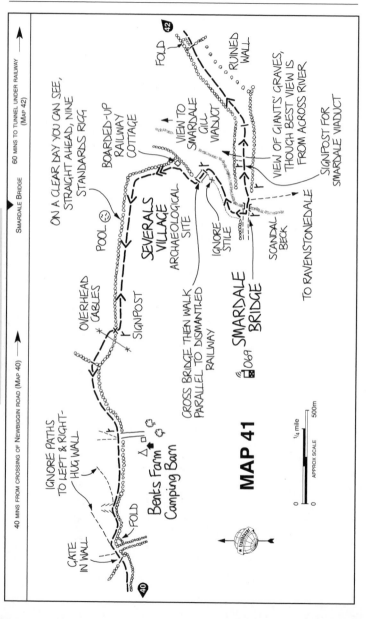

40 MINS FROM CROSSING OF NEWBIGGIN ROAD (MAP 40) ➤

SMARDALE BRIDGE ◀

60 MINS TO TUNNEL UNDER RAILWAY (MAP 42) ➤

42

FOLD

FOLD

RUINED WALL

ON A CLEAR DAY YOU CAN SEE, STRAIGHT AHEAD, NINE STANDARDS RIGG

BOARDED-UP RAILWAY COTTAGE

VIEW TO SMARDALE GILL VIADUCT

VIEW OF GIANTS' GRAVES, THOUGH BEST VIEW IS FROM ACROSS RIVER

SIGNPOST FOR SMARDALE VIADUCT

POOL ☺

SEVERALS VILLAGE ARCHAEOLOGICAL SITE

IGNORE STILE

OVERHEAD CABLES

SIGNPOST

SCANDAL BECK

TO RAVENSTONEDALE

CROSS BRIDGE THEN WALK PARALLEL TO DISMANTLED RAILWAY

SMARDALE BRIDGE

069

IGNORE PATHS TO LEFT & RIGHT- HUG WALL

Bents Farm Camping Barn

FOLD

GATE IN WALL

40

MAP 41

¼ mile

APPROX SCALE

0   500m

trailblazer

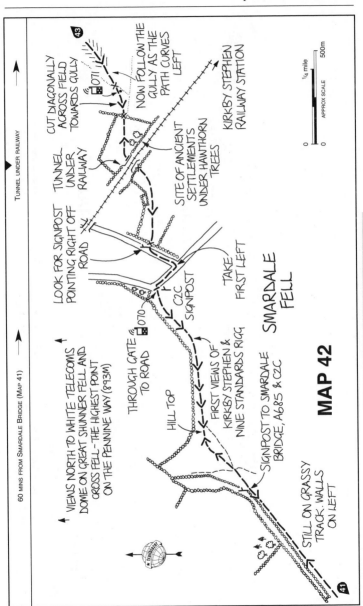

60 MINS FROM SMARDALE BRIDGE (MAP 41) →

TUNNEL UNDER RAILWAY

43

CUT DIAGONALLY ACROSS FIELD TOWARDS GULLY

011

NOW FOLLOW THE GULLY AS THE PATH CURVES LEFT

TUNNEL UNDER RAILWAY

TUNNEL UNDER RAILWAY

LOOK FOR SIGNPOST POINTING RIGHT OFF ROAD

KIRKBY STEPHEN RAILWAY STATION

SITE OF ANCIENT SETTLEMENTS UNDER HAWTHORN TREES

C2C SIGNPOST

TAKE FIRST LEFT

← VIEWS NORTH TO WHITE TELECOMS DOME ON GREAT SHUNNER FELL AND CROSS FELL – THE HIGHEST POINT ON THE PENNINE WAY (893M)

THROUGH GATE TO ROAD

010

SMARDALE FELL

HILL TOP

FIRST VIEWS OF KIRKBY STEPHEN & NINE STANDARDS RIGG

MAP 42

SIGNPOST TO SMARDALE BRIDGE, A685 & C2C

STILL ON GRASSY TRACK. WALLS ON LEFT

41

trailblazer

0   500m

0   ¼ mile

APPROX SCALE

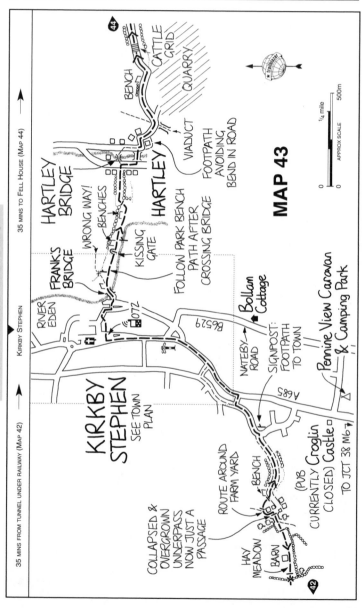

MAP 43

APPROX SCALE

0   ¼ mile
0   500m

44

CATTLE
GRID

QUARRY

BENCH

VIADUCT

FOOTPATH
AVOIDING
BEND IN ROAD

HARTLEY
BRIDGE

WRONG WAY!

BENCHES

FRANKS
BRIDGE

RIVER
EDEN

KISSING
GATE

HARTLEY

FOLLOW PARK BENCH
PATH AFTER
CROSSING BRIDGE

072

Bollan
Cottage

B6529

NATEBY
ROAD

SIGNPOST:
FOOTPATH
TO TOWN

A685

Pennine View Caravan
& Camping Park

KIRKBY
STEPHEN

SEE TOWN
PLAN

ROUTE AROUND
FARM YARD

BENCH

(PUB
CURRENTLY
CLOSED) Croglin
Castle

TO JCT 38 M6

COLLAPSED &
OVERGROWN
UNDERPASS
NOW JUST A
PASSAGE

HAY
MEADOW

BARN

42

walls (see box p191) below Great Ewe Fell will bring you past **Bents Farm** (Map 41; bookings ☎ 01768 774301, information ☎ 01768 371760, 🖳 www .bentscampingbarn.co.uk; toilets but no showers; open all year) with a **camping barn** which sleeps 14 (bed £10pp) and **camping** from £4pp. Booking is recommended as occasionally groups take over the whole barn, which has a well-equipped kitchen. You may also need to book for a minimum of two nights at weekends for the barn – try negotiating with the owner. There is a coin meter (£1) for electricity and sleeping bags can be hired if necessary.

The next prehistoric site lies a short way past the farm where, having crossed a stile, a signpost used to urge you to stick to the recognised path so as not to disturb the archaeological site (the signpost currently lies forlorn by the nearby wall, waiting to be re-erected). This'll probably come as something of a surprise because, no matter how hard you look, there seems to be nothing remarkable. Satellite imagery reveals that what you're actually looking at is the **Severals Village settlement**, said to be one of the most important prehistoric sites in Britain. The fact that it remains unexcavated does nothing to quell the archaeologists' enthusiasm for the place. Without leaving the path, look for irregular or unnatural depressions and bumps in the land here; it's these undulations that have so excited the archaeologists.

On the opposite side of Scandal Beck lies the final ancient site on this stage: the so-called **Giants' Graves** (called 'pillow mounds' on 25k OS maps) are a series of long narrow mounds which, some say, may have been prehistoric rabbit enclosures.

Dropping down to the bridge across Scandal Beck, more recent archeological evidence can be spied in the form of the distant **Smardale Gill viaduct** along a former railway that once joined Kirkby Stephen to what is now the M6 corridor. Climbing to the crest of Smardale Fell, on a clear day the Pennines rise before you like a standing wave with the cairns on Nine Standards Rigg just visible beyond the quarry west of Kirkby Stephen. Looking north across the Eden valley, with less difficulty you may also spot the white dome of the radio station atop Great Shunner Fell and to the left, Cross Fell, at 893m (2930ft), the highest point on the Pennine Way – but that's a walk for another day.

By now, those nearing Kirkby Stephen will not be mindful of such distant prospects, as slowly the town's churches and then other buildings rise from the wooded vale below.

KIRKBY STEPHEN   See map p163
Kirkby Stephen (pronounced 'Kirby' Stephen) vies with Richmond as the biggest town on the route, though don't let that fool you into thinking that this place is a metropolis. In fact, Kirkby Stephen is a pleasant and prosperous market town built along the A685 with a population of around 1900, a figure that's swollen considerably during the summer months by walkers, runners, cyclists and other outdoor *bon*

viveurs. If you're due a rest after the Lakeland stages, a day off in town is the tonic to numerous woes.

There've been **markets** in Kirkby Stephen since at least 1361 when it was granted a market charter. Note the cobbled outline on the market square's floor; it marks the outer limits of a former bull-baiting area, a popular pastime in the town until 1820 when a bull broke free and ran amok, killing a number of bystanders.

The principal tourist attraction in Kirkby Stephen is the 13th-century **church**, which is known locally as the Cathedral of the Dales. The distinctive red sandstone church (part of the same formation found at St Bees) is separated from the market square by the peaceful lawn of the **cloisters**. On entering the main gate, on your right is the **Trupp Stone**, where until 1836 the locals' tithes were collected. Take half an hour or so to wander around inside the church. It is built on the site of a Saxon church, though the earliest feature (the nave) of the present structure dates only to 1220. Features to look out for include the 17th-century **font**, a great stone lump at the rear of the church, and the nearby **bread shelves**, used for distributing bread to the poor. There's also a **Norman coffin** by the north wall, unearthed in 1980 during restoration work, and a glass display cabinet housing old Bibles and, curiously, a **boar's tusk**, said to belong to the last wild boar shot in England. The church's most interesting feature, however, is the 8th-century **Loki Stone** facing the main door, a metre-high block carved by the Vikings with the horned figure of the Norse god Loki.

Other Kirkby Stephen sites of note include the old and much-photographed **signpost** at the southern end of town, where the distances are given in miles and furlongs; and the curious but attractive **stone seats** in the form of sheep, that stand by the door of the visitor centre. Carved by artist Keith Alexander, they're reputed to increase the fertility of any who sit upon them, ovine or otherwise. **Frank's Bridge** is a pretty double-arched stone footbridge, a quiet place to sit by the grassy riverbank and feed the ducks. It's thought to be named after a local brewer, Frank Birkbeck, who lived here in the 19th century.

One other item of note is the flock of **parrots** that fly around town during the day before returning home to their owner, a local resident, at dusk. Since the first edition of our guide we've been writing about these birds, without ever seeing them and beginning to think we'd either been the victim of a hoax or, if they had really existed at one time, we could be fairly certain that they did no longer. However, on our last trip we finally saw three beautiful blue and yellow parrots in the trees near the Pennine View campsite. So keep your eyes peeled!

Services

Kirkby Stephen has become the spiritual (if not *quite* the geographical) heart of the Coast to Coast path. Packhorse (see p29) operate out of the town, and those who opt to take advantage of their 'taxi' service will spend the night in Kirkby Stephen before being shuttled to St Bees the next morning. If you've left your car here, the Packhorse van arrives back in town from Robin Hood's Bay at around 6.15pm.

The **visitor centre** (☎ 017683 71199; 🖳 www.kirkby-stephen.com; Easter to Oct daily 10am-5pm, Nov to Easter Mon, Wed, Fri & Sat 11am-3pm) is crammed with brochures and the staff are knowledgeable. Nearby is the **bookshop**, open Mon/Wed/Fri/Sat, 10am-1pm and 2-5pm. By the church is the **library** (☎ 017683 71775; Mon & Fri 10am-12.30pm & 1.30-5pm, to 6pm on Wed, Sat 10am-1pm) with **internet** connection (£1 for 60 mins). There are two **banks** with **cash machines**. The **post office** (Mon-Fri 9am-5.30pm, Sat 9am-12.30pm) is at the back of Emporium Deli.

The best **supermarket** in the town centre is the Co-op (Mon-Sun 7am-10pm). There's also a Spar (Mon-Sat 8am-10.30pm, Sun 9am-10.30pm) at the southern end of town closer to the campsite and a bigger Co-op at the northern end of town past the chippy. There's a **launderette** down the lane between the Emporium/post office and a chip shop.

Eden Outdoors (☎ 017683 72431; Mon-Sat 9am-5pm) is very well stocked with outdoor gear, maps and books. They also offer out-of-hours emergency help with kit via mobile numbers posted on the shop door. A bigger rival, **Mad About Mountains** (9am-5.30pm) has opened further down the road on the opposite side; the owner usually keeps it open until 7pm in summer, recognising that many C2C walkers often don't arrive in town until late following the long haul from Shap. Blister kits and other medications are on sale at Green Tree **pharmacy** (Mon, Tues, Wed & Fri 9am-5.30pm, Thurs to 5pm, Sat 9am-1pm).

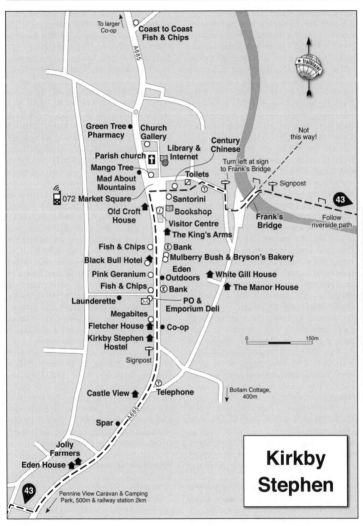

Map labels:
To larger Co-op
Coast to Coast Fish & Chips
Green Tree Pharmacy
Church Gallery
Century Chinese
Not this way!
Parish church
Library & Internet
Turn left at sign to Frank's Bridge
Signpost
Mango Tree
Toilets
Mad About Mountains
072 Market Square
Santorini
43
Old Croft House
Bookshop
Frank's Bridge
Follow riverside path
Visitor Centre
The King's Arms
Fish & Chips
Bank
Black Bull Hotel
Mulberry Bush & Bryson's Bakery
Pink Geranium
Eden Outdoors
White Gill House
Fish & Chips
Bank
The Manor House
Launderette
PO & Emporium Deli
Megabites
Fletcher House
Co-op
Kirkby Stephen Hostel
Signpost
0   150m
Castle View
Telephone
Bollam Cottage, 400m
Spar
Kirkby Stephen
Jolly Farmers
Eden House
43
Pennine View Caravan & Camping Park, 500m & railway station 2km

Where to stay

The Pennine View Caravan and Camping Park (Map 43; ☎ 017683 71717; 🐾; Mar-Oct) is a secure, manicured, no-nonsense spot just on the southern outskirts of town, with a laundry room and a clean ablutions block. Camping costs £9.25pp with a large,

flat grassy area set aside for tents away from the motorhomes and caravans. Use of the shower facilities is included in the charge. Long-term parking (£3.75 per car per day) is available.

Kirkby Stephen Hostel (☎ 017683 71793 or ☎ 07812 558525, 🖥 www.kirk

bystephenhostel.co.uk; 38 beds, 2T/2Qd/3 x 6 beds, 1 x 8 beds; one twin en suite, others share shower facilities; 🐾 by arrangement; WI-FI; (Ⓛ) is an independent hostel grandly housed in a former Methodist chapel in the centre of town and run by the welcoming Denise. Rates are from £20pp; a cooked breakfast is available for £6pp. Evening meals (around £12) can also be provided subject to prior arrangement. However, there are self-catering facilities. Check-in is after 5pm only.

Of the B&Bs on the walk, we've received many recommendations for the *Old Croft House* (☎ 017683 71638, 🖥 www.theoldcrofthouse.com; 1S/2D/1T; all with private facilities; 🛏; WI-FI; Ⓛ £5). It's a lovely old Georgian townhouse with a warm, oak-panelled interior full of books, made all the better by the warmth and generosity of the owners who know what Coasters want, welcoming guests with freshly baked cakes and even providing foot spas in the rooms! They also offer meals in the evenings (if booked in advance), with a choice of 2-/3-course menus for around £16/20. B&B costs £37-40pp.

Next to the hostel and a favourite with many readers, with spacious, well-equipped rooms *Fletcher House* (☎ 017683 71013, 🖥 www.fletcherhouse.co .uk; 2D/1T/1Tr; all en suite; 🛏; WI-FI; Ⓛ £5-6) offers B&B for £37.50pp (sgl occ £55). There's also a drying room, guest lounge and a foot spa.

There's tea and cupcakes on arrival at *Castle View* (☎ 07894 066976, 🖥 castleviewbandb.wordpress.com; 3D or T, all en suite; 🛏, WI-FI; Ⓛ £6) at 21 High Street, with rooms from £38 per person (£60 sgl occ). There's also a drying room. Check-in is after 4pm only.

Towards the southern end of town at 63 High St *The Jolly Farmers Guest House* (☎ 017683 71063; 🖥 www.thejolly farmers.co.uk; 4D/5T; all en suite; 🛏; 🐾 £8; WI-FI; Ⓛ £6) is a converted pub with hydro-spa bath in one room which should help take those aches away, and of course tea and scones on arrival. B&B costs from £38pp (sgl occ £45-55). Next door, *Eden House* (☎ 017683 71891, 🖥 www.eden-housebandb.co.uk; 1D/1T, en suite, 🛏; WI-

FI); is run by Coast to Coast veterans and is a relaxing, welcoming addition to the accommodation scene in Kirkby Stephen. Rates are £32.50pp, single occupancy £45. Note that it is open April to September only.

The Black Bull Hotel (☎ 017683 71237, 🖥 www.blackbullkirkbystephen .co .uk; 1S/5D/3T; all en suite; 🛏; 🐾 £5; WI-FI; Ⓛ £6.50), 38 Market Sq, gets good reports and charges £37.50pp for B&B (sgl £45, sgl occ £65). *The Kings Arms* (☎ 017683 72906, 🖥 www.lakelandinns.net/ thekingsarms; 2T/4D/2F; some en suite; 🛏; 🐾; WI-FI; Ⓛ £6.95), Market St, charges £35pp for B&B in the doubles and twins, £100 for the family rooms.

To the east of the main road on Melbecks, *White Gill House* (☎ 017683 72238, 🖥 barbwgh@onetel.com; 1D/1T; both en suite; 🛏; WI-FI; Ⓛ £5) has been highly recommended by many readers; the B&B's lovely owners, Ken & Barbie (really), charge £37pp. They also have drying facilities. Nearby is *The Manor House* (☎ 017683 72757, 🖥 Jean_Leeson@hotmail .com; 1D/1Qd; en suite; 🐾; WI-FI; Ⓛ £5) offering B&B in their plush Georgian town house for £35pp (sgl occ £50). They're happy to do laundry (£5) and if requested in advance will take you to the station.

A five-minute walk from the very heart of town on Nateby Rd is lovely *Bollam Cottage* (Map 43; ☎ 017683 72038, 🖥 www.bollamcottage.co.uk; 2D or T/1D; all en suite; 🛏; WI-FI; Ⓛ £6; Mar-Oct), with oak beams and a wood burner. B&B costs £38pp (sgl occ from £55). They have drying facilities and are happy to do laundry. Guests also have a separate lounge.

Where to eat and drink

To make up a picnic, you'll find fair value at *Megabite Baguettes* (Mon-Sat 8.30am-2.30pm, Sun 10am-2pm), for filled rolls and salad boxes, and *Bryson's Bakery* (🖥 www.brysonsofkeswick.co.uk; Mon-Sat 8am-4pm, Sun 9am-2.30pm) for a mouth-watering range of speciality breads and sandwiches. More upmarket is *The Emporium Deli* (🖥 www.theedenempori um.co.uk; Mon-Fri 9am-5.30pm, Sat 9am-2pm) nearby, with a great selection of the world's finer foodstuffs.

As for tearooms, *Pink Geranium* (☎ 017683 71586; Wed-Sat 9am-4.30pm, Sun 9am-4pm) gives you a great big pot of tea and there's a good range of cakes and light lunches. *The Mulberry Bush* (☎ 017683 71572) is a popular Kirkby Stephen café (Mon-Sat 9am-5pm, Sun 10am-5pm; winter Mon-Sat 9am-4pm, Sun 10-4pm).

Church Gallery (☎ 017683 72395, 💻 www.church-gallery.co.uk; Mon-Sat 9am-5pm, Sun 11am-5pm) at the top end of town is a bit of a find: pretty much the only place that welcomes dogs, this gift shop has a small, great-value self-service café serving drinks and cakes. They also have a nice little outdoor area facing the church.

On the main street there are no fewer than three **chippies** including the *Coast to Coast* (Thur-Sun 11.30am-1.30pm & 4.30-8pm) dating from 1929 and said to be Wainwright's favourite.

For Chinese, there's *Century Chinese Restaurant* (☎ 017683 72828; Tue-Sun 5-11pm) at the back of the Market Square serving the usual array of Oriental fare. Nearby, *Santorini* (☎ 017683 72323; daily 4-11pm) is Kirkby Stephen's fast-food shack. No town is complete without a curryhouse and Kirkby Stephen's is one of the best places to eat here. It's right in the middle of town by the market square; most dishes in the *Mango Tree* (☎ 017683 74960) are priced around £9.

Currently the best place to eat in town is *The Black Bull* (see Where to stay; daily noon-9pm, lunch menu till 6pm, evening meal from 6pm). Pan roast duck breast with a juniper sausage and bramble sauce is £15 and there's a range of locally-reared steaks (£13.50-19.50) and set menus from £16.

Transport   (see also pp52-5)

Kirkby Stephen is on the Carlisle to Leeds railway line. The **train** station, the only one, apart from St Bees, on the Coast to Coast path, lies over a mile south of the town.

As for **buses**, Grand Prix Coaches' No 563 runs to Penrith (1hr) and back from the Market Square Mon-Sat.

Finally, for a **taxi** call ☎ 017683 71682 or ☎ 017683 72557.

STAGE 7: KIRKBY STEPHEN TO KELD   MAPS 43-50

Introduction

This **13-mile (21km, 5-6hrs via the high routes)** stage is something of a red-letter day. Not only do you cross the **Pennines** – the so-called backbone of the British Isles across whose flanks the Industrial Revolution gathered pace 200 years ago – but in doing so you cross the **watershed** on the Coast to Coast. From the summit at Nine Standards Rigg all rivers, including the infant headwaters of the Swale which you'll track for the next few days, flow eastwards to drain into the North Sea. In a flush of optimism you could say it's downhill all the way (but don't be fooled – it's not!).

You also pass from the county of Cumbria into **Yorkshire**, your home for the rest of the trek and finally, by the end of this stage by our reckoning you're very close to the halfway point, having completed over 90 miles of the 190-odd total.

Yet in spite of these significant landmarks, the one thing that most walkers remember about the transit of the Pennines is the **peat bogs** they have to negotiate along the way. The maps point out the boggiest sections and, on the higher of the **three colour-coded routes** (see pp167-70), it's a good time to don gaiters if you have them. It's not so bad on the way up to Nine Standards. But afterwards it's like a different route, the path (or rather 'paths', there being three of them) all but disappearing and the waymarking minimal, and only really visible by someone with excellent eyesight on a clear day. And then there are the bogs themselves, where many a trekker has been injured and many more have

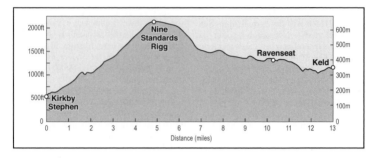

lost boots, dignity – and even the will to carry on – in the moist, tenacious embrace of these silent dangers. If you do succumb to the mires, cheer yourself up with the thought that at the end of this stage you'll be spending the night in the gentle pastoral scenery of **Swaledale**, the most northerly of Yorkshire's Dales and some say its loveliest.

The route
From Kirkby Stephen you cross the Eden river at Frank's Bridge (Map 43) and continue up to **Hartley** village.

From here follow the lane uphill past the huge quarry – a strenuous start to the day. At the end lies a wide dirt track up Hartley Fell where, five miles from town, the path divides (Map 45, WPT 073): the red and blue routes head east up the hill to the Nine Standards, while the green route parallels a stone wall before striking off over a rising moorland path to the quiet, B6270 Kirkby Stephen–Keld road. The three routes are described in more detail below.

The three routes over the moors Due to severe erosion of the peat by walkers as well as a lack of investment to do something about it, there are **three colour-coded paths** across the Pennines to Keld, the exact route you take depending on the time of year or weather conditions, though most walkers continue to ignore the seasonal guidelines. These three routes are marked on Maps 45a, 46 and 47. They initially diverge at a signpost for Nine Standards (Map 45, WPT 073) at which point boggy episodes set in whichever route you take. As we mentioned before, the waymarking is terrible – particularly on the Red and Blue routes – so follow our instructions carefully. Furthermore, the junction where the red and blue paths separate really has been ravaged by erosion from your predecessors' footwear and gets worse year by year. If ever there was a part of the Coast to Coast path that needed lining with stone slabs or duckboards, it's here at the southern end of Nine Standards Rigg which looks like a scene from the Somme, circa 1916.

The **blue and red** high routes are about the same length (4 miles from Nine Standards to the point where all three paths converge just west of Ravenseat). The low-level **green route** is about half a mile shorter (adding up to 12½ miles for this stage) and, with a couple of miles of road, takes about an hour less.

The advice seems to be: if you can't see the Nine Standards by the Mile 5 junction (WPT 073) due to low cloud or mist, you'll see even less when you're up there and may even get lost, so take the green route.

It's possible to have your cake and eat it up here. Should you arrive at the Nine Standards and the weather turns on you, follow a path south for three-quarters of a mile and then head west from the cairns, passing to the west of Rollinson Haggs to pick up Rollinson Gill and so the green route before it reaches the head of Rigg Beck (WPT 075). From there you can follow the road all the way to Keld if you wish.

● **Blue route (Aug-Nov; Maps 45-49; 3hrs 20mins from where the green route separates)** Weather permitting, this is the route to choose to get the full Pennine experience (or should that be immersion?) Up to Nine Standards (WPT 082), just 30 minutes from the junction with the green route it matches the red route. Heading south past the **trig point** (662m) and the low ruins to the end of the ridge, at the key junction marked by the mire-bound signpost (WPT 085) this route then takes an eastern course down to Whitsundale Beck. Irregular and ageing posts daubed with forensic traces of light blue paint guide you east down to the Beck, but if you can't rely on seeing them, a compass bearing of

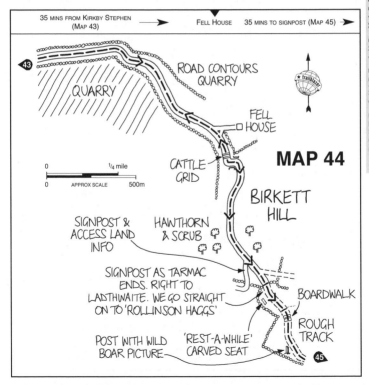

35 MINS FROM KIRKBY STEPHEN (MAP 43) →   FELL HOUSE   35 MINS TO SIGNPOST (MAP 45) →

43

QUARRY

ROAD CONTOURS QUARRY

FELL HOUSE

CATTLE GRID

MAP 44

BIRKETT HILL

0   ¼ mile
0   APPROX SCALE   500m

SIGNPOST & ACCESS LAND INFO

HAWTHORN & SCRUB

SIGNPOST AS TARMAC ENDS. RIGHT TO LADTHWAITE. WE GO STRAIGHT ON TO 'ROLLINSON HAGGS'

BOARDWALK

ROUGH TRACK

POST WITH WILD BOAR PICTURE

'REST-A-WHILE' CARVED SEAT

45

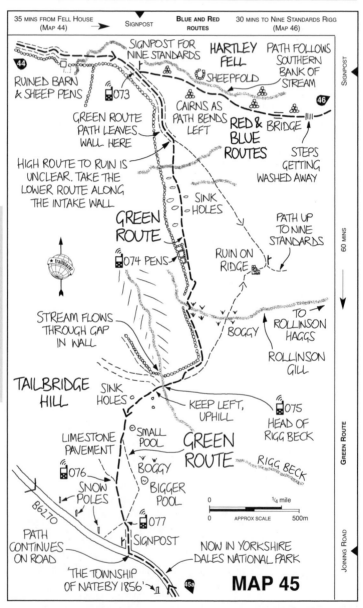

SIGNPOST FOR NINE STANDARDS
HARTLEY FELL
PATH FOLLOWS SOUTHERN BANK OF STREAM
SHEEPFOLD

RUINED BARN & SHEEP PENS

073

GREEN ROUTE PATH LEAVES WALL HERE

CAIRNS AS PATH BENDS LEFT

RED & BLUE ROUTES

BRIDGE

STEPS GETTING WASHED AWAY

HIGH ROUTE TO RUIN IS UNCLEAR. TAKE THE LOWER ROUTE ALONG THE INTAKE WALL

SINK HOLES

GREEN ROUTE

PATH UP TO NINE STANDARDS

★ trailblazer

074 PENS

RUIN ON RIDGE

STREAM FLOWS THROUGH GAP IN WALL

BOGGY

TO ROLLINSON HAGGS

ROLLINSON GILL

TAILBRIDGE HILL

SINK HOLES

KEEP LEFT, UPHILL

075
HEAD OF RIGG BECK

LIMESTONE PAVEMENT

SMALL POOL

GREEN ROUTE

RIGG BECK

076

BOGGY

SNOW POLES

BIGGER POOL

0   ¼ mile

077

0   APPROX SCALE   500m

B6270

PATH CONTINUES ON ROAD

SIGNPOST

NOW IN YORKSHIRE DALES NATIONAL PARK

'THE TOWNSHIP OF NATEBY 1856'

45a

MAP 45

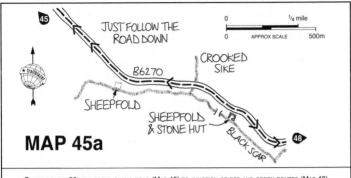

JUST FOLLOW THE ROAD DOWN

CROOKED SIKE

B6270

SHEEPFOLD

SHEEPFOLD & STONE HUT

BLACK SCAR

MAP 45a

0 ¼ mile
0 APPROX SCALE 500m

GREEN ROUTE: 35 MINS FROM JOINING ROAD (MAP 45) TO JUNCTION OF RED AND GREEN ROUTES (MAP 48)

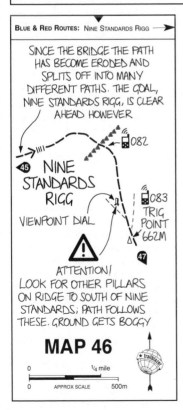

BLUE & RED ROUTES: NINE STANDARDS RIGG

SINCE THE BRIDGE THE PATH HAS BECOME ERODED AND SPLITS OFF INTO MANY DIFFERENT PATHS. THE GOAL, NINE STANDARDS RIGG, IS CLEAR AHEAD HOWEVER

082

NINE STANDARDS RIGG

VIEWPOINT DIAL

083 TRIG POINT 662M

ATTENTION! LOOK FOR OTHER PILLARS ON RIDGE TO SOUTH OF NINE STANDARDS; PATH FOLLOWS THESE. GROUND GETS BOGGY

MAP 46

0 ¼ mile
0 APPROX SCALE 500m

100° or so will do the same job. Once down in the Beck follow its winding course south to a reunion with the other two paths, and just 15 minutes from refreshments at Ravenseat Farm (see p170).

● **Red route (May-July; Maps 45-49; 3hrs 35mins from where the green route separates)** In clear conditions this route is straightforward enough. From the boot-ravaged divergence with the blue route (WPT 085; Map 47) things can get a little boggier still and there are no waymarkers as the route rolls south over the barely noticeable crest of **White Mossy Hill**.

From here you should be able to make out a large **pile of stones** (resembling a ruin) to the south; once there you hope to be able to see a tall stone **pillar** (WPT 096) to the south-south-east. At this point you drop south-east over a small bridge and then south down towards the green route where you turn east onto a track and continue on to the farm at **Ravenseat**. Note that on both these higher routes it's well worth taking your time to **avoid the worst bogs** by all means

ROUTE GUIDE AND MAPS

possible: backtracking, taking a running jump, using a pole, letting your partner go first (always a sensible tactic) or even using them as a plank; whatever works for you. One Trailblazer updater got a bit blasé here and sank down over his knees, while during the last update we met a women on the trail with a broken wrist – caused, so it transpired, by getting her arm caught in the loop of her trekking pole which in turn got caught in the mud. Perhaps those tales of calf-swallowing Pennine bogs were not so exaggerated after all.

● **Green route (Dec-Apr; Maps 45, 45a, 48-49; 3hrs 25mins from where the route separates from the red and blue routes)** This is the simplest route and in inclement weather the best one to take, regardless of the season. Note that we more used path from the junction post at WPT 073 no longer squelches pointlessly halfway up to Rollinson Haggs only to drop down again (as shown on OS maps).

The more practical route follows the intake wall to the moderately impressive head of Rigg Beck which meanders away down its valley.

After Rigg Beck there follows a rise to a section of weathered limestone pavement before you join the B6270. Note too that later on, the point where the green route *officially* leaves the B6270 (Map 48, WPT 078) at a right-hand bend seems to be another pointless hiding to nothing, this time up a gully on all fours. Instead, continue along the road for another minute or so (Map 48) and turn north up the car track. The official path soon joins it. Shortly you'll pass the bootworn scar of the red route coming down from the pillar to join your track (WPT 079), and soon the track ends by a grouse hut.

From here you follow, and occasionally cross, Ney Gill as it wends its way towards the blue route junction at Whitsundale Beck just out of Ravenseat (WPT 080). All in all, on a rainy day keeping below 1700ft (530m) the green route need not be regarded as a 'consolation prize'. Although it's a shame to miss out the mysterious cairns, it's a fine moorland walk in its own right, getting lost is not too great a risk and the road stage along Birkdale is a fine way to appreciate the peaty wastelands without necessarily sinking into them.

Whichever way you've come over the moors, many readers have confirmed that by the time they get to ***Ravenseat Farm*** (Map 49; ☎ 01748 886387; ▢ www .ravenseat.com) they're unable to resist a sit down, **walkers' refreshments** and, when Amanda's around, scones and cream. There's also **camping** (£3.50pp) and for £35pp you can stay (May-Oct) in the delightful **Shepherd's Hut**, a little two-bedded wagon by the river complete with woodburner and breakfast delivered to your door. Evening meals and packed lunches are also available by prior arrangement. There's a separate shower (meter) and toilet 150 yards from the hut.

From Ravenseat the path tracks south alongside the engorged chasm of **Whitsundale Beck**, punctuated with some impressive waterfalls and the finely restored but otherwise unused stone barns or 'laithes' which are a feature of Swaledale. Passing the farmhouse of **Smithy Holme** (Map 50), you can join the B6270 immediately by crossing the bridge, or take the path above the riverside cliff of **Cotterby Scar**. (For once we recommend the road, as it allows you to visit Wainwath Force.) These two paths reunite by the bridge just by ***Park House & Keld Bunk Barn*** (see p175) from where it's a gentle half-mile stroll to what passes for Keld village centre. The tough first half of the Coast to Coast is now behind you; let's just hope your feet are keeping up with the pace.

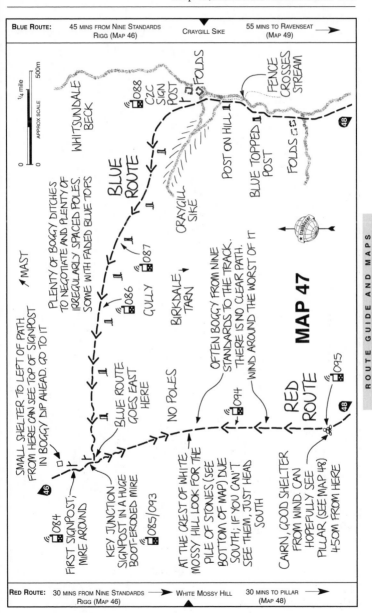

FOLDS

FENCE CROSSES STREAM

☎ 088 C2C SIGN POST

WHITSUNDALE BECK

¼ mile 500m
APPROX SCALE
0   0

POST ON HILL 🚶

BLUE ROUTE

48

BLUE TOPPED POST

FOLDS

▲ MAST

PLENTY OF BOGGY DITCHES TO NEGOTIATE AND PLENTY OF IRREGULARLY SPACED POLES. SOME WITH FADED BLUE TOPS.

CRAYGILL SIKE

☎ 087

☎ 086 GULLY

BIRKDALE TARN

trailblazer

MAP 47

OFTEN BOGGY FROM NINE STANDARDS TO THE TRACK. THERE IS NO CLEAR PATH. WINDS AROUND THE WORST OF IT

RED ROUTE

☎ 095

48

SMALL SHELTER TO LEFT OF PATH FROM HERE CAN SEE TOP OF SIGNPOST IN BOGGY DIP AHEAD. GO TO IT

BLUE ROUTE GOES EAST HERE

NO POLES

☎ 094

46

FIRST SIGNPOST, MIRE AROUND

☎ 084

KEY JUNCTION SIGNPOST IN A HUGE BOOT-ERODED MIRE

☎ 085/093

AT THE CREST OF WHITE MOSSY HILL LOOK FOR THE PILE OF STONES (SEE BOTTOM OF MAP) DUE SOUTH; IF YOU CAN'T SEE THEM, JUST HEAD SOUTH

CAIRN, GOOD SHELTER FROM WIND. CAN HOPEFULLY SEE PILLAR (SEE MAP 48) 450M FROM HERE

ROUTE GUIDE AND MAPS

ROUTE GUIDE AND MAPS

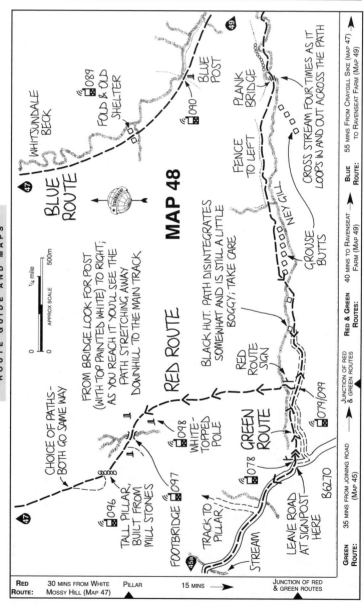

WHITSUNDALE BECK

FOLD & OLD SHELTER 🏕089

BLUE ROUTE 🔵47

BLUE POST 🏕090

MAP 48

CHOICE OF PATHS – BOTH GO SAME WAY

FROM BRIDGE LOOK FOR POST (WITH TOP PAINTED WHITE) TO RIGHT; AS YOU REACH IT YOU'LL SEE THE PATH STRETCHING AWAY DOWNHILL TO THE MAIN TRACK

🔵49

CROSS STREAM FOUR TIMES AS IT LOOPS IN AND OUT ACROSS THE PATH

PLANK BRIDGE

FENCE TO LEFT

NEY GILL

GROUSE BUTTS

RED ROUTE

TALL PILLAR, BUILT FROM MILL STONES 🏕096

🔵47

WHITE-TOPPED POLE 🏕098

FOOTBRIDGE 🏕097

BLACK HUT: PATH DISINTEGRATES SOMEWHAT AND IS STILL A LITTLE BOGGY; TAKE CARE

RED ROUTE SIGN

GREEN ROUTE

🏕078

🏕079/099

TRACK TO PILLAR

🏕45a

STREAM

LEAVE ROAD AT SIGNPOST HERE

B6270

APPROX SCALE
0   1/4 mile
0   500m

RED ROUTE:	30 MINS FROM WHITE MOSSY HILL (MAP 47)	PILLAR ▲	15 MINS ⟶	JUNCTION OF RED & GREEN ROUTES ▲

GREEN ROUTE:	35 MINS FROM JOINING ROAD (MAP 45)	JUNCTION OF RED & GREEN ROUTES ⟶

RED & GREEN ROUTES:	40 MINS TO RAVENSEAT FARM (MAP 49) ⟶

BLUE ROUTE:	55 MINS FROM CRAYGILL SIKE (MAP 47) TO RAVENSEAT FARM (MAP 49) ⟶

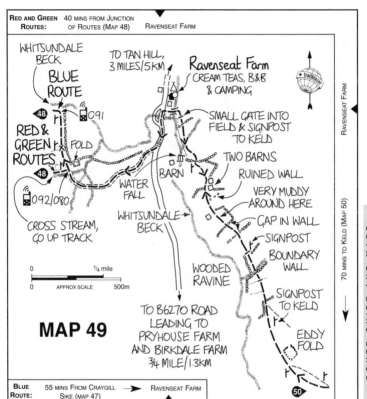

WHITSUNDALE BECK

BLUE ROUTE

TO TAN HILL, 3 MILES/5KM

Ravenseat Farm
CREAM TEAS, B&B & CAMPING

48 [ ]091

RED & GREEN ROUTES [ ] FOLD

48

[ ]092/080

CROSS STREAM, GO UP TRACK

WATER FALL

WHITSUNDALE BECK

BARN

SMALL GATE INTO FIELD & SIGNPOST TO KELD

TWO BARNS

RUINED WALL

VERY MUDDY AROUND HERE

GAP IN WALL

SIGNPOST

BOUNDARY WALL

SIGNPOST TO KELD

EDDY FOLD

WOODED RAVINE

MAP 49

0 ¼ mile
0 APPROX SCALE 500m

TO B6270 ROAD LEADING TO PRYHOUSE FARM AND BIRKDALE FARM ¾ MILE/1.3KM

50

RAVENSEAT FARM

70 MINS TO KELD (MAP 50)

ROUTE GUIDE AND MAPS

KELD   MAP 50, p174

Keld sits at the head of Swaledale where the Coast to Coast dissects the longer, northbound, Pennine Way. Today it's a tiny hill village huddled against the often inclement weather. However, in common with the rest of Swaledale, in the mid-19th century Keld stood at the heart of a local lead-mining industry. Many of the buildings including the two **Methodist chapels** were constructed at this time, as a quick survey of the construction dates carved on the houses' lintels will confirm.

Another building, the old Literary Institute, has been converted into the unstaffed *Keld Countryside & Heritage Centre* (Apr-Oct 8am-9pm, Nov-Mar 8.30am-5pm) which has displays and photographs of local history and farming heritage. One feature allows you to press buttons to hear the thoughts of local people including a farmer and a historian.

Keld is more about water than lead today. The name means 'spring' in Norse and the **Swale River**, dyed brown by the peat, rushes past the village. Do take the opportunity to visit some of the numerous nearby waterfalls – more accurately called cascades or, locally, **forces** (another Norse word) – including Catrake Force, just above the village, and East Gill Force below it.

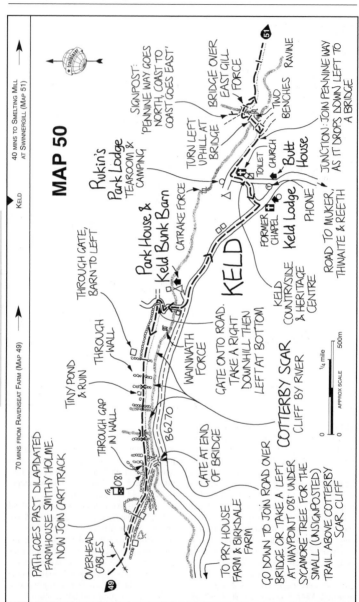

MAP 50

51

BRIDGE OVER EAST GILL FORCE

RAVINE

TWO BENCHES

SIGNPOST: 'PENNINE WAY GOES NORTH, COAST TO COAST GOES EAST'

TURN LEFT UPHILL AT BRIDGE

Rukin's Park Lodge TEAROOM & CAMPING

JUNCTION: JOIN PENNINE WAY AS IT DROPS DOWN LEFT TO A BRIDGE

TOILET

CHURCH

Butt House

Park House & Keld Bunk Barn

THROUGH GATE, BARN TO LEFT

CATRAKE FORCE

FORMER CHAPEL

Keld Lodge PHONE

KELD

KELD COUNTRYSIDE & HERITAGE CENTRE

ROAD TO MUKER, THWAITE & REETH

THROUGH WALL

TINY POND & RUIN

WAINWATH FORCE

GATE ONTO ROAD. TAKE A RIGHT DOWNHILL THEN LEFT AT BOTTOM

THROUGH GAP IN WALL

B6270

COTTERBY SCAR
CLIFF BY RIVER

GATE AT END OF BRIDGE

081

PATH GOES PAST DILAPIDATED FARMHOUSE SMITHY HOLME. NOW JOIN CART TRACK

OVERHEAD CABLES

49

TO FRY HOUSE FARM & BIRKDALE FARM

GO DOWN TO JOIN ROAD OVER BRIDGE OR TAKE A LEFT AT WAYPOINT 081 UNDER SYCAMORE TREE FOR THE SMALL (UNSIGNPOSTED) TRAIL ABOVE COTTERBY SCAR CLIFF

¼ mile

APPROX SCALE

500m

0

0

Being a tiny village at the crossroads of two major long-distance paths, let alone situated in the ever-popular Swaledale, accommodation options in Keld dry up fast if you leave it too late in the high season. Further down the valley the B&Bs in Thwaite and Muker (on the 'low level' route to Reeth) are no less popular. Indeed, such are the charms of Swaledale's rolling scenery, dotted here and there with the distinctive 'laithes' (stone barns for housing hay and livestock) that many hikers forego Wainwright's high route (see p176) via Swinner and Gunnerside gills in favour of the gentle stroll down the Swale valley to Reeth.

The only services in Keld are a **public toilet** and a **phone**. For more details on Keld and the rest of Swaledale visit 🖳 www.swaledale.net.

Where to stay and eat

The village has at least two **campsites**, although level pitches can be scarce once car-borne weekenders with their giant family tents have spread out.

You'll have walked past *Park House* (*Keld Bunk Barn & Yurts*; ☎ 01748 886549; 🖳 www.keldbunkbarnandyurts .com) on the way into the village. Rates in the **bunk barn** (1D/1Tr/1Qd) are £56 for the double room or £21pp in the triple/quad including bedding, towel and a light breakfast. Readers have praised the bunkhouse which has a kitchen plus a cosy lounge area with a TV. **Camping** is £6pp (Mar-Oct) and they have a big shed with a basic kitchen for campers. They also have genuine Mongolian **yurts** (Mar-Oct) which sleep up to four people (£49-89 per night for two). Bedding is provided and there is a wood-burning stove. The shower available for campers and yurt guests has some kick to it; there are also washing and drying facilities. Hot baguettes and tea or coffee (£3-3.50) can be brought to campers in the morning; evening meals (from £6.95; ordered before 6pm) are served and they have an alcohol licence.

Rukin's Park Lodge (☎ 01748 886274; 🖳 www.rukins-keld.co.uk; 🐾) is at the bottom of the village, though their actual **campsites** (Easter to end Oct; walkers £5pp) are in two different places: below Butt House and right by the river. There is

a block with shower and toilet facilities between these campsites; at present there are no laundry facilities. They don't take bookings but walkers will always be accepted. They also have a lovely little **tearoom** (Easter to end Sep; daily 9am-6pm) in the farmhouse with tables and chairs in the front garden. There are bacon rolls and a limited selection of groceries plus beer and wine; they also serve an extra pot of hot water when you order tea – always a sign of a good tearoom in our opinion.

Butt House (☎ 01748 886374, 🖳 www.butthousekeld.co.uk; 1S/1D/2T/1Tr; all en suite; 🛁; 🐾 £7.50; wi-fi; 🕒 up to £7.75) offers a warm welcome and highly praised food. It's a popular place and B&B starts at £40pp (sgl £48) with an à la carte **evening meal** menu from around £3.90 for starters, £9.80 for mains, £4.95 for puddings. Curried parsnip soup (£3.90) is one of their specialities. There is also a washing/drying service for £7.50.

Once the village youth hostel, *Keld Lodge* (☎ 01748 886259, 🖳 www.keld lodge.com; 2S/4T/5D/1Tr/1F, most en suite; 🐾 £7.50; wi-fi; 🕒) has been adapted into a cosy country lodge with an above-average restaurant. There is a drying room and most bedrooms have wonderful views. Rates are from £40pp in the two rooms which aren't en suite, £50pp otherwise (sgl occ £50/70 in the rooms with shared facilities/en suites). The **restaurant** (open during the day for drinks, food served daily noon-2pm & 5.30-8pm) is open to non residents. Mains around £12: beef braised in Black Sheep Bitter with puff pastry (£11.50) is good.

Two miles back up the road to Kirkby (or just a mile back west from where the path joins the B6270 at the gated bridge before Cotterby Scar) is *Pry House Farm* (☎ 01748 886845; 🖳 www.pryfarmhouse .co.uk; 1D en suite/1T private bath; 🛁; wi-fi on request only; 🕒 £5.50) where B&B costs from £37.50pp. They now do evening meals too – at £12.50 for two courses – so there's no need to schlep down a mile to the village centre. You can also get here from Ravenseat: take the single-track road for a mile to the T-junction with the B6270, then turn left over cattle grid and it's on the right-hand side. On the same road, past the

ROUTE GUIDE AND MAPS

turn off north to Ravenseat (a useful short cut avoiding backtracking from Keld) and nearly three miles from the village is *Birkdale Farm* (☎ 01748 886044; 🖥 www .birkdalefarm.com; 1D or T en suite; ➤; Ⓛ £5; Apr-Oct) with a self-contained upstairs studio in a spacious barn conversion (Little Birkdale). The food for dinner and breakfast is provided and guests cook or heat it up whenever it suits. Rates (£50pp; sgl occ full room rate) are on a dinner B&B basis. You may find it a real treat to spread out and enjoy this remote locale in Upper Swaledale. With advance notice they'll pick you up and drop you off the next day (although the OS map shows an interesting path from the farm down to the river, over

Keld Side and around Kisdon Hill to Muker to pick up the valley route to Reeth).

It may also be worth checking out a new place opening in May 2016, 1¼ miles north of Keld on the Pennine Way: *Frith Lodge Keld* (☎ 01748 886489; 🖥 www .frithlodgekeld.co.uk; 3D/2T en suite; Ⓛ £6; evening meal from £15). B&B for £47.50pp.

For more accommodation options in Muker and Gunnerside see p185 and p187.

Transport   (see also pp52-5)
Bus No 30 (Mon-Sat) travels to Reeth and Richmond via Thwaite, Muker and all the Swaledale villages. No 830 (Sun, May-Oct) links Hawes and Richmond via Thwaite, Keld, Muker, Gunnerside and Reeth.

THWAITE   OFF MAP 50
Two miles down the road from Keld, *Kearton Country Hotel* (☎ 01748 886277, 🖥 www.keartoncountryhotel.co.uk; 1S/6D/ 4T/1Tr; all en suite; ➤; WI-FI; Ⓛ £4.50; Feb-Dec) is a good-looking place. B&B costs from £54pp and dinner B&B £66.50pp. Their smart *restaurant* is open to

non-residents; dinner is served daily 6.30-7.30pm. The bar is open daily all day and food is served noon-4pm, though cakes and snacks are available outside these times.

Bus No 30 (Mon-Sat) stops here on its Keld to Richmond route, as does the No 830 on Sundays (May-Oct).

STAGE 8: KELD TO REETH   MAPS 50-56

Introduction
One might rightly assume the **original high-level route** is the way to go but many walkers who've done both find the **low-level (Swaledale Valley) route** (see p185) just as agreeable – though don't be misled into thinking that it's that much easier!

The high-level walk as described in Wainwright's book begins at the foot of Keld village – a bit of a pain to those who've spent the night down in Thwaite or Muker (see p185) from where following the valley alternative to Reeth makes sense. But if you wish to take the high-level route you could catch the No 30 bus back up to Keld. There's one morning service a day Monday to Saturday from Muker to Keld via Thwaite. Note that on this high-level route there's nowhere to buy any food or drink so come prepared.

The high-level route   Maps 51-56
The wildlife along this **11-mile (18km, 4½hr)** walk can be abundant, so try to set off as early as possible to increase your chances of encountering pheasants and deer. However, as with Stage 6 from Shap to Kirkby Stephen, this route is mainly about archaeology and the evidence of man's industrial enterprise in the far north of England. Today's walk takes you through a part of Yorkshire that has been forever scarred by the activities of lead mining. The first sign of this crops up at **Crackpot Hall** (Map 51), 30 minutes from Keld along a pretty trail high

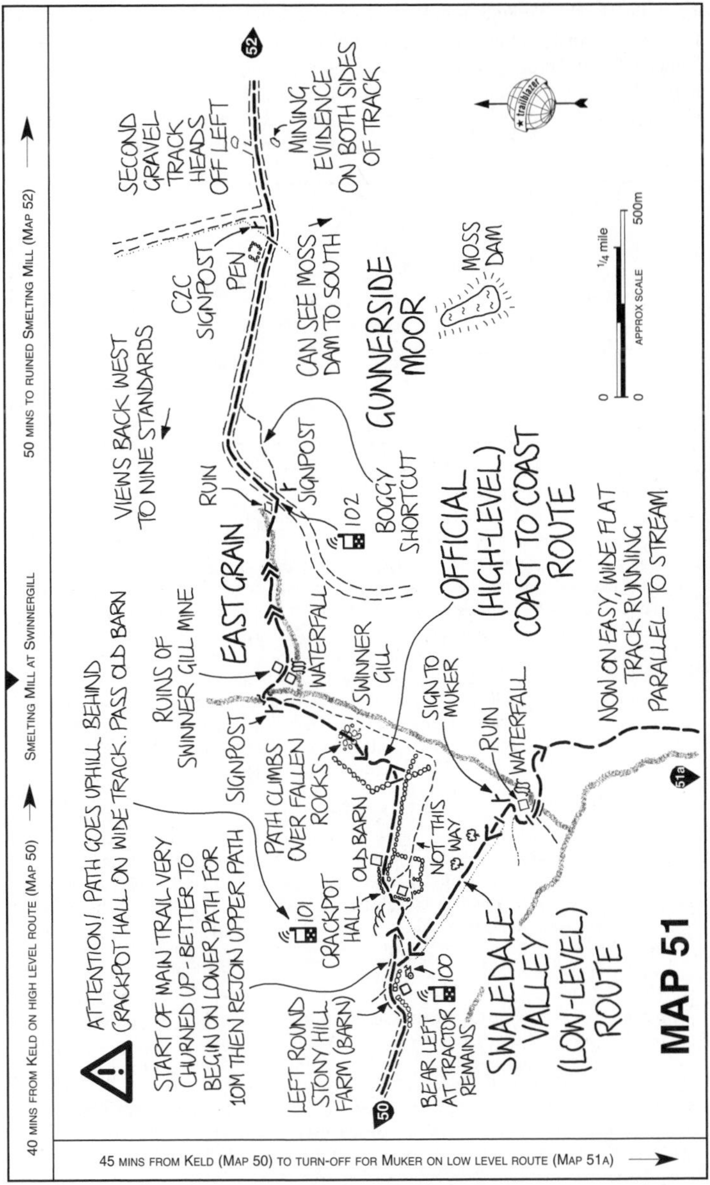
40 MINS FROM KELD ON HIGH LEVEL ROUTE (MAP 50) → SMELTING MILL AT SWINNERGILL 50 MINS TO RUINED SMELTING MILL (MAP 52) →
45 MINS FROM KELD (MAP 50) TO TURN-OFF FOR MUKER ON LOW LEVEL ROUTE (MAP 51A) →
ATTENTION! PATH GOES UPHILL BEHIND CRACKPOT HALL ON WIDE TRACK. PASS OLD BARN
START OF MAIN TRAIL VERY CHURNED UP - BETTER TO BEGIN ON LOWER PATH FOR 10M THEN REJOIN UPPER PATH
LEFT ROUND STONY HILL FARM (BARN)
BEAR LEFT AT TRACTOR REMAINS
100
101
CRACKPOT HALL
OLD BARN
NOT THIS WAY
PATH CLIMBS OVER FALLEN ROCKS
SIGNPOST
RUINS OF SWINNER GILL MINE
EAST GRAIN
WATERFALL
SWINNER GILL
SIGN TO MUKER
RUIN
WATERFALL
VIEWS BACK WEST TO NINE STANDARDS
RUIN
SIGNPOST
102
BOGGY SHORTCUT
C2C SIGNPOST
PEN
CAN SEE MOSS DAM TO SOUTH
SECOND GRAVEL TRACK HEADS OFF LEFT
MINING EVIDENCE ON BOTH SIDES OF TRACK
GUNNERSIDE MOOR
MOSS DAM
OFFICIAL (HIGH-LEVEL) COAST TO COAST ROUTE
NOW ON EASY, WIDE FLAT TRACK RUNNING PARALLEL TO STREAM
SWALEDALE VALLEY (LOW-LEVEL) ROUTE
MAP 51
50
51a
52
0 1/4 mile
0 500m
APPROX SCALE
trailblazer

ROUTE GUIDE AND MAPS

above the Swale. Though there's been a house here since the 16th century, the ruin you see today actually dates from the 18th century and, while not directly connected to the mining industry, the farmhouse was once owned by one of the mine's managers. Quiet and ruined now, the location would be a nice spot for a wild camp were it allowed, as would be many of the mining ruins on this stage. Crackpot', by the way, means 'Deep hole or chasm that is the haunt of crows',

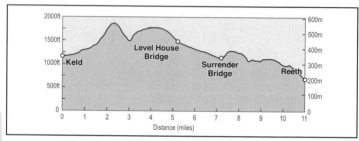

❑ Lead mining in Swaledale

According to the best estimates, lead has been mined in Swaledale since at least Roman times, and very possibly there was some small-scale mining back in the Bronze Age. A couple of pigs (ingots) of lead, including one discovered in Swaledale with the Roman name 'Hadrian' marked upon it, have been found. A versatile metal which oxidises slowly, lead is used in plumbing (indeed the word 'plumbing' comes from the Latin for lead), shipbuilding and roofing as well as in the manufacture of glass, pottery and paint. During medieval times lead was much in demand by the great churches and castles that were being built at that time.

The onset of the Industrial Revolution caused mining in Swaledale to become more organised and developed from the end of the 17th century. The innovation of gunpowder blasting, too, led to a sizeable increase in production, and the Yorkshire sites were at the centre of the British lead-mining industry. Indeed, during the mid-19th century Britain was producing over half the world's lead.

But while some of the mine-owners grew fabulously wealthy on the proceeds, the workers themselves suffered appalling conditions, often staying for a week or more at the mine and spending every daylight hour inside it. Deaths were common as the mines were rarely built with safety in mind and as advances in technology drove the mines ever deeper, so conditions became ever more hazardous. Illnesses from the cramped, damp and insanitary conditions were rife. As if to rub salt into the wounds, many of the workers did not even own their own tools, but instead hired them from an agent. The industry continued to prosper throughout much of the 19th century until the opening of mines in South America led to an influx of cheaper imports sending many British mines into bankruptcy. Many workers drifted away, usually to the coal mines around Durham, or to London and North America, in search of better prospects. By the early 20th century many of the villages were struggling to survive. Indeed, in the words of one resident of Reeth, when the mines closed the village became a 'City of the Dead'. Thankfully, tourism today has gone some way to securing the future of these attractive mining villages, and with the establishment of the Yorkshire Dales National Park the future looks a lot brighter for the villages of Swaledale.

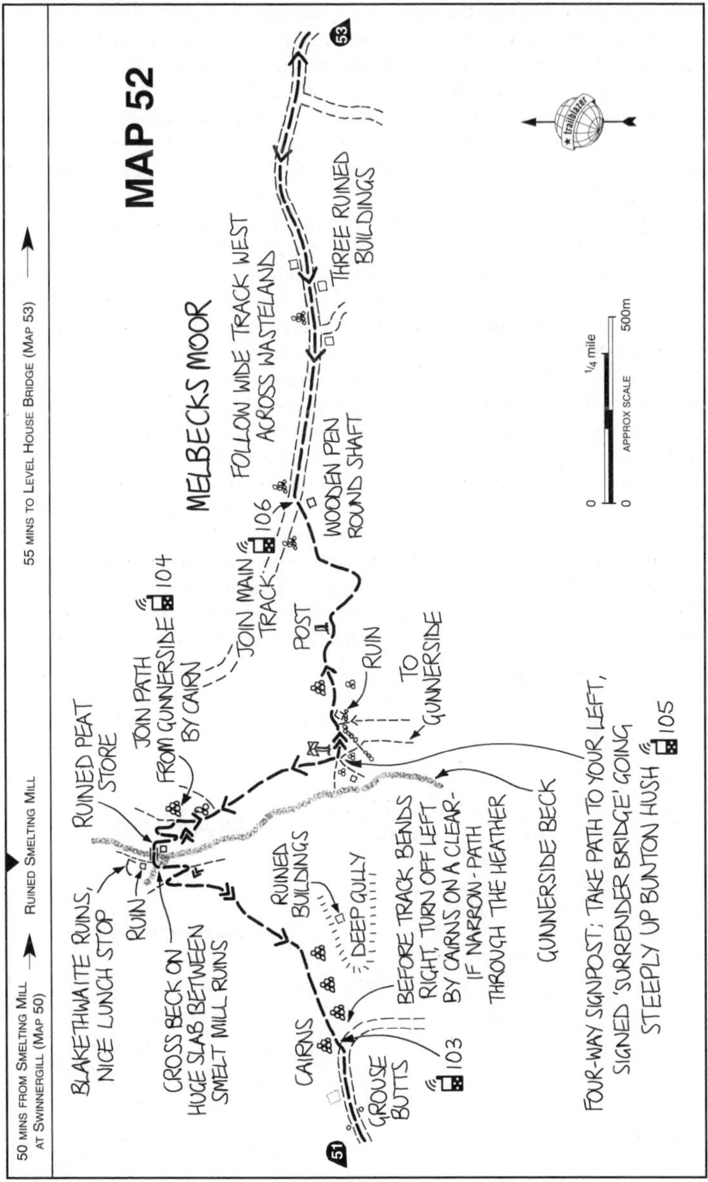

MAP 52

50 MINS FROM SMELTING MILL ← RUINED SMELTING MILL 55 MINS TO LEVEL HOUSE BRIDGE (MAP 53) →
AT SWINNERGILL (MAP 50)

MELBECKS MOOR

FOLLOW WIDE TRACK WEST ACROSS WASTELAND

53

THREE RUINED BUILDINGS

JOIN MAIN TRACK 106

WOODEN PEN
ROUND SHAFT

POST

RUIN

TO GUNNERSIDE

JOIN PATH FROM GUNNERSIDE BY CAIRN 104

RUINED PEAT STORE

BLAKETHWAITE RUINS, NICE LUNCH STOP

RUIN

CROSS BECK ON HUGE SLAB BETWEEN SMELT MILL RUINS

RUINED BUILDINGS

DEEP GULLY

GUNNERSIDE BECK

BEFORE TRACK BENDS RIGHT, TURN OFF LEFT BY CAIRNS ON A CLEAR-IF NARROW-PATH THROUGH THE HEATHER

CAIRNS

103

GROUSE BUTTS

51

FOUR-WAY SIGNPOST; TAKE PATH TO YOUR LEFT, SIGNED 'SURRENDER BRIDGE' GOING STEEPLY UP BUNTON HUSH 105

¼ mile

APPROX SCALE

0 500m

and is not a comment on the value of the endeavours of the former residents.

The path bends north now from behind the Hall to pass an 'old house' on the map and after a gate, traverses the narrow gorge of Swinner Gill. Make sure you head uphill to follow the correct trail or you'll eventually find yourself on a lower, parallel but precipitous sheep track barely two boots wide and clinging to the side of the gorge below the correct route – see Map 51. Whichever route you stumble on, before long you arrive at the eerie remains of **Swinner Gill smelting mill** with waterfalls alongside. Again, from here it's possible to follow a tricky path alongside the north bank of **East Grain Beck** instead of the easier way a little higher up the valley side. Once climbing east, after passing the last mill ruin on your left, look for a higher path after the first stream crossing about 250m on. Either way both paths deliver you with a sweaty brow onto the breezy expanse of **Gunnerside Moor**. There are grouse butts in the area; if people are out shooting you'll be relieved to know that they will stop to let you pass.

Initially climbing and passing **Moss Dam** to the south, on the ensuing descent you leave the track to curve north-east and descend steeply to more picturesque ruins at **Blakethwaite** (Map 52) in the valley of Gunnerside Beck. This is an ideal, if slightly premature, place for a picnic lunch out of the wind. While sitting on the grassy bank behind the large ruined peat store with its impressive arched windows (peat was used with coal to heat the smelting furnace), look for the flue coming down from the hill, finishing near the kiln on the western banks.

From here the path zig-zags east back up onto **Melbecks Moor**. It's not uncommon to lose your way on the final climb onto the moor; we recommend that at the signpost for 'Surrender Bridge' (Map 52, Wpt 105), you either get stuck directly into Bunton Hush gully, or the ascent just to the south which is

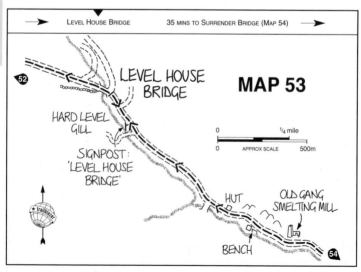

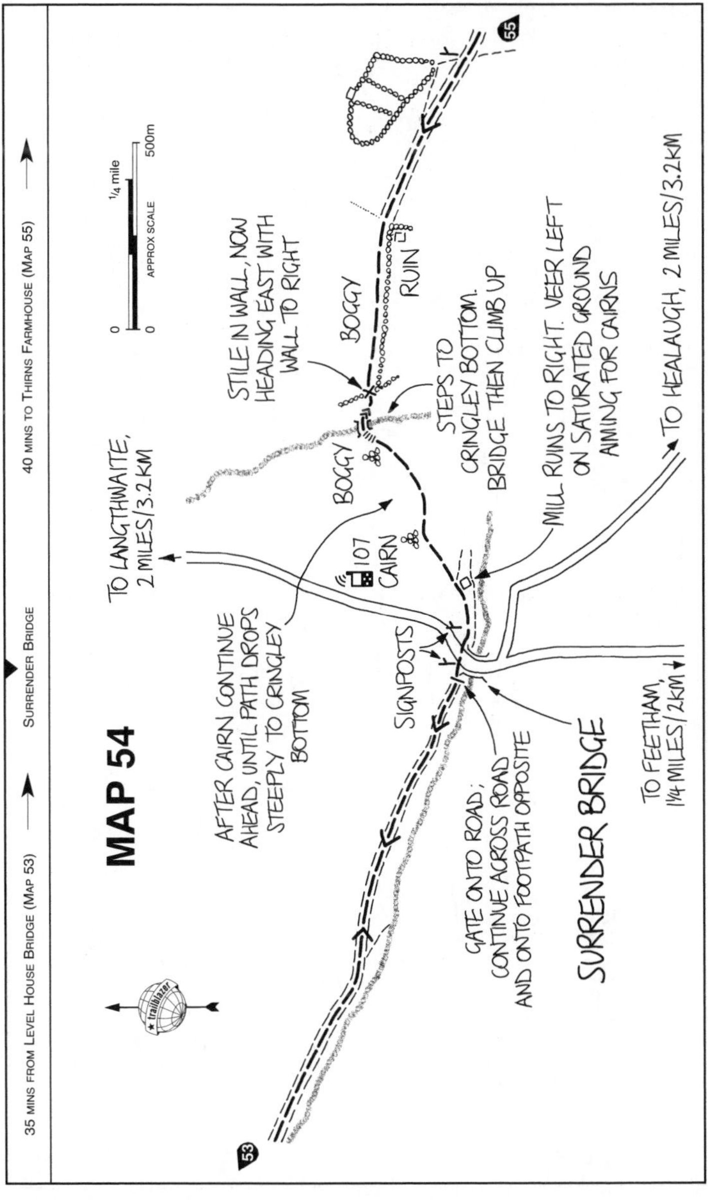
35 mins from Level House Bridge (Map 53)
Surrender Bridge
40 mins to Thirns Farmhouse (Map 55)
MAP 54
0
0
APPROX SCALE
1/4 mile
500m
trailblazer
53
55
AFTER CAIRN CONTINUE AHEAD, UNTIL PATH DROPS STEEPLY TO CRINGLEY BOTTOM
TO LANGTHWAITE, 2 MILES/3.2KM
107 CAIRN
BOGGY
STILE IN WALL, NOW HEADING EAST WITH WALL TO RIGHT
BOGGY
RUIN
STEPS TO CRINGLEY BOTTOM. BRIDGE THEN CLIMB UP
MILL RUINS TO RIGHT. VEER LEFT ON SATURATED GROUND AIMING FOR CAIRNS
TO HEALAUGH, 2 MILES/3.2KM
SIGNPOSTS
GATE ONTO ROAD; CONTINUE ACROSS ROAD AND ONTO FOOTPATH OPPOSITE
SURRENDER BRIDGE
TO FEETHAM, 1¼ MILES/2KM

ROUTE GUIDE AND MAPS

THIRNS FARMHOUSE

40 MINS TO REETH (MAP 56)

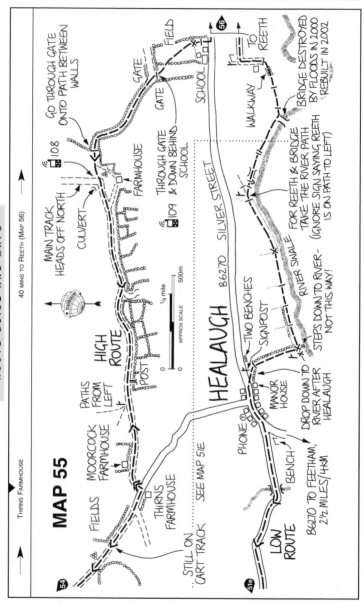

MAP 55

54

FIELDS

STILL ON CART TRACK   SEE MAP 51E

MOORCOCK FARMHOUSE

PATHS FROM LEFT

THIRNS FARMHOUSE

HIGH ROUTE

POST

MAIN TRACK HEADS OFF NORTH

CULVERT

108

GO THROUGH GATE ONTO PATH BETWEEN WALLS

GATE

FARMHOUSE

THROUGH GATE & DOWN BEHIND SCHOOL

109

GATE

FIELD

SCHOOL

56

TO REETH

WALKWAY

BRIDGE DESTROYED BY FLOODS IN 2000, REBUILT IN 2002

FOR REETH & BRIDGE TAKE THE RIVER PATH (IGNORE SIGN SAYING REETH IS ON PATH TO LEFT)

RIVER SWALE

STEPS DOWN TO RIVER - NOT THIS WAY!

TWO BENCHES

SIGNPOST

HEALAUGH   B6270   SILVER STREET

MANOR HOUSE

DROP DOWN TO RIVER AFTER HEALAUGH

PHONE

BENCH

B6270 TO FEETHAM, 2½ MILES/4KM

LOW ROUTE

51E

¼ mile

0

APPROX SCALE

500m

0

trailblazer

less of a landslip. Once on the top, cairns or tracks lead to the wooden-penned shaft on the big track (WPT 106), a key point. Up here the landscape can be a bit of a shock. The mining relics encountered thus far have been rather quaint, but you are now faced by an eerie desolation stripped of topsoil by artificially channelled water to expose the minerals underneath. Such gullies, like the one you just clambered up, are known as a *hush*.

At the end of your 'moon walk' lies **Level House Bridge** (Map 53), where you cross **Hard Level Gill** before following it down to the remains of **Old Gang Smelting Mill**, the most extensive ruins yet where warning notices beseech you not to 'ruin the ruins'. Soon you arrive at **Surrender Bridge** (Map 54) where you cross a minor road leading up to obscure Arkengarthdale and continue past another smelt-mill ruin, dropping down to bridge the finely named **Cringley Bottom** to continue with hopefully fine views of Swaledale's iridescent verdure and dry-stone walls (Map 55) as the track tumbles down to Reeth.

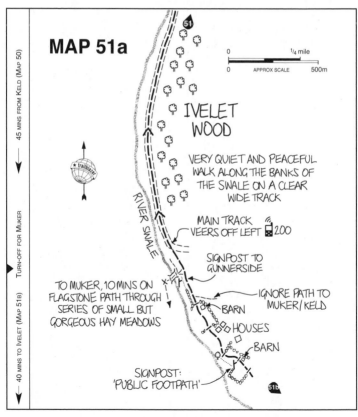

MAP 51a

IVELET WOOD

0   ¼ mile

0   APPROX SCALE   500m

VERY QUIET AND PEACEFUL WALK ALONG THE BANKS OF THE SWALE ON A CLEAR WIDE TRACK

MAIN TRACK VEERS OFF LEFT ▯200

SIGNPOST TO GUNNERSIDE

RIVER SWALE

TO MUKER, 10 MINS ON FLAGSTONE PATH THROUGH SERIES OF SMALL BUT GORGEOUS HAY MEADOWS

IGNORE PATH TO MUKER/KELD

BARN

HOUSES

BARN

SIGNPOST: 'PUBLIC FOOTPATH'

*trailblazer

45 MINS FROM KELD (MAP 50)   TURN-OFF FOR MUKER   40 MINS TO IVELET (MAP 51b)

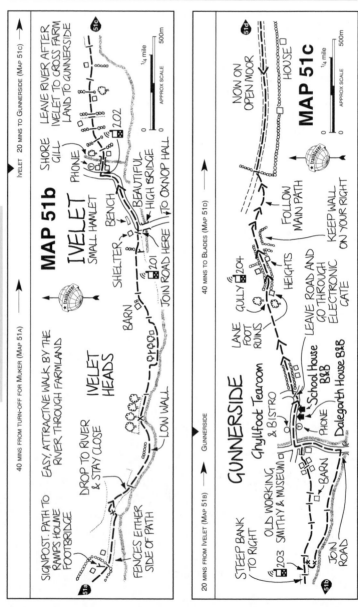

ROUTE GUIDE AND MAPS

MAP 51b

40 MINS FROM TURN-OFF FOR MUKER (MAP 51A) →

IVELET 20 MINS TO GUNNERSIDE (MAP 51c) →

LEAVE RIVER AFTER IVELET TO CROSS FARM LAND TO GUNNERSIDE

51c

Easy, attractive walk by the river through farmland

SHORE GILL

L02

PHONE

IVELET SMALL HAMLET

BENCH

BEAUTIFUL HIGH BRIDGE

SHELTER

TO OXNOP HALL

BARN

L01

JOIN ROAD HERE

IVELET HEADS

DROP TO RIVER & STAY CLOSE

LOW WALL

FENCES EITHER SIDE OF PATH

SIGNPOST. PATH TO RAMPS HOLME FOOTBRIDGE

51a

APPROX SCALE

0 — 500m

0 — ¼ mile

MAP 51c

40 MINS TO BLADES (MAP 51d) →

51d

HOUSE

NOW ON OPEN MOOR

FOLLOW MAIN PATH

KEEP WALL ON YOUR RIGHT

APPROX SCALE

0 — 500m

0 — ¼ mile

GULLY L04

HEIGHTS

LEAVE ROAD AND GO THROUGH ELECTRONIC GATE

LANE FOOT RUINS

GUNNERSIDE

Ghyllfoot Tearoom & Bistro

School House B&B

PHONE

Dalegarth House B&B

OLD WORKING SMITHY & MUSEUM

BARN

JOIN ROAD

STEEP BANK TO RIGHT

L03

51b

20 MINS FROM IVELET (MAP 51B) →

GUNNERSIDE →

The low-level Swaledale Valley alternative route
Map 51 p177, Maps 51a-e pp183-7, Map 56 p193

This option adds up to about 4½ **hours** of *fairly* level walking (**11½ miles, 18.5km**) and you may well end up in Reeth soon after lunch. Some Coasters are tempted to roll it in with the previous stage, making a hefty 23-mile day, but doing so you can expect to hobble into Reeth in a bit of a state. Others in a rush knock out Keld to Richmond in one day; about the same distance and probably with the same consequences.

Our advice? Kick back and enjoy the first leisurely stage for a while, stop frequently to admire the valley and commune with nature. Take the diversion to Muker. Then suppress the urge to press on with a pint or two of Old Peculier while overlooking Reeth's village green. It's a beautiful stroll, particularly in the early morning before the crowds gather. The path is so easy that for once you can fully appreciate your surroundings, looking for riparian wildlife such as herons, ducks and, so it is said, otters. The villages passed on the way are a joy, too.

Muker

Muker (off Map 51a and actually slightly off the route) is a very pleasant little place and one of James Herriot's (see p188) favourites. Pronounced 'Miuker', you'll find a **church** with the Ten Commandments written large upon the wall, and the *Farmers Arms* (☎ 01748 886297; ☐ www.farmersarmsmuker .co.uk; food served daily noon-2.30pm & 6-8.30pm), where dogs and 'muddy boots are welcome'.

Muker has also been the home for 30 years of **Swaledale Woollens** (☐ www.swaledalewoollens.co.uk), their raw material shorn from the hardy Swaledale sheep whose tough wool is considered ideal for carpets. The shop claims that it saved the village following the depression caused by the collapse of the mining industry. Following a meeting in the local pub, a decision was made to set up a local cottage industry producing knitwear, and today over 30 home workers are employed knitting the jumpers, hats and many other items available in the store.

Muker Village Store and Teashop (☎ 01748 886409, ☐ www.mukervil lage.co.uk) comprises the **village shop** (Mar/Apr to end Oct daily 10am-5pm, Nov to Mar/Apr Tue, Thur-Sun 10am-noon, a **tearoom** (Mar/Apr to end Oct, Wed-Mon 11am-ish to 'when it goes quiet'; weekends only in winter) and **B&B** (1D en suite; Ⓛ; from £35pp, in general they don't accept solo walkers).

Accommodation is also available at *Chapel House* (☎ 01748 886822, ☐ www.mukerchapel.co.uk; 1D en suite; Ⓛ; Easter to Nov), just up from Swaledale Woollens, where B&B is from £42.50pp (sgl occ £85).

From Monday to Saturday the No 30 **bus** calls here, and in Gunnerside, and on Sunday the No 830 bus stops in both villages; see pp52-5 for details.

Between Muker and Gunnerside there's more accommodation at *Oxnop Hall* (☎ 01748 886253, ☐ www.oxnophall.com; 1S/1T/2D or T, all en suite; Ⓛ; Easter to Oct), a farm offering B&B from £40pp. They're 800m from Ivelet, off Map 51b. From the trail turn right onto the road over the bridge west of Ivelet, then right at the main road and they're about 300m along on the left.

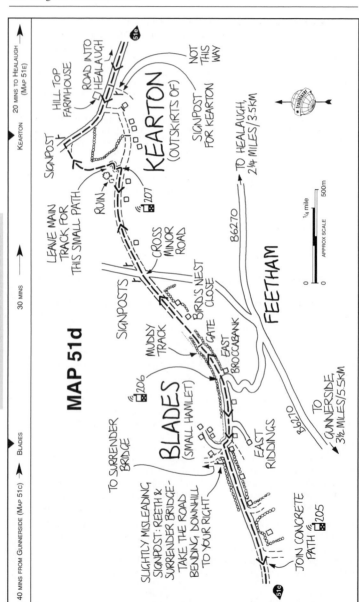

MAP 51d

51e

ROAD INTO HEALAUGH

HILL TOP FARMHOUSE

NOT THIS WAY

SIGNPOST

KEARTON (OUTSKIRTS OF)

SIGNPOST FOR KEARTON

TO HEALAUGH, 2¼ MILES/3.5KM

RUIN

207

LEAVE MAIN TRACK FOR THIS SMALL PATH

CROSS MINOR ROAD

B6270

SIGNPOSTS

BIRD'S NEST CLOSE

FEETHAM

MUDDY TRACK

GATE

EAST BROCCABANK

206

BLADES (SMALL HAMLET)

EAST RIDDINGS

TO SURRENDER BRIDGE

TO GUNNERSIDE 3½ MILES/5.5KM

B6270

SLIGHTLY MISLEADING SIGNPOST: REETH & SURRENDER BRIDGE- TAKE THE ROAD BENDING DOWNHILL TO YOUR RIGHT

JOIN CONCRETE PATH 205

51c

¼ mile

APPROX SCALE

0   500m

0

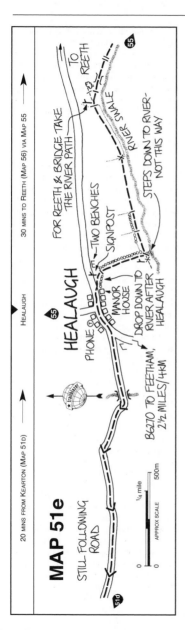

MAP 51e

STILL FOLLOWING ROAD

20 MINS FROM KEARTON (MAP 51d) ← HEALAUGH → 30 MINS TO REETH (MAP 56) VIA MAP 55 →

HEALAUGH

STILL FOLLOWING ROAD

B6270 TO FEETHAM, 2½ MILES/4KM

PHONE

MANOR HOUSE

DROP DOWN TO RIVER AFTER HEALAUGH

SIGNPOST

TWO BENCHES

FOR REETH & BRIDGE TAKE THE RIVER PATH

TO REETH

RIVER SWALE

STEPS DOWN TO RIVER-NOT THIS WAY

¼ mile

500m

APPROX SCALE

0

Gunnerside

Gunnerside (Map 51c; 🖳 www.gunnerside.info) boasts a pub, the *King's Arms* (☎ 01748 886261, 🖳 www.kingsheadgun nerside.com; food served 12-2.30pm, 5.30-8.45pm). There are sandwiches at lunchtime for about £4.25, and mains in the evening cost around £10.

The genteel *Ghyllfoot Tearoom & Bistro* (☎ 01748 886239; 🖳 www.ghyllfoot.co.uk; Feb to Oct, 10.30am-5pm, closed Tue) also serves dinners on Wed and Sat evenings (7-9pm), a roast at lunchtime (12.30-2pm) on Sunday and takeaway curries on the first and third Monday evenings in the month. There's a lounge bar upstairs. Their hiker's brunch (£9.50) is popular.

There's accommodation at *Dalegarth House* (☎ 01748 886275, 🖳 dalegarth@btinternet .com; 1T en suite; WI-FI; Ⓛ) on the way out of the village towards Reeth. B&B costs £30pp (sgl occ £33).

From Gunnerside the path crosses moor and farmland, eventually dropping down to **Healaugh** (Map 51e), from where it returns to the river to continue past the suspension bridge to Reeth (see p188), which it enters via Quaker Rd.

ROUTE GUIDE AND MAPS

REETH   Map 56 p189

Reeth, the 'capital' of Swaledale, is the archetypal Yorkshire dales village: flanked to north and south by mine-scarred valleys and ringed by dry-stone walls. At its heart lies a village green surrounded on all sides by several examples of those twin institutions of Yorkshire hospitality: the **tearoom** and the **pub**. As if to underline its Yorkshire credentials still further, it also has a renowned brass band. Hardly surprising, therefore, that the village was used as a location for many episodes of the quintessential 1980s Yorkshire TV saga *All Creatures Great and Small* based on the books of rural vet, James Herriot.

Mentioned in the Domesday survey nine centuries earlier, the village grew on the profits of the 19th-century mining boom, though unlike other nearby villages it could always claim a second string to its bow as the main market town for Swaledale (the market is still held on The Green on Fridays). After the mines closed tourism gave Reeth a new lease of life and today the town hosts a number of B&Bs and hotels, as well as some **gift shops** and a small museum.

Swaledale Museum (☎ 01748 884118, 💻 www.swaledalemuseum.org; Easter to 30 Sep, Mon-Sat 10am-5pm; £3) is housed in the old 19th-century Methodist school room. It holds some surprisingly intriguing exhibits and is well-worth an hour of your time, particularly if you want to learn more about the local mining and farming industries. The museum also looks at the social history of the area in some detail, attempting to show how the locals used to live a hundred or more years ago.

Services

The **tourist office** and **National Park centre** (☎ 01748 884059, 💻 www.yorkshiredales.org.uk; Apr-Oct daily 10am-5.30pm, Nov-Mar Sat & Sun 10am-4pm) is to the west of The Green in Hudson House. **Internet access** is available here for £1. Tucked round the back of these is Swaledale Outdoors (☎ 01748 880298) full of **outdoor clothing and equipment**.

On the other side of The Green the **general store** (Mon-Sat 8.30am-5.30pm, Sun 10am-4pm) has a **post office** (Mon-Fri 9am-5.30pm, Sat 9am-12.30pm). Otherwise there are **cash machines** (£1) or cashback in both the Black Bull or the **village store** (Mon-Fri 7am-7.30pm, Sat 7am-7pm, Sun 8am-4pm) at the bottom of the hill on the way out of town.

Where to stay

There is no shortage of accommodation in Reeth. The nearest **hostel** is *YHA Grinton Lodge* (off Map 56; ☎ 0845 371 9636, 💻 www.yha.org.uk/hostel/grinton-lodge; 77 beds, 2-/3-/4-/6-bed rooms; beds £15-23, 4-bed rooms £49-79; Ⓛ), a lovely old shooting lodge, but at just over a mile on past Reeth and up a very steep hill, it can be too much to bear. However, it is only half a mile from the path and offers superior lodgings with meals, is licensed and has a TV and a games room. Credit cards are accepted, there are drying facilities and packed lunches can be provided. They also have some camping pods (see 💻 www.thepod.info), three that can sleep 4 people (£59 for the pod) and two with space for three people (£45). They also charge adults £13 for **camping**.

Just half a mile from Reeth and even closer to the path are the converted stone barns of the *Dales Bike Centre* (Map 56; ☎ 01748 884908, 💻 www.dalesbikecentre .co.uk; 3T/2F sleep 4; all bunks; showers available; Ⓛ £5.50) in **Fremington** village. Welcoming all outdoor enthusiasts, not just cyclists, there is a kitchenette, laundry and drying facilities. Bunk and breakfast (cereals and a bacon sandwich) at the Centre costs from £28pp, or it's £38 single occupancy of a twin. There's also a *café/lounge* (9.30am-5pm) with wi-fi and the *Bridge Inn* (Map 56) is just down the road for a steak and a Martini, shaken, not stirred.

Campers pitch up at *The Orchard Caravan Park* (Map 56; ☎ 01748 884475; check-in at the house signed 'Warden Enquiries'; book in advance in peak season; 🐾; mid-March-Oct). The enthusiastic owners have transformed the place and,

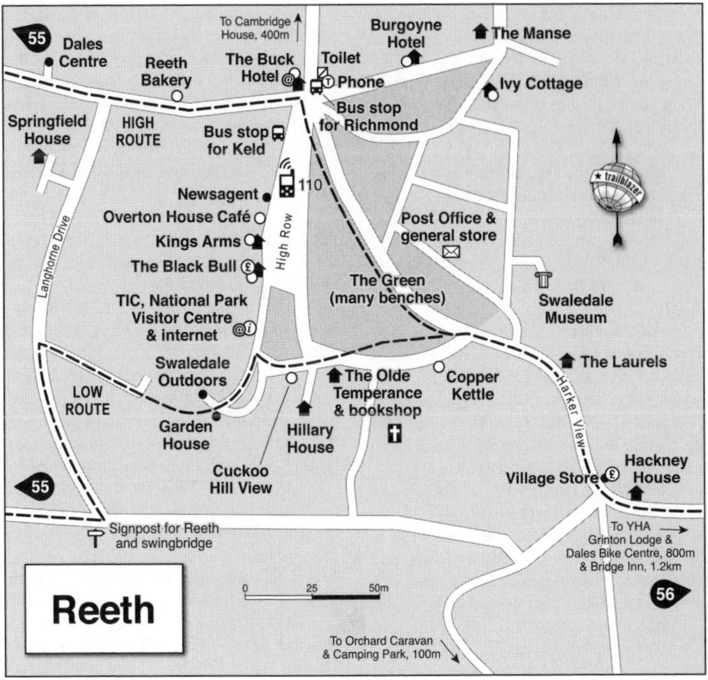

though dominated by caravans, it's still popular with C2Cers. You can camp here for £6pp (shower facilities 20p) and, wonderfully, if it's raining they'll allow you to shelter in one of their old caravans for the same price.

Springfield House (☎ 01748 884634, 💻 www.springfield-house.co.uk; 1D en suite/1T private bathroom; ▼; WI-FI; Apr-Oct) is on Quaker Close, reached via Langhorne Drive. B&B is £35pp (sgl occ £60); they offer complimentary refreshments if you arrive between 3.30 and 5pm.

Hackney House (☎ 01748 884302, 1S shared bathroom, 1T/1D/2D or T/1Tr all en suite; ▼; WI-FI; Ⓛ £6), Bridge Terrace, at the bottom of the village, has received commendations from readers; the breakfasts are big and the welcome friendly. B&B costs from £40pp (sgl £42).

The Laurels (☎ 01748 880257, 💻 www.thelaurelsreeth.com; 2D/1D, T or Tr; en suite; 🐕 £5 which is donated to Swaledale Mountain Rescue; WI-FI) is a very comfortable B&B, in a restored Georgian house. B&B is £42.50pp (sgl occ £75) and there may be a minimum stay of two nights at weekends.

The Olde Temperance (☎ 01748 884401; 1S/1D/1Tr; shared bathroom; ▼; 🐕 £3) is situated above a Christian bookshop and charges £30pp – already the cheapest in Reeth, and they'll reduce it to £25pp if staying two nights or more.

Across The Green and above the tearoom, ***Ivy Cottage*** (☎ 01748 884418, 💻 www.ivycottagereeth.co.uk; 2D en suite; ▼; WI-FI; Ⓛ from £5) charges £40pp (sgl occ £60). There may be a minimum two-night stay at weekends.

The Manse B&B (☎ 01748 884136, 🖳 www.themanseinreeth.co.uk; 1D/2T; all en suite; WI-FI; ⓛ £6) is a comfortable B&B charging from £42.50pp (sgl occ £60). They have a drying room and offer laundry facilities (£8 wash/dry). Complementary tea and cakes are served on arrival.

Enjoying the views from the top of the village, *Burgoyne Hotel* (☎ 01748 884292, 🖳 www.theburgoyne.co.uk; 2T/8D, all en suite or with private bathroom; ➔; 🐾 £10; WI-FI; ⓛ £12.50), is the grandest place to stay here. B&B is from £60pp (sgl occ £102).

For pubs there are three options. *The Buck Hotel* (☎ 01748 884210, 🖳 www.buckhotel.co.uk; 1S/2D/4D or T/2T/ 1Qd; all en suite; ➔; 🐾 £12; WI-FI; ⓛ), which charges £42-49.50pp (sgl £49, sgl occ £59) or £33pp in the triple/quad rooms, with prices rising £5-10 at weekends

The Black Bull (☎ 01748 884213, 🖳 www.theblackbullreeth.co.uk; 4D/2T/2F; all with private facilities; ➔; 🐾; WI-FI in the bar only; ⓛ £6) dates back to 1680 and has rooms overlooking The Green and down Swaledale. B&B costs £40pp.

The Kings Arms (☎ 01748 884259, 🖳 www.the kingsarms.com; 2T/7D/1Qd all en suite; ➔; 🐾; WI-FI; ⓛ from £6.95), next door, charges £35pp for B&B in their rear bedrooms which we found to be bright and clean and with a spacious bathroom, or £40pp for those overlooking The Green. Single occupancy is from £40.

Cambridge House (☎ 01748 884633, 🖳 www.cambridgehousereeth.co.uk; 1S/ 3D/1T; all en suite; ➔; WI-FI; ⓛ from £3) lies about a quarter of a mile (400m) north from Buck Hotel on the road to Arkengarthdale; you'll find it on the left. It is full of antiques and the rooms all face south with views over Reeth. For a night's B&B they charge from £45pp (single £50), are very walker friendly with a full drying room.

Where to eat and drink

It's a real shame *Reeth Bakery* (☎ 01748 884735; Apr-Oct Mon-Sat 10am-4pm, Sun 11am-5pm; Nov-Mar days/hours variable

so check in advance), on Silver St, opens late and closes early most days. Along with a variety of breads and heavenly cakes, the still-warm filled rolls sure make a change from the plastic-cocooned sandwiches found at most village shops. If you can't squeeze into the tiny **tearoom**, take your purchases out onto one of the The Green's many benches.

Ivy Cottage (see Where to stay) has a popular tearoom open daily in the season from noon to 5pm. Toasted teacakes or crumpets with butter are £2.

The *Copper Kettle* (☎ 01748 884748; Apr-Sep Sat-Thur 10am-7.30pm, Fri 10am-3pm; Mar & Oct 10.30am-5pm; closed Nov-Feb) is a traditional establishment serving Swaledale afternoon tea. They also offer more substantial fare throughout the day, with most dishes, including beef lasagne and lamb moussaka, around £8-9.

Cuckoo Hill View (☎ 01748 884929; daily in summer 11.30am-5pm, occasionally up to 8pm, weekends only in winter) is an ice-cream parlour at the foot of The Green serving such flavours as 'rhubarb crumble' and 'chocoholic'. It is delicious.

Next to the Kings Arms the licensed *Overton House Café* (☎ 01748 884045; Mon 10.30am-12.30pm, Tue & Wed, Fri & Sat 10.30am-4pm, Sun 11am-4pm) gets great reviews and offers a take-away service too.

Otherwise the pubs like *The Buck Hotel*, *Kings Arms* (daily noon-2.30pm & 6-9pm; see Where to stay) and *Black Bull* (daily noon-2pm & 6-9pm; see Where to stay) put on the usual spreads with the latter known for its homemade pies from £8.95.

If you've something to celebrate the exclusive *Burgoyne Hotel* (see Where to stay) does a superb four-course dinner for £45. Reservations necessary.

Transport   (see also pp52-5)
From Monday to Saturday **bus** No 30 stops here en route between Keld and Richmond and on Sundays (May-Oct) the No 830 calls here.

STAGE 9: REETH TO RICHMOND   MAPS 56-61

Introduction

There are a couple of lovely tracts of woodland on this rural, **10½-mile (17km, 4½hr)** stage, a simple walk that should allow you time to explore the sights of Richmond at the end of the day if you set off early enough and don't lose your way. A couple of charming villages are passed en route too, as well as the remains of an old priory. Overall, it's not a spectacular day as you leave the Pennines behind but, if the weather's fine, a pleasant one nevertheless.

The route

The walk starts out along the B6270 which you've been tracking since Kirkby Stephen, but soon after leaving Reeth and crossing Arkle Beck, you leave the road and are led along a fence corridor through riverside pastures to meet the road again at Grinton Bridge over the meandering Swale. Over the road you briefly continue along the Swale and then, like a startled badger, dart uphill to

---

❏ Dry-stone walls

I am a Dry Stone Waller
All day I Dry Stone Wall
Of all appalling callings
Dry Stone Walling's worst of all
Pam Ayres, 1978

Along the Coast to Coast path you'll pass hundreds of dry-stone walls out of Britain's estimated 125,000 miles-worth. Beautiful and photogenic, particularly when covered in a layer of velvety green moss, they're probably the most ubiquitous feature of northern England's landscape. That said, few walkers give much thought to who built them, nor have any idea just how much skill and effort goes into making these walls.

Dry-stone walls, so called because they are built without mortar, have been around since Elizabethan times when, as now, they were used to demarcate the boundaries between one farmer's land and another. Many others were built during the Enclosure Acts between 1720 and 1840, when previously large fields shared between a number of farmers were divided into strips of land. A very few of these 18th-century walls are still standing: those nearest to a village tend to be the oldest, as it was this land that was divided and enclosed first. The fact that the walls have lasted so long is largely due to the care that goes into construction.

The first step is to dig some deep, secure foundations. That done, the next step is to build the wall itself, or rather walls, for a typical dry-stone wall is actually made up of two thinner walls built back to back; a design that helps make the wall as sturdy as possible. Every metre or so a through or tie stone is built into the wall to bind the two halves together. It's estimated that one tonne of stone is required for one square yard of wall. Each stone is chosen carefully to fit exactly: a bad choice can upset the pressure loading, leading to an early collapse. Smaller chippings or pebbles are used to fill the gaps and a dry-stone waller we once met in the North Pennines reckoned he could erect just two metres of wall on a good day.

Dry-stone walling has had its heyday; it now faces competition from the wire fence which is a cheaper, simpler and just as effective a way of dividing land, and while the existing dry-stone walls have to be repaired occasionally, more often than not the farmer would rather do it himself than call in a professional. However, the art is certainly not dead; for further information visit the Dry Stone Walling Association's website (🖳 www.dswa.org.uk).

ROUTE GUIDE AND MAPS

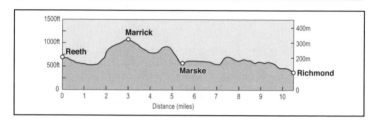

ROUTE GUIDE AND MAPS

meet and cross a minor road and follow more walled pastures to **Marrick Priory** (Map 57), just 40 minutes from Reeth. (Sometimes this route may be blocked, in which case you'll need to turn right and stroll east along the road to the priory.) Though it's visible from a distance, casual visitors are no longer allowed to visit the adjacent ruins which have been incorporated into an Outdoor Education Centre. Nevertheless, it seems that staff don't mind people walking about the drive to inspect the remains. The abbey was founded by local noble, Roger de Aske, for Benedictine nuns who numbered 17 at the priory's dissolution in 1540. There are a couple of tomb slabs in the grounds, including one by the entrance belonging to a Thomas Peacock who died in 1762 at the grand old age of 102.

Those disappointed at not being able to explore the ruins thoroughly will find some consolation in the walk to Marrick village, a pretty uphill amble through the first of this stage's woods, known as Steps Wood and notable as the first dense shade you may have experienced on the trail for several days. The path you're ascending is known as the **Nuns' Steps**, so-called because the nuns are said to have constructed the 375 steps as a walkway to the abbey. At the top, after a couple of fields, lies the village that gave Marrick Priory its name.

From **Marrick** the trail begins a long north-easterly march to Marske through farmland punctuated by any number of tiny stiles and gates. On the way *Elaine's Farmhouse Kitchen* at *Nun Cote Nook Farm* (Map 57; ☎ 01748 884266; **camping** £6pp; **bed** in a static caravan sleeping up to six £12pp; 🐕; Ⓛ from £5) serves **snacks and drinks** (daily 9am to late) overlooking a quiet open field that gives farm camping a good name. They also offer a two-course **evening meal** (with the meat coming from their farm) for campers for just £13. Even if you're not camping here, many Coasters agree Elaine's is well worth a detour for a brew, a snack and a chat about the price of wool.

Nun Cote Nook is just about the last hill farm and so you bid farewell to the Pennines and tramp diagonally across pastures until you join the road to **Marske** and impressive Marske Hall (Map 58) on the right. Continuing up the

---

❏ **Important note – walking times**
Unless otherwise specified, **all times in this book refer only to the time spent walking**. You will need to add 20-30% to allow for rests, photography, checking the map, drinking water etc. When planning the day's hike count on 5-7 hours' actual walking.

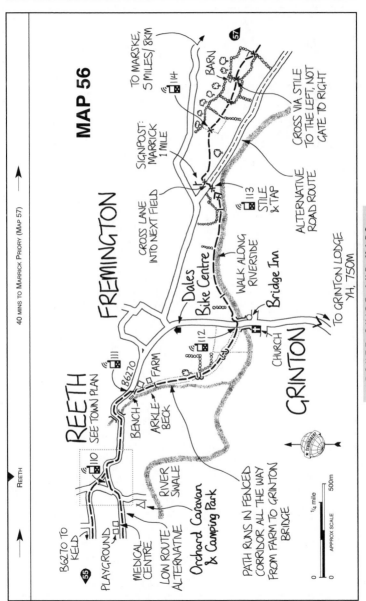

MAP 56

REETH
SEE TOWN PLAN

40 MINS TO MARRICK PRIORY (MAP 57)

REETH

55

B6270 TO KELD

PLAYGROUND

MEDICAL CENTRE

LOW ROUTE ALTERNATIVE

Orchard Caravan & Camping Park

RIVER SWALE

ARKLE BECK

BENCH

FARM

B6270

📷 110

📷 111

FREMINGTON

CROSS LANE INTO NEXT FIELD

Dales Bike Centre

📷 112

Bridge Inn

WALK ALONG RIVERSIDE

CHURCH

GRINTON

TO GRINTON LODGE YH, 750M

PATH RUNS IN FENCED CORRIDOR ALL THE WAY FROM FARM TO GRINTON BRIDGE

📷 113 STILE & TAP

ALTERNATIVE ROAD ROUTE

CROSS VIA STILE TO THE LEFT, NOT GATE TO RIGHT

SIGNPOST: MARRICK 1 MILE

TO MARSKE, 5 MILES / 8KM

📷 114

BARN

57

¼ mile

500m

APPROX SCALE

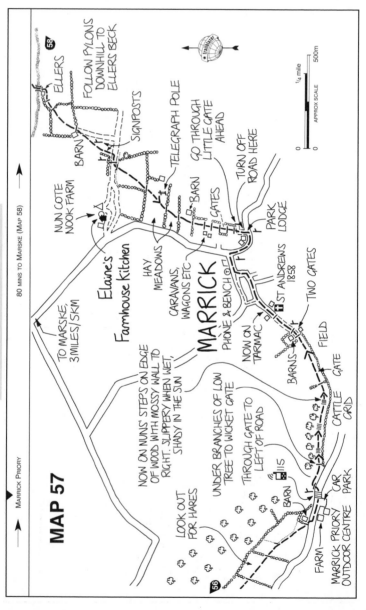

MARRICK PRIORY

MAP 57

80 MINS TO MARSKE (MAP 58)

ELLERS

58

FOLLOW PYLONS DOWNHILL TO ELLERS BECK

TRUE NORTH

APPROX SCALE
0   ¼ mile
0   500m

SIGNPOSTS

BARN

TELEGRAPH POLE

GO THROUGH LITTLE GATE AHEAD

NUN COTE NOOK FARM

BARN

TURN OFF ROAD HERE

GATES

PARK LODGE

TO MARSKE 3 MILES/5KM

Elaine's Farmhouse Kitchen

HAY MEADOWS

CARAVANS, WAGONS ETC

MARRICK

PHONE & BENCH

ST ANDREW'S 1858

NOW ON TARMAC

TWO GATES

FIELD

NOW ON NUNS' STEPS ON EDGE OF WOOD WITH MOSSY WALL TO RIGHT. SLIPPERY WHEN WET, SHADY IN THE SUN

BARNS

GATE

CATTLE GRID

UNDER BRANCHES OF LOW TREE TO WICKET GATE

THROUGH GATE TO LEFT OF ROAD

LOOK OUT FOR HARES

BARN

115

MARRICK PRIORY OUTDOOR CENTRE

FARM

CAR PARK

56

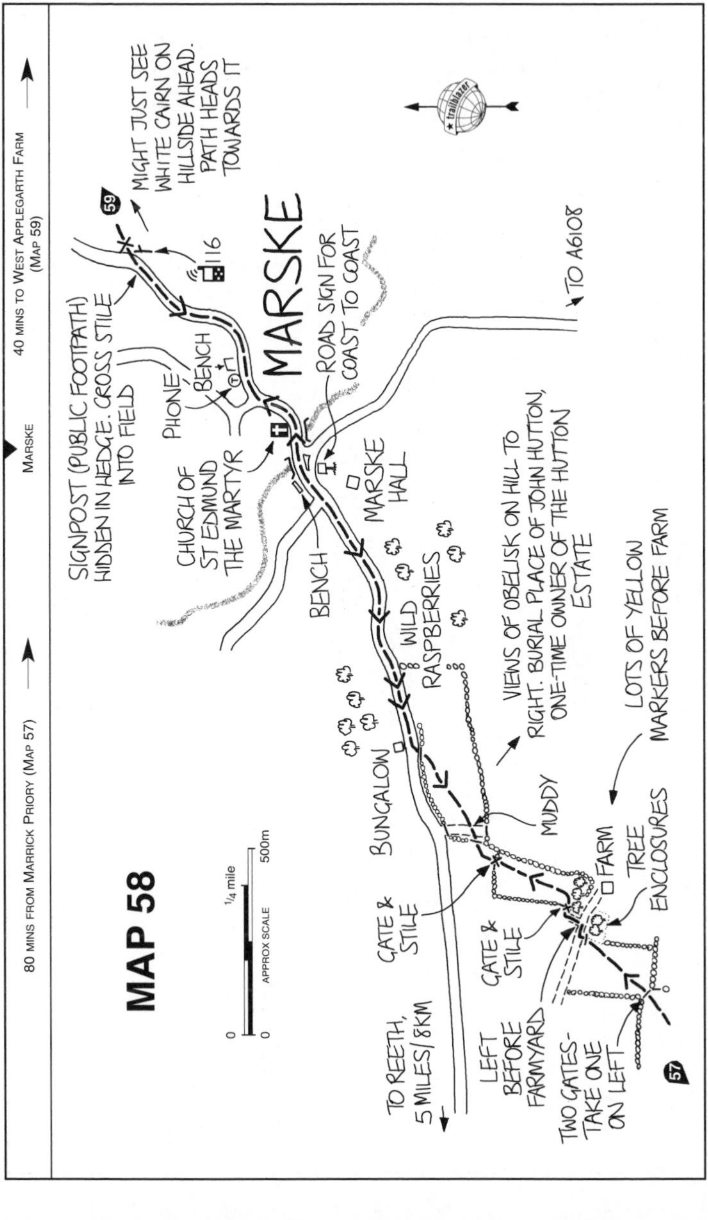
80 MINS FROM MARRICK PRIORY (MAP 57)
MARSKE
40 MINS TO WEST APPLEGARTH FARM (MAP 59)
MAP 58
0
0
1/4 mile
500m
APPROX SCALE
MIGHT JUST SEE WHITE CAIRN ON HILLSIDE AHEAD. PATH HEADS TOWARDS IT
59
116
MARSKE
SIGNPOST (PUBLIC FOOTPATH) HIDDEN IN HEDGE. CROSS STILE INTO FIELD
PHONE
BENCH
ROAD SIGN FOR COAST TO COAST
TO A6108
CHURCH OF ST EDMUND THE MARTYR
MARSKE HALL
BENCH
WILD RASPBERRIES
VIEWS OF OBELISK ON HILL TO RIGHT. BURIAL PLACE OF JOHN HUTTON, ONE-TIME OWNER OF THE HUTTON ESTATE
LOTS OF YELLOW MARKERS BEFORE FARM
BUNGALOW
MUDDY
FARM
TREE ENCLOSURES
GATE & STILE
GATE & STILE
TO REETH, 5 MILES/8KM
LEFT BEFORE FARMYARD
TWO GATES- TAKE ONE ON LEFT
57

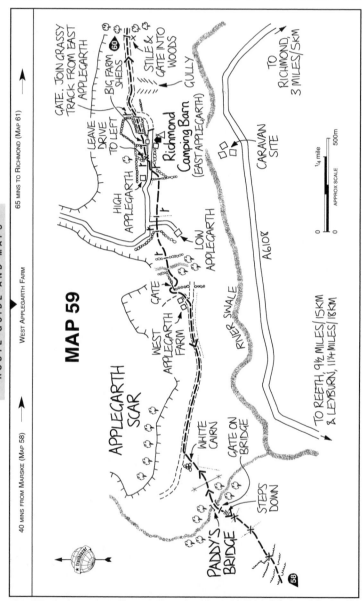

MAP 59

40 MINS FROM MARSKE (MAP 58) →   WEST APPLEGARTH FARM   65 MINS TO RICHMOND   TO RICHMOND (MAP 61) →

GATE. JOIN GRASSY TRACK FROM EAST APPLEGARTH

60

BIG FARM SHEDS

STILE & GATE INTO WOODS

LEAVE DRIVE TO LEFT

GULLY

Richmond Camping Barn (EAST APPLEGARTH)

HIGH APPLEGARTH

TO RICHMOND, 3 MILES/5KM

CARAVAN SITE

¼ mile

APPROX SCALE

0   500m

LOW APPLEGARTH

A6108

APPLEGARTH SCAR

WEST APPLEGARTH FARM

GATE

RIVER SWALE

TO REETH, 9½ MILES/15KM & LEYBURN, 11¼ MILES/18KM

WHITE CAIRN

GATE ON BRIDGE

STEPS DOWN

PADDY'S BRIDGE

58

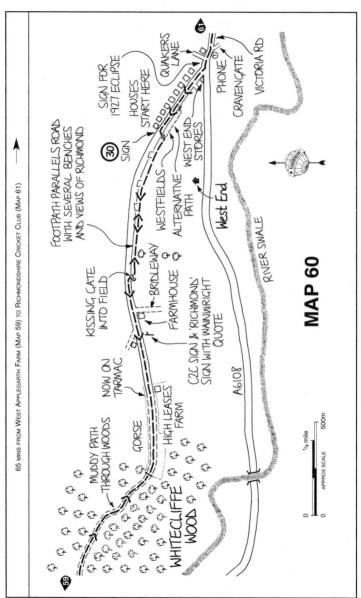

65 MINS FROM WEST APPLEGARTH FARM (MAP 59) TO RICHMONDSHIRE CRICKET CLUB (MAP 61)

MAP 60

FOOTPATH PARALLELS ROAD WITH SEVERAL BENCHES AND VIEWS OF RICHMOND

SIGN FOR 1927 ECLIPSE

HOUSES START HERE

QUAKERS LANE

PHONE

CRAVENGATE

VICTORIA RD

30 SIGN

WEST END STORES

WESTFIELDS

ALTERNATIVE PATH

West End

RIVER SWALE

KISSING GATE INTO FIELD

BRIDLEWAY

FARMHOUSE

C2C SIGN & 'RICHMOND' SIGN WITH WAINWRIGHT QUOTE

A6108

NOW ON TARMAC

GORSE

HIGH LEASES FARM

MUDDY PATH THROUGH WOODS

WHITECLIFFE WOOD

¼ mile

APPROX SCALE

0   500m

hill, you pass the crenellated profile of **St Edmund the Martyr**, built on the site of an earlier church dating back to 1090 from which the north and south doors and hexagonal supporting pillars survive. St Edmund, incidentally, was a Saxon king put to death by the Danes in AD870.

Half a mile out of the village the road is once again forsaken in favour of grassy pasture as the trail unfolds, bending east at the white cairn below **Applegarth Scar** to pick up the farm track to West Applegarth (Map 59).

The farms of Low and High Applegarth are passed before the trail reaches a third farm at **East Applegarth** where, high above the wooded valley, the rustic *Richmond Camping Barn* (Map 59; ☎ 01748 822940; 🐾 by prior arrangement; Mar-Nov) is the nearest cheap accommodation option this side of Richmond, three miles on. However, booking in advance is essential because the barn may be booked for sole occupancy. There's an 8- and a 4-bed **dorm** (from £9pp with bedding). Electricity (including the shower but not lighting) is on a meter (£1 coins only). Subject to prior arrangement food can be made available to cook meals using the facilities provided. There's also a grassy patch for **camping** (from £4pp; campers can use the facilities in the barn unless it has been booked for sole occupancy). If you're a camper and today's hike has been a little short for your tastes, however, then we recommend pushing on beyond Richmond to the Hildyard Arms in Colburn (see p205).

The trail continues into sometimes muddy **Whitecliffe Wood**, emerging 15 minutes later at High Leases Farm where the ensuing road walk can actually be paralleled on a footpath behind the fence on the right. Fine views of Richmond soon emerge; terracotta and slate roofs backed by the distant Cleveland Hills until you enter the town's suburbs.

RICHMOND   MAP 61

Up above a castle! Down below a stream!
Up above a ruin! Down below a dream!
Man made the castle, rude, forbidding, bare.
God made the river, swift, eternal, fair.
From the recollections of **Mr M Wise** as recorded in *Richmond Yorkshire in 1830s* (Wenham Publishers 1977).

This is the largest settlement on the Coast to Coast and feels it. Richmond is a busy market town that evolved around the **castle**, built by one Alan the Red in the 11th century.

As the castle fell into disrepair over time its stones were scavenged to build the surrounding houses, giving the entire town the same sombre hue. During the Georgian era, as the town's fortunes waned still further, Richmond discovered a new source of prosperity as a centre for fine cabinet-making. Many of the buildings leading off the main marketplace date back to this era (indeed, the town museum is housed in a

former cabinet-maker's workshop) and, following its restoration in 2003, the **Georgian theatre** is now said to be the finest in the land.

At the centre of the town is the large, cobbled **marketplace** off which run numerous winding alleys, known as *wynds*. Most of the town's attractions can be found on or near this marketplace, though a couple of the ruins nearby may also warrant further investigation.

Although it's a very pleasant place, the size and scale of Richmond – to say nothing of the noise, the bustle and the traffic – can come as something of a shock to fell-weathered Coasters used to more rural locales. As with so many provincial English towns, Richmond can get rowdy at weekends, but it does have its advantages in terms of the facilities it provides, as well as enough sights to amuse those who decide to rest here for a day.

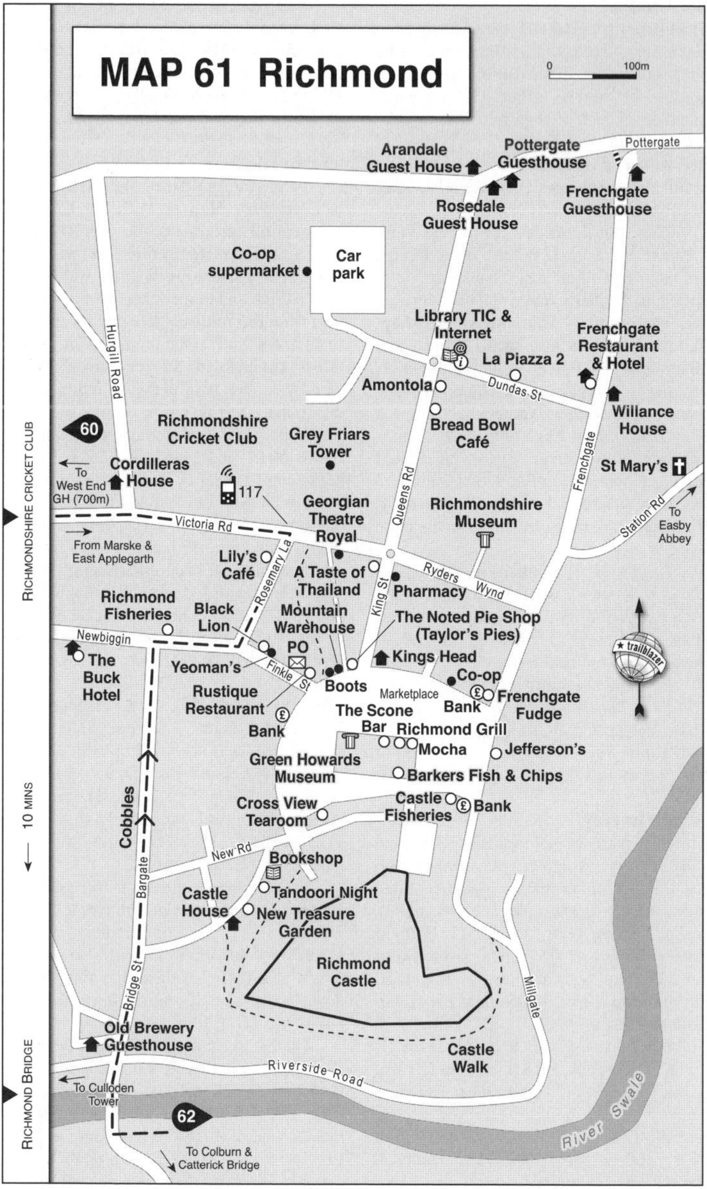

MAP 61 Richmond

0   100m

Pottergate

Arandale
Guest House

Pottergate
Guesthouse

Rosedale
Guest House

Frenchgate
Guesthouse

Co-op
supermarket

Car
park

Library TIC &
Internet

@
i

La Piazza 2

Frenchgate
Restaurant
& Hotel

Amontola

Dundas St.

Richmondshire
Cricket Club

Grey Friars
Tower

Bread Bowl
Café

Willance
House

St Mary's

60

Cordilleras
House

117

Georgian
Theatre
Royal

Richmondshire
Museum

To
West End
GH (700m)

Victoria Rd

Queens Rd

Frenchgate

Station Rd

To
Easby
Abbey

From Marske &
East Applegarth

Lily's
Café

A Taste of
Thailand

Ryders
Wynd

Richmond
Fisheries

Black
Lion

Mountain
Warehouse

Pharmacy

The Noted Pie Shop
(Taylor's Pies)

Newbiggin

PO

King St

Kings Head

The Buck
Hotel

Yeoman's

Boots

Co-op

Rustique
Restaurant

Bank

Marketplace

Bank

Frenchgate
Fudge

The Scone
Bar

Richmond Grill

Cobbles

Green Howards
Museum

Mocha

Jefferson's

Barkers Fish & Chips

Bargate

Cross View
Tearoom

Castle
Fisheries

Bank

New Rd

Bookshop

Castle
House

Tandoori Night

New Treasure
Garden

Bridge St

Richmond
Castle

Old Brewery
Guesthouse

Riverside Road

Castle
Walk

Millgate

To Culloden
Tower

62

To Colburn &
Catterick Bridge

River Swale

RICHMONDSHIRE CRICKET CLUB

10 MINS

RICHMOND BRIDGE

trailblazer

Services

The **library** (☎ 01609 534580, Mon & Thur 10am-6pm, Tue & Fri 10am-5pm, Wed 10am-noon, Sat 10am-1pm; closed Sun) houses the **tourist office** (💻 www.richmond.org) which offers a free accommodation booking service. The library also has free WI-FI and offers **internet** access (eight terminals) and charges £2.50 for 30 minutes to temporary members.

The **post office** (Mon-Fri 9am-5.30pm, Sat 9am-12.30pm) does foreign exchange and all the major banks are represented on the main square and have longed-for **cashpoints**. The **outdoors shop**, Yeoman's (Mon-Sat 9am-5.30pm, Sun 10am-4pm), on Finkle St, is worth checking out for replacement equipment and there's a Mountain Warehouse (Mon-Sat 9am-5.30pm, Sun 10am-5pm) on the northern side of the main square. Next door there's a Boots (Mon-Sat 9am-5.30pm) on the main square and a second **pharmacy**, Richmond Pharmacy, by the roundabout on King St.

Castle Hill **Bookshop** (☎ 01748 824243, 💻 www.castlehillbookshop.co.uk; Mon-Sat 9am-5pm), below the castle, has an excellent range of books and an interesting selection on local history.

For **food shopping** there's a small Co-op (daily 7am-10pm) on the main square, and a larger Co-op superstore (Mon-Sat 6am-10pm, Sun 10am-4pm) to the north of Grey Friars Tower.

Where to stay

Currently there are no hostels in Richmond and the nearest **cheap accommodation** (camping/camping barn) is either three miles back at East Applegarth (see p198), or the *Hildyard Arms* (see p205) in Colburn three miles further along the Coast to Coast path. The ambitious may even want to head on further to the well-appointed *Brompton Camping Barn* (see p205) two miles after Colburn. So if you want to stay in town it's going to have to be a B&B or a hotel. If you haven't pre-booked, your best bet is the free accommodation-booking service at the tourist office. What follows is our selection of the options based on readers' feedback and our own experiences.

Just west of the centre of town and now under new ownership, *West End Guesthouse* (Map 60 p197; ☎ 01748 824783, 💻 www.stayatwestend.co.uk; 1S/2D/1T/1D or T or Tr; all en suite; WI-FI), 45 Reeth Rd, is a comfortable place. For B&B it's £40-42.50pp (sgl £45-50) or £110 for the triple room.

At 11 Hurgill Rd, near the cricket club, is *Cordilleras House* (☎ 01748 824628, www.cordillerashouse.co.uk; 1D/1D or T en suite/1Tr, private facilities; ▾; WI-FI; Ⓛ £6) where walkers are warmly welcomed with a drink and home-made treats. Rooms start from £85 for two sharing (£65 sgl occ) or £110 for three in the family room. A hot tub is available for £5 per person and a laundry service is available in return for a donation to their favourite charity.

Fellow Coasters recommend *Willance House* (☎ 01748 824467, 💻 www.willancehouse.com; 1D/2D or T; all en suite; WI-FI; Ⓛ from £6; Mar-Dec), at 24 Frenchgate, an oak-beamed house (or rather, three houses) dating back to the 17th century. It's named after the first alderman of Richmond. It has a guest lounge; B&B costs from £38pp (sgl occ £56). Almost opposite Willance House is the smart *Frenchgate Restaurant & Hotel* (☎ 01748 822087, 💻 www.thefrenchgate.co.uk; 2S/6D or T/1 suite; all en suite; ▾; WI-FI; Ⓛ), 59-61 Frenchgate. With marble floors, limestone walls, oak-framed beds and showcasing local artists, it's a classy venue for a relaxing stay with B&B from £59pp for a standard room with plusher options at £79pp and the suite from £125pp. Sadly, the weary solo traveller must hand over at least £88.

Further away from the marketplace at No 66 is *Frenchgate Guesthouse* (☎ 07889 768696, 💻 www.66frenchgate.co.uk; 4D/2D or T/1T/1F; all en suite; ▾; WI-FI; Ⓛ), which, like the others, has fine views down across the Swale. B&B costs from £43pp (sgl occ £70).

On the square itself and part of the Best Western chain, there's *The Kings Head Hotel* (☎ 01748 850220, reservations ☎ 0808 178 7666, 💻 www.kingsheadrichmond.co.uk; 6S/19D/1T; all en suite; ▾; 🐾 £10; WI-FI; Ⓛ from £5), probably the smartest hotel in town. Rates start from

£70pp (sgl £85, sgl occ £100) for B&B; however, they can also be quite a bit higher.

The Buck Hotel (☎ 01748 822259, 🖥 www.thebuckhotelrichmond.co.uk; 1S or D/3D or T/2Tr; all en suite; 🐾 £5; WI-FI; ⓛ £5) on Newbiggin is an unpretentious place parts of which are being renovated. However, this is proceeding slowly and the hotel gets mixed reports. B&B costs £35-40pp (sgl £40-50, £100 for three in a room).

To the north on Pottergate is the friendly *Pottergate Guesthouse* (☎ 01748 823826, 🖥 www.pottergateguesthouse.co.uk; 3D/1T/1Tr; all en suite or with private facilities; WI-FI; ⓛ), 4 Pottergate, charging £36pp (sgl occ £50, three in the triple £108) for B&B; a laundry service is also available. Also here is *Rosedale Guest House* (☎ 01748 824465 🖥 www.richmond bedandbreakfast.co.uk; 1T/3D/1F/2 suites ; all en suite; WI-FI; ⓛ £5-6), now under new ownership but still with the silver-starred, high-ceilinged Georgian rooms; the owners also promise to maintain Rosedale's finer touches such as putting sherry and chocolates on the bedside table and maintaining the varied breakfast menu. B&B costs £35-45pp (sgl occ from £70).

Across the road is *Arandale Guest House* (☎ 01748 821282, 🖥 www.aran daleguesthouse.co.uk; 3D/2D or T; all en suite; ➖; WI-FI; ⓛ) which has been recommended, particularly for their hot tub, comfortable beds and great breakfasts. Rates in this Victorian townhouse are £42.50-55pp (sgl occ £55). The hot tub seats up to six people at a time (30-60 mins; swimwear required) and must be booked in advance.

On the small green in the south of the town is *The Old Brewery Guesthouse* (☎ 01748 822460, 🖥 www.oldbreweryguest house.com; 1S/6D/2T; most en suite, others share bathroom; ➖; 🐾 £5; WI-FI; ⓛ £5), another Grade II Georgian building and the nerve centre for Sherpa Van (see p28). B&B costs £39-42pp (sgl/sgl occ from £59).

For a little luxury you could try *Castle House* (☎ 01748 823954, 🖥 www.castle houserichmond.co.uk; 4D/1Tr; all en suite; ➖; WI-FI; ⓛ £7) a boutique B&B on Castle Hill. Rooms start from £80 for two sharing (£10 discount for single occupancy) but if you really want to push the boat out, for £130 you could treat yourself to their Richmond Suite which has an open fire and a four-poster bed with freestanding bath and separate en suite with shower. The attention to detail here is evident, from the complementary glass of wine on arrival to the drying room for wet clothes.

Where to eat and drink
Disregarding fast-food outlets which you won't necessarily have walked across the country to visit, there are lots of good places to eat in Richmond.

On the marketplace, *Cross View Tearoom & Restaurant* (☎ 01748 825897; Mon-Sat 9am-5pm, Sun 10am-5pm) is friendly and good value. Their cottage pie is £7.30. There are a couple of lovely rivals next to each other in the heart of Richmond. First is *The Scone Bar* (☎ 01748 518644; Mon & Tue 10.30am-3.30pm, Fri 10.30am-4pm, Sat 10am-4pm, Sun 11am-4pm; 🐾 on ground floor) which, in addition to the 15 different types of scones on offer, also boasts the title of having the best hot chocolate in town, though this claim is disputed by *Mocha* (Mon-Tue & Thur-Sat 9.30am-5pm, Sun 11am-4pm), ostensibly a chocolate shop but one which serves up some real sweet treats including jaffa cake ice cream and a fantastic chilli hot chocolate.

Lily's Café (☎ 01748 822633, 🖥 www.lilyscafe.co.uk; Tue-Sat 9.30am-4pm), on Rosemary Lane, does great coffee and tea, scones and a scrumptious range of cakes and cupcakes as well as light lunches.

On Queens Rd, German dishes sit alongside roast beef and Yorkshire pudding at *The Bread Bowl Café* (☎ 01748 850625; Mon-Wed & Fri-Sat 10am-4pm, Wed 10am-7.30pm). It's very good value, too; jager schnitzel is £6.95.

Richmond is well served by fish and chipperies with two of them, *Castle Fisheries* (Mon & Tues 4-9.30pm, Wed & Thu noon-9.30pm, Fri & Sat noon-10pm, Sun noon-8pm) and *Barker's Fish & Chips* (Sun-Wed 11am-9.30pm, Thu-Sat to 10pm), both residing on the market square.

If you can't face the thought of another pub meal, a top class curry is a possibility so point yourself towards *Amontola Tandoori* (☎ 01748 826070; 🖥 amon tola.co.uk; Sun-Thur 5-10.30pm, Fri-Sat to 11pm) up on Queen's Rd and now under new management. There's plenty of space, the service is great and there's a three-course deal for £9.95. There's another curry house, **Tandoori Night** (☎ 01748 826677, 🖳 www.tandoorinight-restaurant.co.uk; daily 5-10pm) south of the marketplace, which also gets good reviews.

Another option is Italian fare, for which try **La Piazza 2** (☎ 01748 825008, www.lapiazzaitalianrichmond.co.uk/; daily 5-10pm, Fri-Sun also noon-3pm); with its fountains and statuary, it's certainly doing its best to recreate the atmosphere of the Mediterranean on Richmond's Dundas St. Pizzas start at £8.95.

The **Black Lion** (☎ 01748 826217; food daily noon-2.30pm and 5-9.30pm) on Finkle St near the marketplace, does good pub grub. Their steak pie (£8.50) has been recommended. They also do a decent afternoon tea for two (2.30-5pm) for £9.95.

New Treasure Garden (☎ 01748 825827; Sun, Mon, Wed & Thur 6-10.30pm, Fri & Sat 6-11pm), 7 Castle Hill, is a Cantonese restaurant with an interesting Szechuan selection.

A Taste of Thailand (☎ 01748 829696; daily 5-11pm), on King St, is a quirky little place that's nevertheless popular. They do excellent red and green curries and have a BYO policy with corkage £1.

The **restaurant** at **The Kings Head** (see Where to stay; daily 7-9pm, Sun noon-2pm) is very smart but pricey. They also do meals at the **bar** (daily 9am-9pm) which are less expensive.

One of the best places to eat in Richmond is **Rustique** (☎ 01748 821565, 🖳 www.rustiquerestaurants.co.uk, daily noon-9pm), on Finkle St and French-gate. For the full Gallic experience start with half a dozen snails for £6.25. It's all good value and you can get an excellent three-course set meal for £16.95.

Also highly recommended is **Richmond Grill & Brasserie** (☎ 01748 822602, 🖳 www.richmondgrillandbrasserie .co.uk; Tue-Sat noon-2pm and 5.45-9pm) on the marketplace. Main dishes are around £13.90 on the imaginative menu (eg braised ox cheek with horseradish mash or Asian

marinated swordfish) and you can kick off the evening with a stylish RG&B martini for £7.50. You'll probably need to book.

Frenchgate Restaurant & Hotel (see Where to stay; daily noon-2pm & 7-9pm) is another good, if expensive, choice for a relaxed evening's dining. Venison, turbot and your old friend, Swaledale lamb, may be on the regularly changing menu. Their three-course set meal costs £39; booking recommended.

For drinking, there are some pubs lining Market Place, but they can be extremely noisy with a couple catering largely to groups of local lads looking for a fight. A safe option is **The Buck Hotel** (see Where to stay; food Tue 6-9pm, Wed-Fri noon-3pm & 6-9pm, Sat noon-7pm, Sun noon-6pm), on Newbiggin, which, though it still has live music some Saturday nights, is a lot more friendly and relaxed, with great views across the river.

If you need something for your lunch-box, on the marketplace try **Taylor's Noted Pie Shop** (☎ 01748 464716, Mon-Sat 7.30am-4.30pm) for their famous pies or the deli, **Jefferson's** (☎ 01748 821258, 🖳 www.jeffersonsofrichmond.co.uk; Mon-Sat 8am-4.30pm), which also has a small café; dogs are OK here too. Round it all off with a visit to **Frenchgate Fudge & Chocolate Makers** (Mon, Tue & Thur-Sat 10am-5pm, Sun 2-5pm), at 1 Frenchgate.

What to see and do

Richmond is a great town to walk around, with plenty of twisting 'wynds' to explore and plaques installed here and there pointing out places of historical interest.

● **Richmond Castle** (☎ 01748 822493; 🖳 www.english-heritage.org.uk; daily 10am-4pm; £5/4.50 adult/concs, English Heritage members free) Without Richmond Castle it's arguable there would be no Richmond and while it ceased performing its castellian duties centuries ago, in the middle of the 1800s it found a new purpose as a tourist attraction and has been welcoming visitors ever since. Visitors are, however, advised not to rush headlong at the ruins like a troupe of marauding barbarians, but instead first acquaint themselves with the **exhibition** in the reception building; it gives a thought-provoking account of the history of the castle and the town as well as a display on how the castle was originally built. There's also an interesting section on World War I conscientious objectors (absolutists) who were held captive here. Their poignant graffiti still exists on the cell walls, though for protection these cells are today kept locked; copies of the graffiti can be seen in the exhibition.

Now advancing to the ruins in an orderly and newly informed manner, you may be a little disappointed at first by the lack of surviving structures within the castle walls, though by reading the information boards dotted around, you should get a reasonable idea of how the castle once looked.

Scholars may be similarly entranced by the ruins of **Scolland Hall**, the finest ruins surviving from Alan the Red's time; most visitors, however, will find the views from the **keep** overlooking the town far more engrossing.

● **Georgian Theatre Royal** (☎ 01748 825252, 🖥 www.georgiantheatreroyal.co .uk) Built in 1788 by actor-manager Samuel Butler and now beautifully restored, this is the most complete Georgian theatre in the country as well as being the oldest working theatre in its original form. It's well worth a visit for a performance (check the website for what's on) or a fascinating backstage tour. From mid-Feb (after the pantomime season) to mid-Nov small guided tours run on the hour from 10am until 4pm; suggested donation £3.50. You'll get to see the oldest surviving painted scenery in Britain as well as the theatre museum.

● **Richmondshire Museum** (☎ 01748 825611, 🖥 www.richmondshiremuseum .org.uk; April to end Oct daily 10.30am-4.30pm; £3/£2.50 concs) Another surprisingly absorbing local museum, similar in content to Reeth's Swaledale Museum (see p188), though bigger and with even more impressive exhibits. Highlights include **Cruck House**, a 15th-century building moved wholesale from Ravensworth in 1985, an exhibition tracing the history of transport (including an original penny farthing bicycle), and tellingly, most popular of all, the set of the vet's surgery from the TV series of *All Creatures Great and Small*.

● **Green Howards Museum** (☎ 01748 826561; 🖥 www.greenhowards.org.uk; Mon-Sat 10am-4pm, summer also Sun 12.30-4.30pm) Richmond has a long military association and is the garrison town of Catterick, now many times larger than Richmond itself. The town's regiment, the Green Howards, have their own museum and headquarters in this former Holy Trinity Church. With a history spanning the Crimean and Boer wars, as well as military engagements on the North-West Frontier of India and more recent operations in neighbouring Afghanistan, the story of the regiment is a fascinating one. Highlights include the staggering 3750-strong medal collection awarded to members of the regiment.

● **Easby Abbey** Formerly and more properly known as **St Agatha's Monastery**, Easby Abbey lies about a mile to the east of Richmond Castle. You may get a distant view of it from across the Swale during the next stage of the walk, but if you've got the time we strongly advise you make a detour and pay a proper visit. Like those at Shap, the ruins at Easby were once part of a Premonstratensian Abbey, this one built in 1152, just 31 years after the founding of the order by St Norbert in Prémontré in Picardy, northern France. The monastery served the community for almost 400 years because, unlike many other orders who chose to cut themselves off from the outside world, the Premonstratensians saw it as their duty to minister to and serve the laity until Henry VIII brought about the dissolution. Unwilling to bow to Henry's demands, they joined the Pilgrimage of Grace in 1536, the most popular rebellion against Henry. Many monasteries were briefly restored by the rebels – St Agatha's at Easby among them. They were subsequently defeated and Henry set about exacting a chilling revenge on those who had dared to defy his orders, instructing his forces in the north to '*cause such dreadful execution upon a good number of inhabitants, hanging them on trees, quartering them and setting their heads and quarters in every town, as shall be a fearful warning*'. While visiting, be sure to check out the **parish church** here at Easby, which has survived in remarkable condition and plays host to some wonderful 13th-century **wall paintings**. Look, too, for the 12th-century **panel of glass** depicting St John.

Other sights There are a couple of magnificent ruined towers in town. The first you'll come across is **Grey Friars Tower**, in the gardens opposite off Queens Rd. This was once part of a Franciscan monastery, founded in 1258, though the tower itself wasn't built until sometime around 1500. The second, clearly visible to the west of town from Richmond Castle, is **Culloden Tower**, a folly dating back to 1746. Amazingly, it's now a novelty holiday cottage (💻 www.landmarktrust.org.uk).

Transport (see also pp52-5)
The nearest **railway station** is in Darlington, but there are plenty of **buses** from Market Place. Bus No 29 goes to Darlington, as does the No X26/X27 (via Catterick), taking about an hour. The No 30 service runs up Swaledale (Mon-Sat), calling at Reeth, Gunnerside and Keld, and their No 54 and No 55 go to Northallerton.

Those who wish to skip some of the next section can catch one of the many buses to Catterick Bridge or the No 55 to Bolton-on-Swale – your conscience may torment you but the truth is you won't have missed much.

For a **taxi** call Amalgamated (☎ 01748 825112).

STAGE 10: RICHMOND TO INGLEBY CROSS   MAPS 61-72

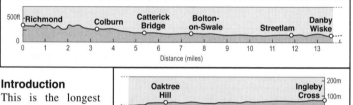

ROUTE GUIDE AND MAPS

Introduction
This is the longest stage in this book but it's also the flattest so there's something to be said for Wainwright's suggestion of traversing the **Vale of Mowbray** in one fell day, rather than overnighting at Danby Wiske. It's a fairly uneventful trudge by the standards of the Coast to Coast, much of it conducted on back roads and with barely a hill to grimace at, so the **22½ miles* (36km, 8½hrs)** to Ingleby Cross are actually achievable. What you may want to factor in is the pounding your trail-weary feet may get along the roads as well as the following stage; a notably more gruelling 21-miler to Blakey Ridge. There's more on p221 to help make up your mind how you stage the next couple of days.

The fell-loving Wainwright lost little love on this tepid agricultural tract, not least the innocent hamlet of Danby Wiske, cruelly claiming it to be a low point in his project in more than just elevation. Things have obviously changed for the better (and were probably never that bad), and now there are two B&Bs, and a pub to tempt you. So, in our opinion, there's a lot to be said for spending a morning ticking off a couple of sights in Richmond before setting out on the 13½ mile* to Danby Wiske in the afternoon.

* Note that the A1 (M) roadworks diversion (see p205) currently adds 1 mile (1.6km) to this.

❑ **Temporary route diversion** Around Catterick Bridge and Brompton-on-Swale the **A1 (M) road works and bridge replacements** which began in 2014 are unlikely all to be completed until late 2016/early 2017 and you may still have to take a detour. This adds about a mile to this stage, and you swap some gentle field strolling for a tedious pavement-based trudge beside the fast-ish A6136. See **Maps 63-4 (pp207-8)**.

The route

Starting off from **Richmond Bridge** with a stroll along the Swale's southern bank, you leave the river for a terrace of houses and join the A6136, leaving it in turn along a lane to the left that passes a sewage works and subsequently a dark, occasionally muddy stretch of riverside woodland. When you finally pop out of the trees – quite possibly to the sound of gunfire from the nearby garrison at Catterick – you traipse over or around more fields and farms to Catterick Bridge.

COLBURN, CATTERICK BRIDGE & BROMPTON-ON-SWALE
MAP 63 p207, MAP 64 p208

The village of **Colburn** (Map 63) has little to distract the eastbound hiker apart from *The Hildyard Arms* (☎ 01748 832353, 🖥 thehildyardarms.wordpress.com; food daily noon-3pm, Mon-Sat 6-9pm; 🐾; ⓛ £4.95, breakfasts £6.95). As well as Richmond ales on tap, they do soup and sandwiches outside the main food times and will make up packed lunches and breakfasts for campers. **Camping** is free if you phone ahead, a decent shower is 50p. The long-planned conversion of the barn into a bunkhouse has still not left the drawing board but this is our only niggle, for this place comes highly recommended for friendliness and convenience; if you're camping you won't find better in the area.

From Colburn at one point the path skirts past the former site of St Giles Hospital that flourished alongside the river some 800 years ago, although if any trace of it remains today, it's best observed following a prolonged session at the Hildyard Arms.

More conspicuous is *St Giles Farm* (☎ 01748 811372; 1T/1D/1F; all en suite; 🐾; ⓛ from £2.50) providing **B&B** (booking essential) from £40pp, and **camping** for £6pp including shower/toilet facilities.

From here the path continues above the river past *Thornborough Farm* (Map 64; ☎ 01748 811421; 🐾 by prior arrangement) where very basic **camping** (£5pp inc toilet/washing facilities, no shower; book-

ing appreciated) is offered, and under the throbbing A1 trunk road to **Catterick Bridge**. Famed for its racecourse and army camp, the name Catterick reaches back 2000 years when a strategic Roman garrison and town developed where Dere Street (today's A1(M) or Great North Road) bridged the Swale.

There are other pubs offering accommodation in **Brompton-on-Swale**, as well as *Brompton Camping Barn* (arrivals confirmation ☎ 01748 818326; 🐾). The barn has three rooms (each sleeping four) with bunk beds including bedding (sleeping sacks cost £1); the rate is £10pp. There's a fully equipped kitchen, dining/lounge area and shower facilities (10p). Electricity is metered (£1 coins only). There's also **camping** (£5pp inc shower) for half a dozen tents. Book through the YHA (see p22; ☎ 0800 019 1700, 🖥 www.yha.org.uk/barn/brompton-camping-barn) or direct. Right opposite the Barn there's a mini **supermarket** open very early till late. To get to the Barn from the original route, continue north once over the bridge, turn left down Bridge Rd, passing under the A1 and join West Richmond Rd; it's on the right, a 15-minute walk from the bridge. Or take a daring short cut by scrambling down to the small bridge over the Swale River by Colburn Beck Woods (see Map 63); you won't miss much.

Dales & District's No 55 **bus** stops in Brompton-on-Swale (Mon-Sat), and the No 54 goes via Catterick Bridge; see pp52-5.

ROUTE GUIDE AND MAPS

Having flirted with the river for much of the past five miles since leaving Richmond, you finally leave it for good to march into the hamlet of **Bolton-on-Swale** (Map 65). There are no refreshments here other than those to be found in the church but, if you can be bothered, you could walk the 400 metres north to **Scorton** where *Joan's Tearooms* (off Map 65; Tues-Fri 10am-4pm) serves scones and cakes and other treats in the Community Hall. In Bolton-on-Swale it's worth visiting the churchyard, famous for its **monument to Henry Jenkins**, a local man who lived an unremarkable life except for its length. He claimed he was 169 when he died, a fact which may explain the popularity of the village with retirees. (cont'd on p212)

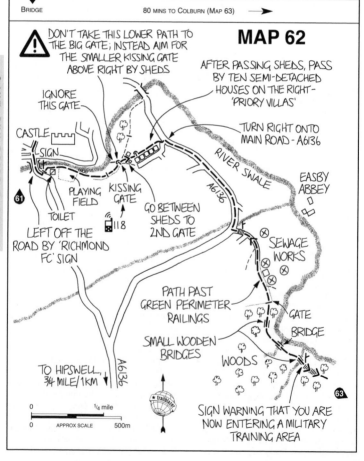

BRIDGE   80 MINS TO COLBURN (MAP 63) ⟶

MAP 62

DON'T TAKE THIS LOWER PATH TO THE BIG GATE; INSTEAD AIM FOR THE SMALLER KISSING GATE ABOVE RIGHT BY SHEDS

AFTER PASSING SHEDS, PASS BY TEN SEMI-DETACHED HOUSES ON THE RIGHT- 'PRIORY VILLAS'

IGNORE THIS GATE

CASTLE
SIGN

TURN RIGHT ONTO MAIN ROAD - A6136

RIVER SWALE

A6136

EASBY ABBEY

61

PLAYING FIELD

KISSING GATE

TOILET

118

GO BETWEEN SHEDS TO 2ND GATE

SEWAGE WORKS

LEFT OFF THE ROAD BY 'RICHMOND FC' SIGN

PATH PAST GREEN PERIMETER RAILINGS

GATE

BRIDGE

SMALL WOODEN BRIDGES

WOODS

TO HIPSWELL, ¾ MILE/1KM

A6136

63

0   ¼ mile
0   APPROX SCALE   500m

trailblazer

SIGN WARNING THAT YOU ARE NOW ENTERING A MILITARY TRAINING AREA

ROUTE GUIDE AND MAPS

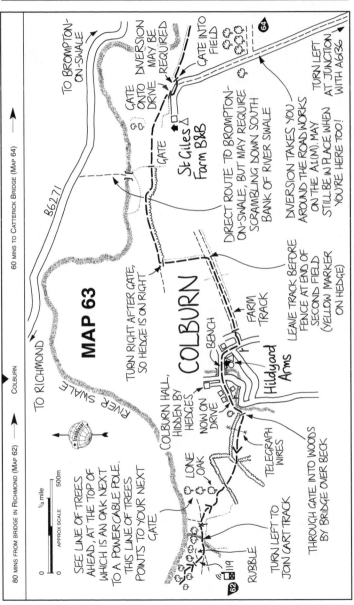

80 MINS FROM BRIDGE IN RICHMOND (MAP 62) → | COLBURN | 60 MINS TO CATTERICK BRIDGE (MAP 64) →

0
0   ¼ mile
     500m
APPROX SCALE

trailblazer

MAP 63

TO RICHMOND

RIVER SWALE

B6271

TO BROMPTON-ON-SWALE

TO BROMPTON-ON-SWALE

DIVERSION MAY BE REQUIRED

GATE INTO FIELD

GATE ONTO DRIVE

GATE

GATE ONTO DRIVE

St Giles Farm B&B

TURN LEFT AT JUNCTION WITH A6136

TURN RIGHT AFTER GATE, SO HEDGE IS ON RIGHT

DIRECT ROUTE TO BROMPTON-ON-SWALE, BUT MAY REQUIRE SCRAMBLING DOWN SOUTH BANK OF RIVER SWALE

DIVERSION TAKES YOU AROUND THE ROADWORKS ON THE A1(M). MAY STILL BE IN PLACE WHEN YOU'RE HERE TOO!

COLBURN

FARM TRACK

LEAVE TRACK BEFORE FENCE AT END OF SECOND FIELD (YELLOW MARKER ON HEDGE)

COLBURN HALL, HIDDEN BY HEDGES

NOW ON DRIVE

BENCH

Hildyard Arms

LONE OAK

TELEGRAPH WIRES

SEE LINE OF TREES AHEAD, AT THE TOP OF WHICH IS AN OAK NEXT TO A POWER/CABLE POLE. THIS LINE OF TREES POINTS TO YOUR NEXT GATE

THROUGH GATE INTO WOODS BY BRIDGE OVER BECK

TURN LEFT TO JOIN CART TRACK

RUBBLE

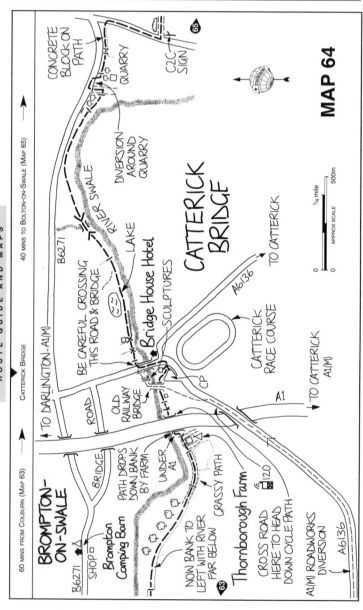

MAP 64

APPROX SCALE

¼ mile · 500m

CONCRETE BLOCK ON PATH

QUARRY

C2C SIGN

DIVERSION AROUND QUARRY

RIVER SWALE

TO DARLINGTON- A1(M)

B6271

BE CAREFUL CROSSING THIS ROAD & BRIDGE

LAKE

Bridge House Hotel

SCULPTURES

CATTERICK BRIDGE

TO CATTERICK

A6136

CATTERICK RACE COURSE

TO CATTERICK A1(M)

A1

CP

OLD RAILWAY BRIDGE

ROAD

BRIDGE

PATH DROPS DOWN BANK BY FARM

UNDER A1

GRASSY PATH

NOW BANK TO LEFT WITH RIVER FAR BELOW

Thornborough Farm

CROSS ROAD HERE TO HEAD DOWN CYCLE PATH

A1(M) ROADWORKS DIVERSION

A6136

BROMPTON-ON-SWALE

SHOP

Brompton Camping Barn

B6271

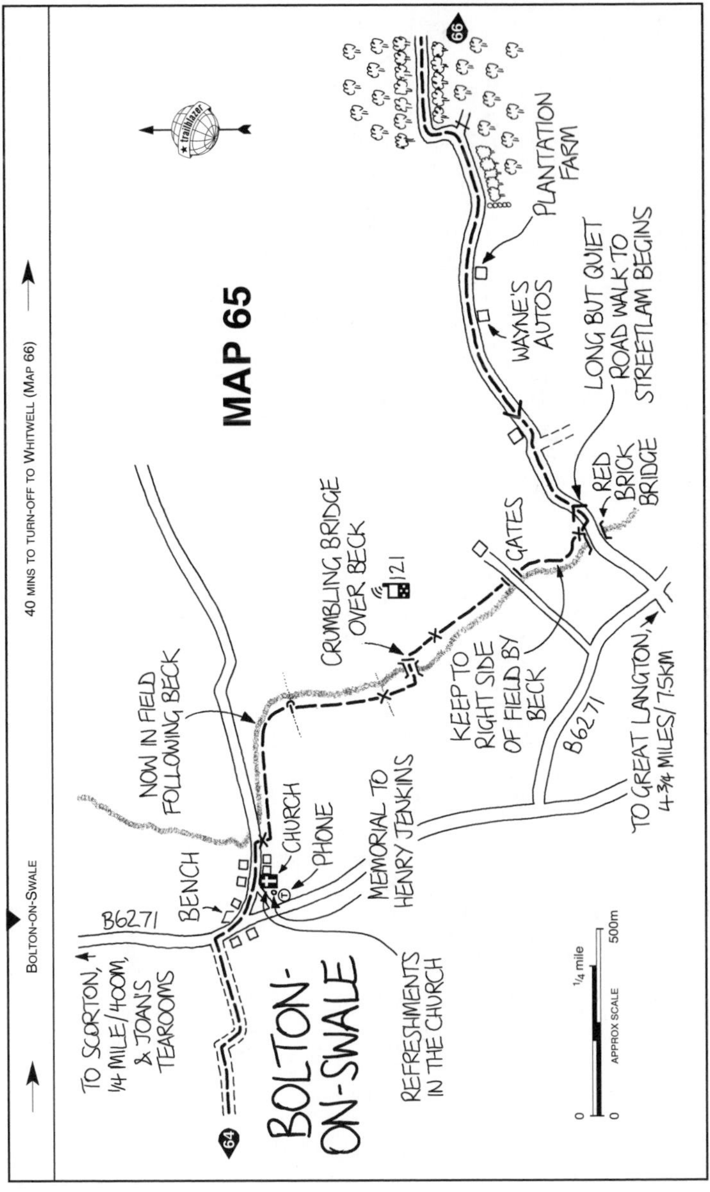
40 MINS TO TURN-OFF TO WHITWELL (MAP 66)
BOLTON-ON-SWALE
MAP 65
trailblazer
64
TO SCORTON, 1/4 MILE/400M, & JOAN'S TEAROOMS
B6271
BENCH
CHURCH
PHONE
MEMORIAL TO HENRY JENKINS
REFRESHMENTS IN THE CHURCH
BOLTON-ON-SWALE
NOW IN FIELD FOLLOWING BECK
CRUMBLING BRIDGE OVER BECK
121
KEEP TO RIGHT SIDE OF FIELD BY BECK
B6271
TO GREAT LANGTON, 4 3/4 MILES/7.5KM
GATES
RED BRICK BRIDGE
LONG BUT QUIET ROAD WALK TO STREETLAM BEGINS
WAYNE'S AUTOS
PLANTATION FARM
66
APPROX SCALE
0
1/4 mile
0
500m

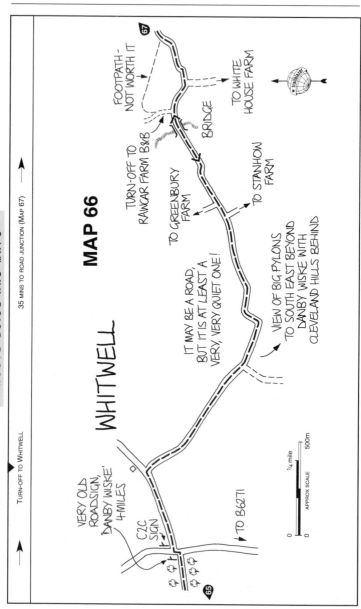

MAP 66

WHITWELL

FOOTPATH -
NOT WORTH IT

TURN-OFF TO
RAWCAR FARM B&B

TO GREENBURY
FARM

BRIDGE

TO WHITE
HOUSE FARM

TO STANHOW
FARM

IT MAY BE A ROAD,
BUT IT IS AT LEAST A
VERY, VERY QUIET ONE!

VIEW OF BIG PYLONS
TO SOUTH EAST BEYOND
DANBY WISKE WITH
CLEVELAND HILLS BEHIND

VERY OLD
ROADSIGN,
'DANBY WISKE'
4 MILES

C2C
SIGN

TO B6271

¼ mile
APPROX SCALE   500m
0
0

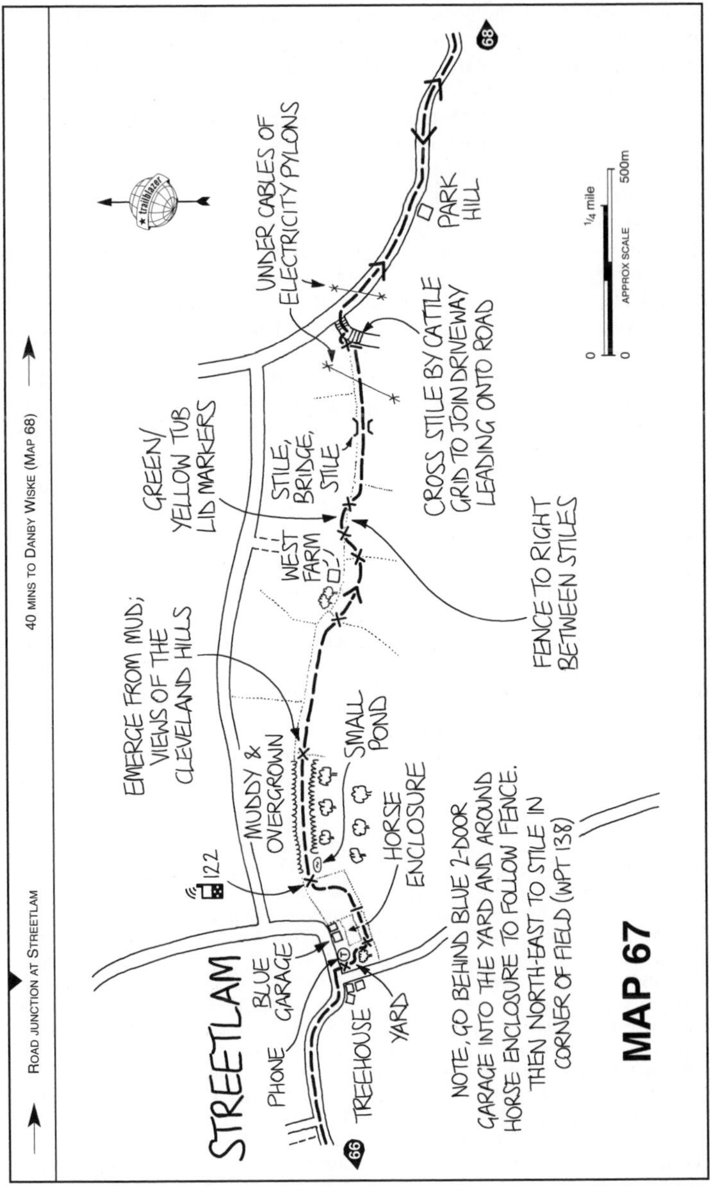
Road junction at Streetlam
40 mins to Danby Wiske (Map 68)
STREETLAM
66
Phone
Blue Garage
Treehouse
Yard
122
Muddy & overgrown
Small pond
Horse enclosure
Emerge from mud; views of the Cleveland Hills
West Farm
Fence to right between stiles
Green/Yellow tub lid markers
Stile, bridge, stile
Cross stile by cattle grid to join driveway leading onto road
Under cables of electricity pylons
Park Hill
68
Approx scale
0
0
1/4 mile
500m
Note, go behind blue 2-door garage into the yard and around horse enclosure to follow fence. Then north-east to stile in corner of field (WPT 138)
MAP 67

(*cont'd from p206*) Bolton-on-Swale church itself is of course older, dating back to the 14th century, with Norman and Saxon ancestors; you can see various bits of masonry from these earlier churches inside, including part of an Anglo-Danish cross shaft in the vestry and part of a pointed arch in the vestry roof. If you need a break Dales & District's No 55 **bus** calls here (Mon-Sat); see p55.

More unexceptional field-tramping ensues followed by a 3½-mile stretch of road-walking, the longest on the entire trail (Maps 65-68). With an OS map you might string together a network of footpaths but here in the Vale, is it worth it? The roads are nearly as quiet as they were in Wainwright's day, while the intrusive odours and hum of intensive farming will be present whichever route you take. Furthermore, we've had people writing to us saying that they either got lost or stuck in a bog trying to follow an 'alternative' route to Wainwright's original!

Sticking to the road, there's accommodation available at the 100-acre organic ***Rawcar Farm*** (☎ 01325 378297, 💻 www.rawcar.co.uk; 2D or T; 🛏; WI-FI), though it is only open in the summer months, April or May to September, the exact times depending on the farming year. The place has been recommended by our readers as a convenient place to interrupt the long-haul schelp through the Vale of Mowbray. Rates are from £52.50 (sgl occ full room price).

At **Streetlam** (Map 67) there's an opportunity to hack along an overgrown footpath towards more fields of pasture and livestock. One gets the feeling that some of the residents hereabouts aren't too happy with thousands of walkers trooping through their fields year after year. The path is unkempt, stiles are sometimes overturned and greetings are sometimes met with stony silence. Our advice: don't antagonise them any more than we and our walking brethren already have: stick to the path, keep disturbances to their livestock to a minimum, take all your litter away with you – and if all that fails, should you meet one, just give them a cuddle. You'll shortly rejoin the road into Danby Wiske.

DANBY WISKE   MAP 68

Chances are you'd never heard of Danby Wiske before you set your sights on the Coast to Coast, but this tiny village with an 11th-century Norman church and a tidy village green is a renowned staging post on your trek. Having long outgrown the hurtful comments in Wainwright's guide, the proud villagers welcome trail-weary Coasters.

The White Swan (☎ 01609 775131, 💻 www.thewhiteswandanbywiske.co.uk) does **B&B** (2T/1Qd en suite; 3T shared facilities; WI-FI; Ⓛ £5) for £39.50pp (sgl occ £46) in the rooms with shared facilities, £44pp (single occ £55) in the en suites, and **camping** (£6pp inc shower; breakfast from £7.50 if prebooked) is also available in a field. They also have drying facilities. **Food** is available in the bar (daily 6-8pm but call first as it depends on demand). Snacks are available most of the day.

The previous owners of the pub now run ***The Old School*** (☎ 01609 774227, 💻 oldschooldanbywiske@yahoo.co.uk; 1D en suite/2T private facilities; 🛏; Ⓛ £5; Easter to end Sep). A 19th-century schoolhouse as its name implies, all the rooms are bright, neat and smart; if only two people book a twin room it is effectively en suite. Rates are from £40pp (sgl occ £45).

The other choice is ***Ashfield*** (☎ 01609 771628, 💻 jeannorris@btinternet.com; 2T/1Tr, all with private facilities; 🛏; Apr-Sep) where B&B is from £80pp (sgl occ £50), £37pp in the triple. They also offer drying facilities.

As for the **church** – one of the very few in England that has no known dedication – only the solid oak door and the font are 11th-century originals, though much of the north aisle is only slightly younger. Look above the main door at the tympanum

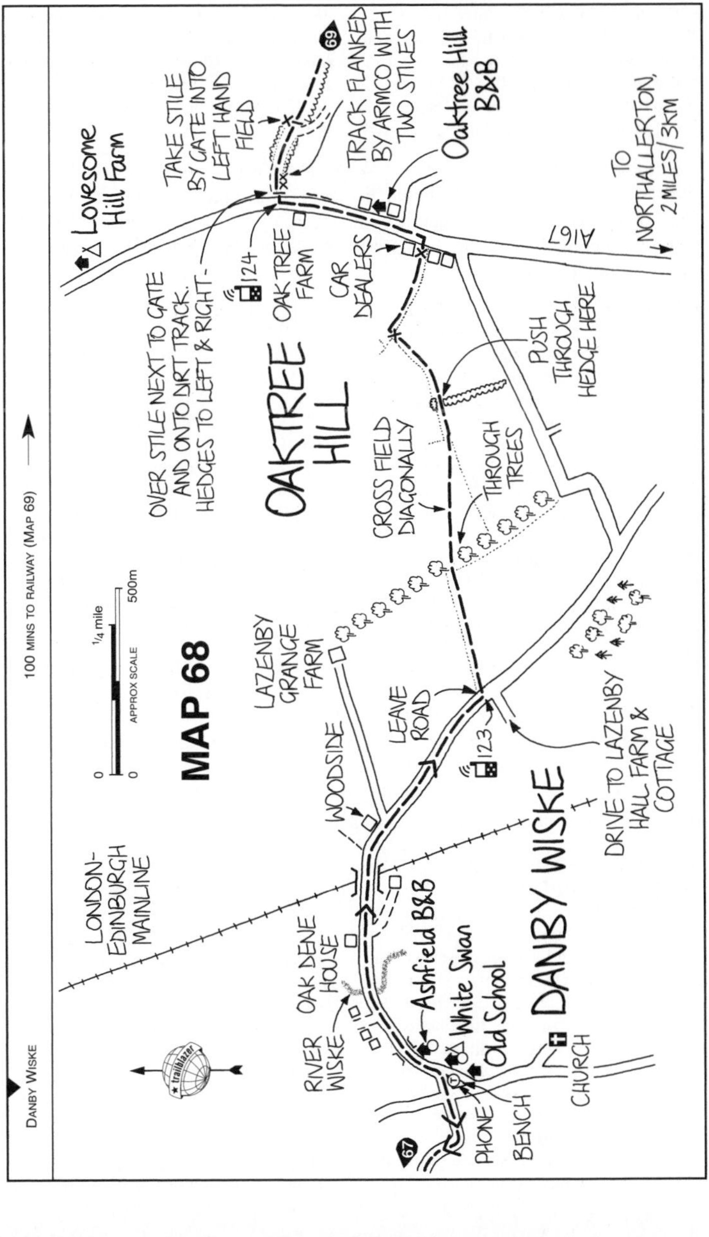
DANBY WISKE
100 MINS TO RAILWAY (MAP 69)
MAP 68
APPROX SCALE
0
0
1/4 mile
500m
trailblazer
LONDON-EDINBURGH MAINLINE
WOODSIDE
LAZENBY GRANGE FARM
OVER STILE NEXT TO GATE AND ONTO DIRT TRACK. HEDGES TO LEFT & RIGHT-
OAKTREE HILL
124
OAK TREE FARM
CAR DEALERS
Lovesome Hill Farm
TAKE STILE BY GATE INTO LEFT HAND FIELD
TRACK FLANKED BY ARMCO WITH TWO STILES
69
Oaktree Hill B&B
TO NORTHALLERTON, 2 MILES/3KM
A167
PUSH THROUGH HEDGE HERE
CROSS FIELD DIAGONALLY
THROUGH TREES
LEAVE ROAD
123
DRIVE TO LAZENBY HALL FARM & COTTAGE
DANBY WISKE
OAK DENE HOUSE
Ashfield B&B
White Swan
Old School
RIVER WISKE
CHURCH
PHONE
BENCH
67

and you should be able to make out the outlines of three weathered figures. They've been interpreted as follows: the Angel of Judgement is weighing the soul of the figure on the right using the scales that he holds in his other hand, and though the evil deeds in one of the scales' pans outweigh the other, the third figure, the Angel of Mercy (Jesus Christ), has slipped his fingers under the pan containing the bad deeds, thus causing the good deeds to seem heavier.

From the bridge crossing the River Wiske outside the village, you can see the outline of the Cleveland Hills in the distance. Unfortunately the other half of the Vale of Mowbray still lies before you (it's 8½ miles from Danby to Ingleby Cross), much of it as before on roads, but with a nifty back route sneaking up on Oaktree Hill.

OAKTREE HILL   MAP 68

This is not much more than a car dealership and a string of houses lining the A167 but there are a couple of accommodation options. Right by the trail is the eponymous *Oak Tree Hill B&B* (01609 761658; www.oaktreehillbedandbreakfast.co.uk; 1D/1T; shared bathroom; ☎; WI-FI; ⏰ £2-5) a friendly B&B charging £32pp (£42 sgl occ). Evenings meals are £12 by prior arrangement, and there's a laundry service (£5). Half a mile further north is *Lovesome Hill Farm* (Map 68; ☎ 01609 772311, 🖳 www.lovesomehillfarm.co.uk; 1S/1D/2D or T/1Tr; all en suite; ☎; WI-FI; ⏰ from

£3). Despite the noise of the road, it's been praised by walkers for the quality of its accommodation, the food and the opportunity to take a tour of the 165-acre farm. **B&B** rates are £40-45pp (sgl £42). They also have a luxury cottage (1D) with spa bath (£40-45pp); a **bunk barn** (🐾) with two rooms each sleeping four (from £13pp inc shower; bedding £4.50; 🐾) and offer **camping** (£5pp). Both **evening meals** (from £14) and breakfast (£6.50) for campers can be provided if requested in advance. They also have a hot tub (30 mins/£15 up to 6 people) so bring your swimwear. It's run by keen walkers.

Here more tracks and quiet backroads link a series of busy farms as you cross a railway line and a beck or two to finally meet the busy A19 (Map 71) at **Exelby Services**. Campers should note that, unless you pop into Osmotherley, from here on there are no village shops along the path until Glaisdale, two days and over 30 miles away. However, if you traipsed all the way from Richmond, a more pressing concern will be finding the energy to dash across four lanes of the A19 without causing a pile-up. Be patient and take extreme care crossing.

INGLEBY CROSS   MAP 72, p219
& INGLEBY ARNCLIFFE

Sandwiched between two busy 'A' roads, Ingleby Cross and its twin Ingleby Arncliffe are actually surprisingly peaceful places if you're not camping. Ingleby Cross is said to be named after its war memorial and has nothing more than the **post office** (Mon-Wed 9.30am-noon), situated in the Blue Bell Inn. Abbots No 80/89 **bus** services (Northallerton–Stokesley) stop here.

Where to stay and eat

In **Ingleby Arncliffe**, *Elstavale* (☎ 01609 882302, 🖳 www.elstavale.co.uk; 1D or

T/1Tr; en suite; WI-FI; ⏰ from £6) is situated right on the path and offers B&B at £32.50pp (sgl occ £60, £90 for three in room). The facility-filled rooms are in a separate annexe and come with foot spas. There are great breakfasts and a most welcome cream tea on arrival.

Conveniently located near the path is *Ingleby House Farm* (☎ 01609 882500, www.inglebyhousefarm.co.uk; 1S or D/1T /1D, all en suite; 🐾; WI-FI; laundry service £5; ⏰ £2.50-4.50) where B&B in the twin and double rooms is £32.50pp in a separate building; the single is £45. Run by friendly people you'll be welcomed with a cream

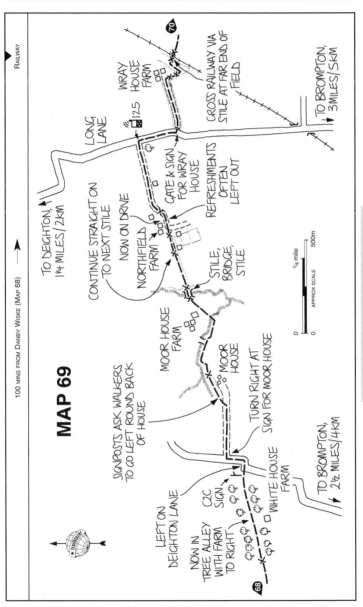

RAILWAY

MAP 69

TO DEIGHTON, 1¼ MILES / 2KM

CONTINUE STRAIGHT ON TO NEXT STILE

NOW ON DRIVE

NORTHFIELD FARM

SIGNPOSTS ASK WALKERS TO GO LEFT ROUND BACK OF HOUSE

MOOR HOUSE FARM

STILE, BRIDGE, STILE

LONG LANE

12.5

WRAY HOUSE FARM

70

CROSS RAILWAY VIA STILE AT FAR END OF FIELD

GATE & SIGN FOR WRAY HOUSE

REFRESHMENTS OFTEN LEFT OUT

TO BROMPTON, 3 MILES / 5KM

MOOR HOUSE

TURN RIGHT AT SIGN FOR MOOR HOUSE

LEFT ON DEIGHTON LANE

NOW IN TREE ALLEY WITH FARM TO RIGHT

C2C SIGN

WHITE HOUSE FARM

TO BROMPTON, 2½ MILES / 4KM

68

¼ mile

500m

0

0

APPROX SCALE

ROUTE GUIDE AND MAPS

ROUTE GUIDE AND MAPS

20 MINS FROM RAILWAY (Map 69) → HARLSEY GROVE FARM → 80 MINS TO A19 (MAP 71) →

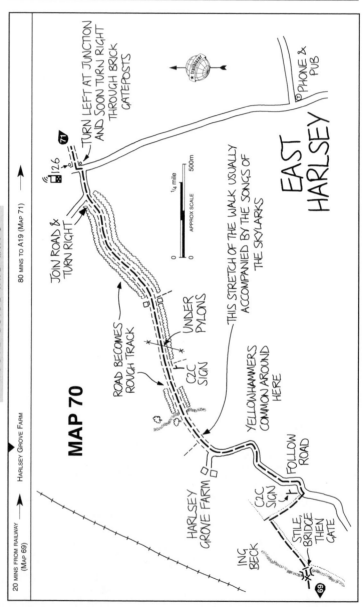

MAP 70

TURN LEFT AT JUNCTION AND SOON TURN RIGHT THROUGH BRICK GATEPOSTS

71

126

JOIN ROAD & TURN RIGHT

ROAD BECOMES ROUGH TRACK

UNDER PYLONS

C2C SIGN

THIS STRETCH OF THE WALK USUALLY ACCOMPANIED BY THE SONGS OF THE SKYLARKS

PHONE & PUB

EAST HARLSEY

¼ mile
APPROX SCALE
500m

YELLOWHAMMERS COMMON AROUND HERE

FOLLOW ROAD

HARLSEY GROVE FARM

C2C SIGN

STILE, BRIDGE THEN GATE

ING BECK

69

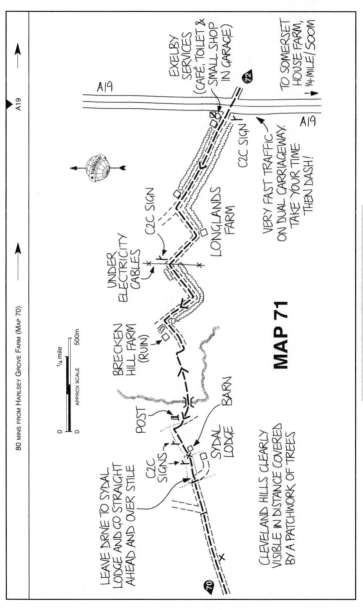

80 MINS FROM HARLSEY GROVE FARM (MAP 70)

A19

¼ mile

500m

APPROX SCALE

A19

EXELBY SERVICES
(CAFÉ, TOILET &
SMALL SHOP
IN GARAGE)

TO SOMERSET
HOUSE FARM,
¼ MILE/ SOOM

A19

C2C SIGN

VERY FAST TRAFFIC
ON DUAL CARRIAGEWAY.
TAKE YOUR TIME
THEN DASH!

C2C SIGN

LONGLANDS
FARM

UNDER
ELECTRICITY
CABLES

BRECKEN
HILL FARM
(RUIN)

MAP 71

POST

BARN

SYDAL
LODGE

C2C
SIGNS

LEAVE DRIVE TO SYDAL
LODGE AND GO STRAIGHT
AHEAD AND OVER STILE

CLEVELAND HILLS CLEARLY
VISIBLE IN DISTANCE COVERED
BY A PATCHWORK OF TREES

ROUTE GUIDE AND MAPS

tea on arrival here, too, and given an excellent breakfast next day.

Somerset House Farm (☎ 01609 882555, 🖥 www.somersethousefarm.co .uk; 2T/4D; all en suite; 🛏; small 🐾 £6; WI-FI; ⓛ £6) charges £35pp. They also do laundry (£4); no evening meals are available but they are licensed. To get there, at the water tower in the village walk south, or walk down the A19 (see Map 71) for five minutes though this is not recommended; the farm's on the left.

The Blue Bell Inn (☎ 01609 882272, 🖥 www.the-blue-bell-inn.co.uk; 2S/2T/1D; en suite; 🐾 in bar area only; WI-FI; ⓛ £5) in the centre of **Ingleby Cross** serves real ales and standard **bar meals** (daily noon-2pm & 6-9pm) sometimes including the Middlesborough staple, chicken parmesan, which is less Italian than it sounds. You can

also **camp** in the field out back for just £5 including shower; breakfast (£7.50) is available in the mornings if booked the night before. **B&B** is £65 for the double or twin rooms, single £45.

Although it's just over a mile further along the path and agonisingly uphill too, from what readers tell us **Park House** (☎ 01609 882899, 🖥 www.parkhousecountry guesthouse.com; 2D/2T/2F; all en suite; WI-FI downstairs; 🐾 £10; ⓛ £6) is well worth the effort. With a lovely lounge and grounds that hopefully you'll have the energy to appreciate, there's also a laundry service (£5 a load) and drying facilities. If enough people have requested they will provide an evening meal (book 24 hrs in advance; main courses £9.50-12.50); this is a good option as they are also licensed. B&B costs £40pp (sgl occ £60), family room £105.

❑ Mount Grace Priory   Map 72
April-Oct Mon & Thur-Sun 10am-6pm, Nov-Mar Sat-Sun 10am-4pm; £5.40/4.90 adult/concessions, free for English Heritage and NT members.

Mount Grace Priory was built in 1398, by the ascetic **Carthusian** order, founded in 1084 by St Bruno, a canon of the Cathedral Church of Rheims. He established a religious community that settled at La Grande Chartreuse near Grenoble, from which the name Carthusian (and also the word for all Carthusian monasteries, which are known as charterhouses) comes. St Bruno and his followers saw the world as inherently wicked so lived as hermits undistracted by temptation. The monastic order that evolved from this community followed much the same principles. The prior was the only person in the monastery allowed access to the outside world, while each monk lived an essentially solitary existence, eating his meals alone and spending much of his life in his cell. The monk's day was fairly hard, rising at 5.45am and returning to bed only at 2.30am the next morning, following a day spent mainly in prayer or contemplation.

There are two people to thank for the preservation of Mount Grace. Following the priory's dissolution on 18 December 1539, James Strangways bought the land from the government but did not destroy the church as required by law at that time. Instead he let it stand as it was, intact save for the roof, possibly because his parents and grandparents had all been buried on the site. In 1899, 260 years later, Sir Lowthian Bell bought the adjoining 17th-century house, and during the course of his 30-year residency did some restoration to the priory, including the first attempt to rebuild cell number 8, one of 25 cells in total.

The priory today, though definitely a ruin, is an absorbing one, and one that clearly shows in its foundations the basic layout of the place. The restoration of **cell number 8** also makes clear that, for their time, these cells were remarkably comfortable, built on two floors with cabinets, a loom, a small bed, water closet and a small garden.

And the **drainage system**? Well with latrines fitted and clean water piped into every cell, the plumbing was indeed ahead of its time. Little of the system remains today save for the channels in which the water flowed around the priory.

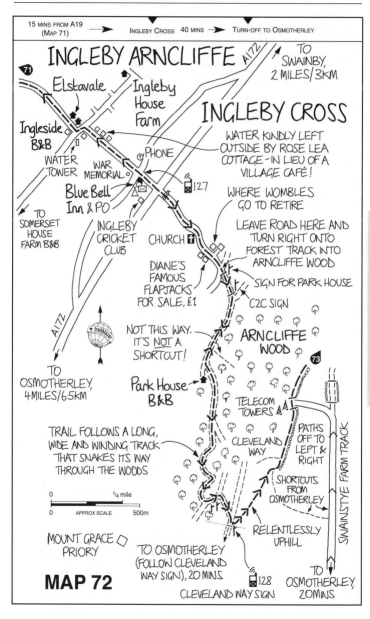

INGLEBY ARNCLIFFE

TO SWAINBY, 2 MILES/3KM

INGLEBY CROSS

Elstavale

Ingleby House Farm

Ingleside B&B

WATER TOWER

WAR MEMORIAL

PHONE

WATER KINDLY LEFT OUTSIDE BY ROSE LEA COTTAGE – IN LIEU OF A VILLAGE CAFÉ!

127

WHERE WOMBLES GO TO RETIRE

Blue Bell Inn & PO

TO SOMERSET HOUSE FARM B&B

INGLEBY CRICKET CLUB

CHURCH

DIANE'S FAMOUS FLAPJACKS FOR SALE, £1

LEAVE ROAD HERE AND TURN RIGHT ONTO FOREST TRACK INTO ARNCLIFFE WOOD

SIGN FOR PARK HOUSE

C2C SIGN

NOT THIS WAY. IT'S NOT A SHORTCUT!

ARNCLIFFE WOOD

73

TO OSMOTHERLEY, 4 MILES/6.5KM

Park House B&B

TELECOM TOWERS

PATHS OFF TO LEFT & RIGHT

TRAIL FOLLOWS A LONG, WIDE AND WINDING TRACK THAT SNAKES ITS WAY THROUGH THE WOODS

CLEVELAND WAY

SHORTCUTS FROM OSMOTHERLEY

0 ¼ mile
0 APPROX SCALE 500m

RELENTLESSLY UPHILL

SWAINSTYE FARM TRACK

MOUNT GRACE PRIORY

TO OSMOTHERLEY (FOLLOW CLEVELAND WAY SIGN), 20 MINS

MAP 72

128 CLEVELAND WAY SIGN

TO OSMOTHERLEY, 20 MINS

OSMOTHERLEY
OFF MAP 72 p219 & MAP 73, p223

Though a 20-minute walk off the Coast to Coast trail, Osmotherley is a delight and energetic walkers may want to visit, even if they're not staying there. In the centre stands a **market cross** and a **barter table**, believed to be the same one from which John Wesley preached. Indeed, in Chapel Yard you can find what's believed to be Britain's oldest practising **Methodist chapel**, constructed in 1754.

There's also the church, **St Peter's**, built on Saxon foundations. The most distinctive things about Osmotherley, however, are its beautiful, **sand-coloured terraced cottages**, built for the workers who laboured at the flax mill that now houses the hostel. **Thompson's**, for years a time-warp shop that was once described as a 'mini Harrods', has been in the same family since 1786. It was recently sold by Grace Thompson with a restrictive covenant that it must continue to serve the community as a local shop. It hasn't reopened yet.

There's a **post office** (Mon & Fri 9am-noon, Wed 1-4pm) inside the village hall and the small **village store** (Mon-Sat 8.30am-5.30pm, Sun 9am-5pm) where they sell basic provisions and sandwiches.

To rejoin the trail, you needn't return to the junction with the Cleveland Way, but can take a short-cut up along Swainstye Farm track (on the left as you walk from the village towards Cote Ghyll caravan park), meeting up with the Cleveland and Coast to Coast paths at the Telecom Tower (see Map 72) or at Scarth Wood Moor (Map 73).

Where to stay

YHA Osmotherley is now operated by the owners of Cote Ghyll Caravan Park (see below) as part of their franchise Enterprise scheme. It has also been renamed: *Cote Ghyll Mill* (☎ 01609 883425, 🖳 www .coteghyll.com; 64 beds, 1x2-, 5x4-, 7x6-bed rooms; beds £20-22, rooms £39-51 for two; ⓛ £5.50; breakfast £5.50; WI-FI; Feb-Oct). Virtually all beds are bunk beds; some 6-bed rooms are en suite and have a double bed. Meals are available but check in advance. The hostel is licensed and accepts credit cards. Coming from Arncliffe Wood,

at the top end of the village turn left when you hit the road, rather than right down the hill into town. Just before the hostel, *Cote Ghyll Caravan Park* (contact details as above; 🐾; WI-FI £3/day; book in advance in summer; Mar-Oct) has **camping** for £8-9.50pp inc toilet/shower facilities. Breakfast may be available at Cote Ghyll Mill. As its name suggests, its main business is caravans and during the school holidays it can be crammed with sugar-high kids, though they do have a few places to pitch a tent on the far side of the site.

Back in the centre of the village, *Queen Catherine Hotel* (☎ 01609 883209, 🖳 www.queencatherinehotel.co.uk; 1S/1D/2T; all en suite; dogs; WI-FI; ⓛ £5), 7 West End, charges £35pp (sgl £35, sgl occ £50) for B&B. The pub is actually named after Henry VIII's wife, Catherine of Aragon, who is believed to have sheltered with monks at Mount Grace Priory (see p218). It is, surprisingly, the only pub in England named after her.

Back up the hill a little way is *Vane House* (☎ 01609 883448, 🖳 www.vane house.co.uk; 4T/3D/1Qd; all en suite; 🐾£10; WI-FI; ⓛ around £8), 11A North End, with B&B from £45-50pp (sgl occ £60). They are happy to do laundry (wash and dry £10). Unfortunately, this place has been getting mixed reports lately from our readers. Let's hope this is merely temporary as the building is lovely.

The Three Tuns (☎ 01609 883301, 🖳 www.threetunsrestaurant.co.uk; 3D/1T; all en suite; 🐾 £10; WI-FI; ⓛ £7.50) is a restaurant that offers pleasant rooms. B&B starts at £47.50pp (sgl occ £70). They also have two cottages (1D/1D or T) with 🛏.

The Golden Lion (☎ 01609 883526, 🖳 www.goldenlionosmotherley.co.uk; 2D/5D or T, all en suite; 🐾; WI-FI) charges £47.50pp in the twins, £50 in the doubles (sgl occ £75) for B&B.

Where to eat and drink

The Three Tuns (see Where to stay; food served Mon-Sat noon-2.30pm & 5.30-9.30pm, Sun noon-6pm), opposite The Green, is a surprisingly smart establishment with by some distance the best food in town, with starters from around £5.50 and mains from £11.25; the menu changes frequently but we can vouch for the quality of the braised rabbit short crust pie (£9.50).

For pub food, we've had good reports about the food at *The Golden Lion* (see above). The bar is open Mon-Tue 5-11pm & Wed-Sun noon-11pm, food is served Wed-Sat noon-3pm & daily 6-9pm.

Queen Catherine Hotel (see Where to stay) has the most popular bar in town, with occasional live jazz music and some great homemade meals (daily Mon-Sat noon-2.30pm & 6-9pm, Sun noon-4pm & 6-9pm) including Whitby crab salad and new potatoes for £12.95. For something lighter try

The Coffee Pot (☎ 01609 883536; Mar-Oct Mon-Thur 10.30am-2pm, school hols and Fri-Sun 10.30am-5pm, Nov-Feb Sat & Sun 10am-4.30pm), a pleasant little café which also does soups and light lunches.

Cheapest of all is *Osmotherley Fish and Chip Shop* (☎ 01609 883557; summer Fri-Sat noon-2.30pm, Wed & Thur 5-9pm, Fri & Sat 5-9.30pm), where it's £5.80 for a large haddock and chips or £1.40 for a chip bun.

Transport   **(see also pp52-5)**
Abbott's No 80/89 **bus** services stop here en route to Stokesley and Northallerton.

STAGE 11: INGLEBY CROSS TO BLAKEY RIDGE   MAPS 72-81

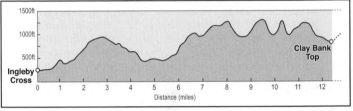

ROUTE GUIDE AND MAPS

Introduction
At **21 miles (34km, 8hrs)**, this is another stage that many walkers consider splitting in two, particularly as

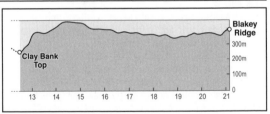

there are five big climbs separating you from Blakey Ridge. Unfortunately, unless wild camping, it's less easily done than Stage 10 which is one reason you might want to spare yourself if coming from Richmond; you'll need to be in good shape to arrive at Blakey Ridge without looking like an extra from a George Romero zombie movie.

If you do divide the walk at **Clay Bank Top** and spend the night in one of the nearby villages, such as Great Broughton to the north or Urra to the south, the next day (having returned to Clay Bank Top) is a relatively effortless 8½ miles (14km) to Blakey Ridge so you can easily add the 9½ downhill miles to Glaisdale so needn't lose much time. Providing you book in advance, the B&Bs at Great Broughton, Urra and the other nearby villages are more than happy to collect you at Clay Bank Top and return you there next morning.

Weather and willpower depending, the all-in-one option has its plus points, however. For one thing, although the first half is a bit of a rollercoaster as the gradient profile reveals, once you've climbed one last time onto Urra Moor, some 12 miles (19.5km) from Ingleby Cross and following well over 1000 metres (nearly 3800ft) of accumulated ascent, the second half feels blessedly level and straightforward. Furthermore, many consider the Lion Inn at Blakey to be one of the more memorable pubs on the route, an isolated but busy tavern stranded atop a mist-bound moor with camping for Coast to Coasters only.

Thus our advice is as follows: if your feet are in good shape and there's room at the Inn (or elsewhere, see p232), grab it and attempt the 21 miles in a day. If that doesn't suit your schedule, organise a B&B near Clay Bank Top and if necessary catch up by pushing on to Glaisdale – an 18-mile day.

One final thing: campers should note that there's **camping** at Lord Stones Café (see p224 though it's no longer free but they do also have some pods) and the Lion Inn has camping for Coast to Coasters only.

As for the walk itself, this stage takes us into the **North York Moors National Park** with, it is said, the world's largest expanse of heather. Depending on the weather, this could be a pleasant stage as you tramp merrily along, stopping only to admire the iridescent plumage of the clucking pheasant or savour the views south to the valleys of Farndale and north to the industrial glories of Teeside and your first view of the North Sea. Or it could be a miserable, claggy rain-soaked trudge with all views obscured by a bone-chilling mist while paramotors buzz menacingly overhead. Let's hope it's the former but either way, on the bright side the waymarking is good so you're unlikely to get lost.

The route

From Ingleby Cross the walk begins with a climb up past the **church** (note the triple-decker pulpit and purple box pews) and on up into **Arncliffe Wood**, where the path takes a turn to the south.

Having passed the turn-off for Park House (see Map 72, p219) you climb steeply and at the southernmost point of the wood a hairpin bend sees Wainwright's climbing trail meet the Cleveland Way, established two years before Wainwright's original book was published and which you follow for almost the entire way to Blakey Moor. For Osmotherley, turn off south through the gate.

The route continues steeply up through Arncliffe Wood (get used to it, there's plenty more of it on this stage), with cleared forestry providing views back to the Vale of Mowbray as you pass a humming telecoms station to emerge onto the heather-clad **Scarth Wood Moor** (Map 73). You soon join the Lyke Wake Walk (see box p263) in **Clain Wood** before joining the road briefly to pretty **Huthwaite Green**. Here, haul yourself up a steep, wooded climb onto **Live Moor** (Map 74), duly noting the first appearance of a number of stone boundary markers along the wayside.

The path now drops slightly and then ascends to **Carlton Moor** (Map 75), with its gliding club, runway and paragliders. At the far end of the moor is a trig point and another boundary marker, from where you may see the **North Sea** beyond the industrial installations of Teeside, and where the path drops steeply

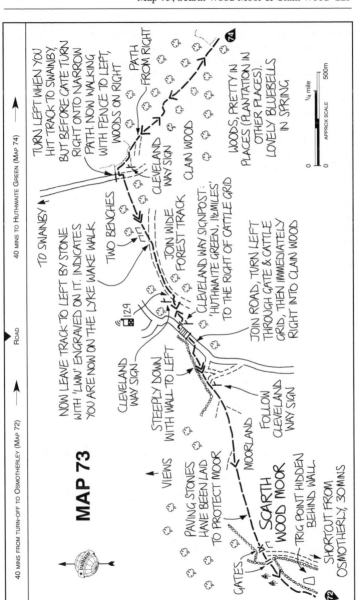

TURN LEFT WHEN YOU HIT TRACK TO SWAINBY, BUT BEFORE GATE TURN RIGHT ONTO NARROW PATH. NOW WALKING WITH FENCE TO LEFT, WOODS ON RIGHT

PATH FROM RIGHT

CLEVELAND WAY SIGN

CLAIN WOOD

WOODS, PRETTY IN PLACES (PLANTATION IN OTHER PLACES). LOVELY BLUEBELLS IN SPRING

TO SWAINBY

NOW LEAVE TRACK TO LEFT BY STONE WITH 'LWW' ENGRAVED ON IT. INDICATES YOU ARE NOW ON THE LYKE WAKE WALK

TWO BENCHES

129

JOIN WIDE FOREST TRACK

CLEVELAND WAY SIGNPOST: 'HUTHWAITE GREEN, 1½ MILES' TO THE RIGHT OF CATTLE GRID

CLEVELAND WAY SIGN

STEEPLY DOWN WITH WALL TO LEFT

JOIN ROAD, TURN LEFT THROUGH GATE & CATTLE GRID, THEN IMMEDIATELY RIGHT INTO CLAIN WOOD

FOLLOW CLEVELAND WAY SIGN

MOORLAND

MAP 73

VIEWS

PAVING STONES HAVE BEEN LAID TO PROTECT MOOR

SCARTH WOOD MOOR

TRIG POINT HIDDEN BEHIND WALL

SHORTCUT FROM OSMOTHERLEY, 30MINS

GATES

APPROX SCALE
¼ mile
500m

around a quarry to a road. Crossing this and its adjacent stile, by a car park *Lord Stones Café, Grill & Camping* (Map 76; ☎ 01642 778482, 🖥 www.lord stones.com; summer daily 8am-9pm or to 4pm Sun, winter 9am-5pm or to 4pm Sun; 🐾; WI-FI;) is well staged for a break, a busy hub serving both day and dog walkers who you'll meet and greet between here and Clay Bank Top. Old hands will rue the changes here since redevelopment in 2013. Camping is no longer free but the facilities are much improved. The shop is more of a deli and there's now a swanky **restaurant**. There are several **camping** pitches at £17 per pitch, five furnished **pods** (sleep 4) with loo and basin en suite for £60-74 and ablutions block. They have also now invested in a couple of bell tents, yurts and a tube tent too, each with proper beds, log-burning stoves and electricity – expect to pay between £55-75 for two people per night to stay in one of these. It's also the only place on this stretch where **tap water** is available.

From here, the cunning amongst you will have noticed that there is a low-level path that avoids all the steepness of the next few hours, all the way to Clay Bank Top. Take it if you must; the path is such that you can pretty much join it after every descent, allowing you to choose how many of the steep climbs to tackle, and circumnavigating any others. But for those of you with an ounce of integri-

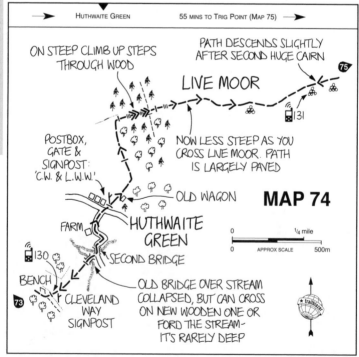

ROUTE GUIDE AND MAPS

⟶ HUTHWAITE GREEN   55 MINS TO TRIG POINT (MAP 75) ⟶

ON STEEP CLIMB UP STEPS THROUGH WOOD

PATH DESCENDS SLIGHTLY AFTER SECOND HUGE CAIRN

75

LIVE MOOR

131

NOW LESS STEEP AS YOU CROSS LIVE MOOR. PATH IS LARGELY PAVED

POSTBOX, GATE & SIGNPOST: 'C.W. & L.W.W.'

OLD WAGON

MAP 74

FARM

HUTHWAITE GREEN

0   ¼ mile
0   APPROX SCALE   500m

130

SECOND BRIDGE

BENCH

73

CLEVELAND WAY SIGNPOST

OLD BRIDGE OVER STREAM COLLAPSED, BUT CAN CROSS ON NEW WOODEN ONE OR FORD THE STREAM – IT'S RARELY DEEP

★ trailblaze

ty (!) and who want to keep to Wainwright's path, another steep climb follows – this time up to **Cringle Moor** (Map 76), with the superbly situated **Alec Falconer Memorial Seat** from where you can take in more views over the smokestacks of Teeside, the outlying cone of Roseberry Topping, and just ahead of it, an obelisk on Easby Moor commemorating locally born Captain James Cook.

Follow the bends south then east (towards and then away from the summit of Cringle Moor), skirt the cliffs of **Kirby Bank** and then tackle a steep descent.

The **Wain Stones** are clearly visible on top of your next moor, the outcrops (a favourite of Wainwright's) resembling cake decorations atop **Hasty Bank** (Map 77). If staying at Great Broughton (see p228), you may wish to divert from the path on the signposted low-level trail before the climb up to the stones as the road walk is said to be no fun. Otherwise, from the Wain Stones the path continues east to **Clay Bank Top** steeply dropping one more time to the B1257 and, for those staying in the nearby villages, a possible rendezvous with your hosts. Moorsbus usually has a Sunday service calling here (Apr-Oct), see p52-5.

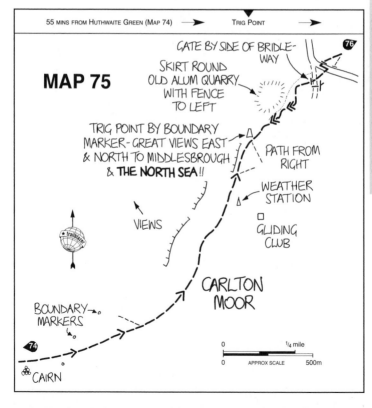

55 MINS FROM HUTHWAITE GREEN (MAP 74) ⟶   TRIG POINT   ⟶

MAP 75

GATE BY SIDE OF BRIDLE-WAY

SKIRT ROUND OLD ALUM QUARRY WITH FENCE TO LEFT

76

TRIG POINT BY BOUNDARY MARKER - GREAT VIEWS EAST & NORTH TO MIDDLESBROUGH & **THE NORTH SEA !!**

PATH FROM RIGHT

WEATHER STATION

GLIDING CLUB

VIEWS

★ trailblazer

CARLTON MOOR

BOUNDARY MARKERS

74

0   1/4 mile
0   APPROX SCALE   500m

CAIRN

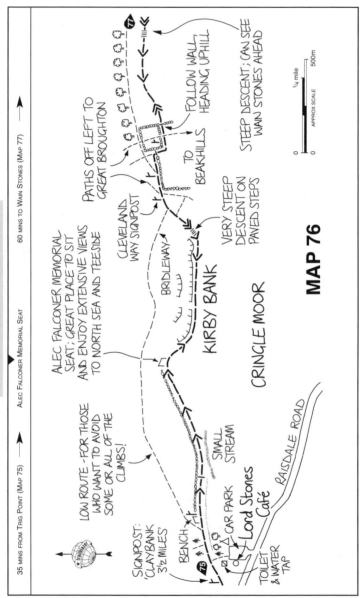

MAP 76

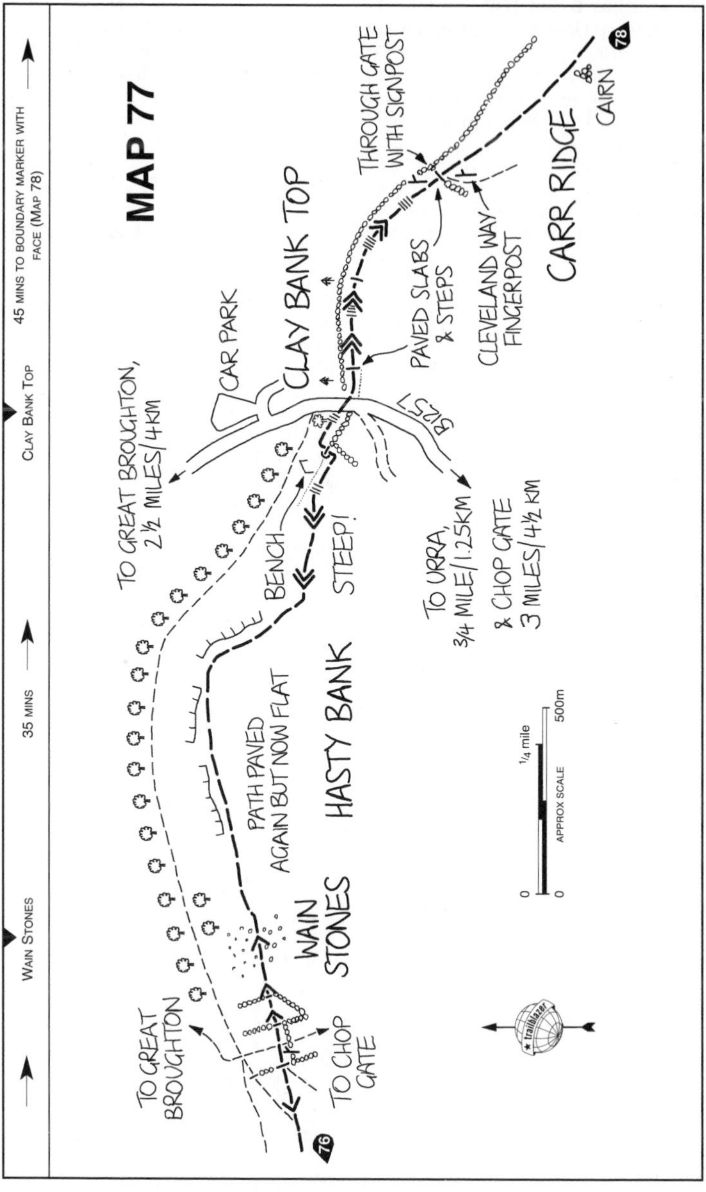
Wain Stones
35 mins
Clay Bank Top
45 mins to boundary marker with face (Map 78)
MAP 77
TO GREAT BROUGHTON
TO CHOP GATE
WAIN STONES
PATH PAVED AGAIN BUT NOW FLAT
HASTY BANK
TO GREAT BROUGHTON, 2½ MILES/4KM
BENCH
STEEP!
CAR PARK
CLAY BANK TOP
B1257
TO URRA, 3/4 MILE/1.25KM
& CHOP GATE 3 MILES/4½ KM
PAVED SLABS & STEPS
CLEVELAND WAY FINGERPOST
THROUGH GATE WITH SIGNPOST
CARR RIDGE
CAIRN
76
78
APPROX SCALE
¼ mile
500m
0
0
trailblazer

NEAR CLAY BANK TOP   MAP 77
(Urra, Chop Gate & Great Broughton)
Accommodation-wise the nearest place to Clay Bank Top, where the B1257 bisects the Coast to Coast path, is **Urra** a mile to the south. Gerry and Wendy have been running *Maltkiln House* (☎ 01642 778216; 2T/1D; en suite/shared; wi-fi; ⓛ £5) for many years and charge from £33pp for B&B, from £16 for dinner. One of the twin rooms is en suite and the other rooms share a shower room. They'll also show you the short cut from the back of the house directly onto Urra Moor the next morning.

Chop Gate is three miles south of Clay Bank Top and not an enjoyable walk even if you can find the overgrown footpaths. Most accommodation options in Chop Gate offer free lifts from/to Clay Bank Top, as does (after 4pm) *The Buck Inn* (☎ 01642 778334, 🖳 www.the-buck-inn.co.uk; 1S/2D/3T/1Tr or Qd, en suite; 🐾 £10; wi-fi in lounge; ⓛ £3.45-6.95). B&B is from £39.50pp in the double/twin rooms (sgl £69), while it's £37.50pp in the family room. **Camping** is £8.50pp – or free if you eat in the inn! (Note there's no shower but

you can use the toilets while the pub is open.) Run by a German-English couple, we've had great reports from readers, about the local beer and the food (Mon-Tue 3-9pm, Wed-Sun 11am-9pm in summer, shorter hours in winter) in particular. Their game casserole (£12.95) is especially good.

Near the pub and also offering free lifts to and from Clay Bank there's the very hospitable *Forge House* (☎ 01642 778166, 🖳 www.coast2coast.co.uk/forgehouse; 1S/1T/2D, shared facilities; 🐾 £3; wi-fi; ⓛ £4.50). B&B is from £30pp (sgl £35); their sandwiches were voted by one of the blogs as the best on the path and indeed a couple of readers have written in to praise the helpfulness of the owners.

Great Broughton lies 2½ miles to the north of Clay Bank Top. There's a **shop** (9.30am-5.30pm but closed Wed/Sat pm) and **post office** (Mon & Thur 9am-5.30pm). Most B&Bs offer lifts to/from Clay Bank Top. *Newlands House* (☎ 01642 712619, 🖳 www.newlandshouse.co.uk; 1D/1T/1Tr; all en suite; 🐾; wi-fi; ⓛ £5) is at 7 Ingleby Rd; B&B starts at £40pp (sgl occ £50).

(cont'd on p232)

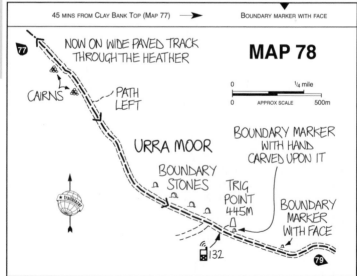

45 MINS FROM CLAY BANK TOP (MAP 77) →   BOUNDARY MARKER WITH FACE

NOW ON WIDE PAVED TRACK THROUGH THE HEATHER

MAP 78

0 ————— ¼ mile
0 ———— APPROX SCALE ———— 500m

CAIRNS

PATH LEFT

URRA MOOR

BOUNDARY STONES

TRIG POINT 445M

BOUNDARY MARKER WITH HAND CARVED UPON IT

BOUNDARY MARKER WITH FACE

📱132

79

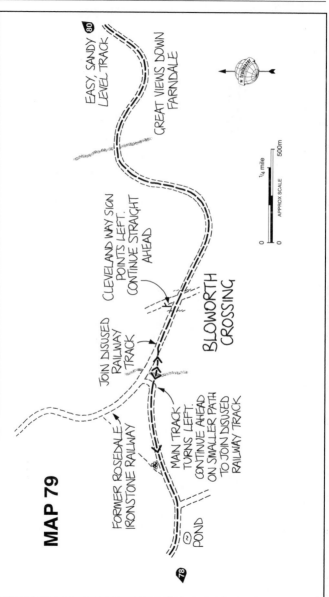

MAP 79

EASY, SANDY LEVEL TRACK

GREAT VIEWS DOWN FARNDALE

CLEVELAND WAY SIGN POINTS LEFT. CONTINUE STRAIGHT AHEAD

JOIN DISUSED RAILWAY TRACK

BLOWORTH CROSSING

MAIN TRACK TURNS LEFT. CONTINUE AHEAD ON SMALLER PATH TO JOIN DISUSED RAILWAY TRACK

FORMER ROSEDALE IRONSTONE RAILWAY

POND

¼ mile

500m

0

0

APPROX SCALE

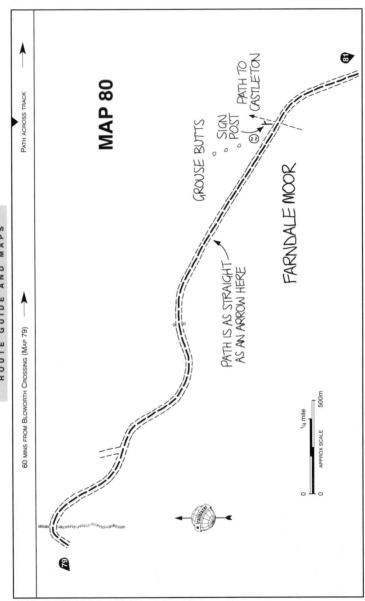

MAP 80

PATH ACROSS TRACK

60 MINS FROM BLOWORTH CROSSING (MAP 79)

GROUSE BUTTS

SIGN POST

PATH TO CASTLETON

FARNDALE MOOR

PATH IS AS STRAIGHT AS AN ARROW HERE

¼ mile

500m

APPROX SCALE

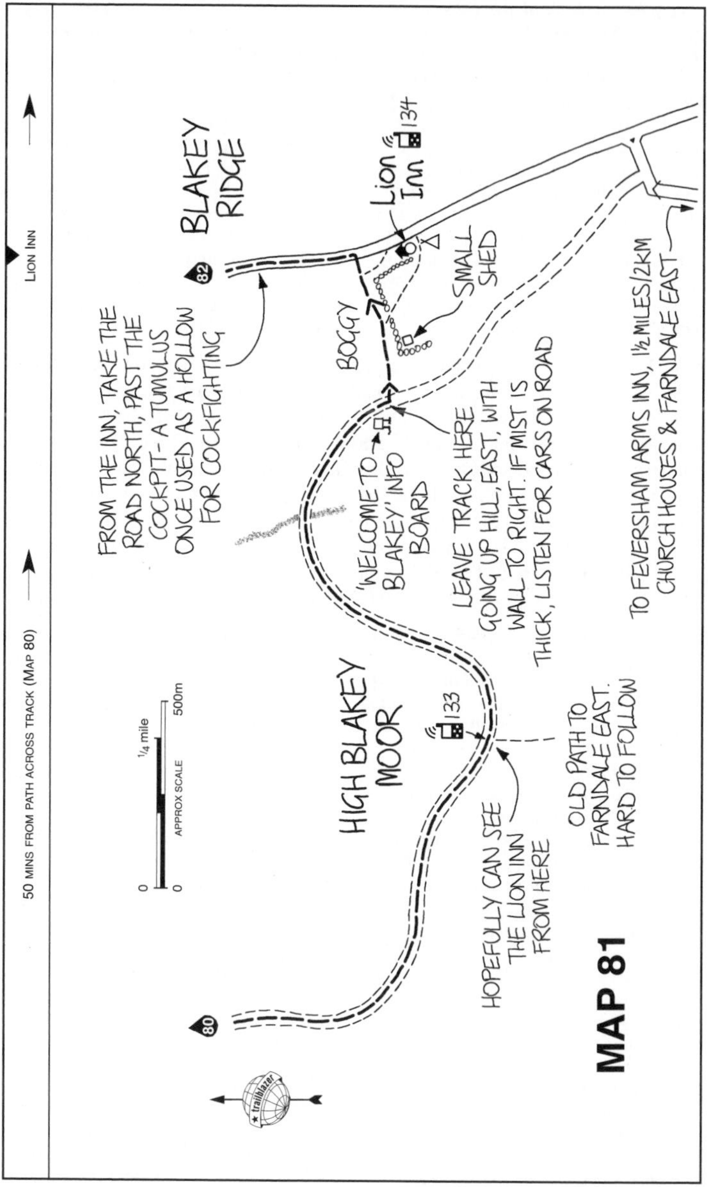

50 MINS FROM PATH ACROSS TRACK (MAP 80)

LION INN

BLAKEY RIDGE

Lion Inn 🍺 ▤ 134

SMALL SHED

82

BOGGY

FROM THE INN, TAKE THE ROAD NORTH, PAST THE COCKPIT - A TUMULUS ONCE USED AS A HOLLOW FOR COCKFIGHTING

'WELCOME TO BLAKEY' INFO BOARD

LEAVE TRACK HERE GOING UP HILL, EAST, WITH WALL TO RIGHT. IF MIST IS THICK, LISTEN FOR CARS ON ROAD

TO FEVERSHAM ARMS INN, 1¼ MILES/2KM CHURCH HOUSES & FARNDALE EAST

HIGH BLAKEY MOOR

▤ 133

¼ mile

500m

0

0

APPROX SCALE

OLD PATH TO FARNDALE EAST. HARD TO FOLLOW

HOPEFULLY CAN SEE THE LION INN FROM HERE

80

MAP 81

(cont'd from p228) **The Wainstones Hotel** (☎ 01642 712268, ☐ www.wainstone shotel.co.uk; 3S/14D/7T; all en suite; ✆; WI-FI; ⓛ £5.50) is more upmarket: B&B is £69.50 in the single rooms, £44.75pp in the double or twins. Food is served daily Mon-Sat noon-2pm & 5-10pm, Sun noon-9pm; main courses start at around £10. There's also the walker-friendly **Bay Horse** (☎ 01642 712319; ☐ www.thebayhorse-great broughton.co.uk; food Mon-Fri noon-2pm & 6-930pm, Sat noon-9.30pm, Sun noon-9pm), on the High St. Abbotts No 89 **bus** stops in Great Broughton en route between Stokesley and Northallerton.

Just under a mile west of Great Broughton at **Kirkby** there's *Dromonby Bridge B&B* (☎ 01642 712226, ☐ www.dromonbybridge.com; 1D/3D or T or Tr/1Qd, all en suite; ✆; ✞; WI-FI; ⓛ) where B&B costs £32pp (sgl occ from £38) and £24pp for the quad. An excellent value place, they have self-service laundry facilities (no charge, donations welcome) and will pick up and drop off booked guests at Clay Bank and also take them to the pub for an evening meal. At breakfast times they also bring in sandwich ingredients so you can make your own packed lunch, for which a donation only is requested.

From Clay Bank Top the penultimate climb the Coast to Coast follows is paved with steps and after 20 minutes the top of **Urra Moor** is reached where the gradient relents to what feels like nothing. A wide track unrolls over the moor past a **trig point** (Map 78) and after the **boundary marker with a face** carved onto it, you arrive at a junction of tracks. It's here that the Cleveland Way breaks away to the north, to return as you reach the sea cliffs north of Robin Hood's Bay, while you continue on the wide track of the former Rosedale Ironstone Railway (Map 79) that used to serve the nearby iron mines a century and a half ago. Passing above the head of pretty **Farndale**, renowned for its daffodils, the track curves round High Blakey Moor to your probable destination, the isolated Lion Inn.

BLAKEY RIDGE   MAP 81, p231
For everybody, be they a walker or a motorist, Blakey Ridge *is* the *Lion Inn* (☎ 01751 417320, ☐ www.lionblakey.co.uk; 1T private bath/8D/4T or F; all en suite; ✆; ✞ £5; WI-FI; ⓛ £5.25), the fourth highest inn in Britain (the highest, the Tan Inn, lies near Keld) and one of the most charming on the route. The inn is nothing much to look at on the outside. Indeed, its orange-tiled roofs are rather disappointing for those expecting the rustic image suggested by the website. But inside, with its dark time-worn beams and open fires, it looks like the inn back nearly 500 years and is a great place to end the day. The (small) twin is from £24pp, but most other rooms cost £42-49pp (sgl occ £49.50-56.50) for **B&B**. The **food**, served at the bar or in the restaurant (daily noon-10pm), is tailor-made for walkers, being hearty and tasty.

Camping is allowed in the adjacent field for £2.50pp, with a bit of shelter offered by the walls; toilet and showers are accessible when the pub's open. They pre-fer you book your pitch in advance to help filter out beery louts intent on mischief, but as long as you rock up in a suitably drenched cagoule and not a Middlesbrough FC outfit, they'll probably let you stay.

As the Lion Inn is often booked up, readers have recommended an alternative. *Feversham Arms Inn* (☎ 01751 433206, ☐ www.fevershamarmsinn.co.uk; 3D or T/cottage; all en suite; ✞; WI-FI; ⓛ about £6.50) in **Church Houses**, down the hill in **Farndale**, can be reached by heading south away from the Lion Inn along the road, taking the first right (west) down Blakey Bank and Long Lane for about 1½ miles. B&B costs £34.50-40pp (sgl occ £45); the cottage (self-catering) costs from £105/£125 for two/four sharing. Note that guests can check-in only when the pub is open (see below). The **food** (Mon-Sat noon-2pm, to 2.30pm in summer, then daily 6-9pm; daffodil season open from 12.30pm all day) is reportedly excellent and the owner will drive walkers back up the hill in the morning if convenient; or they can arrange a taxi.

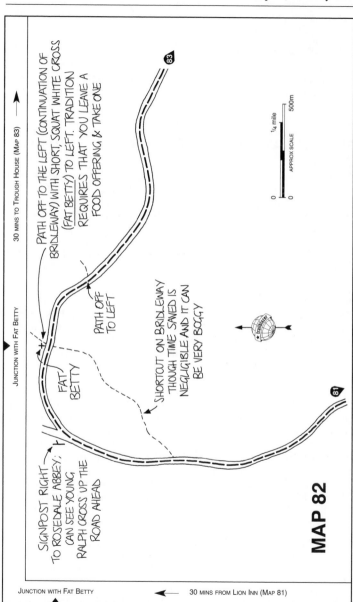

30 MINS TO TROUGH HOUSE (MAP 83)

PATH OFF TO THE LEFT (CONTINUATION OF BRIDLEWAY) WITH SHORT, SQUAT WHITE CROSS (FAT BETTY) TO LEFT. TRADITION REQUIRES THAT YOU LEAVE A FOOD OFFERING & TAKE ONE

JUNCTION WITH FAT BETTY

FAT BETTY

PATH OFF TO LEFT

SHORTCUT ON BRIDLEWAY THOUGH TIME SAVED IS NEGLIGIBLE AND IT CAN BE VERY BOGGY

SIGNPOST RIGHT TO ROSEDALE ABBEY; CAN SEE YOUNG RALPH CROSS UP THE ROAD AHEAD

MAP 82

APPROX SCALE

¼ mile

500m

JUNCTION WITH FAT BETTY

30 MINS FROM LION INN (MAP 81)

ROUTE GUIDE AND MAPS

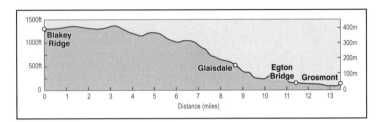

ROUTE GUIDE AND MAPS

STAGE 12: BLAKEY RIDGE TO GROSMONT   MAPS 81-87

Introduction

For those who enjoy cosy English villages hidden amongst the gentlest, most bucolic scenery this fine country has to offer, the **13½-mile (22km, 5hr)** stroll down the **Esk Valley** to Glaisdale and on to Grosmont may be the best section of this walk. For charm, only the lakeland villages of Borrowdale and Grasmere come close to matching Egton Bridge and Grosmont, and it comes as no surprise that the nostalgic '60s village bobby TV show, *Heartbeat*, was filmed nearby.

As a final destination on this stage, either Egton Bridge or Grosmont will do nicely. But first you have to get to the valley, and that means getting down off the moors.

The route

The walk begins by following the tarmac north towards **Young Ralph Cross** (off Map 82), which just pokes its head over the horizon as you turn off right onto another road, this one signposted to Rosedale Abbey.

Soon you pass the stumpy white landmark known as **Fat Betty** off the path to the left, where tradition requires you both take and leave a snack or a sweet; here's your chance to finally cash in those galling muesli bars! (That said, some walkers have written to tell us that they found nothing when they arrived.) Perhaps suitably revived, you then turn north-east into the wonderfully named **Great Fryup Lane** (Map 83 and where one suspects Betty spent too much time) and leave the road to pass **Trough House**. The path can clearly be made out continuing eastwards round the southern side of Great Fryup Dale until the end of **Glaisdale Moor** where, on rejoining the road, the **North Sea** ought to be obvious at the far end of the valley.

After a mile of road walking, Coast-to-Coasters take to the track along **Glaisdale Rigg** (Map 85) past various standing stones (and a particularly well-hewn **boundary marker** to the right of the path. Continue on down to a gated junction by a small pool. Descend through farmland to the houses of Glaisdale.

GLAISDALE   MAP 86, p238

Ten miles (16km) from Blakey, the village of Glaisdale sprawls across its lofty perch above the Esk Valley.

The terraced houses that are a feature of the town were originally built for the workers in the ironstone mines of the late 19th century. Today the **Robinson Institute** is a village hall that also acts as a small theatre. The late 18th-century **Church of St Thomas the Apostle**, near the upper end of

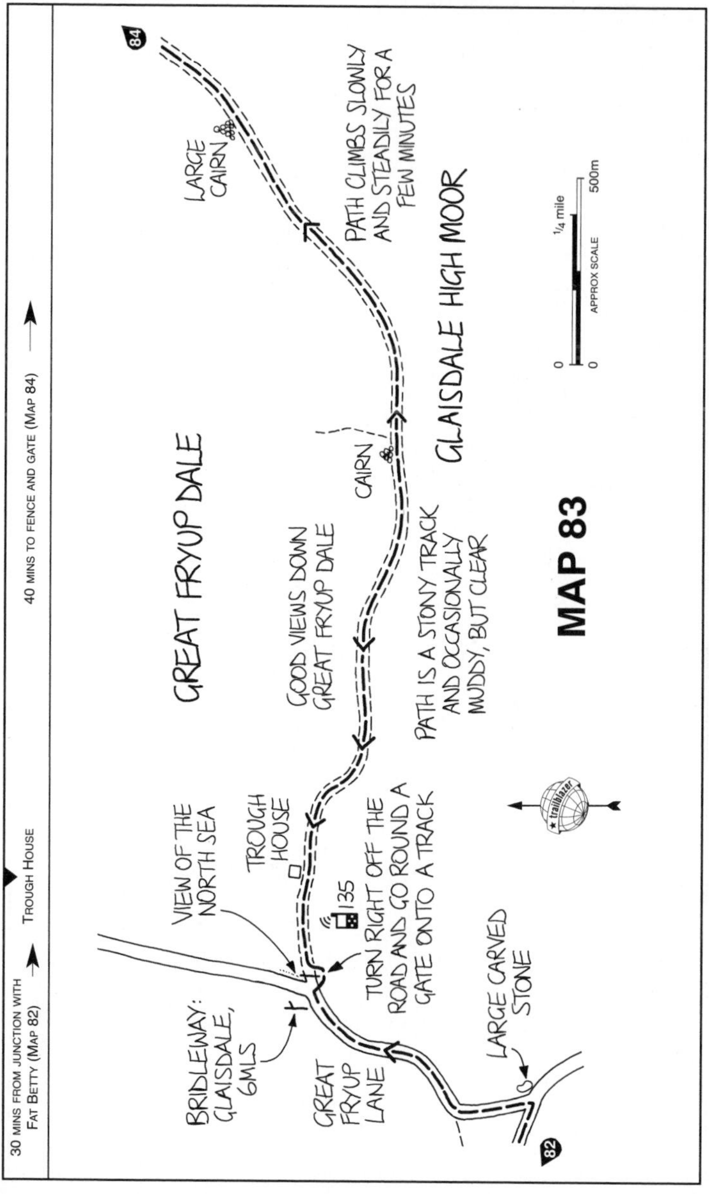

MAP 83

30 MINS FROM JUNCTION WITH FAT BETTY (MAP 82) → TROUGH HOUSE → 40 MINS TO FENCE AND GATE (MAP 84) →

84

GREAT FRYUP DALE

LARGE CAIRN

PATH CLIMBS SLOWLY AND STEADILY FOR A FEW MINUTES

GLAISDALE HIGH MOOR

GOOD VIEWS DOWN GREAT FRYUP DALE

CAIRN

PATH IS A STONY TRACK AND OCCASIONALLY MUDDY, BUT CLEAR

VIEW OF THE NORTH SEA

TROUGH HOUSE

35

TURN RIGHT OFF THE ROAD AND GO ROUND A GATE ONTO A TRACK

BRIDLEWAY: GLAISDALE, 6MLS

GREAT FRYUP LANE

LARGE CARVED STONE

82

¼ mile

APPROX SCALE

500m

trailblazer

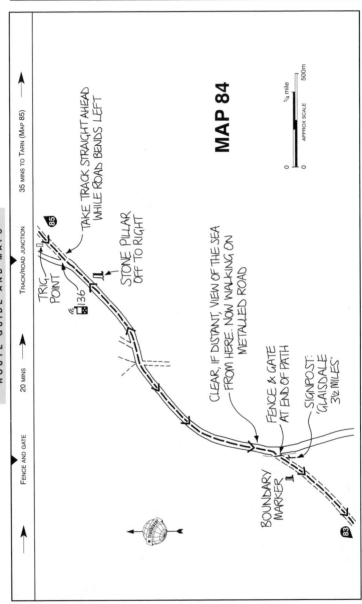

FENCE AND GATE

20 MINS

TRACK/ROAD JUNCTION

35 MINS TO TARN (MAP 85)

TAKE TRACK STRAIGHT AHEAD WHILE ROAD BENDS LEFT

STONE PILLAR OFF TO RIGHT

TRIG POINT

136

CLEAR, IF DISTANT, VIEW OF THE SEA FROM HERE. NOW WALKING ON METALLED ROAD

FENCE & GATE AT END OF PATH

SIGNPOST: 'GLAISDALE 3½ MILES'

BOUNDARY MARKER

83

MAP 84

APPROX SCALE

0   ¼ mile

0   500m

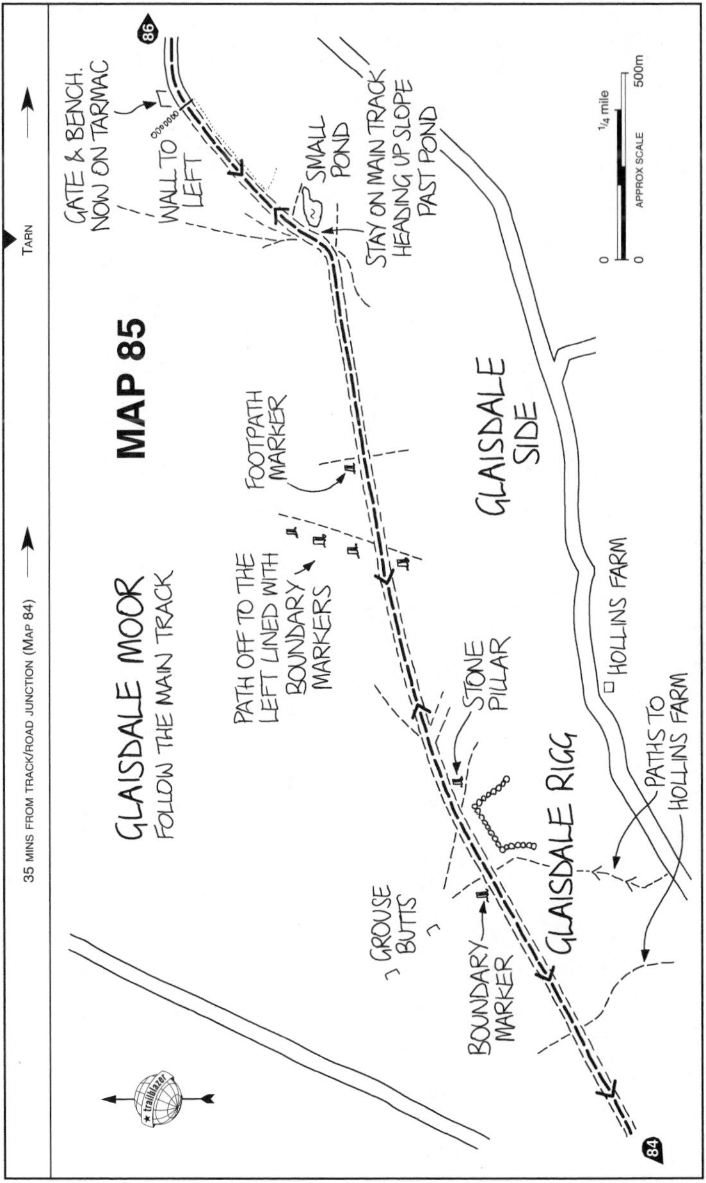

MAP 85

GLAISDALE MOOR
FOLLOW THE MAIN TRACK

35 MINS FROM TRACK/ROAD JUNCTION (Map 84)

TARN

86

GATE & BENCH.
NOW ON TARMAC

WALL TO
LEFT

SMALL
POND

STAY ON MAIN TRACK
HEADING UP SLOPE
PAST POND

FOOTPATH
MARKER

PATH OFF TO THE
LEFT LINED WITH
BOUNDARY MARKERS

GLAISDALE SIDE

STONE
PILLAR

HOLLINS FARM

GLAISDALE RIGG

PATHS TO
HOLLINS FARM

GROUSE
BUTTS

BOUNDARY
MARKER

84

APPROX SCALE

¼ mile

500m

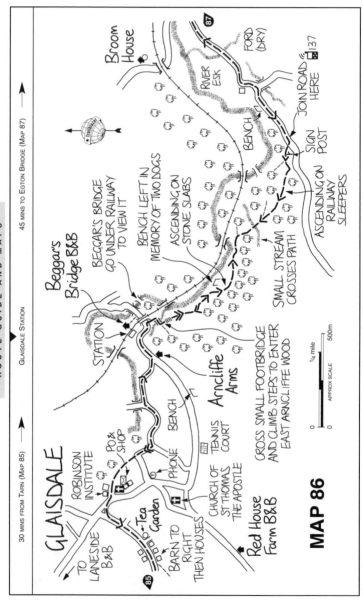

MAP 86

GLAISDALE

TO LANESIDE B&B

ROBINSON INSTITUTE

PO & SHOP

PHONE

BENCH

TENNIS COURT

BARN TO RIGHT THEN HOUSES

Tea Garden

CHURCH OF ST THOMAS THE APOSTLE

Red House Farm B&B

CROSS SMALL FOOTBRIDGE AND CLIMB STEPS TO ENTER EAST ARNCLIFFE WOOD

Arncliffe Arms

STATION

Beggar's Bridge B&B

Beggar's Bridge

BEGGAR'S BRIDGE GO UNDER RAILWAY TO VIEW IT

BENCH LEFT IN MEMORY OF TWO DOGS

ASCENDING ON STONE SLABS

SMALL STREAM CROSSES PATH

ASCENDING ON RAILWAY SLEEPERS

SIGN POST

JOIN ROAD HERE

BENCH

RIVER ESK

Broom House

FORD (DRY)

87

85

137

★ trailblazer

¼ mile

0   APPROX SCALE   500m

Glaisdale, is notable for its 16th-century wooden font cover and communion table. (Don't be fooled by the '1585' date stone in the side of the steps leading to the tower, it's from an earlier chapel). The church also contains a picture of Thomas Ferris, the beggar made famous in Glaisdale's other main sight, the **Beggar's Bridge** at the other end of the village. In the 17th century, Ferris, a humble pauper, was courting the daughter of the wealthy local squire. In order to win her hand Ferris thought he needed to improve his standing in the community so with this in mind he struck upon a plan to set sail from Whitby and seek his fortune on the high seas. The night before he put this plan into action, Ferris went to visit his beloved who lived across the river. Unfortunately, the river was swollen by heavy rains and Ferris's dreams of a romantic farewell were dashed. The story, however, does have a happy ending: Thomas returned from his adventures on the sea a wealthy man and married his sweetheart, and with part of his fortune built the Beggar's Bridge so that other young lovers from the neighbourhood would not suffer the same torment as he had that stormy night.

As for facilities, the **shop** (Mon-Sat 7am-6pm, Sun 9am-noon) is also home to the **post office** (Mon, Tues, Thur & Fri 8.30am-12.30pm & 1.30-5.30pm, Wed & Sat 8.30am-12.30pm).

Where to stay and eat
On the path as you enter Glaisdale you'll find *Glaisdale Tea Garden* (☎ 01947 897521; Thur-Sun 10am-5pm) which serves hot and cold drinks, sandwiches, home-made cakes and pastries.

About half a mile north of the path is *Laneside B&B* (☎ 01947 897272, ▨ www.glaisdalebedandbreakfast.co.uk; 3D or T; en suite; WI-FI; ▮ for free; Ⓛ £5.50). B&B is from £35pp (sgl occ £50). Free transport to the pub for supper is provided if required.

Down near the railway station *The Arncliffe Arms* (☎ 01947 897555; ▨ www.arncliffearms.com; 2S/1D/1T/1D or T/1Tr; all en suite; ▮£5; WI-FI; Ⓛ £6) charges from £35pp (sgl £42, sgl occ £52, three in triple £105). It also lays on **food** (Mon-Fri noon-2.30pm & 6-8.30pm, Sat noon-9pm, Sun noon-8pm). They accept credit cards and can do cashback as long as you buy a drink; they serve tea, coffee & cakes noon-6pm and have drying facilities.

Half a mile from the village centre is the award-winning 17th-century *Red House Farm* (☎ 01947 897242, ▨ www .redhousefarm.com; 2D/1T or Tr; en suite; ▬; WI-FI; Ⓛ £6.50 if requested 24hrs in advance). Once a working farm and still the home of a number of farm animals, it's been tastefully converted to retain many of the original features to the point where it would be a shame to spend only one night here. B&B costs from £40pp (sgl £60).

At the very end of the village just across the tracks from the railway station is *Beggar's Bridge* (☎ 01947 897409, ▨ www.beggarsbridge.co.uk; 2D en suite; Ⓛ £5), close to the lovelorn bridge. B&B rates are from £35pp (sgl occ £55).

Transport (see also pp52-5)
Bus No 99 (Mon-Sat) travels up and down the Esk Valley from Lealholm to Whitby. **Trains** stop here en route between Middlesbrough and Whitby.

From Glaisdale you enter **East Arncliffe Wood**, walking along the river until the path winds up at a road where a left leads down the hill and into Egton Bridge.

EGTON BRIDGE MAP 87, p241
A strong competitor for the accolade of prettiest village on the Coast to Coast, Egton Bridge is a delight, a hamlet of grand houses surrounding an uninhabited island on the Esk. Everything about the place is charming, from the bridge itself – a 1990s'

copy of the original 18th-century structure washed away in a flood in 1930 – to the stepping stones that lead across to the island and the mature trees that fringe the settlement. The Catholic **St Hedda's Church**, too, is incredibly grand given the tiny size of

❏ **St Hedda**
The seventh-century British saint, Hedda, crops up a few times on the Coast to Coast walk, even though he is these days more closely associated with Winchester, Hampshire. He began his episcopal career at Whitby Abbey (whose striking remains you'll have spied from Glaisdale Moor), where he was educated and rose to become abbot.

His big break came in 676AD when he was consecrated as the Bishop of Wessex by St Theodore of Tarsus, at that time the Archbishop of Canterbury. He ruled over the diocese for thirty years, during which time he moved the see from Dorchester to Winchester and became chief advisor to King Ina. Described by the Venerable Bede as 'a good and just man, who in carrying out his duties was guided rather by an inborn love of virtue than by what he had read in books', he died in 705AD and is buried at Winchester Cathedral.

Egton Bridge. On the exterior are a series of friezes while inside, behind glass to the right of the altar, are the relics of Nicholas Postgate, a local Catholic priest and martyr hung, drawn and quartered for continuing to practise his faith in 1679. See box above for details about St Hedda himself.

There are public **toilets** and a **telephone** in the village centre.

Where to stay and eat
It would be a surprise indeed if somewhere like Egton Bridge didn't have decent accommodation, and the village doesn't disappoint. *The Horseshoe Hotel* (☎ 01947 895245, 🖥 www.egtonbridgehotel.co.uk; 4D/2T; all en suite; ✆; WI-FI; Ⓛ £4.95), right on the walk at the start of the village, fulfils every expectation of a country inn, with an expansive beer garden, a lavish array of local ales and a snug interior. Main courses are from £10 (hot baguettes cost £6-7) and are served daily noon-2pm & 6-9pm. B&B costs from £39.75pp (sgl occ £69.50).

A little way to the west of the village, the four-star *Broom House* (Map 86, p238; ☎ 01947 895279, 🖥 www.broom-house.co.uk; 1T/6D; all en suite; ✆; WI-FI; Ⓛ £6.95;

Mar-Nov) is a 19th-century farmhouse described by one reader as more of a country house hotel with a touch of class. They charge £45-75pp for B&B.

Aka 'The Black Dog' in *Heartbeat*, *The Postgate Inn* (☎ 01947 895241, 🖥 www.postgateinn.com; 1D/1D or T/1Qd; all en suite; ✆; 🐾; WI-FI; Ⓛ) is another top choice with **food** served daily (light lunches daily noon-2.30pm, meals 6.30-9pm), and **B&B** around £42.50pp, £25-30pp for four/three in the quad. To get there, head up the hill from the church past the point where the Coast to Coast path turns down the track.

On Broom House Lane by the banks of the Esk is *The Old Mill* (☎ 01947 895351; 🖥 theoldmillegtonbridge@live.co.uk; 1D or T en suite, 1D or T private facilities; ✆; Ⓛ £5). B&B is from £37.50pp (sgl occ £66).

Transport   (see also pp52-5)
Egton Bridge is on the **railway** line between Whitby and Middlesbrough. In addition, **bus** No 99 travels from Whitby up the Esk Valley to Glaisdale and Lealholm.

The next mile or so from Egton Bridge to Grosmont takes you past the elegant **Egton Manor** along an old toll road (the original toll charges are still written on a board hanging from **Toll Cottage**, halfway along). It's an easy walk now, taking you under the railway and along the Esk, past Priory Farm (see p242), and into Grosmont.

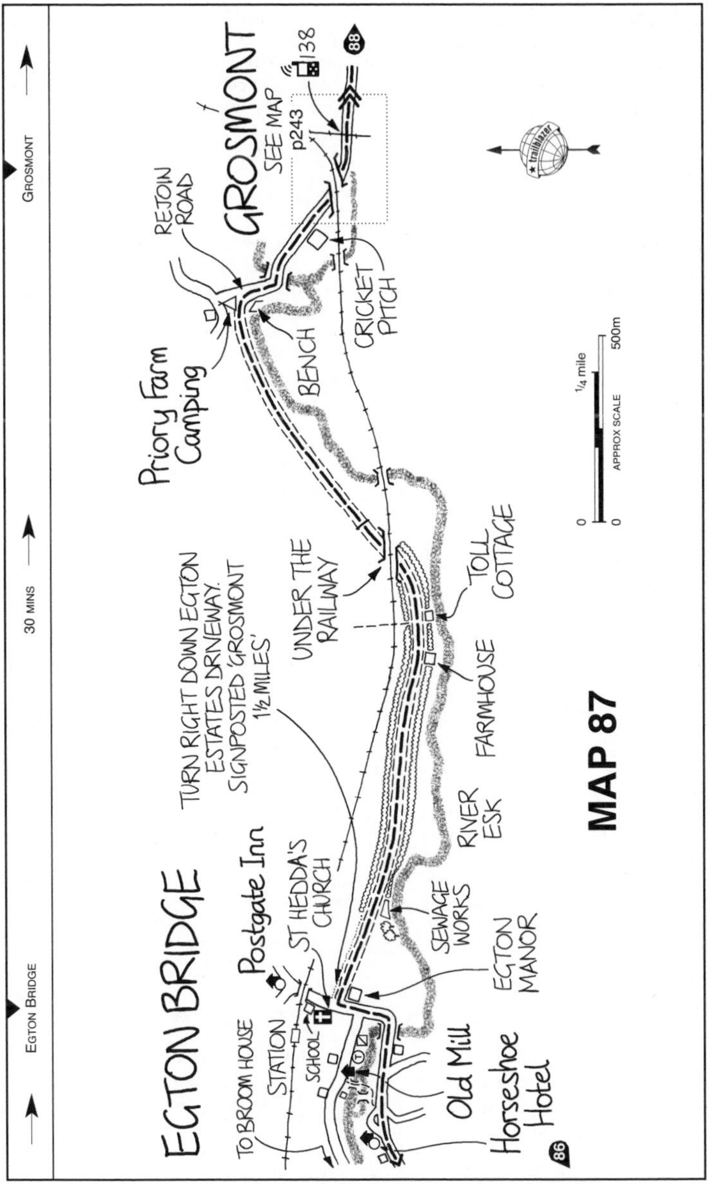

MAP 87

EGTON BRIDGE

TO BROOM HOUSE

STATION

SCHOOL

Horseshoe Hotel

Old Mill

Postgate Inn

ST HEDDA'S CHURCH

EGTON MANOR

SEWAGE WORKS

RIVER ESK

TURN RIGHT DOWN EGTON ESTATES DRIVEWAY. SIGNPOSTED 'GROSMONT 1½ MILES'

UNDER THE RAILWAY

FARMHOUSE

TOLL COTTAGE

Priory Farm Camping

REJOIN ROAD

GROSMONT

SEE MAP

p243

p138

88

BENCH

CRICKET PITCH

30 MINS

EGTON BRIDGE

GROSMONT

86

0   ¼ mile
0   500m
APPROX SCALE

ROUTE GUIDE AND MAPS

GROSMONT   MAP 87, p241

After the quaint, picture-perfect settlements of the preceding few miles, Grosmont emerges as a grittier and more distinctive sibling. Indeed literally so as from the rail crossing in the village centre, a row of soot-stained terraces claw their way up the hill, caked by the acrid fumes that once belched from three ironstone smelting furnaces 150 years ago. These days this less glamorous heritage is all but forgotten as tourists and steam rail enthusiasts alike flock to ride the locomotives of the **North York Moors Railway**. Featured as the 'Hogwarts Express' in the original *Harry Potter* movie, it's definitely worth hanging about to see at least one loco in motion before leaving Grosmont, if not timing your arrival to take a return ride to Pickering or Whitby. By now you deserve to take the weight off your feet; see 'Transport' opposite.

While you're waiting, follow the alleyway leading through a long train tunnel to the **sidings and loco sheds** to gain an insight into what it takes to keep these engines on track. The tunnel is thought to be the oldest passenger train tunnel in the world, hewn out around 1829 to serve a horse-drawn railway designed by none other than George Stephenson. Regarded as the 'Father of Railways', it was Stephenson who foresaw a future in a network of inter-linked rail lines along which engines powered by steam would go on to span and help consolidate the riches of the British Empire. During the tunnel excavations viable quantities of iron ore were unearthed, leading to the ironstone mining boom along the Esk Valley.

There's a **church**, too, with a boulder of Shap granite outside the west door, deposited here by a glacier which lost its way back in the Ice Age.

The settlement, originally known as 'Tunnel', went on to gain the name Grosmont and is today a one-street village where both modern and heritage rail lines intersect, and that has all of the essentials a weary trekker needs: a **store**, **pub** (the Station Tavern, of course!), several **tearooms** and a few B&Bs. The Co-op (Mon-Fri 7.30am-5.30pm, Sat 8am-5.30pm, Sun

9am-5.30pm) is one of the oldest community-run village shops in the country. It's also home to the **post office** (Mon-Fri 9am-noon). As well as the post office, the Station Tavern does **cashback**.

Where to stay and eat

In high season if there's some sort of rail event happening, accommodation in Grosmont is scarce. One option is to catch the train to Whitby (25 mins) and stay there.

A little before the village, **campers** stop at *Priory Farm* (Map 87, p241; ☎ 01947 895324, 🖳 prioryfarmwhitby.word press.com) offering 'back-to-basic' facilities (a little too back-to-basic for one reader, though perhaps because the toilet had broken down when he visited) for just £4pp including a small room alongside the farmhouse with a toilet, sink, kettle and toaster.

Highly recommended B&B is on offer above the *Geall Gallery* (☎ 01947 895007, 🖳 www.chrisgeall.com; 1D/4D or T en suite; ➾; WI-FI) on Front St. The comfortable rooms (from £45pp) are decorated with atmospheric artwork from the gallery downstairs. The Art/Artisan Café, also downstairs, is an excellent place to eat, recommended several times by readers.

Just over the rails *Linten House* (☎ 01947 895386; 1D or T with private bathroom; ➾; WI-FI; Apr-Oct) offers plain B&B accommodation in an old terrace house from £35pp (sgl occ £40). Over the road is *The Station Tavern* (☎ 01947 895060, 🖳 www.stationtavern-grosmont.co.uk; 1S/1D/1Tr; all with private facilities; ➾; ✝ £10; WI-FI; ⏰ up to £5.95) which serves **pub grub** (daily noon-9pm) and has become something of a venue for spontaneous Coast to Coast banquets before people go their separate ways at Robin Hood's Bay. B&B costs £37.50-42.50pp (sgl from £43). A refurb is in progress – expect all rooms to be en suite by the time you read this. As it's pretty much the only place in Grosmont to eat in the evening, you'll almost certainly meet your fellow Coast to Coasters here.

Further on, *Grosmont House* (☎ 01947 895539, 🖳 www.grosmonthouse .co.uk; 5D en suite/1T/1Tr or Qd; shared bathroom; ➾; WI-FI; ⏰ about £5) is a delightfully quirky old place whose gardens also have wonderful views down over the railway. The two double rooms on the top floor are particularly good for a group of four people. They also have two cottages (for two people each) that can be rented out when the house is full. Rates are from £35pp (sgl occ £45) or £40pp in the cottages. **Dinner** (daily around 7pm) is available if you pre-book (even if you're not staying there). One reader pointed out that Grosmont House 'needs a bit of a declutter' and another remarked that the 'shower wasn't very modern'. But the general consensus of opinion seems to be that this is a grand old place full of character run by a charming and hospitable couple.

Grosmont boasts several excellent tearooms. Long-running *Hazelwood House* (☎ 01947 895292; daily Easter to Oct 10.30am-5pm) is on the right before the rail crossing. Nearby is the *Artisan Café & Geall Gallery* (see above; daily Apr-Nov 11am-4pm, Dec-Mar Thur-Sun 11am-4pm; WI-FI) with an interesting menu in addition to the standard teatime favourites. The *Old School Coffee Shop* (☎ 01947 895167, 🖥 www.grosmontcoffeeshop.co.uk; daily Easter to Oct 10.30am-4.30pm but closed some Fridays; 🐾 outside; WI-FI) was formerly the village primary school and has a great view of the steam railway. They welcome walkers, don't mind muddy boots and even have shower facilities as well as a flask-filling service. There's also *Signals Tea Room*, on the railway platform.

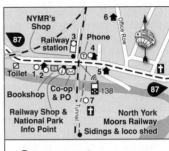

Grosmont

Where to stay, eat and drink
1 Hazelwood House Tearooms
2 Artisan Café & Geall Gallery
3 Signals Tearoom
4 Station Tavern
5 Linten House B&B
6 Grosmont House B&B
7 Old School Coffee Shop

Transport   (see also pp52-5)
North York Moors Railway's **steam train** (☎ 01751 472508, 🖥 www.nymr.co.uk) to Pickering (70 mins), or Whitby (25 mins) leaves Grosmont between four and eight times a day. Some of the trains are drawn by a diesel rather than a steam engine, so if you want that authentic chuff-chuff sound check the timetable. Northern Rail's ('normal') **trains** go to Whitby (20 mins) and to Middlesbrough (70 mins). **Bus** No 99 also goes to Whitby (15 mins) from here.

STAGE 13: GROSMONT TO ROBIN HOOD'S BAY   MAPS 87-95
Introduction
Time to saddle up for the last stage, but don't be fooled into thinking this last stage is a mere formality – as the savage climb out of Grosmont will soon demonstrate. It's a long stretch totalling **15½ miles (25km, 6hrs)** with enough ups and downs, lefts and rights and ins and outs to ensure that you arrive in

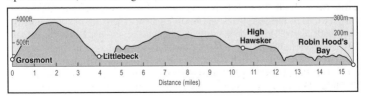

Robin Hood's Bay suitably dishevelled. The scenery is largely similar to what's gone before: desolate moorland punctuated with short road stages and, in a superior echo of the first leg, a grand finale along the sea cliffs prior to the final descent to the Bay. The most pleasant surprise, especially on a hot day, is the transit of Little Beck Wood, a narrow belt of the most heavenly woodland in North Yorkshire.

The route

First, there's that calf-popping 700ft (230m) climb up to **Sleights Moor**, part of the intriguingly named Eskdaleside Cum Ugglebarnby, which is how you may feel if you missed breakfast. With views north-east to the well-ventilated ruins of **Whitby Abbey** or back down into misty Eskdale, you pass the **High Bride Stones** – five ancient standing monoliths – to the right of the road. (Incidentally, the confusing jumble of the Low Bride Stones stands just below them on a terrace, to your right as you pass over the cattle grid.)

Opposite a car park turn left onto a path (Map 88, WPT 139) and cut a corner down to the A169 where you turn left again along the road for a few hundred metres until a Coast to Coast sign heralds the path dropping down through more heather to Littlebeck.

LITTLEBECK MAP 89, p246

Littlebeck is another tiny hamlet with a lengthy past; it's hard to imagine today's picturesque rural idyll was actually once a centre of alum mining in the 17th to 19th centuries. Alum, by the way, is used in dyeing as well as tanning leather. A hundred tons of shale would be produced in order to extract just one ton of alum, so it seems remarkable the surrounding land appears so unscarred.

The village has one other minor claim to fame as the home of master woodcarver Thomas Whittaker who died in 1991 (his house, now called **Woodcarver's Cottage**, is on the bend above the **Old Mill**). Whittaker exclusively used English oak and would 'sign' every piece of his furniture with a gnome; in German folklore the oak tree's guardian. Above the cottage is **Kelp House**, where kelp, used in the processing of alum, was stored.

Fifteen minutes south of the village and half a mile from the path, staying at ***Intake Farm*** (☎ 01947 810273, 🖳 intakefarm.com; 2D/1T/1Tr; one en suite, others private/shared facilities; ☕; 🐕; WI-FI; Ⓛ £5) is regularly and warmly recommended by readers who want to spin out the last day into an easy 12-miler. **B&B** costs £30-35pp (sgl occ £40, £30pp for three in the triple) – and £5 to **camp** (£1 for a shower). It's a way to the nearest pub but they'll happily lay on an evening meal (£15, three courses, book in advance). Whilst you can reach the farm from the centre of the village, it's quicker to join the track to the right (south) of the Coast to Coast path heading off the A169 via both High Quebec Farm and Low Quebec Farm.

Pretty as Littlebeck is, it's nothing when compared to the beauty that awaits in **Little Beck Wood**. This really is a stunning 65 acres of woodland, filled with oak trees, deer, badgers, foxes and birdlife galore. There are also a couple of man-made features to see on the way including the mysterious **Hermitage** (Map 89), a boulder hollowed out to form a small cave. Above the entrance is etched the year '1790'. More delights await as the path from the Hermitage leads you down to **Falling Foss** (Map 90), a 20m-high waterfall alongside the former ruins of **Midge Hall**, a former gamekeeper's cottage now enterprisingly converted

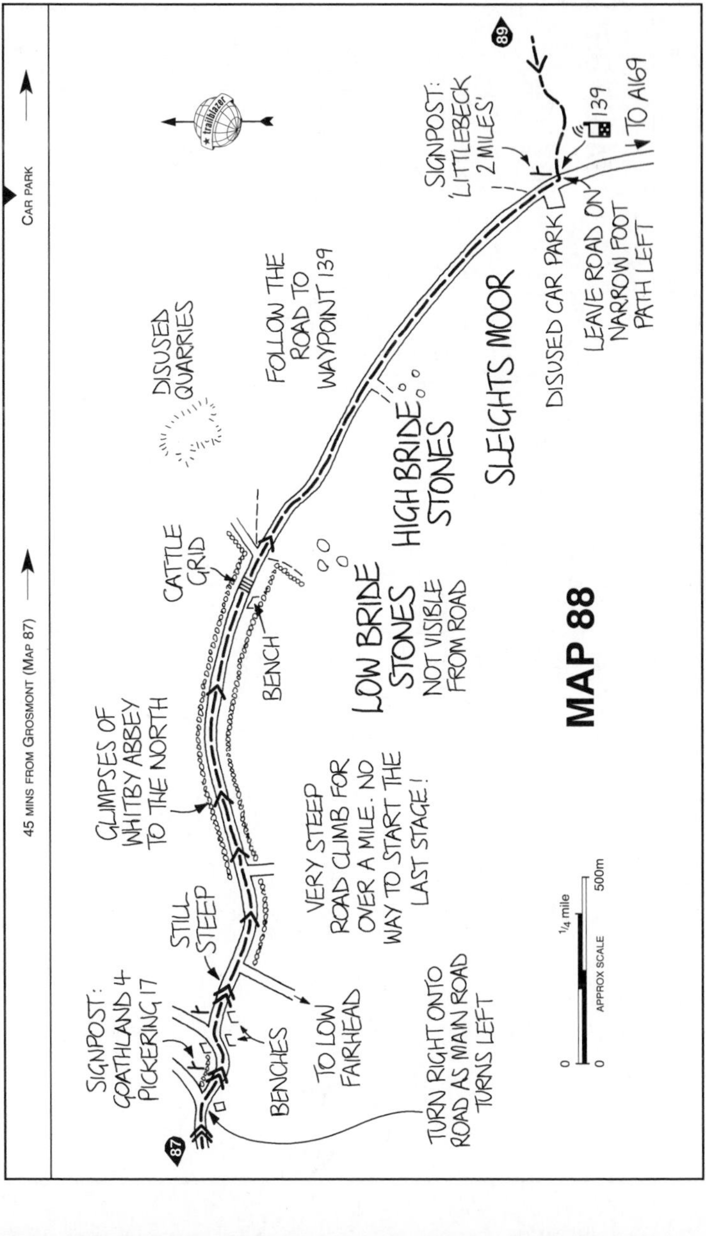

45 MINS FROM GROSMONT (MAP 87) →

CAR PARK

87

SIGNPOST:
GOATHLAND 4
PICKERING 17

STILL
STEEP

BENCHES

TO LOW
FAIRHEAD

TURN RIGHT ONTO
ROAD AS MAIN ROAD
TURNS LEFT

VERY STEEP
ROAD CLIMB FOR
OVER A MILE. NO
WAY TO START THE
LAST STAGE!

GLIMPSES OF
WHITBY ABBEY
TO THE NORTH

CATTLE
GRID

BENCH

DISUSED
QUARRIES

FOLLOW THE
ROAD TO
WAYPOINT 139

LOW BRIDE
STONES
NOT VISIBLE
FROM ROAD

HIGH BRIDE
STONES

SLEIGHTS MOOR

MAP 88

DISUSED CAR PARK

LEAVE ROAD ON
NARROW FOOT
PATH LEFT

SIGNPOST:
'LITTLEBECK
2 MILES'

139

TO A169

89

trailblazer

¼ mile

500m

APPROX SCALE

0

0

ROUTE GUIDE AND MAPS

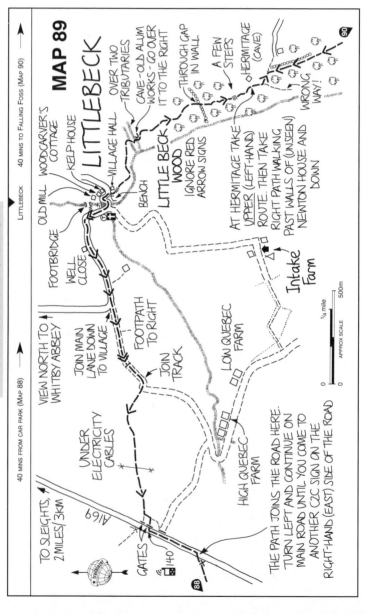

ROUTE GUIDE AND MAPS

40 MINS FROM CAR PARK (MAP 88) →   LITTLEBECK   40 MINS TO FALLING FOSS (MAP 90) →

MAP 89

LITTLEBECK

VIEW NORTH TO WHITBY ABBEY ↑

TO SLEIGHTS, 2 MILES/3KM

A169

UNDER ELECTRICITY CABLES

JOIN MAIN LANE DOWN TO VILLAGE

FOOTPATH TO RIGHT

JOIN TRACK

FOOTBRIDGE

WELL CLOSE

OLD MILL

WOODCARVER'S COTTAGE

KELP HOUSE

VILLAGE HALL

BENCH

OVER TWO TRIBUTARIES

CAVE – OLD ALUM WORKS – GO OVER IT TO THE RIGHT

THROUGH GAP IN WALL

A FEW STEPS

◇ HERMITAGE (CAVE)

WRONG WAY!

90

LITTLE BECK WOOD

IGNORE RED ARROW SIGNS

AT HERMITAGE TAKE UPPER (LEFT-HAND) ROUTE. THEN TAKE RIGHT PATH WALKING PAST WALLS OF (UNSEEN) NEWTON HOUSE AND DOWN

Intake Farm

LOW QUEBEC FARM

HIGH QUEBEC FARM

GATES

140

88

THE PATH JOINS THE ROAD HERE. TURN LEFT AND CONTINUE ON MAIN ROAD UNTIL YOU COME TO ANOTHER C2C SIGN ON THE RIGHT-HAND (EAST) SIDE OF THE ROAD

1/4 mile

APPROX SCALE

500m

0   0

trailblazer

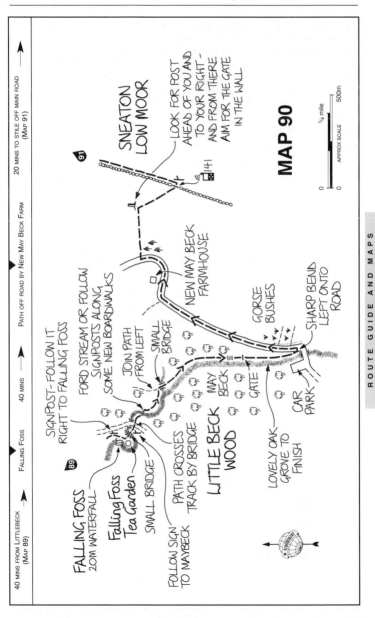

SNEATON LOW MOOR

LOOK FOR POST AHEAD OF YOU AND TO YOUR RIGHT - AND FROM THERE AIM FOR THE GATE IN THE WALL

91

MAP 90

0   ¼ mile
0   500m
APPROX SCALE

SIGNPOST- FOLLOW IT RIGHT TO FALLING FOSS

FORD STREAM OR FOLLOW SIGNPOSTS ALONG SOME NEW BOARDWALKS

NEW MAY BECK FARMHOUSE

JOIN PATH FROM LEFT

SMALL BRIDGE

GORSE BUSHES

SHARP BEND LEFT ONTO ROAD

FALLING FOSS 20M WATERFALL

89

Falling Foss Tea Garden

SMALL BRIDGE

PATH CROSSES TRACK BY BRIDGE

MAY BECK

GATE

LITTLE BECK WOOD

CAR PARK

FOLLOW SIGN TO MAYBECK

LOVELY OAK GROVE TO FINISH

★ Trailblazer

ROUTE GUIDE AND MAPS

into the *Falling Foss Tea Garden* (☎ 07723 477929, 🖳 www.fallingfosstea garden.co.uk; Apr-Sept daily 10.30am-5pm, closed Oct-Mar). It's a great place for a coffee and cake, an ice cream or a light lunch before you leave the woods for the final hike to the sea. Suitably refreshed, head along **May Beck** to the car park at the southern extremity of the wood. Here you turn back north and walk along the road, looking back over the valley you've just walked through and the moors beyond. A traverse of two other moors, Sneaton Low Moor and the innocuously named Graystone Hills, follows. The former is now fairly easy to negotiate, the new diversion that's been introduced for once helping rather than

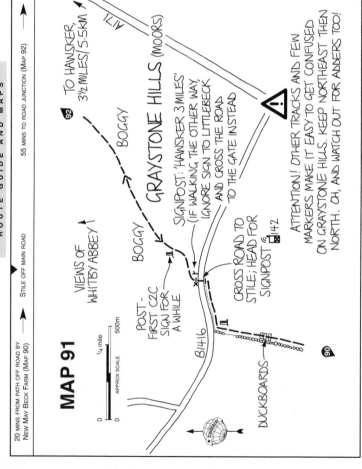

MAP 91

20 MINS FROM PATH OFF ROAD BY NEW MAY BECK FARM (MAP 90) — STILE OFF MAIN ROAD — 55 MINS TO ROAD JUNCTION (MAP 92)

¼ mile / 500m APPROX SCALE

VIEWS OF WHITBY ABBEY

POST-FIRST C2C SIGN FOR A WHILE

BOGGY

BOGGY

GRAYSTONE HILLS (MOORS)

TO HAWSKER, 3½ MILES/5.5KM

B1416

DUCKBOARDS

CROSS ROAD TO STILE; HEAD FOR SIGNPOST 🏠142

SIGNPOST: 'HAWSKER 3 MILES' (IF WALKING THE OTHER WAY, IGNORE SIGN TO LITTLEBECK AND CROSS THE ROAD TO THE GATE INSTEAD)

ATTENTION! OTHER TRACKS AND FEW MARKERS MAKE IT EASY TO GET CONFUSED ON GRAYSTONE HILLS. KEEP NORTHEAST THEN NORTH. OH, AND WATCH OUT FOR ADDERS TOO!

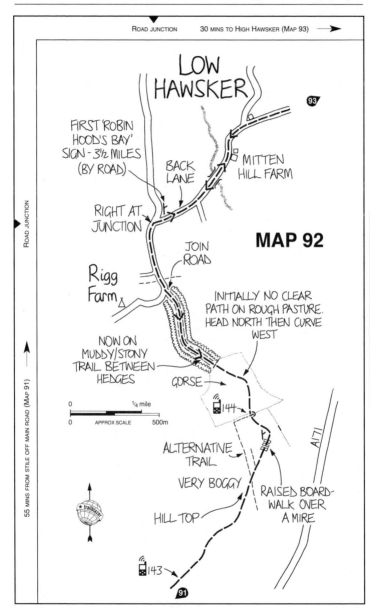

ROAD JUNCTION   30 MINS TO HIGH HAWSKER (MAP 93) →

LOW
HAWSKER

93

FIRST 'ROBIN
HOOD'S BAY'
SIGN - 3½ MILES
(BY ROAD)

BACK
LANE

MITTEN
HILL FARM

RIGHT AT
JUNCTION

JOIN
ROAD

MAP 92

Rigg
Farm

INITIALLY NO CLEAR
PATH ON ROUGH PASTURE.
HEAD NORTH THEN CURVE
WEST

NOW ON
MUDDY/STONY
TRAIL BETWEEN
HEDGES

GORSE →

144

0   ¼ mile
0   APPROX SCALE   500m

ALTERNATIVE
TRAIL

VERY BOGGY

HILL TOP

RAISED BOARD-
WALK OVER
A MIRE

A171

★ trailblaze

143

91

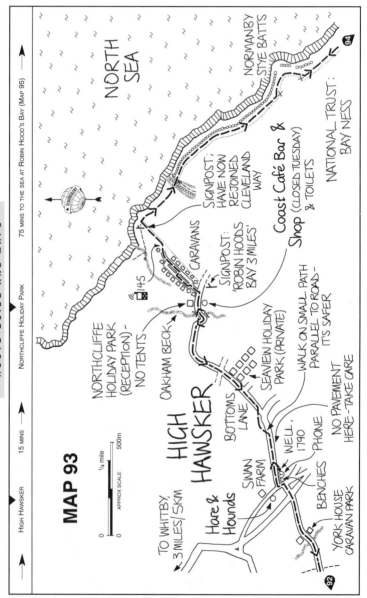

← HIGH HAWKSER ← 15 MINS → ▶ NORTHCLIFFE HOLIDAY PARK ← 75 MINS TO THE SEA AT ROBIN HOOD'S BAY (MAP 95) →

MAP 93

¼ mile
0   500m
0
APPROX SCALE

NORTH SEA

NORMANBY STYE BATTS

94

SIGNPOST; HAVE NOW REJOINED CLEVELAND WAY

NATIONAL TRUST: BAY NESS

CARAVANS

SIGNPOST: 'ROBIN HOODS BAY 3 MILES'

Coast Café Bar & Shop (CLOSED TUESDAY) & TOILETS

145

NORTHCLIFFE HOLIDAY PARK (RECEPTION) – NO TENTS

OAKHAM BECK

WALK ON SMALL PATH PARALLEL TO ROAD – IT'S SAFER

BOTTOMS LANE

HIGH HAWSKER

SEAVIEW HOLIDAY PARK (PRIVATE)

TO WHITBY, 3 MILES/5KM

SWAN FARM

WELL, 1790

PHONE

NO PAVEMENT HERE – TAKE CARE

Hare & Hounds

BENCHES

YORK HOUSE CARAVAN PARK

92

hindering navigation, though the rather lean waymarks and confusing paths across Graystone Hills to Normanby Hill Top (north of the B1416) can require a good sense of direction or some luck, even in bright sunshine; see box p93.

All being well, you'll eventually emerge on a road and should turn left here if planning to camp at Rigg Farm (see below). If not, continue down the road where before long you will no doubt be thrilled to spot the first road sign to Robin Hood's Bay indicating it's only '3½ miles' by road. But for you, my friend, the walk is not over; turn right to follow Back Lane past York House Caravan Park and into the village of **High Hawsker** (Map 93) on the A171 Whitby road.

HIGH HAWSKER   MAP 93

In the village the *Hare & Hounds* (☎ 01947 880453, 🖥 www.hareandhound shawsker.co.uk; Mon-Thur noon-3pm & 5-9pm, Fri-Sun noon-9pm) serves hot meals as well as sandwiches. If you're set on **camping**, the smaller *Rigg Farm Caravan Park* (Map 92; ☎ 01947 880430, 🖥

www.riggfarmcaravanpark.co.uk; 🐾; Mar-Oct), a couple of minutes' walk west from where you rejoined the road, charges £12-17 per pitch to camp. There's limited space so phone in advance. The site has toilet/shower facilities but no shop.

Arriva's **bus** No X93 (daily) calls here; see pp52-5 for details.

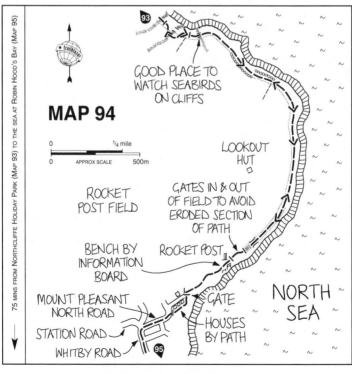

MAP 94

93

GOOD PLACE TO WATCH SEABIRDS ON CLIFFS

0   ¼ mile
0   APPROX SCALE   500m

LOOKOUT HUT

ROCKET POST FIELD

GATES IN & OUT OF FIELD TO AVOID ERODED SECTION OF PATH

BENCH BY INFORMATION BOARD

ROCKET POST

MOUNT PLEASANT NORTH ROAD

GATE

HOUSES BY PATH

NORTH SEA

STATION ROAD

WHITBY ROAD

95

75 MINS FROM NORTHCLIFFE HOLIDAY PARK (MAP 93) TO THE SEA AT ROBIN HOOD'S BAY (MAP 95)

ROUTE GUIDE AND MAPS

From Hawsker, the remains of your eastward marathon takes you down past sprawling caravan parks and **Coast Café Bar** (Map 93; Mon, Wed & Thur 10am-4pm – or 6pm in July and Aug – Fri & Sat 10am-10pm-ish, Sun 9am-4pm, WI-FI), where you can get a last-minute snack for the final stretch.

And so you arrive at the **North Sea** to rejoin the Cleveland Way and stride weary but unbeaten along the blustery clifftops towards Robin Hood's Bay. Though the tiny beach at Robin Hood's Bay appears half an hour before you actually set foot on it, the village itself, tucked away by the headland, is concealed until the very last moment. But eventually, having passed a coastguard station and **Rocket Post Field** (Map 94) from which coastguards used to practise aiming their rescue rockets, you join Mount Pleasant North Rd at the top end of Robin Hood's Bay. Take a left at the end of the road and at the roundabout follow either the cliff path or the steep street down, down, down to the bay.

You arrive at the slipway, or Dock as it's known, and all that remains is to liberate that pebble you've carried from St Bees beach and then toast your fine achievement in Wainwright's Bar at Bay Hotel (see p254 for opening hours), not forgetting to sign their book.

And that's it. Your Coast to Coast walk is over. Congratulations: you've walked the width of England, and quite probably more than 200 miles in all, which is certainly something to be pleased about. But not quite as satisfying as knowing there's no more walking on the agenda for a while.

ROBIN HOOD'S BAY   MAP 95, p255

Robin Hood's Bay is the perfect place to finish: a quaint, cosy little fishing village that in high summer becomes a busy seaside resort that is entirely in keeping with the picturesque theme of the walk. Though fishing has declined since its heyday in the 19th century, there's been a revival thanks to its crab grounds, said to be amongst the best in the north.

The old town huddles around the Dock, row after row of terraced, stone cottages arranged haphazardly uphill with numerous twisting interconnecting alleyways and paths to explore. Within them are a number of pubs and tearooms where you can celebrate. There are also gift, souvenir and antique shops aplenty, as well as certificates (see Bay Hotel, p254) for newly ennobled Coast to Coasters. If that's not enough to commemorate your achievement you could get a personalised plaque (from £45) from **Cromwells** (🖳 www.cromwell splaques.com), opposite the Bay Hotel.

The **Old Coastguard Station National Trust Visitor Centre** (☎ 01947 885900; Easter-Sep daily 10am-5pm, Oct-Easter weekends only 11am-4pm) sits right by the end of the trail and has some great displays including a mini wind machine and an aquarium of marine life. There's also a small **museum** (🖳 museum.rhbay.co .uk; June & Sep and school hols Sun-Fri 2-4pm, July-Aug Tues-Sun noon-4pm).

Services

The official tourist information **website** (🖳 www.robin-hoods-bay.co.uk) has plenty of useful information, including a comprehensive list of **accommodation**. The **post office** (Mon-Fri 9am-5.30pm, Sat 9am-12.30pm) **and general store** (same times – though open to 6pm on Sat) offers **cashback**. There's another **general shop** in the lower town.

If you've any aches and pains after the walk visit **Treat Therapy** (🖳 www.treat therapy.co.uk) for their Relax and Unwind package, including a foot soak, reflex foot massage, Swedish back massage and Aroma facial (including scalp, hand and arm massage), a two-hour treatment for £70.

Finally, several residents have asked us to emphasise the fact that there is **no cashpoint in town**.

Where to stay

Robin Hood's Bay is divided into Upper Bay, the development dating from the Victorian era at the top of the hill, and the quainter and more congested 17th-century Lower Bay or 'Old Town' down by the sea, where there are fewer accommodation options and rooms are less spacious. Not since Grasmere have you paused to stay in such a busy tourist 'honeypot', and as most Coasters end their walk on a Thursday or Friday, it's worth knowing that rooms at weekends and in holiday periods may be hard to come by and some places may even insist on a **minimum of two nights stay** for advance bookings.

There are two **campsites** and both can be pretty crowded in summer with families, dogs and caravans. The first, *Middlewood Farm Holiday Park* (☎ 01947 880414, 🖳 www.middlewoodfarm.com; 🐾; 🐕 £2; Easter-Oct) is a smart and efficient operation with a laundry room and the finest ablutions block in North Yorkshire. Camping costs from £8pp (£10 on bank holidays); showers and toilets are free but for £1 you can even take a bath. They are very 'pro' Coast to Coasters and will always try to accommodate campers arriving on foot even at busy times, but prefer 24 hours warning of your arrival if possible. They also now offer 'gypsy cabins' – wool-insulated wooden pods sleeping two with microwave and fridge for £40-55 (🐕 £5) – though they may request a two- or three-night minimum stay over busy periods. To get there, from the end of the walk by the Bay Hotel head up Albion Rd past the chippy for 10 minutes along the path.

High on a hill above the town, you may want to check into the no less popular *Hooks House Farm* (☎ 01947 880283, 🖳 www.hookshousefarm.co.uk; 🐕 on a lead; Mar-Oct) before walking the last mile or two down to the sea as the walk back can be quite an effort. **Camping** here costs £8-10pp including showers and use of kitchen.

YHA Boggle Hole (☎ 0845 371 9504, 🖳 www.yha.org.uk/hostel/boggle-hole; 85 beds, 1 x single, 2-/3/4-/5/6-/8-bed rooms; beds £15-18.50, 4-bed rooms £49-109; WI-FI; ⓛ £5.50; Mar-Oct daily, Nov-Feb weekends only) has two main buildings. The first

is a former corn mill with 42 beds and the usual facilities plus a sandpit, mermaid, old boat and pirates. The second, built in 2015, the Crow's Nest, is an environmentally friendly building with 44 beds up some steep steps. Both are located in a ravine about a mile south of the village and reachable either along the shore or the inland road past Middlewood Farm Holiday Park. The hostel serves meals and has a bar and drying room. Credit cards are accepted.

Back in town there are nearly three dozen hotels, guesthouses and B&Bs to choose from; the official town website (see opposite) has a fuller list. Accommodation is most prolific in Upper Bay, where *Thackwood* (☎ 01947 880858, 🖳 www.thackwood.com; 2D/1T, all en suite; 🐾; WI-FI) is the first B&B you spot as the trail comes into town. B&B is from £37.50pp (sgl occ £60). This is followed by *Northcliff* (☎ 01947 880481, 🖳 www.north-cliff.co.uk; 2D/1T; all en suite; WI-FI) a Victorian villa also on Mount Pleasant North Rd. B&B rates are from £32.50pp (sgl occ £40). Next door, *Manning Tree* (☎ 01947 881042, 🖳 www.manningtreebnb.co.uk; 2D/1T; all en suite; WI-FI) offering a similar standard of accommodation; B&B costs from £35pp (sgl occ £45).

On Mount Pleasant Rd there's more of the same with the pick of the bunch including *Lee-Side* (☎ 01947 881143, 🖳 lee-side.rhbay.co.uk; 3D/1T; all en suite or private facilities; 🐾; WI-FI) with B&B for £37.50-40pp (sgl occ £50), and *Streonshalh* (☎ 01947 881065, 🖳 www.streonshalh.co.uk; 2S/2D/2D or T; all en suite; WI-FI), costing £37.50-40pp for B&B (sgl £43). Credit cards are accepted. The name, by the way, is apparently what the Vikings called Whitby.

On Station Rd is *The Grosvenor Hotel* (☎ 01947 880320, 🖳 www.thegrosvenor.info; 6D/1T/3Tr; all en suite; 🐾; WI-FI) with B&B from £32.50pp (sgl occ £50, three in triple £85), while still on Station Rd, *The Villa* (☎ 01947 881043, 🖳 www.thevillarhb.co.uk; 2D/2D or T, all en suite; 🐾; WI-FI) is another Victorian property. They have retained the period features such as the cast-iron fireplaces and the servant bells. B&B rates are from £37.50pp (sgl occ £50).

All dietary requirements, coeliac in particular, catered for by these friendly people.

Below, a further string of B&Bs on Station Rd leads down towards the old town. They're all pretty similar. Readers have recommended the rooms – and the food – at *The Wayfarer* (☎ 01947 880240, 💻 www.wayfarerbistro.co.uk; 4D/1D or T; all en suite; WI-FI; Feb-Dec). B&B costs £38pp (sgl occ £50). The elegant *West Royd* (☎ 01947 880678, 💻 www.westroyd.co.uk; 2D/1Tr; all en suite; ➤; 🐾 for free; WI-FI) was built in 1897 and maintains its Victorian charm. B&B from £75pp (sgl occ £50).

This is followed by *Devon House* (☎ 01947 880062, 💻 www.devonhouserhb.co .uk; 2D/1D or T/1T; all en suite; ➤; WI-FI) with B&B from £37.50pp (sgl occ £50); *Birtley House* (☎ 01947 880566, 💻 www .birtleyhousebedandbreakfast.co.uk; 3D/ 1T/1Tr, all with private facilities; ➤) charging £32.50-42.50pp (sgl occ £50) and *Lynnfield* (☎ 01947 881253, 💻 www.lynn fieldbedandbreakfast.co.uk; 3D/1T; en suite; ➤; WI-FI), the first house in Upper Bay to offer B&B, way back in 1955. B&B in the bright rooms is from £37-42.50pp (sgl occ from £54 but not at weekends).

Alongside these *The Victoria Hotel* (☎ 01947 880205, 💻 www.victoriarhb.com; 12D/3D or T/1D or Tr; all en suite; ➤; WI-FI) charges £40-70pp (sgl occ from £60-120). The alleyway next to The Victoria leads onto a road with great views down to the old town. This is where you'll find *Raven House* (☎ 01947 880444, 💻 raven house.rhbay.co.uk; 1S/2D/1Tr; all en suite; WI-FI), which more than one reader has recommended. Most of the rooms enjoy great panoramas. B&B starts at £40pp (sgl/sgl occ from £40).

In the **old town**, most of the accommodation has been given over to self-catering holiday apartments for those intending to stay for a week or more, such as *Ingleby House* (☎ 01947 880887, 💻 www.ingleby-houseinrobinhoodsbay.com; 1D en suite; 🐾 £10; WI-FI) although it does also have a room available for one-night stays for £32.50-40pp (sgl occ £40-55). Tea, coffee, milk and cereal are provided in the room. They also have an en suite room with basic cooking facilities that could accommodate

two singles; contact them for details.

Of the old town B&Bs, many request a two-night minimum stay. If you can't stay that long, try the *The Boathouse* (☎ 01947 880099, 💻 boathouserhb.co.uk; 2D/3T, studio and apartment both with 1D; all en suite; WI-FI). Right in the centre of the action, B&B is from £40pp (sgl occ £65). Most rooms can be booked for a single-night stay except over bank holiday weekends.

Close to the Dock, *Bramblewick* (☎ 01947 880187, evenings ☎ 01947 881186, 💻 www.bramblewick.org; 4D; all en suite), 2 King St, retains the feel of its 17th-century origins with B&B from £40pp (sgl occ £60); and finally, as close to the walk's end as the tides will allow, *Bay Hotel* (☎ 01947 880278, 💻 www.bayhotel.info; 3D all with private facilities; ➤; WI-FI; 🐾) where B&B is £40-45pp (sgl occ £80-90).

Where to eat and drink

It has to be said that Robin Hood's Bay is not the easiest place to celebrate your monumental achievement with fine dining. The cuisine here seems strictly seaside traditional: pubs, takeaways and bucket 'n' spade snackeries, but there are a few notable exceptions.

There are plenty of good tea rooms to relax in should you arrive early and need to spin down. *Swell* (💻 www.swellcafe.co.uk; 10am-3.30pm, to 4 or 5pm in summer), in the heart of the old-town alleyways, is the smartest place. Formerly a Wesleyan chapel it's now also a wedding venue. Up near the top of the hill, *Candy's Café* (☎ 01947 880961; Sun-Wed 9am-5pm, Thurs-Sat 9am-7pm in summer) has a flagstone terrace where you can devour a big breakfast, ice-cream or cake whilst admiring the great sea view. *Pie Parlour* (☎ 01947 881152; daily 10am-6pm) also serves full English breakfasts, served until 12.30pm daily.

A visit to the *Bay Hotel* (see Where to stay; food served daily noon-2pm & 6.30-9pm, 2.30-5pm soup and sandwiches) is almost obligatory. The main **bar** is upstairs (daily 11am-midnight) and in peak periods they open the so-called **Wainwright's Bar** downstairs. The pub sells mementos of the walk including certificates (£2.50); don't forget to sign their book to record your suc-

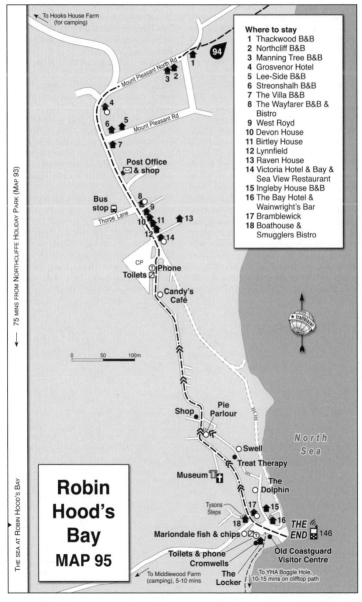

To Hooks House Farm
(for camping)

94

Mount Pleasant North Rd

3 2

1

4

Mount Pleasant Rd

6

5

7

Post Office
✉ & shop

Bus
stop 🚌

Thorpe Lane

8

9

10 11   13

12 14

CP

ℹ️ Phone
Toilets 🚻

Candy's
Café

0   50   100m

Shop

Pie
Parlour

Swell
Treat Therapy

Museum 🏛️✝️

The
Dolphin

Tysons
Steps   17   15

18   16

Mariondale fish & chips 🍴🚻

Toilets & phone
Cromwells

The
Locker

To Middlewood Farm
(camping), 5-10 mins

THE
END 🚌 146

Old Coastguard
Visitor Centre

To YHA Boggle Hole,
10-15 mins on clifftop path

North
Sea

trailblazer ⭐

Where to stay
1 Thackwood B&B
2 Northcliff B&B
3 Manning Tree B&B
4 Grosvenor Hotel
5 Lee-Side B&B
6 Streonshalh B&B
7 The Villa B&B
8 The Wayfarer B&B &
   Bistro
9 West Royd
10 Devon House
11 Birtley House
12 Lynnfield
13 Raven House
14 Victoria Hotel & Bay &
   Sea View Restaurant
15 Ingleby House B&B
16 The Bay Hotel &
   Wainwright's Bar
17 Bramblewick
18 Boathouse &
   Smugglers Bistro

Robin
Hood's
Bay
MAP 95

75 MINS FROM NORTHCLIFFE HOLIDAY PARK (MAP 93)

THE SEA AT ROBIN HOOD'S BAY

ROUTE GUIDE AND MAPS

cess (the log book will be in the upstairs bar if Wainwright's Bar is closed). Also in the old town, the best place to eat is *Smugglers Bistro* (see The Boathouse, p254; daily from 5pm; booking advised). The menu includes seafood dishes from £12.95.

The best place to eat at the top of town – indeed, some reckon this to be the best place to eat in the whole area – is *The Wayfarer Bistro* (🖳 www.wayfarerbistro .co.uk; see p254; Feb-Oct Tue-Sun from 6pm; Nov-Dec Thur-Sun from 6pm). It features grills and seafood and booking is advised. Also in the higher part of town, Victoria Hotel's (see Where to stay) *Bay & Sea View Restaurant* is popular, as is *The Grosvenor Hotel* (see Where to stay, food served Apr-Oct daily noon-9pm, Nov-Mar Mon-Fri 6-9pm, Sat & Sun noon-9pm) which serves a varied menu of traditional favourites for £7.95-12.95. Down in the old town, *Bramblewick* (see Where to stay; café 9.30am-5pm, restaurant 6-9.30pm) serves a small but varied menu with main courses for around £13-20. During the day their café menu includes all-day breakfast.

Further up King St *The Dolphin* (food served noon-2pm & 6.30-9pm) serves local fish dishes, as well as boasting a good range of real ales and live music sessions on Fridays and Mondays.

Fish and chips under a mashed pea sludge never did Alfred Wainwright any harm, so the like-minded will queue expectantly at *Mariondale Fisheries'* chippy (Mon-Wed & Sun noon-7pm, Thur to 7.30pm, Fri & Sat to 8.30pm) up an alleyway by The Boathouse. This is certainly one of the best chippies in the area but get there early: there are few things more disheartening than finishing a two-week trek then finding the chippy has run out of fish!

Transport (see also pp52-5)

Arriva's **bus** No X93 runs daily, once an hour, north to Whitby (20 mins) and on to Middlesbrough (90 mins) for trains to Darlington – or south to Scarborough (40 mins), the nearest place for a train to York. The bus stop is on Thorpe Lane, just north of the main car park. For a **taxi**, call Bay Private Hire on ☎ 01947 880603.

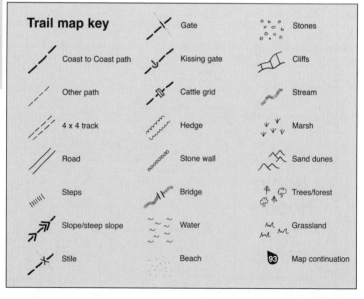

Trail map key

Coast to Coast path	Gate	Stones
Other path	Kissing gate	Cliffs
4 x 4 track	Cattle grid	Stream
Road	Hedge	Marsh
Steps	Stone wall	Sand dunes
Slope/steep slope	Bridge	Trees/forest
Stile	Water	Grassland
	Beach	93 Map continuation

APPENDIX A – TAKING A DOG

COAST TO COAST WITH A DOG

Many are the rewards that await those prepared to make the extra effort required to bring their best friend along the trail. You shouldn't underestimate the amount of work involved, though. Indeed, just about every decision you make will be influenced by the fact that you've got a dog: how you plan to travel to the start of the trail, where you're going to stay, how far you're going to walk each day, where you're going to rest and where you're going to eat in the evening etc.

If you're also sure your dog can cope with (and will enjoy) walking 12 miles or (significantly) more a day for several days in a row, you need to start preparing accordingly. You also need to be sure that your dog will be able to negotiate the many stiles on the path – or that you'll be able to lift them over if they can't! Extra thought also needs to go into your itinerary. The best starting point is to study the village and town facilities table on pp36-7 (and the advice below), and plan where to stop and where to buy food.

Looking after your dog

To begin with, you need to make sure that your own dog is fully **inoculated** against the usual doggy illnesses, and also up to date with regard to **worm pills** (eg Drontal) and **flea preventatives** such as Frontline – they are, after all, following in the pawprints of many a dog before them, some of whom may well have left fleas or other parasites on the trail that now lie in wait for their next meal to arrive. **Pet insurance** is also a very good idea; if you've already got insurance, do check that it will cover a trip such as this.

On the subject of looking after your dog's health, perhaps the most important implement you can take with you is the **plastic tick remover**, available from vets for a couple of quid. These removers, while fiddly, help you to remove the tick safely (ie without leaving its head behind buried under the dog's skin).

Being in unfamiliar territory also makes it more likely that you and your dog could become separated. For this reason, make sure your dog has a **tag with your contact details on it** (a mobile phone number would be best if you are carrying one with you); if it wasn't **microchipped** as a puppy you could consider having this done for further security.

When to keep your dog on a lead

● **On mountain tops** It's a sad fact that, every year, a few dogs lose their lives falling over the edge of steep slopes.

● **When crossing farmland**, particularly in the lambing season (around May) when your dog can scare the sheep, causing them to lose their young. Farmers are allowed by law to shoot at and kill any dogs that they consider are worrying their sheep. During lambing, most

Town plan key					
		📖	Library/bookstore	●	Other
♠	Where to stay	@	Internet	CP	Car park
O	Where to eat and drink	🏛	Museum/gallery	🚌	Bus station/stop
Λ	Campsite	✚	Church/cathedral	▬☐▬	Rail line & station
✉	Post Office	☉	Telephone	▨	Park
£	Bank/ATM	☑	Public toilet	📱082	GPS waypoint
ⓘ	Tourist Information	☐	Building		

farmers would prefer it if you didn't bring your dog at all. The exception to the dogs on leads rule is if your dog is being attacked by cows. Each year in the UK there are deaths caused by walkers being trampled as they tried to rescue their dogs from the attentions of cattle. The advice in this instance is to let go of the lead, head speedily to a position of safety (usually the other side of a gate or stile) and call your dog to you.

● **Around ground-nesting birds** It's important to keep your dog under control when crossing an area where certain species of birds nest on the ground. Most dogs love foraging around in the woods but make sure you have permission to do so; some woods are used as 'nurseries' for game birds and dogs are only allowed through them if they are on a lead.

What to pack
You've probably already got a good idea of what to bring to keep your dog alive and happy, but the following is a checklist:

● **Food/water bowl** Foldable cloth bowls are popular with walkers, being light and taking up little room in the rucksack. You can get also get a water-bottle-and-bowl combination, where the bottle folds into a 'trough' from which the dog can drink.

● **Lead and collar** An extendable one is probably preferable for this sort of trip. Make sure both lead and collar are in good condition – you don't want either to snap on the trail, or you may end up carrying your dog through sheep fields until a replacement can be found.

● **Medication** You'll know if you need to bring any lotions or potions.

● **Bedding** A simple blanket may suffice, or you can opt for something more elaborate if you aren't carrying your own luggage.

● **Poo bags** Essential. ● **Hygiene wipes** For cleaning your dog after it's rolled in stuff.

● **A favourite toy** Helps prevent your dog from pining for the entire walk.

● **Food/water** Remember to bring treats as well as regular food to keep up the mutt's morale. That said, if your dog is anything like mine the chances are they'll spend most of the walk dining on rabbit droppings and sheep poo anyway.

● **Corkscrew stake** Available from camping or pet shops, this will help you to keep your dog secure in one place while you set up camp/doze.

● **Tick remover** See above. ● **Raingear** It can rain! ● **Old towels** For drying your dog.

When it comes to packing, I always leave an exterior pocket of my rucksack empty so I can put used poo bags in there (for deposit at the first bin we come to). I always like to keep all the dog's kit together and separate from the other luggage (usually inside a plastic bag inside my rucksack). I have also seen several dogs sporting their own 'doggy rucksack', so they can carry their own food, water, poo etc – which certainly reduces the burden on their owner!

Cleaning up after your dog
It is extremely important that dog owners behave in a responsible way when walking the path. Dog excrement should be cleaned up. In towns, villages and fields where animals graze or which will be cut for silage, hay etc, you need to pick up and bag the excrement.

Staying with your dog
In this guide we have used the symbol 🐕 to denote where a hotel, pub or B&B welcomes dogs. However, this always needs to be arranged in advance and some places make an additional charge (usually per night but occasionally per stay) while others may require a deposit which is refundable if the dog doesn't make a mess. Hostels (both YHA and independent) do not permit them unless they are an assistance (guide) dog; smaller campsites tend to accept them, but some of the larger holiday parks do not. Before you turn up always double check whether there is space for them; many places have only one or two rooms suitable for people with dogs. In some cases dogs need to sleep in a separate building.

When it comes to eating, most landlords allow dogs in at least a section of their pubs, though few restaurants do. Make sure you always ask first and ensure your dog doesn't run around the pub but is secured to your table or a radiator.

APPENDIX B – GPS WAYPOINTS

Each GPS waypoint below was taken on the route at the reference number marked on the map as below. This list of GPS waypoints is also available to download from the Trailblazer website – 🖳 www.trailblazer-guides.com.

MAP NO	WAY-POINT	OS GRID REF	DESCRIPTION
Stage 1		**St Bees to Ennerdale Bridge (14 miles)**	
1	001	NX 96042 11791	Mile Zero; Coast to Coast sign on St Bees beach
3	002	NX 97898 14269	Gate on right, then downhill to railway tunnel
3	003	NX 98500 14189	Plank bridge over stream
4	004	NX 98932 14175	By woods continue N then E to disused railway/ cycle route
4	005	NX 99608 14346	Cross A595 and pass Coast to Coast statue; east into Moor Row
4	006	NY 00768 13923	Turn E into field
5	007	NY 01558 13494	Cleator Stores, Main St; cross road into Kiln Brow
5	008	NY 02295 13356	Black How Farm. Backroad N to Ennerdale or track E to Dent Hill
5	009	NY 03055 13338	Stile in fence; follow wall ESE towards Dent Hill summit
5	010	NY 03743 13052	Cairn along walls; not the summit
5	011	NY 04148 12893	Dent Hill summit (353m), small cairn
5	012	NY 04352 12765	Stile in fence, continue SE
6	013	NY 04535 12668	Junction, follow track going ENE to tall stile
6	014	NY 05532 12979	Having crossed over Kirk Beck continue NE along stream
6	015	NY 05744 13873	Opposite gorse hillside head NE
7	016	NY 06942 15811	Ennerdale Bridge over river
Stage 2		**Ennerdale Bridge to Borrowdale (Rosthwaite) low route (15 miles)**	
9	017	NY 12493 13874	Bridge at eastern end of Ennerdale Water
10	018	NY 14564 14122	Turn off north for high-level route via Red Pike
10	019	NY 17713 13216	A path leads E up to Scarth Gap Pass (Hay Stacks)
11	020	NY 19118 12508	Path comes down from Scarth Gap
12	021	NY 20278 12033	Cross Loft Beck by two cairns and ascend
12	022	NY 20548 12383	Top of Loft Beck at boggy saddle; turn E for stile in fence
12	023	NY 20802 12417	Stile in fence
12	024	NY 21135 12465	Cairns; now head NE
13	025	NY 21366 12632	Join bigger track coming from Brandreth
13	026	NY 21593 13455	Drum House
14	027	NY 25825 14939	At bridge turn off by bus stop in Rosthwaite
Stage 3		**Borrowdale to Grasmere (9 miles)**	
16	028	NY 28313 11202	Top of Lining Crag; bogs & cairns to Greenup Edge
16	029	NY 28602 10526	Greenup Edge; twin cairns just after fence post
17	030	NY 29558 10287	Top of Easedale; two routes separate
17	031	NY 30160 10411	Top of Calf Crag (538m)
18	032	NY 32744 09202	Near Helm Crag summit
18	033	NY 32712 08536	Gate on left for Poet's Walk route
18	034	NY 33260 08458	At road just E of Thorney How Hostel

MAP NO	WAY- POINT	OS GRID REF	DESCRIPTION
Stage 4 Grasmere to St Sunday Crag to Patterdale (8½ miles)			
19	035	NY 33952 09817	Two Tongue paths separate
19	036	NY 34908 11680	Grisedale Hause
21	037	NY 36932 13393	Summit of The Cape (841m); head N briefly to cairn
21	038	NY 36975 13678	Cairn; descent NE from St Sunday Crag begins
24	039	NY 37927 14728	Wall joins from E
24	040	NY 38680 15699	Turn right (SE) at oak tree
Stage 5 Patterdale to Shap (15½ miles)			
25	041	NY 40053 16146	Behind Rooking, path heads off SE uphill to Boredale Hause
25	042	NY 40793 15619	Boredale Hause; grassy flat by two drain covers
25	043	NY 41104 14953	Paths diverge but soon join up near Angle Tarn
26	044	NY 42550 13650	Wall ends; continue E on path
26	045	NY 42761 13574	By wall, turn SE
26	046	NY 43106 13121	Cross stream before gap in wall
27	047	NY 43629 12849	Walls meet; path becomes track and curves to the S
27	048	NY 43924 12259	Turn left (NE) at cairn for track to Kidsty Pike
27	049	NY 44735 12583	Kidsty Pike summit (784m)
28	050	NY 45900 12588	Minor path to N; continue E to start of steep descent
28	051	NY 46839 11894	End of descent at Haweswater reservoir
30	052	NY 50559 16134	E of dam, a gate leads through trees to Burnbanks
30	053	NY 51132 16000	Out of woods; ladder stile near stream
30	054	NY 52026 16221	Turn right up side of field by gully
31	055	NY 53372 16466	After bog, turn right, SE, just before Rosgill Bridge
32	056	NY 53868 15625	Head E here across fields to Shap Abbey
33	057	NY 56210 15555	Shap (northern end by The Hermitage)
Stage 6 Shap to Kirkby Stephen (20½ miles)			
34	058	NY 57700 13950	Path turns SE away from motorway
34	059	NY 57916 13829	Cross wall by farm and head E across farm drive
35	060	NY 58568 13573	Steps to and from quarry access road
36	061	NY 59961 11826	Southern corner of plantation. Head ESE towards twin tree landmark
36	062	NY 60406 11733	Limestone pavement near two isolated trees; track soon curves to S
36	063	NY 60836 10784	E at wall corner then NE past gully near Robin Hood's Grave
39	064	NY 67383 07661	Join road near Sunbiggin Tarn
40	065	NY 67138 07336	Leave road to S
40	066	NY 67101 06984	Faint, unmarked junction; turn E across Ravenstonedale Moor
40	067	NY 67621 06930	Wooden bridge
40	068	NY 69342 06501	Drain by the road with a hilltop reservoir to the E
41	069	NY 72068 05957	Smardale Bridge over Scandal Beck
42	070	NY 74695 07269	Through gate to road
42	071	NY 75630 07479	Head for corner of the field towards gully to Green Riggs Farm
43	072	NY 77423 08375	Kirkby Stephen Market Square
45	073	NY 81047 06732	Signpost for Nine Standards; Red and Blue routes go E, Green route goes S

MAP NO	WAY-POINT	OS GRID REF	DESCRIPTION

Stage 7 Kirkby to Keld
● Green route (12½ miles)

45	074	NY 81305 05950	Stone pens by wall
45	075	NY 81278 05146	Head of Rigg Beck
45	076	NY 80800 04633	Path joins from NW; continue S to road
45	077	NY 80810 04467	Four paths meet, head S then SSE to B6270
48	078	NY 83106 02787	Leave road; or carry on a bit and take easier track left uphill.
48	079/099	NY 83542 02774	Red route comes down from pillar cairn to N

● Blue route (13 miles)

46	082	NY 82495 06561	Nine Standards
46	083	NY 82544 06111	Trig point 662m
47	084	NY 82689 05836	Signpost
47	085/093	NY 82736 05728	Blue and Red routes diverge
47	086	NY 83608 05632	Waypoint on Blue route
47	087	NY 84157 05563	Waypoint on Blue route
47	088	NY 84635 05204	Signpost at descent to Whitsundale Beck
48	089	NY 84873 03745	Old shelter
48	090	NY 85250 03380	Vicinity of blue post by fence
49	091	NY 85536 03263	Turn S

● Red route (13 miles)

46	082	NY 82495 06561	Nine Standards
46	083	NY 82544 06111	Trig point 662m
47	084	NY 82689 05836	Signpost
47	093/085	NY 82736 05728	Blue and Red routes diverge
47	094	NY 82830 04950	White stick nearby
47	095	NY 82823 04381	Cairn. Can see pillar cairn S of here
48	096	NY 83098 03785	Pillar cairn; head SE here
48	097	NY 83280 03636	Footbridge; ignore 'no access' sign to E and head for next waypoint
48	098	NY 83352 03582	White-topped pole; descent continues to Green route track
48	099/079	NY 83542 02774	Point where Red route joins Green route; turn E on track

● All routes

49	080/092	NY 85583 03012	Signpost; all three routes converge by beck and wall
50	081	NY 87689 01633	Leave track for indistinct scar-top path (or descend to road)

Stage 8 Keld to Reeth

51	100	NY 90464 00863	Fork; high route goes left, low route goes downhill

● High route (11 miles)

51	101	NY 90594 00864	Crackpot Hall; turn N towards spoil heaps then E onto stony track
51	102	NY 91865 01300	Climb out of East Grain ends and path joins track
52	103	NY 93189 01309	Leave track to NE; descent to Gunnerside Beck
52	104	NY 93782 01747	Point above Blakethwaite ruins on zigzag path
52	105	NY 93988 01332	Signpost for Surrender Bridge; turn E up Bunton Hush (gully)

MAP NO	WAY-POINT	OS GRID REF	DESCRIPTION
● **High route (11 miles)** *(cont'd)*			
52	106	NY 94709 01420	Join track near wooden pen around mine shaft
54	107	NY 99363 00007	Cairn after Surrender Bridge
55	108	SE 02712 99739	Cairn; head ENE for wall corner
55	109	SE 03321 99494	Cross field SE to the east side of the school buildings
56	110	SE 03813 99295	Reeth village green
● **Low route (11½ miles)**			
51a	200	SD 91014 98674	Main track goes left, take path to right
51b	201	SD 93295 97817	Join road
51b	202	SD 93600 97989	Leave road in Ivelet, cross Shore Gill, head E
51c	203	SD 94488 98054	Direct route to Gunnerside unclear; take river path
51c	204	SD 96355 98286	Gully
51d	205	SD 97385 98160	Join concrete path
51d	206	SD 98420 98436	Leave road, follow muddy track
51d	207	SD 99535 98999	Leave main track for small path
56	110	SE 03813 99295	Reeth village green
Stage 9 Reeth to Richmond (10½ miles)			
56	111	SE 04272 99087	Leave main road to right, take path along river behind farm
56	112	SE 04647 98581	Cross road by bridge and continue along northern side of Swale
56	113	SE 05412 98630	Tap by gate; cross road and enter field to N
56	114	SE 05708 98625	Head for this stile
57	115	SE 06622 97883	Field path rejoins road at Marrick Abbey farm
58	116	NZ 10897 00916	Leave road to right for path NE up to white cairn
61	117	NZ 17033 01012	Turn right into Rosemary Lane
Stage 10 Richmond to Ingleby Cross (22½ miles)			
62	118	NZ 17494 00656	Gate on right leads to sheds and path to houses
63	119	SE 18611 99429	Continue SE past junction before stream; at the track head E then SE
64	120	SE 22732 99420	North of bridge turn right (E) along river bank
65	121	SE 26050 98454	Crumbling bridge over beck
67	122	SE 31230 98932	Join muddy, overgrown path at stile
68	123	SE 34873 98550	Leave the road and head ENE along edge of field
68	124	SE 36146 99166	Turn E off the A167
69	125	SE 38890 99773	No obvious sign but turn S here onto road
70	126	NZ 41763 01057	Brick gateposts
72	127	NZ 44962 00629	Crossroads opposite Blue Bell Inn
Stage 11 Ingleby Cross to Blakey Ridge (21 miles)			
72	128	SE 45403 98603	Footpath for Osmotherley
73	129	NZ 47460 00404	Join track, leave woods, head ENE
74	130	NZ 48952 00288	Leave track and turn NE down across field
74	131	NZ 50499 01301	Cairn (324m)
78	132	NZ 59411 01512	Near trig point (445m)
81	133	SE 66677 99442	A path leads S to Farndale East; not easy to follow
81	134	SE 67914 99725	Lion Inn pub

MAP NO	WAY-POINT	OS GRID REF	DESCRIPTION

Stage 12 Blakey Ridge to Grosmont (13½ miles)

83	135	NZ 69990 01919	Turn E off road for Glaisdale Moor
84	136	NZ 73998 04022	Junction near trig point
86	137	NZ 79303 04644	Path emerges from Arncliffe Wood by road
87	138	NZ 82819 05246	Grosmont level crossing

Stage 13 Grosmont to Robin Hood's Bay (15½ miles)

88	139	NZ 85514 04255	Leave moorland road here and take path E to A169
89	140	NZ 86174 04720	Turn E off A169 for descent to Littlebeck
90	141	NZ 89912 03519	Coast to Coast signpost; solitary tree visible to NNE
91	142	NZ 90712 03993	Turn NE off B1416 at stile
92	143	NZ 91778 04649	Open moor
92	144	NZ 92088 05505	Post by stile and gate
93	145	NZ 94062 08147	NE end of caravan park, just before sea cliffs
95	146	NZ 95325 04849	Slipway by Bay Hotel in Robin Hood's Bay

---

❏ **The Lyke Wake Walk** (see p222)

The Lyke Wake Walk, which the Coast to Coast trail joins for part of the stretch across the moors, was the invention of one man. Local farmer and journalist Bill Cowley came up with the idea in 1955 when he claimed that, with the exception of one or two roads that run across the moors, one could walk the entire 40 miles over the North York Moors from east to west (or vice-versa) on **heather**. Several walkers were keen to see if Mr Cowley was right, and it was agreed that the trail should start on Scarth Wood Moor, near Osmotherley, and finish in Ravenscar. To make the challenge tougher, the whole 40 miles had to be completed in 24 hours.

The curious name comes from the Lyke Wake Dirge, possibly the oldest verse in the Yorkshire dialect and starts:

This yah neet, this yah neet, *When thoo frae hence away art passed*
Ivvery neet an' all, *Ivvery neet an' all,*
Fire an' fleet an' cannle leet, *Ti Whinny Moor thoo cums at last*
An' Christ tak up thy saul. *An' Christ tak up thy saul.*

'Lyke' was the local term for corpse and the song recounts the passage of the soul through the afterlife. Bill himself became the chief dirger and handed out black-edged cards to those who successfully completed the trail. There was also a Wake Club which he founded for those who completed the walk.

Unfortunately, the trail has suffered from hard times recently. Firstly, the popularity of the walk through the '60s and '70s, led to a fair amount of environmental damage. These days there are a number of different paths to choose from to limit the damage caused by the walkers. The death of Bill Cowley in 1994 dealt another blow to the trail and the demise of the original Lyke Wake Club in 2005 was a further setback. However, a New Lyke Wake Club (🖳 www.lykewake.org) has been set up to continue along much the same lines as the original organisation. See the website for details.

INDEX

TRAILBLAZER'S LONG-DISTANCE PATH (LDP) WALKING GUIDES

We've applied to destinations which are closer to home Trailblazer's proven formula for publishing definitive practical route guides for adventurous travellers. Britain's network of long-distance trails enables the walker to explore some of the finest landscapes in the country's best walking areas. These are guides that are user-friendly, practical, informative and environmentally sensitive.

● **Unique mapping features** In many walking guidebooks the reader has to read a route description then try to relate it to the map. Our guides are much easier to use because walking directions, tricky junctions, places to stay and eat, points of interest and walking times are all written onto the maps themselves in the places to which they apply. With their uncluttered clarity, these are not general-purpose maps but fully edited maps drawn by walkers for walkers.

● **Largest-scale walking maps** At a scale of just under 1:20,000 (8cm or 3¹/₈ inches to one mile) the maps in these guides are bigger than even the most detailed British walking maps currently available in the shops.

● **Not just a trail guide – includes where to stay, where to eat and public transport** Our guidebooks cover the complete walking experience, not just the route. Accommodation options for all budgets are provided (pubs, hotels, B&Bs, campsites, bunkhouses, hostels) as well as places to eat. Detailed public transport information for all access points to each trail means that there are itineraries for all walkers, for hiking the entire route as well as for day or weekend walks.

Coast to Coast *Henry Stedman*, 7th edition, £11.99
ISBN 978-1-905864-74-4, 268pp, 110 maps, 40 colour photos

Cornwall Coast Path (SW Coast Path Pt 2) 5th edition, £11.99
ISBN 978-1-905864-71-3, 3526pp, 142 maps, 40 colour photos

Cotswold Way *Tricia & Bob Hayne* 3rd edition, £11.99
ISBN 978-1-905864-70-6, 204pp, 53 maps, 40 colour photos

Dales Way *Henry Stedman* 1st edition, £11.99 – **due June 2016**
ISBN 978-1-905864-78-2, 192pp, 50 maps, 40 colour photos

Dorset & South Devon (SW Coast Path Pt 3) *Stedman & Newton*, £11.99
ISBN 978-1-905864-45-4, 336pp, 88 maps, 40 colour photos

Exmoor & North Devon (SW Coast Path Pt I) *Stedman & Newton*, £11.99
ISBN 978-1-905864-43-0, 192pp, 68 maps, 40 colour photos

Hadrian's Wall Path *Henry Stedman*, 4th edition, £11.99
ISBN 978-1-905864-58-4, 224pp, 60 maps, 40 colour photos

Offa's Dyke Path *Keith Carter*, 4th edition, £11.99
ISBN 978-1-905864-65-2, 240pp, 98 maps, 40 colour photos

Peddars Way & Norfolk Coast Path *Alexander Stewart*, £11.99
ISBN 978-1-905864-28-7, 192pp, 54 maps, 40 colour photos

Pembrokeshire Coast Path *Jim Manthorpe*, 4th edition, £11.99
ISBN 978-1-905864-51-5, 224pp, 96 maps, 40 colour photos

Pennine Way *Stuart Greig*, 4th edition, £11.99
ISBN 978-1-905864-61-4, 272pp, 138 maps, 40 colour photos

The Ridgeway *Nick Hill*, 3rd edition, £11.99
ISBN 978-1-905864-40-9, 192pp, 53 maps, 40 colour photos

South Downs Way *Jim Manthorpe*, 5th edition, £11.99
ISBN 978-1-905864-66-9, 192pp, 60 maps, 40 colour photos

Thames Path *Joel Newton*, 1st edition, £11.99
ISBN 978-1-905864-64-5, 256pp, 99 maps, 40 colour photos

West Highland Way *Charlie Loram*, 6th edition, £11.99
ISBN 978-1-905864-76-8, 208pp, 60 maps, 40 colour photos

'The same attention to detail that distinguishes its other guides has been brought to bear here'.
THE SUNDAY TIMES

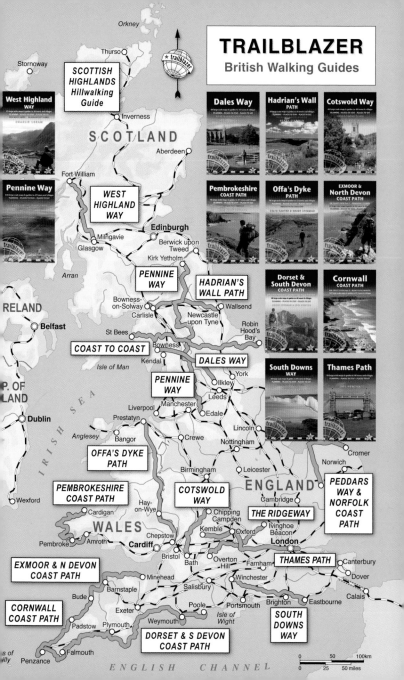

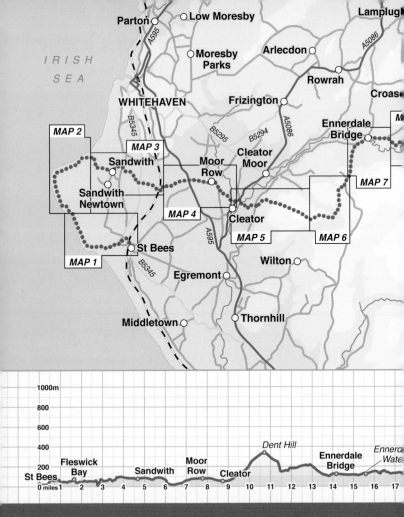

Maps 1-7 – St Bees to Ennerdale Bridge

14 miles/22.5km – 6¼hrs

Maps 7-14 – Ennerdale Bridge to Rosthwaite (Borrowdale)

15 miles/24km – 6½hrs (low route)

NOTE: Add 20-30% to these times to allow for stops

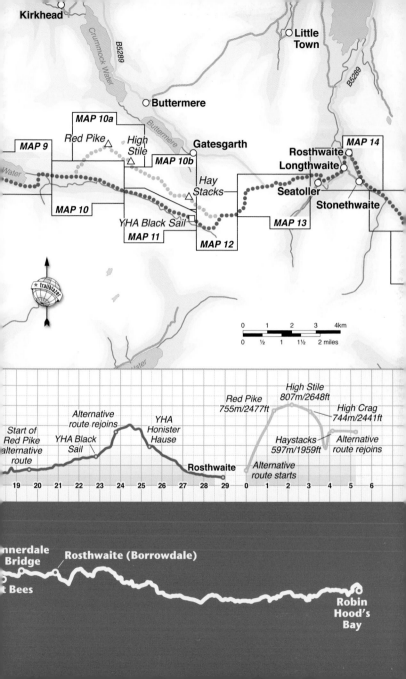

Kirkhead

Little Town

B5289

Crummock Water

B5289

Buttermere

Buttermere

Gatesgarth

MAP 10a

MAP 9   Red Pike △   High Stile △   MAP 10b

Rosthwaite   MAP 14

Longthwaite

Water

Hay Stacks

Seatoller

MAP 10   △   **Stonethwaite**

YHA Black Sail

MAP 11   MAP 12   MAP 13

★ trailblazer

Water

| 0 | 1 | 2 | 3 | 4km |

| 0 | ½ | 1 | 1½ | 2 miles |

Alternative route rejoins

YHA Black Sail

Start of Red Pike alternative route

YHA Honister Hause

Red Pike 755m/2477ft

High Stile 807m/2648ft

High Crag 744m/2441ft

Haystacks 597m/1959ft

Alternative route rejoins

Rosthwaite

Alternative route starts

19 20 21 22 23 24 25 26 27 28 29 0 1 2 3 4 5 6

nnerdale Bridge

Rosthwaite (Borrowdale)

t Bees

Robin Hood's Bay

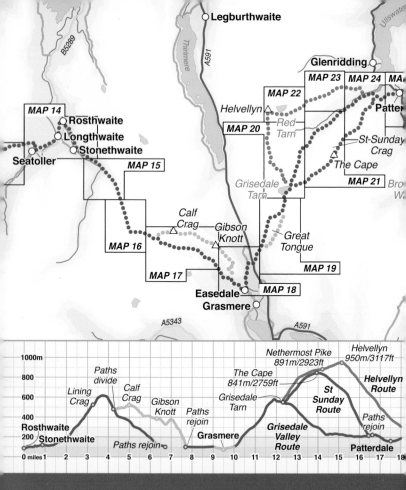

Maps 14-18 – Rosthwaite to Grasmere

9 miles/14.5km – 4-5½hrs (low route)

Maps 18-25 – Grasmere to Patterdale

8½ miles/13.5km – 3-4hrs (via Grisedale Pass)

Maps 25-33 – Patterdale to Shap

15½ miles/25km – 6½hrs
NOTE: Add 20-30% to these times to allow for stops

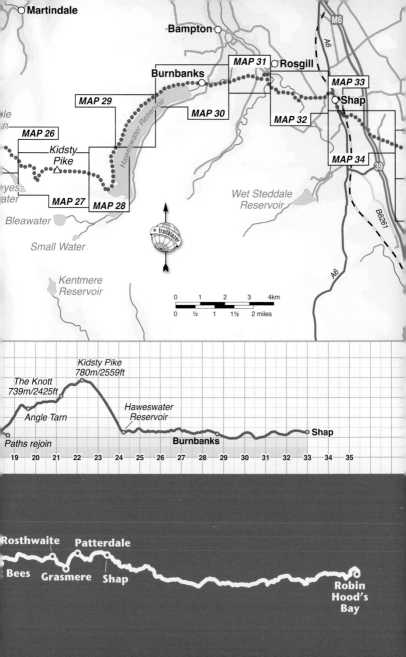

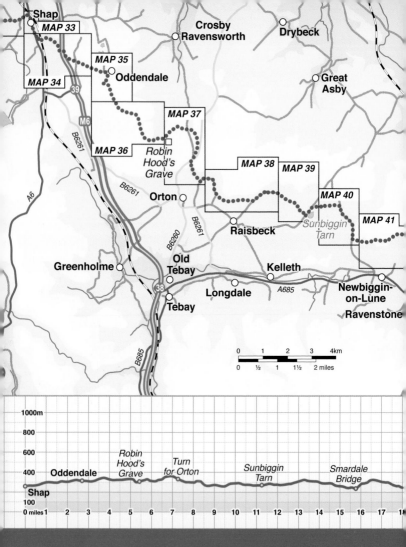

Maps 33-43 – Shap to Kirkby Stephen
20½ miles/33km – 7hrs

Maps 43-50 – Kirkby Stephen to Keld
13 miles/21km – 5-6hrs
NOTE: Add 20-30% to these times to allow for stops

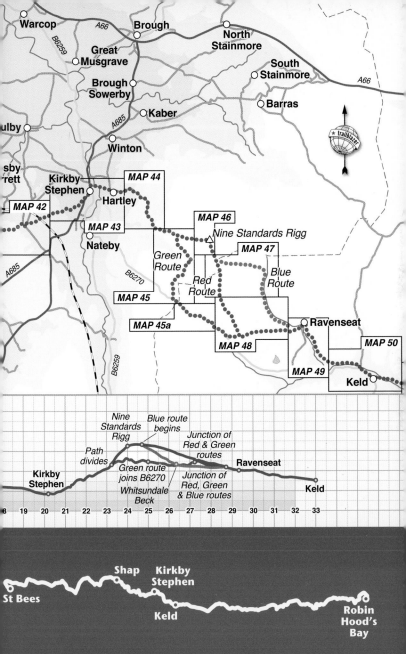

Warcop
_A66_
Brough
North Stainmore

Great Musgrave

South Stainmore
_A66_

Brough Sowerby
Barras

Kaber
★ trailblazer

_A685_
Winton

ulby
sby
rett
Kirkby Stephen
MAP 44
Hartley

MAP 42
MAP 43
Nateby

MAP 46
Nine Standards Rigg
MAP 47

_A685_
Green Route
Blue Route

_B6270_
Red Route

MAP 45

MAP 45a
Ravenseat
MAP 50

MAP 48
MAP 49
_B6259_
Keld

Nine Standards Rigg
Blue route begins
Junction of Red & Green routes
Path divides
Ravenseat
Green route joins B6270
Junction of Red, Green & Blue routes
Kirkby Stephen
Whitsundale Beck
Keld

18 19 20 21 22 23 24 25 26 27 28 29 30 31 32 33

Shap **Kirkby Stephen**
St Bees
Keld
Robin Hood's Bay

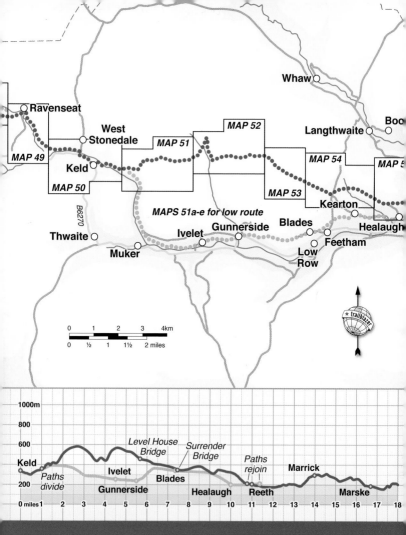

Maps 50-56 – Keld to Reeth
11 miles/18km – 4½hrs (Official path)

Maps 56-61 – Reeth to Richmond
10½ miles/17km – 4½hrs
NOTE: Add 20-30% to these times to allow for stops

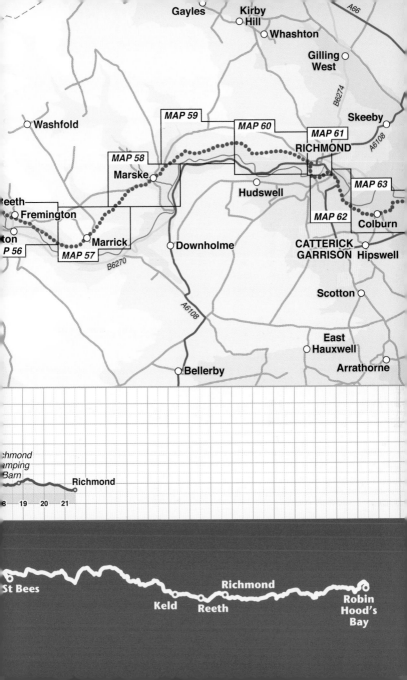

Gayles

Kirby
Hill

Whashton

Gilling
West

Skeeby

Washfold

MAP 59

MAP 60

MAP 61

RICHMOND

MAP 58

Marske

Hudswell

MAP 63

eeth

MAP 62

Fremington

Colburn

ton

MAP 57

Marrick

CATTERICK
GARRISON

P 56

B6270

Downholme

Hipswell

Scotton

East
Hauxwell

Arrathorne

Bellerby

*chmond
mping
Barn*

Richmond

8 19 20 21

St Bees

Keld

Reeth

Richmond

Robin
Hood's
Bay

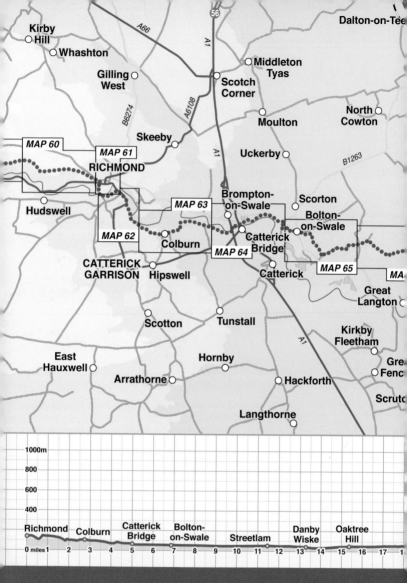

Kirby Hill
Whashton
Gilling West
Dalton-on-Tees
A66
A1
56
Middleton Tyas
Scotch Corner
Moulton
North Cowton
A6108
Skeeby
Uckerby
B1263
B6274

MAP 60
MAP 61
RICHMOND
Hudswell
A1
MAP 63
Brompton-on-Swale
Scorton
Bolton-on-Swale
MAP 62
Colburn
Catterick Bridge
MAP 64
MAP 65
MA
CATTERICK GARRISON
Hipswell
Catterick
Great Langton
Scotton
Tunstall
A1
Kirkby Fleetham
East Hauxwell
Hornby
Gre
Fenc
Arrathorne
Hackforth
Scrut
Langthorne

1000m
800
600
400

Richmond   Colburn   Catterick Bridge   Bolton-on-Swale   Streetlam   Danby Wiske   Oaktree Hill

0 miles 1   2   3   4   5   6   7   8   9   10   11   12   13   14   15   16   17   1

Maps 61-72 – Richmond to Ingleby Cro:

22½ miles/36km – 8½hrs
NOTE: Add 20-30% to these times to allow for stops

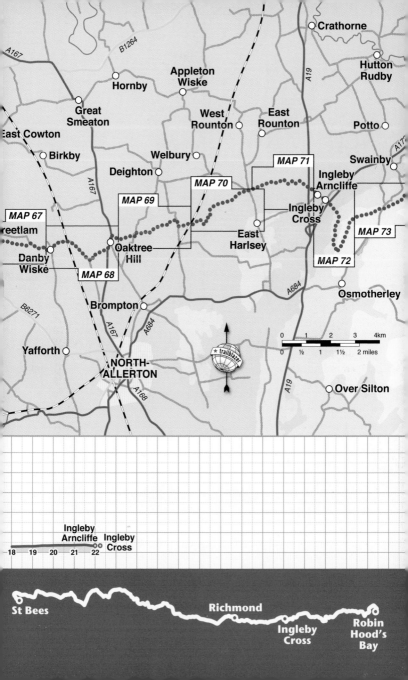

Crathorne

Hutton
Rudby

A19

A167

B1264

Appleton
Wiske

Hornby

Potto

A172

Great
Smeaton

East Cowton

West
Rounton

East
Rounton

Birkby

Welbury

Swainby

Deighton

MAP 71

Ingleby
Arncliffe

A167

MAP 70

Ingleby
Cross

MAP 69

MAP 67

reetlam

East
Harlsey

MAP 73

Danby
Wiske

Oaktree
Hill

MAP 68

MAP 72

A684

Osmotherley

Brompton

B6271

A167

A684

Yafforth

trailblazer

A19

NORTH-
ALLERTON

A168

Over Silton

0   1   2   3   4km
0   ½   1   1½   2 miles

Ingleby
Arncliffe

Ingleby
Cross

18 19 20 21 22

St Bees

Richmond

Robin
Hood's
Bay

Ingleby
Cross

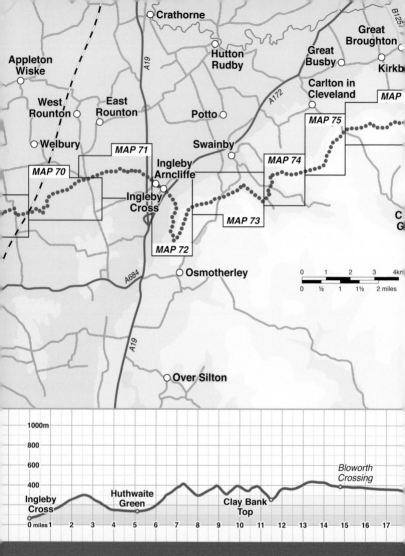

Maps 72-81 – Ingleby Cross to Blakey Ridge

21 miles/34km – 8hrs

NOTE: Add 20-30% to these times to allow for stops

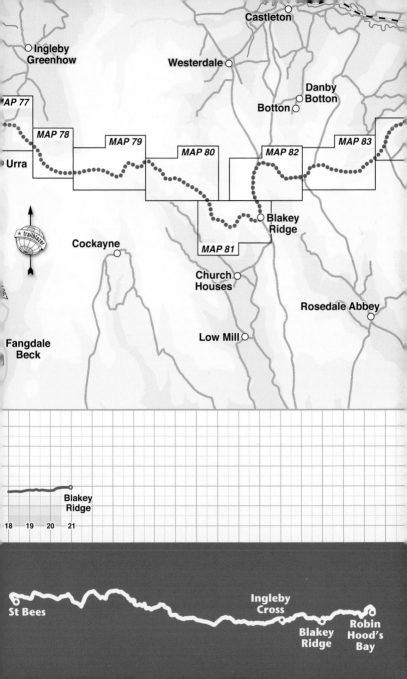

Ingleby
Greenhow

Castleton

Westerdale

Danby
Botton

Botton

MAP 77

MAP 78

MAP 79

MAP 80

MAP 82

MAP 83

Urra

MAP 81

Blakey
Ridge

Cockayne

Church
Houses

Rosedale Abbey

Fangdale
Beck

Low Mill

Blakey
Ridge

18   19   20   21

St Bees

Ingleby
Cross

Blakey
Ridge

Robin
Hood's
Bay

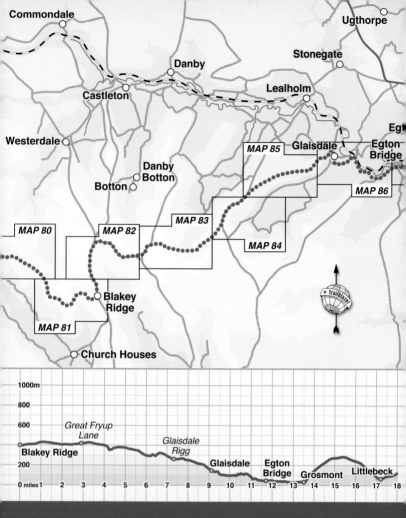

Maps 81-87 – Blakey Ridge to Grosmon

13½ miles/22km – 5hrs

Maps 87-95 – Grosmont to Robin Hood's Bay

15½ miles/25km – 6hrs

NOTE: Add 20-30% to these times to allow for stops

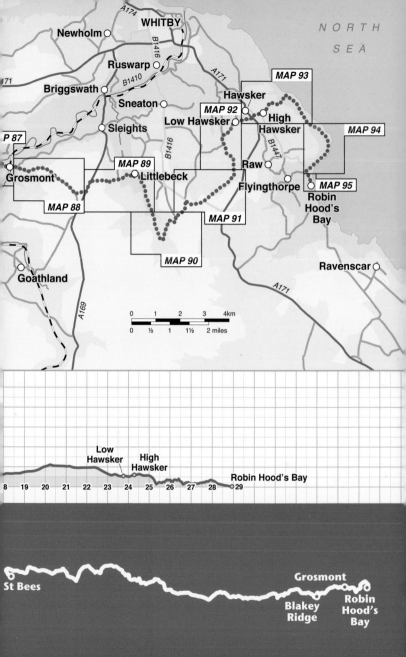

P 87

NORTH

SEA

WHITBY

Newholm

Ruswarp

Briggswath

Sneaton

Sleights

Hawsker

MAP 92

Low Hawsker

High
Hawsker

MAP 93

MAP 94

Raw

MAP 95

Grosmont

MAP 89

Littlebeck

Flyingthorpe

Robin
Hood's
Bay

MAP 88

MAP 91

MAP 90

Goathland

Ravenscar

0   1   2   3   4km

0   ½   1   1½   2 miles

Low
Hawsker

High
Hawsker

Robin Hood's Bay

18   19   20   21   22   23   24   25   26   27   28   29

St Bees

Grosmont

Blakey
Ridge

Robin
Hood's
Bay

	St Bees	Sandwith	Moor Row	Cleator	Ennerdale Bridge	Ennerdale YH	Black Sail YH	Honister Hause	Seatoller	Rosthwaite	Easedale	Grisedale Tarn	Patterdale	Burnbanks	Shap	Broadfell Farm	Ravenstonedale
St Bees	0																
Sandwith	5	0															
Moor Row	8	3	0														
Cleator	9	4	1	0													
Ennerdale Bridge	14	9	6	5	0												
Ennerdale YH	19	14	11	10	5	0											
Black Sail YH	23	18	15	14	9	4	0										
Honister Hause	26	21	18	17	12	7	3	0									
Seatoller	30	25	22	21	16	11	7	4	0								
Rosthwaite	32	27	24	23	18	13	9	6	2	0							
Easedale	42	37	34	33	28	23	19	16	12	10	0						
Grisedale Tarn	46	41	38	37	32	27	23	20	16	14	4	0					
Patterdale	53	48	45	44	39	34	30	27	23	21	11	7	0				
Burnbanks	64	59	56	55	50	45	41	38	34	32	22	18	11	0			
Shap	69	64	61	60	55	50	46	43	39	37	27	23	16	5	0		
Broadfell Farm	77	72	69	68	63	58	54	51	47	45	35	31	24	13	8	0	
Ravenstonedale	84	79	76	75	70	65	61	58	54	52	42	38	31	20	15	7	0
Kirkby Stephen	89	84	81	80	75	70	66	63	59	57	47	43	36	25	20	12	5
Ravenseat	99	94	91	90	85	80	76	73	69	67	57	53	46	35	30	22	15
Keld	102	97	94	93	88	83	79	76	72	70	60	56	49	38	33	25	18
Reeth	113	108	105	104	99	94	90	87	83	81	71	67	60	49	44	36	29
Marrick	118	113	110	109	104	99	95	92	88	86	76	72	65	54	49	41	34
Richmond	124	119	116	115	110	105	101	98	94	92	82	78	71	60	55	47	40
Colburn	127	122	119	118	113	108	104	101	97	95	85	81	74	63	58	50	43
Catterick Bridge	129	124	121	120	115	110	106	103	99	97	87	83	76	65	60	52	45
Bolton on Swale	130	125	122	121	116	111	107	104	100	98	88	84	77	66	61	53	46
Danby Wiske	138	133	130	129	124	119	115	112	108	106	96	92	85	74	69	61	54
Oaktree Hill	140	135	132	131	126	121	117	114	110	108	98	94	87	76	71	63	56
Ingleby Cross	147	142	139	138	133	128	124	121	117	115	105	101	94	83	78	70	63
Arncliffe Wood	148	143	140	139	134	129	125	122	118	116	106	102	95	84	79	71	64
Carlton Bank	155	150	147	146	141	136	132	129	125	123	113	109	102	91	86	78	71
Clay Bank Top	159	154	151	150	145	140	136	133	129	127	117	113	106	95	90	82	75
Blakey Ridge	168	163	160	159	154	149	145	142	138	136	126	122	115	104	99	91	84
Glaisdale	178	173	170	169	164	159	155	152	148	146	136	132	125	114	109	101	94
Egton Bridge	180	175	172	171	166	161	157	154	150	148	138	134	127	116	111	103	96
Grosmont	181	176	173	173	167	162	158	155	151	149	139	135	128	117	112	104	97
Littlebeck	185	180	177	176	171	166	162	159	155	153	143	139	132	121	116	108	101
High Hawsker	192	187	184	183	178	173	169	166	162	160	150	146	139	128	123	115	108
Robin Hood's Bay	198	193	190	189	184	179	175	172	168	166	156	152	145	134	129	121	114

Coast to Coast Path
DISTANCE CHART
miles (approx)

	Kirkby Stephen	Ravenseat	Keld	Reeth	Marrick	Richmond	Colburn	Catterick	Bolton on Swale	Danby Wiske	Oaktree Hill	Ingleby Cross	Arncliffe Wood	Carlton Bank	Clay Bank Top	Blakey Ridge	Glaisdale	Egton Bridge	Grosmont	Littlebeck	High Hawsker	Robin Hood's Bay
Kirkby Stephen	0																					
Ravenseat	10	0																				
Keld	13	3	0																			
Reeth	24	14	11	0																		
Marrick	29	19	16	5	0																	
Richmond	35	25	22	11	6	0																
Colburn	38	28	25	14	9	3	0															
Catterick	40	30	27	16	11	5	2	0														
Bolton on Swale	41	31	28	17	12	6	3	1	0													
Danby Wiske	49	39	36	25	20	14	11	9	8	0												
Oaktree Hill	51	41	38	27	22	16	13	11	10	2	0											
Ingleby Cross	58	48	45	34	29	23	20	18	17	9	7	0										
Arncliffe Wood	59	49	46	35	30	24	21	19	18	10	8	1	0									
Carlton Bank	66	56	53	42	37	31	28	26	25	17	15	8	7	0								
Clay Bank Top	70	60	57	46	41	35	32	30	29	21	19	12	11	4	0							
Blakey Ridge	79	69	66	55	50	44	41	39	38	30	28	21	20	13	9	0						
Glaisdale	89	79	76	65	60	54	51	49	48	40	38	31	32	23	19	10	0					
Egton Bridge	91	81	78	67	62	56	53	51	50	42	40	33	32	25	21	12	2	0				
Grosmont	92	82	79	68	63	57	54	52	51	43	41	34	33	26	22	13	3	1	0			
Littlebeck	96	86	83	72	67	61	58	56	55	47	45	38	37	30	26	17	7	5	4	0		
High Hawsker	103	93	90	79	74	68	65	63	62	54	52	45	44	37	33	24	14	12	11	7	0	
Robin Hood's Bay	109	99	96	85	80	74	71	69	68	60	58	51	50	43	39	30	20	18	17	13	6	0

TRAILBLAZER TITLE LIST

Adventure Cycle-Touring Handbook
Adventure Motorcycling Handbook
Australia by Rail
Azerbaijan
Coast to Coast (British Walking Guide)
Cornwall Coast Path (British Walking Guide)
Corsica Trekking – GR20
Cotswold Way (British Walking Guide)
The Cyclist's Anthology
Dales Way (British Walking Guide) – due mid 2016
Dolomites Trekking – AV1 & AV2
Dorset & Sth Devon Coast Path (British Walking Gde)
Exmoor & Nth Devon Coast Path (British Walking Gde)
Hadrian's Wall Path (British Walking Guide)
Himalaya by Bike – a route and planning guide
Inca Trail, Cusco & Machu Picchu
Japan by Rail
Kilimanjaro – the trekking guide (includes Mt Meru)
Moroccan Atlas – The Trekking Guide
Morocco Overland (4WD/motorcycle/mountainbike)
Nepal Trekking & The Great Himalaya Trail
New Zealand – The Great Walks
Offa's Dyke Path (British Walking Guide)
Overlanders' Handbook – worldwide driving guide
Peddars Way & Norfolk Coast Path (British Walking Gde)
Pembrokeshire Coast Path (British Walking Guide)
Pennine Way (British Walking Guide)
Peru's Cordilleras Blanca & Huayhuash – Hiking/Biking
The Railway Anthology
The Ridgeway (British Walking Guide)
Sahara Overland – a route and planning guide
Scottish Highlands – The Hillwalking Guide
Siberian BAM Guide – rail, rivers & road
The Silk Roads – a route and planning guide
Sinai – the trekking guide
South Downs Way (British Walking Guide)
Thames Path (British Walking Guide)
Tour du Mont Blanc
Trans-Canada Rail Guide
Trans-Siberian Handbook
Trekking in the Everest Region
The Walker's Anthology
The Walker's Haute Route – Mont Blanc to Matterhorn
West Highland Way (British Walking Guide)

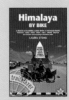

For more information about Trailblazer and our
expanding range of guides, for guidebook updates or
for credit card mail order sales visit our website:

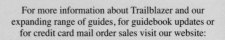

www.trailblazer-guides.com

Coast to Coast
EASTERN SECTION

North Sea

FINISH

Robin Hood's Bay

Whitby

High Hawsker

Grosmont

Egton Bridge

Glaisdale

Littlebeck

Blakey

Clay Bank Top

Redcar

Middlesbrough

Sedgefield

Stockton on Tees

Darlington

Bishop Auckland

Staindrop

Barnard Castle

D U R H A M

Osmotherley

Ingleby Cross

Northallerton

Oaktree Hill

Danby Wiske

Bolton-on-Swale

Catterick Bridge

Colburn

Richmond

Marske

Reeth

Gunnerside

Ivelet

Keld

Ravenseat

N O R T H   Y O R K S H I R E

Leyburn

0   5   10km
0   2½   5 miles

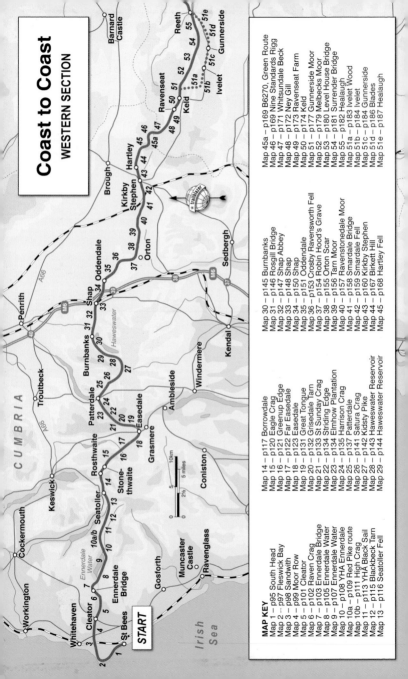

Coast to Coast
WESTERN SECTION

CUMBRIA

Irish Sea

START